"America and her sons paid a great price during the Vietnam War, and *Dr. Tom's War—A Daughter's Journey* helps depict the enormity of their sacrifice. I thoroughly enjoyed getting to know Dr. Tom Viti, a man among many "unsung heroes" who served in a time of need, making a huge difference to those he served. *Dr. Tom's War—A Daughter's Journey* provides the reader a unique insight into this bloody war. The anecdotes were real, from real people and used effectively. Ms. Viti did a superb job pulling the story together, telling it like only the child of someone who served can. Well done!"
— Chris Cortez, Major General, U.S. Marine Corps (Ret.)

"While stories of our fighting men are legion, the tales of our caregivers— doctors, corpsmen, and chaplains are rare. Lucia Viti addresses this with a remarkable journey back in time to capture the Viet Nam service of her father, Doctor Tom Viti, who served as battalion surgeon with the 2nd Battalion, 5th Marines during one of the bloodiest campaigns of the Viet Nam War. Ms. Viti's effort, detailed and emotional, is a great personal tribute to her beloved father. *Dr. Tom's War—A Daughter's Journey* fills a gap in the literature of the Viet Nam War." — Otto Lehrack, Lt.Col. USMC, (Ret.) Author of *No Shining Armor: The Marines at War in Vietnam.*

"*Dr. Tom's War—A Daughter's Journey* is the story of a woman's journey into her father's past as she learns of war and those who are called to fight it. Ms. Viti learns the meaning of the core values of honor, courage, and commitment shared by Marines and those, like her father, who wore Marine green if only for a short time. *Dr. Tom's War—A Daughter's Journey* displays the cold reality of deceit by those who "want to be." Take this incredible journey with her. You will not be disappointed." — Ron Christmas, Lieutenant General, USMC (Ret), Former Commanding Officer, "Hotel" Company, 2/5

"*Dr. Tom's War—A Daughter's Journey* is a marvelous piece of detective work; a fascinating story of a daughter's search and discovery for the Viet Nam father she truly never knew or understood. Dr. Tom Viti was a true hero. Although Dr. Tom Viti rarely shared Viet Nam's trauma with loved ones, had he chosen to, his daughter would have been too young to understand its meaning. Years later, Lucia Viti has skillfully and successfully placed the many pieces of the Viet Nam puzzle together." — Jan K. Herman, Historian, Navy Medical Department, Washington D.C.

D1569455

"The definition of love is what this *Dr. Tom's War—A Daughter's Journey* represents. The journey that we are taken on by the daughter of a battalion surgeon leaves behind the contentious political discussions of the legitimacy and efficacy of the war, and instead focuses on the humanity and heroics of her father, LT Tom Viti USN (MC). Dr. Viti is brought to life by the first hand accounts of the Marines and sailors that served with him. Dr. Tom's remarkable acts of heroism, compassion, and kindness are a testament to his legacy and his Catholic faith; a remarkable account of a genuine American Hero."
— R.W. Koeneke, Colonel, U.S.Marine Corps (Ret)

"*Dr. Tom's War—A Daughter's Journey* delivers every imaginable experience surrounding the Vietnam War. Lucia Viti takes the reader on a journey so personal, you yearn to meet Dr. Tom as both a father and a physician. Sometimes heart-breaking, often funny, and always fascinating, *Dr. Tom's War—A Daughter's Journey* is a must read for those who wish to experience the Vietnam War as a first-hand perspective from those who served on the front-line." — James T. Denton, Actor/Desperate Housewives/Threat Matrix Musician/The Band From TV

"The catalog of Nam Lit is ever crowded with early booming writers who missed it, real vets who didn't and wished they did, and canonical scribes looking to make sense of the insensible. Every theme and narrative approach is covered, it seems. And we care, and we read them because after all, it was a shitty war and we shit on its soldiers.

"But on occasion a gem appears; something fresh and unnamable that necessarily reopens the discourse and the wounds and the war. Lucia Viti's vivisection of the Vietnam War is, like her subject father/physician's tour, focused, driven, and altruistic. It's a unique perspective of a daughter caught in the echo-booming period when so many want to forget the Nam. And so many desperately need to remember.

"What drives this tale is what is not said. Behind the relentless research, gushing quotes, and years of digging gopher holes in her mind, Viti can be seen as the little girl trying to make sense of not only of an absent father but of an abject ethic, a country her family came to for solace and was itself, loss in misguided leadership and ideology.

"The reader need only glance at the details and images to realize that Viti has sought to separate the map from the territory but in the end finds that she, like most of the affected, just missed her dad and wants only to tell them that, "hu rah . . . luv ya, dad. I'm okay, after all." — Scott Tinley, Professional Ironman Athlete, Author

Dr. Tom's War

Dr. Tom's War
A Daughter's Journey

Lucia Viti

Rogue Books
Bedazzled Ink Publishing Company • Fairfield, California

978-1-934452-51-6 paperback
978-1-934452-60-8 ebook

Library of Congress Control Number 2010932178

Photo Reproductions/ Illustrations
By
Sgt. Roger D. McDowell, USMC, 65 -71.

Cover Design
by
C.A. Casey

Canaday, Angela. "Tribute to a War Hero." *Home Reporter and Sunset News*, Long Island, New York, May 28, 1982.

Daily News Photo. "This is for Your Daddy . . ." *Daily News*, October 30, 1968. Copyright © 1968 by *Daily News*. Reprinted with permission.

Daily News Photo. "A Nation Remembers--And So Does She." *Daily News*, March 19, 1969. Copyright © 1969 by *Daily News*. Reprinted with permission.

Dzubak, Susan L. "Operating Room Nurses Share With Readers Inspiring Reports From Vietnam," *The Herald Statesman*, 1967. Copyright © 1967 by *The Herald Stateman*. Reprinted with permission.

"Fifth Regiment Aid Station Aiding Marines and Villagers : Da Nong." *The Sea Tiger*, November 17, 1967, vol. III, no. 46. Copyright © 1967 by *The Sea Tiger*. Reprinted with permission.

Haber, Michael. "War Hero Wins Award 15 Years After Service." *Parkchester News*, October, 1982. Copyright © 1982 by *Parkchester News*. Reprinted with permission.

Krulak, Victor H. from First to Fight: An Inside View of the U.S. Marine Corps. Copyright © 1999 by Victor H. Krulak. Reprinted with permission of Naval Institute Press.

Lowe, Lance Cpl. Lucas G. "Former Corpsman honored for Heroism." *The Quantico Sentry*, April 4, 2010. Copyright © 2010. Reprinted with permission.

Noah, Dennis L. "A Grunt Corpsman's Prayer." "An Old Corpsman's Dream." from *Reflections on the Vietnam War: Experience of a Marine Corpsman*. unpublished manuscript. Copyright © 2005 by Dennis L. Noah. Reprinted with permission.

"Thumbing a Boat Ride." *The Sea Tiger*, February 8, 1967, vol. III, no. 6. Copyright © 1967 by *The Sea Tiger*. Reprinted with permission.

Viti, Tom. "Nurses at St. John's Hospital Send Ex-Interne Supplies Needed in Vietnam." Letter by Dr. Tom Viti. *The Herald Statesman*, Sseptember, 1967. Copyright © 1967 by *The Herald Stateman*. Reprinted with permission.

Weinraub, Bernard. "Navy Doctor from the Bronx is 'No. 1' to South Vietnamese Village Children; An Incident Last March." *New York Times*, November 24, 1967, sec 11/24/67, page 4. Copyright © 1967 by the *New York Times*. Reprinted with permission.

United States Marine Corp. "Release No. CS-243-68." October 29, 1968. Copyright © 1968.

U.S. Congress. "Tribute to Dr. Gaetano Thomas Viti: A Viet Nam War Hero Gets Long Overdue Recognition." *Congressional Record*. 97th Cong., 2d sess., 1982, Vol. 128, pt. 43. Copyright © 1982.

Rogue Books
a division of
Bedazzled Ink Publishing Company
Fairfield, California
http://www.bedazzledink.com/roguebooks

For You
Daddy

To Chris
My Love
My Life
My Gift

*Many thanks to Roger McDowell for his
overwhelming generosity and talent in re-touching
every old photograph and newspaper clipping
that had become worn with age
living inside the now
infamous Harry & David box.*

Acknowledgements

To acknowledge is to appreciate through recognition. I'd like to recognize kind gestures, kudos, and "life as normal" love and support systems that enabled me to persevere through days that were filled with the magic of discovery, the sadness of loss, and the joy of completion.

C. A. Casey—where do I start? A thank you seems so utterly inept. Honestly, there aren't enough words in the English language to thank you and Claudia Wilde and Carrie Tierney at Bedazzled Ink for believing in me. Thank you for enabling me to share this testament of love to my father, Dr. Tom. Thank you, thank you, thank you.

A very special shout-out goes to Jennifer Blum and Erin Barnes for selflessly sharing your Dad with me. Thanks to the Barnes, Bond, and McCardle families for heartwarming holidays. And I wouldn't dream of forgetting John Hackett for sharing our football Sundays.

Thank you Jane for your love, friendship and never-ending reminder that my Heavenly Father loves me just as much as my Daddy does and that I am—as we all are—God's somebody.

To John, Carol, Thomas, John-Luke, and Sophia; may the legacy of Dr. Tom inspire you to always be your best Viti.

Special thanks to my Aunt Aggie and Aunt Pepe for sharing memories of our youthful "Tommy."

Oodles of gratitude to my New York gal pals—Gina, Aileen, Lori, and Megan for your allegiance, kindness and years of memorable holidays, beach Sundays, and one-heck-of-a-New York City nightlife.

Kitty hugs to Lori, Mo, and the Goddesses of Carpenteria for a tapestry of friendship woven between the mountains of West Virginia and the beaches of southern Cal.

Bear hugs to Erin O'Brien and the Denton brood for being such good people.

A huge thank you to Brenda McNally for never, ever giving up.

I am truly grateful for Pacific Athletic Club of San Diego. Phil Sanchez, my PAC San Diego colleagues, and PAC San Diego members fueled these marching orders in more ways than you know.

Special thanks to Kimberly for always making me feel like a princess.

Cheers to Naomi and the women of San Diego's roundtable for your unyielding support.

Loud applause goes to Lisette, Jamie, Janet, Barb, Lori and the Boot Campaign for the coolest pictures—ever!

I'd like to toast the Joye's and the Sterk's for their cherished friendships.

Hugs to the Tinley family for always making my day.

Malaki hugs to the Schuler family for being such cool neighbors.

I'm truly appreciative for the warm welcome of Naomi Esau, Janet Newton, Susan Noah, Carol Bowers, Khahn Marengo, and Susan Meyers.

Special thanks also goes to General James T. Conway, 34th Commandant, U.S. Marine Corps (Ret.); Wesley Lee Fox, Colonel, U.S. Marine Corps (Ret.); Ron Christmas, Lieutenant General, U.S. Marine Corps (Ret.); Chris Cortez, Major General, U.S. Marine Corps (Ret.); R.W. Koeneke, Colonel, U.S. Marine Corps (Ret); William L. Buchanan, Captain, U.S. Marine Corps (Ret.); Otto Lehrack, LtCol. U.S. Marine Corps (Ret.); Roger McDowell, Sgt, U.S. Marine Corps; LtCol Christian Wortman U.S. Marine Corps; Colonel Fred Milburn U.S. Marine Corps, Jan K. Herman U.S. Naval Historian; Bernie Weinraub; Warren Duffy; the Graham Family; Mrs. Joseph Donnelly, James Denton, and Scott Tinley. To every librarian and historian that crossed my path—thank you.

And last but not least, special thanks to Chris—my best pal in the whole world.

TABLE OF CONTENTS

Foreword

The Vietnam War involved many Americans, directly and indirectly, and so much of the reality of the events that occurred during the Vietnam War remains unknown or was misrepresented to our fellow Americans at home. Our news media was the first cause of this problem, and our supposed political leaders making decisions for the combat commanders on the ground was another major contribution to our supposed loss of the Vietnam War. Actually, America won the Vietnam War on the ground, in Vietnam; our politicians and news media gave the win away. Lucia Viti covers these points well as she references her father's commitment to America during the Vietnam War as well as Dr. Tom's commitment to his Marines and the Vietnamese civilians in his battalion's assigned area.

Lucia Viti's father, Dr. Tom Viti, was a naval surgeon assigned (by his choice) to the Marines serving in Vietnam. All medical personnel, surgeons, doctors, and corpsmen, serving Marines are Navy personnel. I am so impressed with their service that I say that the Marine battle cry is CORPSMAN UP! *Dr. Tom's War—A Daughter's Journey* supports my thoughts with the revelation that six hundred corpsmen were killed during the Vietnam War; three received Medals of Honor; twenty-nine received Navy Crosses; one hundred and twenty-seven received Silver Stars; two hundred and ninety received Bronze Stars, and five thousand plus received the Purple Heart for wounds received in action against the enemy of our country. What was the total number of naval corpsmen assigned to the Marines in that war? What is the percentage of corpsmen killed in action considering the six hundred mentioned above?

Lucia's work is an emotional read for Marines because she provides her thoughts on the subject of the U.S. Marine: what is a Marine, from where is the Marine coming, and a discussion on the always positive, direct, individual Marine's movement forward. Ms. Viti expresses in her writing what I have stated for years: There is no such thing as a former Marine! A Marine is a Marine for life, "former" as well as "ex" does not fit with the word Marine; there is no such thing in our world.

Lucia Viti traveled America to interview 2nd Battalion 5th Marine Regimental Marines and corpsmen who served with her dad. This was her effort to re-connect with the man she loved more than life itself. Dr. Tom, unlike most physicians assigned to infantry battalions in combat, spent more time in the "bush" than his fellow officers; his dealings with most of his counterparts were short, concise, and medical. Lucia gathered quips and quotes from those he served with and those who knew her dad best, and she provides these interviews in her story. *Dr. Tom's War* is a narrative memoir that depicts a unique journey of discovery, not only of Lucia's father's life as the battalion surgeon in one of America's most controversial wars, but of the Marines and corpsmen that served with him. These men were a silent majority who are now willing to share untold stories of their involvement in that war.

Hanoi Jane Fonda is justifiably placed within her position as a national traitor explained by several of the Marines interviewed in *Dr. Tom's War—A Daughter's Journey*; and in my opinion, most deservedly so. Also included were the Marine reflections concerning the accounts of a non-American identified as John Kerry and his despicable conduct during the Vietnam War, in country and in America. Add Oliver Stone and his distorted depiction of our conduct during the Vietnam War, particularly of Marine personalities portrayed in his phony Hollywood movie. Contrary to my comments above, it is correct to show Oliver Stone as an ex-Marine; he may have worn the uniform, but he is no Marine. Walter Cronkite is also covered herein as one of the contributors to our countrymen's receipt of misinformation by incorrectly referencing the conduct and accomplishments of our warriors, our gunfighters in the Vietnamese War. The Marine interviews of *Dr. Tom's War* tell it the way it really was; their contributions to the facts will be greatly appreciated by our countrymen.

Dr. Tom's War is a testament of a daughter's love of her father. Lucia Viti's words introduce the courageous men who fought with her father against communist aggression in the Vietnam War. These pages are fueled by personal determination, endurance, and resolve; they capture the courage, fortitude, and bravery of our gunfighters in a place named Vietnam. Weaving the Marine Corps Esprit de Corps with the horrors of war, the author provides a first-hand perspective on combat life in a Marine infantry battalion in Vietnam during 1967.

The contents of *Dr. Tom's War* will not only appeal to veterans, it will also attract an audience that may be hesitant to embrace a military read. This manuscript is for every family member associated with the thousands of Vietnam veterans. The interviewed individuals herein provide an understanding with their own words of what these men endured and sacrificed, our young warriors described by the ignorant and misinformed as "baby killers" who were fighting a dirty war.

The author separates the chapters with a Dear Daddy title on each chapter's first page. That first page of each chapter bridges her present voice to her memories of 1967 and her father. Lucia's dad has long since moved on from taking care of Marines to guarding the gates into heaven. Nevertheless, her words to her dad on these pages concern her thoughts, memories, and how much she misses him. On these lead-in chapter pages she also introduces the interviewed Marine or corpsman who, served with her dad and, is covered in that chapter. She still communicates with the most important man in her life. She is a remarkable young lady as well as a great writer and author. I admire her work; not only is it all about Marines, our great nation's gunfighters but it reinforces my feelings of our Marine Battle Cry: CORPSMAN UP!

Colonel Wesley Fox, USMC (Retired)
1950-1993
Medal of Honor Recipient
Operation Dewey Canyon, 1969

Bronze Star w/Valor Device
Purple Heart (4)
Navy Commendation Medal (2) w/ Valor Device
United Nations Service Medal

❧ Dear Daddy ❧

How do I find myself here today, four-plus decades post your Vietnam tour, weaving the final threads of Dr. Tom's War? How did I discover a seemingly ancient Harry & David fruit box stuffed with your Vietnam memorabilia—the contents of which left me breathless—and stare at it for years before plunging into a world alien to the core of my being? Why did I—the creative wild child—commit myself to the rigors of writing within a media frenzy of yet another unfavorable war? You, Daddy, you. I went searching for you. The you who left me more than twenty-three years ago. The you I continue to love more than life itself.

Thinking that I could re-connect and give you life, I decided to create my Hollywood Field of Dreams. *I built this so you would come and ease my pain. And the news is good, for I went the distance. But truth be known, I've resembled more Forrest Gump than Shoeless Joe Jackson. I thought—in my hero as father Forrest Gump naiveté—that I could explore that war—discover everyone's favorite "Doc" and magically fill the void of your absence. Although my efforts to resuscitate you were successful, the hole in my heart is now bigger than ever. Dear Lord, what was I thinking?*

And hardly reminiscent of a baseball diamond built in an Iowa cornfield, I lay buried by government papers, Command Chronologies, Marine Corps and Naval Orders, documentaries, movies, magazines, books, websites, interviews, and transcriptions. Consequently, after four years of diligent and tedious research, I can merit the arguments of America's involvement in Southeast Asia; question the competence of Washington, DC's political strategists; describe the ironies of this living-room war of aggression; expose the reality of bush combat and infantry camaraderie; portray enemy savagery and burn Jane Fonda at the public stake. But no need to dwell on the details. Today's book market is saturated with many factual—and some not so honest—accounts.

So today, Daddy, I've decided to surrender my Vietnam passage to a higher purpose. I believe that my gatherings were pre-ordained, by you, to allow those willing to share a cathartic healing. My diligence in the study of Vietnam—although impressive—mattered little. My ability to listen patiently, sans judgment mattered most. You served as the common dominator, and I as the conduit. I really was Forrest Gump and you were my "best good friend."

Dr. Tom's War—A Daughter's Journey is a scrapbook of short stories, quotes, and confessions by those who proudly served their country 11,000 miles away from home. That which I have collected neither annuls nor justifies the Vietnam War; respectively, I refuse. And my journey depicts but a single year—1967; a time frame described by most as a "different war." But I chose the year of your tenure—one year within eleven very long ones. Civilians may wince at this exposé, for it lacks Hollywood's macho romanticism. And that's okay. Let this slice of humanity attached to the Second Battalion Fifth Marines, First Marine Division stationed in An Hoa, Republic of South Vietnam during 1967 with you, speak for itself.

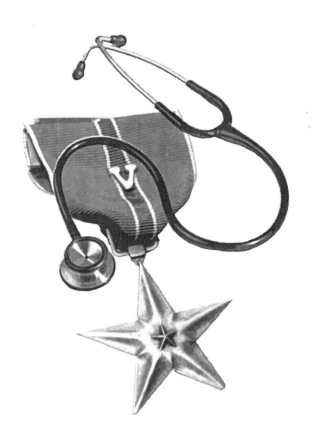

D r. Gaetano Thomas Anthony Viti was born at home in Brooklyn, New York on April 22, 1935. He was the eldest of five siblings and the only son of Dr. Felice "Phil" Raphael Viti and Helen Colucci. Tommy, an intelligent and boisterous lad, grew up in a lively, classy, traditional Catholic-Italian household when Brooklyn was as famous for housing Mafia notables as it was for its bakeries, dairies, and butcher shops.

Dr. Phil, described as regimented but fair, shipped his protégé to La Salle Military Academy in the eighth grade—a military boarding school

Gaetano Thomas Anthony Viti, Brooklyn, NY, 1936.

in New York's Long Island. Senior worried that Tommy's smothering from Mamma, Grandma Joya, and his sisters would soften him. La Salle Military Academy showcased Tommy as a gifted athlete in football and baseball and as a member of the debate team. Destined to lead, he graduated as captain of his company, an honor comparable to valedictorian.

Washington, DC's Georgetown University followed La Salle but Tommy who carried a summer and winter tuxedo to Georgetown—was more successful with his social life than his grades. Senior wasted no time shipping Junior to St. Michael's— an all male Catholic College in Vermont.

Helen Colucci Viti, Tommy Viti, Josephine "Joya" Colucci, Brooklyn, NY, circa 1948.

In 1956, the summer of his graduating year, Tommy met Louise Joan Sellitto, a Bronx-bred, Catholic-Italian in Villagio Italia, a popular Italian summer resort in Haines Falls, New York. The two married within a year. Tommy worked as a bacteriologist at Memorial Sloan-Kettering Institute in Manhattan while completing his graduate degree at Hunter College.

In 1958, Tommy entered Medical School at the University of Bologna in Italy. He transferred to the University of Padua in 1959 where he earned a degree in Medicine and Surgery in November of 1963. The now father of four moved back to America to begin his residency in Family Medicine and Surgery. In 1965, this Acting Chief Resident in New York's Goldwater Memorial Hospital passed all exams required by the Education Council for Foreign Medical Graduates.

PHONE SAYVILLE 900

LA SALLE MILITARY ACADEMY

OAKDALE, LONG ISLAND
NEW YORK

11 August 1951

Mr. Thomas Viti
65 Cranberry Street
Brooklyn 2, New York

Dear Thomas:

It gives me great pleasure to inform you that you have been appointed to the rank of Captain in The Cadet Battalion for the scholastic year 1951-1952.

This you have achieved by your attention to detail, your scholastic attainment, and your willingness to cooperate in all academic matters. This position carries with it not only the privileges of office, but also the heavy responsibilities of having a direct hand in guiding the Battalion during the coming year. I know you are fully capable of handling this position in an effective and efficient manner.

Please see Mr. Maher at 11 West 25th Street, New York, on or before Friday, August 24th, so that your uniforms may be altered, chevrons sewed on, or new uniforms ordered in time to have them ready when you return to school in September. This matter must be taken care of before August 24th. If for any reason you cannot see Mr. Maher before the above date, please inform me beforehand with your reasons outlined.

We will expect you to report in the Principal's office at 10:00 A.M. on Saturday, September 15th.

With my best wishes that you may continue to enjoy a pleasant summer, I remain,

Sincerely

Brother Amian, F.S.C.
Headmaster

BA:C

La Salle Military Academy Graduation Photo, Long Island, NY, June 1952.

La Salle Military Academy Captain's Letter, Long Island, NY, 1951.

Military Training Certificate
RESERVE OFFICERS' TRAINING CORPS

This is to certify that _____ THOMAS ANTHONY VITI _____ has completed _TWO_ years of instruction in the Senior Division Reserve Officers' Training Corps, in which he was enrolled, from _18 SEPTEMBER_ 19 _50_ to _12 JUNE_ 19 _52_, and if otherwise qualified, is eligible to enter an Army Officer Candidate Course, or reenlist in the Enlisted Reserve Corps, in the grade of _PRIVATE FIRST CLASS_, this _TWELFTH_ day of _JUNE_ in the year of our Lord, one thousand nine hundred and _FIFTY-TWO_.

La Salle Military Academy Reserve Officer Training Corps Certificate, Long Island, NY, June 12, 1952.

La Salle Military Academy Graduation Day, Brooklyn, NY, June 1952.

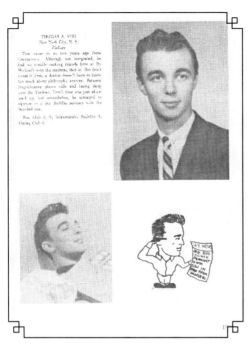

St. Michael's College Senior Yearbook Photo,
Colchester, Vermont, June 1956.

Louise Joan Sellitto and Tommy Viti,
Brooklyn, NY, 1956.

Louise Joan Sellitto-Viti and Tommy
Viti, Bronx, NY, February 1957.

Tommy Viti and Cousin Eugenio, Padua, Italy, circa 1961.

Dr. Viti graduation from Medical School, University of Padua, November 1963.

Dr. Viti and Lucia Viti in Padua, Italy, 1962.

Dr. Viti and Lucia Viti in Padua, Italy, 1962.

While working as an Intern in St. John's Riverside Hospital in Yonkers, New York, the young physician received a letter from Army Headquarters advising him of his name submission as a reserve officer to the Department of the Navy. Refusing to wait, the maverick applied for active/inactive commission in the U.S. Navy/Naval Reserve. He listed the Fleet Marine Force as his first field of choice.

Dr. Viti and Louise Viti on the day of his departure in front of his apartment, Bronx, NY, October 1966.

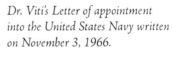

Dr. Viti's Letter of appointment into the United States Navy written on November 3, 1966.

Dr. Viti, on the day of his departure in front of his apartment, Bronx, NY, October 1966.

In November of 1966, Navy
Lieutenant Gaetano "Tom" Viti, MD,
trained at Camp Pendleton's Field
Medical School for active duty with
the Fleet Marine Force. Assigned to
the Second Battalion Fifth Marines
(2/5), First Marine Division, Lieutenant
Viti, MD, landed in An Hoa, Republic
of South Vietnam (RSVN) in early
December of 1966. He would remain
in An Hoa until his departure on
December 3, 1967.

*Dr. Viti, USN, Field Medical School
training in Camp Pendleton, San Diego,
CA, November 1966.*

The Vietnam War was in full
swing in 1967. Fighting against the
backdrop of the Cold War and threatened by the Domino Theory, the United
States remained on a course chartered by Presidents Eisenhower and Kennedy.
The Vietnamese, seasoned from one thousand years of combat against the
Chinese, Japanese, and French, regarded America's presence in South Vietnam
as foreign aggression. Ho Chi Minh, North Vietnam's dictator, collaborated
with South Vietnam's Viet Cong to re-unify his country separated at the 17th
parallel by the Geneva Accords as President Lyndon B. Johnson renewed his
commitment to stunt godless communism.

South Vietnam, its topography, people, language, and culture, was as
convoluted to America's military as the region's diverse political factions. Some
locals were loyal to North Vietnam's communists and the Viet Cong while
others rejected communism and supported a U.S. military presence.
Vietnamese religious beliefs, ranging from atheist and pagan to Catholic and
Buddhist, created even more complexity.

By the end of 1967's Haight and Ashbury's summer of love, five hundred
thousand American troops were stationed in Vietnam. The KIA rate had
escalated from six hundred and thirty-six in December of 1965 to sixteen
thousand. More than fifty-eight thousand would succumb to the same fate by
1974.

The 2/5 South Vietnam Tactical Area of Responsibility (TAOR) spanned
one hundred and forty-four square miles, twenty-five miles southwest of the
coastal city of Da Nang. Surrounded by the majestic Que Son Mountains and
meandering rivers and tributaries, this TAOR included three Vietnamese
districts—Quan Duc Duc, Quan Duy Xuyen, and Quan Dien Ban; the An
Hoa Industrial Complex; the An Hoa Combat Base; the perimeter outposts of
Mau Chanh (1) and (2); My Loc (2); Phu Lac (6) and the Nong Son Coal Mine.
Included within the An Hoa's combat base arms and elbows were Logistics
Support Activity (LSA), the Battalion Aid Station (BAS), an Amtrac Tractor
Park, a Motor Transport Park, a Tank Platoon, 2/5 supply, a reinforced

artillery battery, a platoon of combat engineers, a military/civilian airstrip, a watch tower, and the Seabees. Due to the excessive bulges, 2/5 operated under the First Marine Division, as opposed to the Fifth Marines Regiment. The 2/5 reported directly to General Nickerson, dubbed Herman the German.

This TAOR was later manned by the entire Fifth Marines Regiment.

The Second Battalion Fifth Marines' myriad of operations were intended to secure the east end of the Thong Duc Corridor—an access route from the Ho Chi Minh Trail—and flush out the enemy infiltrated areas of the Arizona Territory, Antenna Valley, and the VC R & R retreat at Go Noi Island.

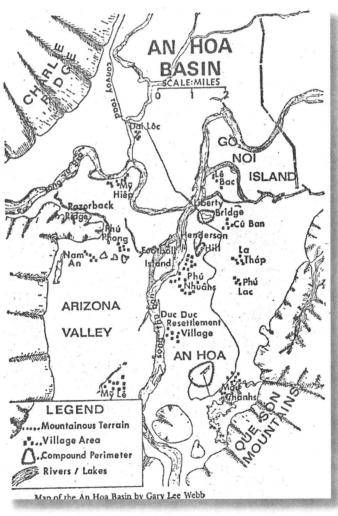

Official Map of The An Hoa Basin by Gary Lee Webb.

🌺 *Dear Daddy* 🌺

Dr. Tom's War began with a visit to the consummate Marine, your pal, Richard H. Esau, Jr., a.k.a. The Colonel. Armed with a suitcase stuffed with Vietnam documentation, I hustled to Virginia Beach seeking guidance, direction, and knowledge from the man who knew you best. I asked, and the colonel answered.

I quickly learned the ground rules:

• Once a Marine, always a Marine. There's no such thing as an ex-Marine or a former Marine.

• Marines are guided by principles of virtue, integrity, and a love of God, Country, and Corps.

• Marines adhere to higher standards, so they are a cut above the rest.

• Marines just don't become Marines. Marines accept the challenge and earn the privilege of wearing the eagle, globe, and anchor.

• Marines conduct themselves under a code of ethics—honor, courage, and commitment.

• Marines are elite combat warriors.

• Marines are a unique band of brothers that demand and deliver excellence.

• Marines are Semper Fidelis.

• So what part of Marine don't you understand?

Oh and by the way, Marines are never referred to as soldiers. Marines are Marines.

Pops, the colonel exudes an extraordinary aura of what it means to be a Marine. Shuffle unwavering leadership, guts, tenacity, spirit, selfless determination, and relentless dedication with excellence in achievement, and Richard reigns supreme among The Few . . . The Proud . . . The Marines!

One afternoon, as pelting rain kept us indoors, I presented the good colonel with an impressive list of political questions stemming from Robert McNamara's book, In Retrospect. *I expected a deluge of information but Richard answered in mono-syllable grunts and barely audible grumbles. I blamed the Yankees Game as the culprit of distraction until I realized that the Yankees were losing by a football score.*

I hesitantly pursued until the good colonel politely but sternly said, "Lucia, McNamara was one of the many no-good Washington, DC politicians who curtailed and ultimately destroyed our success in Vietnam. I won't answer questions pertaining to those men responsible for Vietnam combat veterans bearing the burden and the wrath for the Vietnam War."

"My apologies, Colonel."

"No apologies necessary. Your efforts are commendable. But you, like most civilians who lived through that war, only know of the distortions presented by the media, Hollywood, and our political press. Hindsight is a wonderful gift, isn't it? Admission of any kind will not bring back my dead men; my boys. I have no desire to listen to McNamara's rhetoric. And that book you bought at the PX today . . ."

"Which one?"

"It doesn't matter. Don't believe everything you read. Read **Stolen Valor.***"*

"Will do. Should we break? Have I exhausted you?"

"No, I'll tell tales about your Dad or any other noble compatriot until the moon's blue. The world needs to read about men like Doctor Tom who could have easily deferred his deployment, but instead chose to honor America by caring for her finest on the other side of the world. Dr. Tom Viti was a hero who lived the very definition of the Hippocratic Oath."

"I believe that Vietnam gave my father a benchmark to which life was never the same again."

"Maybe so. Vietnam forever changed many lives."

"I'm honestly overwhelmed. I've committed myself to an arduous task. Between grieving Daddy and the controversy surrounding Vietnam, I'm not sure how to start this thing called Vietnam. Despite reading an enormous amount of research material, I've yet to make a dent in this eleven-year monstrosity."

"Lucia, it may be time to stop. Simply celebrate your father's presence in Vietnam, and the book will write itself."

Not a moment too soon Naomi—a.k.a. Mrs. Colonel—rang the dinner bell. Retired Marine Ken Noonan—your patient from St. Alban's Naval Hospital joined us. And as fact is often stranger than fiction, I kept the tape recorder on during dinner. Thus began the written word.

Dinner with the Colonel

Colonel Richard H. Esau, Jr.,
USMC, 1982.

Major Richard H. Esau, Jr., USMC.

I sheepishly carried the tape recorder into the dining room and wondered how the colonel would react to an informal, dinnertime interview. A gale force downpour threatening to implode the floor-to-ceiling windowpanes echoed in the background. "Do you mind if I keep the tape recorder on during dinner?"

"Again with that thing?" Rich asked.

"You won't even know it's on, I promise."

Ken chuckled. "This could be dangerous; we're drinking."

"Ahhh." I grinned. "What better time to catch a few gems."

"Settle down all of you," Naomi said. "Of course it's okay, Lucia. Set it here. No one will be the wiser."

"Thanks, Naomi."

Rich smirked. "More questions? You should be an expert by now. You've certainly read enough."

"Yes, that's true. But I'd rather ask you. You're an incredible storyteller. You don't simply tell a story, you infuse life into a backdrop of history."

"Sounds like a snow job to me," Ken said.

"We'll keep it light and simple," I added with a cheeky grin.

"Is that so?" Rich said. "Like how?"

"Like why are Marines referred to as Leathernecks?"

"Oh that's an easy one," Ken jumped in. "The nickname dates back to the Revolutionary War, days of wooden ships and iron men in hand-to-hand combat. Marines wore thick pieces of leather beneath their uniform collars to protect themselves from having their throats slashed."

"You see, that was painless," I said. "Besides, Rich, you love talking about Pops. And I'm truly proud of what I've discovered about Dr. Tom's Vietnam tour."

Rich leaned forward with a gleam in his eye and eased into an answer. "Rightfully so, young lady. Tom Viti understood his vocation in Vietnam and dedicated himself to the Marines and the Vietnamese. Although highly unusual, An Hoa's Second Battalion Fifth Marines Battalion Aid Station, otherwise known as 2/5's BAS, provided medical assistance to the military and the Vietnamese civilian populous. Dr. Tom, Dr. Flip Gonder, and Chief Hospital Corpsman Lou LeGarie worked tirelessly to improve the lives of the local citizenry who were important to the accomplishment of our mission. Although I will say Tom Viti could be unorthodox. But senior people never bitched. And if they did, we invited them to our combat base in An Hoa to make changes, which of course never happened."

An Hoa, Combat Base, RSVN, 1967.

"Major Esau, as he was then called, served as 2/5's S3 operations officer in An Hoa with more authority and less interaction with higher brass," Ken said. "Rich requested permission from the higher ups with his military agenda ready to rock and roll like so: 'Hey, Colonel so and so, does such and such work?' The generals and visiting morons in Da Nang would never have tolerated such behavior."

Rich nodded. "Kenny makes an interesting point."

I smiled. "About the visiting morons?"

"Well, almost, but no. Point being that 2/5 remained under the operational control of the division, not the regiment because we were so far out on a limb."

"No one," Ken said, "thought 2/5 would be assigned to An Hoa for long."

"That's right," Rich said. "But General Nickerson realized 2/5 exceeded all military expectations—oddball or not—and therefore used us as a role model. Doctor Tom and Chief LeGarie did their part by building An Hoa's BAS into a model complex; although good ol' Tom could make me crazy. Christ, he wouldn't listen. We'd be under mortar attack, and out of nowhere I'd hear, 'Umph grunt, umph, grunt, ouch.' Tom, God love him, carried extra canteens for the wounded around his cartridge belt which inevitably bounced off his groin."

Rich transformed his demeanor, posture, and voice, and laid his hands on his hips. Major Esau then bellowed at the rebel doctor drenched by a monsoon rain that made our howling thunderstorm look like an afternoon Caribbean sun shower.

> "Doc, is that you?"
> "Hey, Rich. What's up?"
> "What's up? What's up? What the hell do you mean what's up? In case you haven't noticed, it's raining like the dickens, and we're under intense enemy mortar fire. That's what's up. And you're not supposed to be here. Now get the hell out of here."

"Half an hour later he'd be in my face all cheery," Rich said.

> "Hey, Major. What's up?"
> "Are you still here? What the hell are you doing here when I told you to get lost? You don't belong here, and I can't afford to lose you so get back to the BAS where you belong. I mean it. Get the hell out of here."
> "Okay, Major."

"It quickly became nothing more than a game," Rich said.

"Your father showed the same defiant compassion in St. Albans Naval

Hospital," Ken said. "Doctor, lawyer, Indian chief, it didn't matter. Did you know he almost strangled a colleague?"

"Yes, I've heard the choke story," I said.

"That's a good story, tell Naomi."

Without hesitation I shared an all-too-familiar Dr. Tom tale that boasted of a head-strong Italian compassion. "A physician assisted Dad in amputating the leg of a young Marine and regretfully commented about his lack of financial compensation in a VA Hospital like St. Albans. I say regretfully because Dad pinned the

Major Richard H. Esau, Jr. and Dr. Viti, USN, RSVN, 1967.

guy by the throat against the wall and threatened to squeeze the life out of him if he ever again dared to degrade his boys by placing a price tag on their health and well-being."

Rich chuckled. "A mere suggestion of a firsthand visit to Vietnam."

"That asshole doctor never stepped foot in Vietnam," Ken said. "And a pansy like that never would. Nothing meant more to Dr. Viti than caring for his Marines. Nothing. Dr. Viti showed us pictures of his field surgical kits. I never saw another doctor in Vietnam with so much medical equipment out of the Battalion Aid Station. Never."

"Well, how about the amtrac we transformed into a hospital?" Rich asked.

"I have a picture of an amtrac attached to the BAS," I said as I left the table to search through one of the albums organized from slides recently discovered in the Vietnam treasure chest masquerading as an old Harry & David fruit box. I handed Naomi the photo. "How cool is that?"

"Impressive." Naomi turned to Rich. "How did you attach this amtrac to the BAS?"

"We connected it to a wall inside the BAS," Rich said. "The amtrac should have been sent to Da Nang for refurbishing but Dr. Tom decided it would better suit his need as an operating room. Mortar fragments can't penetrate amtracs. Chief Lou painted the inside mint green, and we added sandbagged walls for further protection. But hell, that didn't keep Tom from going where he didn't belong. He took dicey chances even from the BAS."

Rich looked at me with a twinkle in his eyes. "Do you know your father borrowed Brigadier General Frosty LaHue's helicopter?"

"Borrowed a helicopter?" I was shocked. My father's presence on an airplane was virtually non-existent. And when required—although rare—for the occasional medical conference or junket trip to a Vegas Casino, Dr. Tom

Amtrac Dr. Viti converted into an emergency room attached to An Hoa's BAS.

two-fisted two Bloody Marys throughout the entire flight. "He was petrified of flying."

"Helicopters could be scary," Ken said.

Rich eyed me in disbelief. "We were fighting the main force VC in Antenna Valley while Tom was stuck in An Hoa's BAS. So Tom sold the visiting general's pilot a bill of goods, choppered into Antenna Valley—under heavy fire, and medevaced the wounded. That was probably the first and only time anyone borrowed the general's bird."

Amused, Naomi toasted her glass of Napa Valley Merlot toward the heavens. "Tom Viti was certainly surrounded by guardian angels."

"Here, here." Rich raised his glass. "The good Lord protects children, fools, and doctors of which Tom wore the last two hats rather well. Ahh, but we all survived Vietnam with a touch of the macabre."

"How so?" I also raised my glass.

"We added humor to the circumstances beyond the norm and out of our control," Rich said. "For example, we'd kid Tom about digging up a young Vietnamese woman whose parents, unfortunately, buried her alive. 'Hey, Tom, dig anybody up today?' Although that was a prime example of what a pain-in-the-ass he could be, running where no man goes—alone—to save her."

"Oh do tell," I piped up, all ears.

"Tom bolted *through* An Hoa's protective mine field instead of running *around* it on a quest for a missing patient in the ville outside the wire. The distance between the two was maybe five minutes, but for Tom it was an eternity. But, for Christ's sake, no one runs through a mine field, especially if you don't know where the mines are."

"I'm not sure I understand," I said.

"A young female patient was removed from the BAS by her parents who thought she was dead," Rich said. "Ballistic, Tom did the unthinkable. I ordered him to the COC."

"You wanted to see me, Major?" Tom asked.

"God damn it, what the hell are you doing? Where the hell were you going?"

"I was attending to one of my patients."

"By running through our mine field? For Christ's sake, you don't run *through* a mine field, you run *around* the goddamn thing."

"I couldn't afford the time," Tom said.

"That truly is admirable, really, but tell me who do I pick as party to retrieve your body strewn across our mine field? Or better yet, how do I tell your wife you gallantly galloped *through* a mine field, alone, with not a clue as to where a single mine lay, to un-dig with his bare hands a patient whose parents buried her?"

"Can you believe they buried her alive?"

"What was wrong with her?"

"Severe dysentery and dehydration," Tom said. "The meds caused a sedative-induced sleep. Her parents took her home from the BAS and buried her, thinking she was dead."

"And you dug her up with your bare hands to perform CPR?"

"I was trying to save the life of a young woman."

"Yeah, and I'm trying to keep my battalion surgeon alive."

"Well, I'm alive so what's your problem?"

"Your father was a pisser, and it was easy to love him," Rich said.

"Yes, Pops was incredibly loveable." I sighed, grateful the gaping hole in my heart caused by his absence was not open for public viewing. "Tell Naomi and Ken the watch story you told me this afternoon."

"I can't remember the kid's name," Rich said, "but he was an A-gunner who got himself in trouble whenever he spoke to anyone so he decided to talk to his watch. 'Hello, watch. Good morning, watch. How are you? I see that you're ticking this morning, and hopefully by day's end, we'll both still be ticking.' It was a bit strange, but what the hell. He unfortunately got wounded, and was transported to our naval hospital ship the *USS Repose*. While on board, the surgeon noted that he spoke to his watch, and was therefore, *non compos mentis*."

"Not mentally comprehending," Ken explained.

"Yes, not mentally comprehending. So Division ordered the lad home, which was completely unacceptable to him and us. This kid knew his gunner couldn't function without him. Tom tried to convince the division surgeon that conversing with one's watch wasn't all that unusual."

"Do you talk to your watch?" the division surgeon asked.

"On occasion, certainly," Dr. Tom said.

"Be real. Are you comfortable talking to your watch?"

"Of course. I would only be uncomfortable if the watch talked back."

"Needless to say the division surgeon second-guessed Tom's way of thinking, insisting that this kid wasn't sane," Rich said. "So Tom fetched him from the *USS Repose* and brought him back to An Hoa. Division ordered both to Da Nang. Tom refused."

> "With all due respect, sir, there's nothing life threatening concerning the health status of this young Marine," Dr. Tom said. "He will soon be well enough to resume his duties and complete his tour of duty."
>
> "I'm not sure which I find more disturbing," the division surgeon said. "The fact that this kid talks to his watch or that you, a Navy physician serving as a battalion surgeon for the Marine Corps in a war zone, finds nothing wrong with this scenario."
>
> "Sir, I invite you to An Hoa to make your own assessment."

Rich had a twinkle in his eye. "This again, of course, never happened."

"So was he brave or perhaps just a little nuts?" I asked, already more than familiar with my father's ability to add levity to the absurd.

"Brave. Brave. Brave." Rich boomed. "During one operation, Tom jumped from a bird under fire into a flooded rice paddy. His medical knapsack and extra canteens restricted his arms—which didn't make his exit easy—as he stumbled to a corpsman crouched behind a paddy dike one hundred meters away. This medic, desperately trying to keep a wounded Marine alive, said, 'I lost him, Dr. Viti.' 'Let me look at him, son.' Undaunted by the surrounding machine gun and mortar fire, Tom massaged the heart of this dead kid and brought him back to life."

"That's my pops," I said proudly. "How did the Vietnamese civilians react to the good doctor?"

"The locals loved the *Bac-si* but the Viet Cong retaliated," Rich said. "Tom treated a pregnant woman at the BAS who we later found staked to her home. Her stomach had been sliced open and her fetus lay on the ground as a declaration to not seek assistance from the American doctor."

Ken groaned in disgust. "The main force VC were very, very crummy."

"The main force Viet Cong were hardened communists striving to turn

Vietnam into a communist nation," Rich continued. "They asked no quarter, they gave no quarter; they were a formidable enemy. But over time Tom won the hearts and minds of everyone, including the insurgents."

"How so?" Naomi asked as she refilled glasses running low on Merlot.

"A chance occurrence sparked a chain of events that shifted civilian allegiance from the VC to the Marines," Rich said. "Some twenty-three hundred villagers requesting asylum joined a Marine unit returning to An Hoa. The VC had since levied a seventy-five percent tax on their rice crop and forcibly inducted into its army all boys thirteen years and older. Resistors were killed. The refugees were taken to Duc-Duc District Headquarters and welcomed by Major Ham, the District Chief. The Seabees and the Marines built housing and USAID supplied food, but medical assistance was another story. The Vietnamese housed but a single nurse. The neighboring German Red Cross Clinic—run by an authentic German baroness—couldn't handle the multitudes. So Tom and his medical staff began treating five hundred Vietnamese a day. As the VC lost their clutch on the civilian populace, Dr. Tom was cited as public enemy number one, complete with a bounty for his capture. Circulars were posted in every hamlet. But that didn't stop Tom and the onset of refugees. Requests to aid those too sick to transport doubled. Despite the bounty, Tom accompanied battalion patrols into enemy territory to aid the elders, women, and children. Yet another mother, ignoring the VC's imposing threat, sought aid for her dying baby. The Viet Cong savagely murdered her and her four children. Medical supplies soon ran short. Refugees seeking asylum swelled Duc Duc's population to more than twenty thousand Vietnamese. A lesser man would have crumbled. But Tom being Tom, always found a way through the labyrinth of obstacles.

"Well, on one patrol, the good doctor administered medical aid to a Vietnamese girl suffering from spinal meningitis. Happenchance, this woman was the daughter of a Viet Cong district chief. Tom saved her life. So the VC chief lifted the bounty and declared that no one could harm the American *Bac-si*. And Tom forged on. He wrote to the staff at St. John's Riverside Hospital in New York, requested, and received immunizations for the village children. He also opened three clinics protected by Marine CAP Units."

Rich turned to me. "Do you know what a CAP Unit is?"

"If I remember correctly, CAP stands for a Marine Combat Action Platoon."

"Very good. A Marine Combat Action Platoon unit included a Marine squad, a Navy corpsman, and Vietnamese Popular Force soldiers designated to provide hamlet security. As word of Tom's humanitarian exploits spread, the local populace understood that the Americans had come to help, not colonize them. Six months after Dr. Viti's arrival to An Hoa, the locals were alerting Marines to the presence of booby traps. This radical change was a direct result of medical aid from Drs. Viti, Gonder, and Donnelly."

"Fearless, Lucia, fearless," Ken interrupted. "Dr. Viti was fearless."

"Your father even refused a spot to transfer to the relative safety of Division

"Bac-si" Dr. Viti, sitting outside of the BAS in An Hoa, RSVN, 1967.

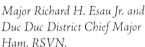

Major Richard H. Esau Jr. and Duc Duc District Chief Major Ham, RSVN.

Headquarters," Rich continued. "He told Division, 'I'd rather ride a helicopter into a hot zone than fly a rear area desk any time.'"

"Did you ever see the good doctor lose his cool?" I asked.

"Tom didn't have a temper; he simply had no patience for stupidity," Rich said. "And he, like most of us, endured truly heart-wrenching losses. One night a five-year-old boy was peppered with shrapnel from H&I fire. I never understood what the hell he was doing out at three a.m., but nonetheless, we brought him into the BAS. Dr. Viti couldn't save him. It was terrible. Tom did everything to help this little guy, and when he expired, so did a piece of Tom. It's one thing to kill people who are trying to kill you. It's another to witness the death of innocent children."

Ken shifted. "The kids were stuck in a no-win situation. Kids threw grenades or walked around strapped with explosives. I mean little kids, three- and four-year-olds. The VC didn't care. And we, as Marines, couldn't discern child as bad guy. That is, the kid needed to chuck the grenade before we could react. Since Marines couldn't comprehend a child was trying to kill them, they often ended up dead. It's not easy to shoot a child."

"Here's a sad story," Rich said. "One Marine sniper at Liberty Road's checkpoint three shot a VC planting a mine. He kicked over the dead body only to discover a fourteen-year-old girl. The Marine was done. He could never fire a rifle again."

Naomi sighed. "How sad."

"Terrible things happen in war," Ken said. "Like watching your buddy ravaged by a booby trap outside a ville you're protecting while the villagers know it's there."

Public Opinion

Nurses At St. John's Hospital
Send Ex-Interne Supplies
Needed In Vietnam

To The Herald Statesman:

Last July 1 a terrible accident happened on the New York State Thruway at the Yonkers exit.

Thirteen persons were seriously injured, and they were brought to St. John's Riverside Hospital. The call went out—and physicians and nurses and staff responded. They gave their time and knowledge unselfishly. There was no thought of payment of any kind. They just responded and gave of themselves.

NOW I WANT to tell you of something that happened just a few weeks ago.

Another call went out — this call was for medical supplies that I needed here in Vietnam.

I did not write to anyone here, but I did write to my friends— the nurses of the operating room and the physicians of St. John's Hospital.

I needed special supplies over here. They answered again a call for help — unselfishly. I received my much - needed special supplies in less than three weeks' time. These arrived in more than enough time.

THEY HAVE the thanks of many of the men who will benefit from the supplies from Yonkers. These men probably will never know who sent them, but I will thank God and ask His blessing on those who sent them — and will do so every time I use them.

I am very proud to have been associated with the physicans and surgeons, the nurses and staff of St. John's. I believe the people of Yonkers should also be proud to know what their hospital has done. That hospital answered a call again — a call by which they gave of themselves unselfishly once again.

GAETANO THOMAS VITI,
Lieutenant, U.S. Marine Corps,
Wtih First Marine Division
in Vietnam.

EDITOR'S NOTE — Lt. Viti was an interne at St. John's Riverside Hospital at the time he went to Vietnam, and he was one of the medical men who rushed to help during the time of the July 1 accident. When he left, within two weeks of completing his internship, the hospital nurses and staff presented him a survival kit. Within the last few days student nurses at the hospital carried out help - Vietnam project of their own, sending off 85 pounds of supplies, magazines, candy, shaving materials and books.

Letter written by Dr. Viti to the Herald Statesman, *Riverside, New York—1967 thanking St. John's Riverside Hospital for supplies donated to medical clinics in An Hoa, RSVN.*

Rich nodded in agreement. "We'd sweep through a village—without firing, question the elders about VC activity and invariably get the party line, 'No, no, no see VC, no see VC.' And of course, we'd receive fire from that village. That's why John Kerry is full of baloney."

Sensing Rich's agitation, I hesitated to pursue the John Kerry hot button during dinner. But I knew I had to seize this fervent moment. The answer would lead to a better understanding of the scourge ignited by the mere mention of the man, shrouded by his controversial Vietnam tour of duty. "Would you be kind enough to explain the why behind the disdain for John Kerry?"

"John Kerry slandered an entire generation of Vietnam veterans," Rich said. "John Kerry accused me, my men, and Dr. Viti of genocide. John Kerry compared your father to the likes of Genghis Khan. As a leader in the Vietnam Veterans Against the War, John Kerry told the U.S. Senate Foreign Relations Committee that Marines arbitrarily killed innocent Vietnamese. John Kerry portrayed my men as murderers and rapists ravaging the countryside of South Vietnam. His testimony was based on veterans, like himself, who claimed to witness war crimes that occurred on a daily basis while officers in all levels of command knew. Hogwash."

"Many of these so-called honorably discharged men were later exposed as phonies," Ken said.

Rich leaned in. "Let me set the record straight. Despite receiving VC fire while waiting outside a ville, we held our fire, aware that civilians were scrambling into bunkers. We removed Vietnamese from bunkers—*without firing a single shot*—filled with caches of enemy weapons and food. And if they refused to leave, we threw in tear gas grenades. Now exit the children, the elders, the mamma-sans, and invariably the Viet Cong with his rifle. And if we couldn't transport the contraband, we blew it to hell. We risked Marine casualties to ensure we didn't kill Vietnamese. John Kerry traveled on a Swift Boat for less than four months—"

"And received three purple hearts and his ticket home," Ken cut in.

Rich grunted. "John Kerry is full of donkey dust, the Irish term for bullshit."

Naomi shook her head. "The civilians were certainly caught between a rock and a hard place."

I pressed on. "Dare I ask about Jane Fonda?"

Ken flushed. "Oh, the traitor perched on a North Vietnamese anti-aircraft gun wearing an NVA helmet, laughing while American Air Force Pilots captured as POW's were being tortured? Jane Fonda and Tom Hayden provided aid and comfort to the enemy and should be in jail for treason. Jane Fonda betrayed America of her own free will and deserves to be plastered as decal on VA urinals so every Vietnam veteran who walks into the men's room in a VA building can pee on her."

Rich grabbed the table as if to restrain himself from throwing a punch into the pages of history. "Jane Fonda clapped and cheered on a 37mm enemy anti-aircraft gun that killed Americans. That leftist broad lauded the efforts of the VC and the NVA and encouraged South Vietnamese military soldiers to desert and mutiny. She accused American pilots of being war criminals and claimed tortured POW's were in good health. Well, who's better qualified to bear witness than the self-proclaimed military and political expert known as Jane Fonda? The same dame who lectured POW's on Hanoi radio with statements scripted by the North Vietnamese—"

> "What are you doing? Accept no ready answers fed to you
> by rote from basic training on up but as men, as human
> beings. Can you justify what you are doing? Do you know why
> you are collecting extra combat pay on Sunday?"

"Isn't that just wonderful?" Rich said. "Somebody please tell Hanoi Jane that Sundays didn't exist in Vietnam. Jane Fonda and Tom Hayden did nothing but aggravate the already inhumane and barbaric treatment of American POW's." Rich leaned toward me, his body still tense with anger. "Do you know what it was like to serve with men like your father, return to America as a Marine Corps officer recruiter and have snot-nose, college-campus hippies, inspired by the likes of Ms. Hanoi Jane, spit on me? I watched baby-faced, pseudo-intellectuals—who didn't know what the hell they were talking about—burn American flags while proudly waving NVA flags. 'Ho Ho Ho Chi Minh, NLF is gonna' win.' My blood boils just thinking about it."

Rich could not suppress his resentment. "Ms. Fonda preached her communist gospel at a multitude of colleges. 'If you understood what communism was, you would hope, you would pray on your knees that we would someday become communist.'"

Rich exhaled. "Jane Fonda is a communist who betrayed her country."

"The dame should be in jail," Ken said.

Defeated, Rich leaned back in his chair. "The Vietnam War was fought on foreign soil and lost to American dissidents. Even the legendary Walter Cronkite was disingenuous to the U.S. military."

That was the last name I expected to hear. "Walter Cronkite?"

"Yes, Walter Cronkite. America's revered news anchor reported that the Marines lost the battle of Huế City when in fact 2/5 proved victorious in Huế City. God Bless Lieutenant General Ernie Cheatham, the man who led 2/5's Fox, Golf, and Hotel Company Marines to victoriously recapture the citadel in Huế City."

"Why would Walter Cronkite say such a thing?" I asked.

"Good question," Rich said. "I'm sure Walter Cronkite, like so many other Americans at the time, had little factual information concerning the events taking place in the heart of South Vietnam."

"And the media complicated the issue by using propaganda morsels against Marines," Ken said.

"Damn right," Rich said. "A reporter once accused me of using chemical warfare after throwing tear gas to sweep an area owned by the enemy. 'Is that right?' I responded. 'What would you have me do? Throw a fragmentation grenade into a family bunker, killing everyone, instead of a tear gas grenade? Is that what you want me to do so you can't accuse me of using chemical warfare?' "

"How often did the media tag along?" I asked.

"Too often," Rich said without hesitation. "During Operation Union II, a helicopter deposited so-and-so writer during a lull in the fighting. When the NVA resumed their mortar attack this jerk demanded immediate evacuation. No bird could have landed under such intense fire. So this member of the fourth estate screamed, hollered, and upset everyone around him."

Naomi looked a bit puzzled. "The fourth estate?"

"Me," I said, "the press."

"That's right," Rich said. "The executive, legislative, and judicial are recorded as the first three. As the media seems to wield as much power, they're listed as the fourth estate. One Marine requested permission to shoot and ultimately silence the guy. I denied his request; although I did clock the media moron with my .45 when he became uncontrollable. The possible repercussions compared little to the safety of my men. The next morning as he boarded a chopper *after* we medevaced our wounded, I cringed, fearful of the tale he would tell. But the journalist reported he aided 2/5 in defeating the NVA and even he had been wounded. So there. Although there is one female correspondent to whom I am forever grateful. As Tom and I administered to a dying Marine crying for his mother, this female reporter knelt down, cradled his head, and removed her helmet. Her long hair surrounded his face. This kid died smiling, thinking he was in his mother's arms."

Naomi sighed. Rich gulped his Merlot, and Ken toyed with inedible slivers of soft-shell crabs. I knew I had to lighten the now heavy mood. I affectionately rubbed Rich's arm. "Hey, tell us your favorite, comical Dr. Tom story."

"They're all my favorites. The lasagna story's a typical Tom story."

"Lasagna in Vietnam?" Naomi asked.

"No, honey, in the Bronx. But the story parallels Tom's military career as a physician with his life as a civilian doctor. Tom was removing Mrs. Vericcio's gall bladder, a woman gravely concerned with the family's inability to pay the cost that Medicaid would not. Tom tolerated no such worry."

"Mrs. Vericcio, *non pre-ocuparre*. Is it true you make the best lasagna in the Bronx?"

"*Si, dottore*. I make a very good lasagna."

"Well that will cover my fee; one tray of your very best lasagna."

"Do you know Mrs. Vericcio cooked dinner for us every Friday night for years?" I said.

"That doesn't surprise me," Rich said. "Pulling shrapnel out of Captain Marsden's ear was a lighter Vietnam moment. While sweeping the Antenna Valley, Captain Dick Marsden looked through his binoculars directly at a sniper firing. I'll never understand why the hell he didn't get down. 'Oh look, there's a sniper. Wow, he's looking straight at me!' Boom. The sniper shot the metal lock of Captain Marsden's helmet strap which steered the bullet outboard, but not before shredding the copper jacket which caused bits and pieces of shrapnel to rip his ear. The next day the captain visited Dr. Viti with a very swollen ear. Tom called me into the BAS."

> "Hey, Major, grab those tweezers and help."
> "Sure, I'd be glad to help."
> I turned to Marsden. "You're one lucky SOB."
> "Yeah, yeah."
> Tom nodded. "We'll take turns."

"So Tom began pulling the shrapnel from Marsden's ear. 'She loves me.' To which I responded, 'She loves me not.' Then he said, 'She loves me.' And I said, 'She loves me not.' And that's how we got the shrapnel out of Captain Marsden's ear."

Ken pointed to his head. "I still take shrapnel and sand out of my head and body."

"Does it hurt when it surfaces?" I asked.

"No, but I was lucky, the explosion backfired more sand than shrapnel."

I couldn't resist. "And not a grain ruined the handsome chap you are."

"Oh, listen to this," Ken said.

"But you lost a little hair maybe?" I kidded.

"This is a Marine cut—high and tight."

"It's amazing how shrapnel travels through the body," Rich said. "A sliver of black metal oozed out of my calf while working out on my Nordic Trac just the other day. Naomi thought it was a tick."

"But after closer inspection, I realized it was a tiny piece of metal," Naomi said.

"I still have fragments behind my eye."

"Oh, don't I know," Ken said. "We're cowboy-ing down the turnpike at seventy, and the colonel starts driving funny."

> "Colonel, are you all right?"
> "Not really. I can't see."
> "What do you mean you can't see?"
> "I have a piece of shrapnel floating in my eye."
> "Shrapnel?"

Ken looked at Rich and laughed. "So I looked for an anchor to throw outside the damn car."

"Honey, did you know Tom before Vietnam?" Naomi asked. "You were both from New York, and your families knew each other, but did you know he was the battalion surgeon stationed in An Hoa?"

"No," Rich said. "I knew nothing about Tom but our friendship was destined to be."

"I thought you knew my mom," I said.

"I knew your mom and your grandpa Viti but not your dad," Rich said. "But Tom knew who I was. Our introduction was Tom's little game."

> "Hi, Major Esau, my name is Tom Viti."
> "Gee that's unusual. My father works with a Dr. Felice Viti at Madison Square Garden. They're good friends."
> "Well, wouldn't you know? Dr. Felice Viti's my dad. Hey, do you know this woman?"

"And of course, Tom shows me a photo of his svelte wife, Louise, my former classmate. Tom knew we went to St. Benedict's Grammar School together, but Louise was chubby in her younger years."

> "I've never seen this woman before."
> "Yes, you have."
> "No, sir, I can assure you, I've never laid eyes on this woman."

"So he hands me a second, pudgy school photograph," Rich said.

> "Why that's Louise Sellitto. We went to school together in the Bronx. She was the smartest girl in the entire class."
> "Well, Louise Sellitto is now Louise Viti."

"We bonded immediately," Rich said.

"Did you know that Pops described you as his big German leprechaun who stood up to carry wounded to the chopper while getting shot at?"

Rich smiled. "No."

"That's a direct quote from one of his many newspaper clippings I found in the now infamous Harry & David box."

"Let's just say we thought alike, and sometimes too much alike," Rich said. "One night in An Hoa's officer's club, which was really just a little hootch, the German Red Cross people joined us for a beer. It wasn't long before we heard, *krump, krump, krump.* Tom, me, and two officers bolted out of that hootch and into a trench in a heartbeat, knowing those mortars would walk right across our combat base, *krump, krump, krump*. We quickly realized we forgot the Red Cross civilians. Now, we had to leave the damn trench and get back into the club to rescue them. We knew exactly what krump, krump, krump meant but they had no clue. We kidded each other. 'What the hell kind of people are we that we didn't grab them to begin with?' Vietnam was truly survival of the fittest."

"Honey, share a funny story that wasn't a close call," Naomi said.

"The Donnelly story's a good one," Rich said.

"Dr. Donnelly was the dentist?" I asked.

"And a popular one at that," Rich said. "Dr. Donnelly removed more rotten teeth in Vietnam than he ever did in his years of practice in the U.S. Well, Dr. Donnelly was bound and determined to get home alive, so he built a sliding board that connected his hootch to a trench that enabled quick access into his foxhole during mortar attacks. We walked by one night after a mortar attack and decided, 'A trench like this must be a urinal.' So we peed on him."

Naomi shrieked.

"Here's another funny story," Rich said. "While checking my men in the field at two a.m., I stumbled on a young black Marine wearing sunglasses. 'Son, what the hell are you doing with those shades on?' This kid cocked his chest and said, 'Sir, when you're cool, you're cool all of the time.'"

Ken chuckled. "There aren't too many majors you can say that to."

"This kid was too funny," Rich said, "but I had to ask, 'Can you see?' 'Yes, sir, you don't worry about me, I can see, sir.'"

"That had to be a city slicker," Ken said.

I gave Ken a curious look. "Was there a difference between a country Marine and a city Marine?"

"During the initial stages southerners had a leg up on their northern counterparts because they understood field craft and survival from camping in the woods," Ken said. "Most city kids didn't instinctively understand nature. You're not likely to find a New York street kid camping at the juncture of 14th Street and Seventh Ave."

"I remember one southern kid who returned from a road sweep with a puppy sticking out of his shirt," Rich said. "So again I had to ask, 'Son, where did you get that?' To which the reply dripped with a southern drawl. 'Sir, in the village with no one around to care for him. I brought him back because I knew we could look after him, sir.' And of course the puppy grows up into a dog."

"And finds its way into a villager's pot as lunch," Ken said with a snicker. "I'll tell you a funny story. Marines wore stateside leather, not jungle boots during my first tour in May of 1965. The soles were sown with strings that rotted immediately, leaving nothing more to the shoe than a flip-flop. It was terrible but we were Marines, less is more. Hoorah! So we twisted C-rat carton wires to hold the boot and sole together. Well, my unit had the one seldom, complete shit-bird-big-private-you-know-what-nobody Marine. A *Life Magazine* photographer took a picture of this crumb-bun sitting on a riverbank with the wire sticking out of his boots and the bird-brain became famous; absolutely famous. If we got four bags of mail, three were for him. Offers of marriage, the equivalent of pornographic pictures, boots, socks, you name it. That stupid picture made the biggest nincompoop in the whole company a hero."

Rich grimaced. "C rats! Yuk. I didn't like C rations. Kenny did. I ate C rats to stay alive."

"They weren't so bad. It was different for the colonel." Ken turned to Rich. "How long were you in the Marine Corps before you went to Vietnam?"

"Nine-and-a-half years."

"Now here's a grown man, married, not eating in the mess hall for almost ten years. At that point it's crap, but at eighteen it's, 'Yeah, I'm hard.' C'mon, Rich, when you ate C rations in PLC they were okay. Tell the truth."

"I always hated C rats," Rich said.

"Oh, c'mon."

"C rations were nothing but a glob of greasy, bubbling fat. The fruit wasn't so bad. That's what I survived on in Vietnam. Fruit would magically appear outside of my foxhole, and I knew that my troops appreciated me. Trust me, that fruit meant as much to them as it did to me."

Ken cocked his head in surprise. "You didn't even like the chicken noodles? They tasted like chicken soup. We spiced C rats with hot sauce. I guess hot sauce masks everything."

"Hot sauce helped. I added onions, potatoes, and whatever I could get my hands on. But forget about dining from the can. Here's a good story. While working for General Lew Walt in Da Nang, I received U.S. military CARE packages. A Wisconsin woman mailed fudge to 'Whom It May Concern.' I wrote Mrs. Wisconsin so-and-so a thank you note that said, 'Happiness is receiving a can of delicious fudge from Wisconsin. Sincerely, R. H. Esau, Jr., Major, USMC.' Well, this woman nabbed every Wisconsin Mrs. to mail fudge because we received pounds of it daily. And of course the boys loved it. The fudge even followed me to An Hoa."

Ken reached his fork into Rich's plate. "Speaking of food, what are you doing? These are soft shell crabs, you eat the whole thing."

"I don't break this apart?" Rich asked.

"No. Boy, I did a great job of cooking this fish. I nailed every clam."

Rich grimaced. "I think the last clam I ate was bad."

"Not to worry, Colonel, there's enough garlic to kill all foreign bodies."

"Honey, tell Lucia and Ken the mosquito story," Naomi said.

"Vietnam mosquitoes were big, bad, and ugly," Rich said. "A Vietnam mosquito gave me malaria. I woke up to one mother biting a vein in my hand. This clown filled up with blood so fast he exploded. Wvhoooooom! It was beautiful."

I flinched. "Gross. What was the average age of the enlisted Marine in 1967?"

"Eighteen for a private first class Marine, plus the officers—minus the staff sergeants, throw in some old bastards, and it still didn't get any older than twenty-three, including the lieutenants," Ken said.

Rich nodded. "War is fought by young men."

"I love what Eleanor Roosevelt said about Marines," Ken chuckled. "And I quote, 'The Marines I have seen around the world have the cleanest bodies, the filthiest minds, the highest morale, and the lowest morals of any group of animals I have ever seen. Thank God for the United States Marine Corps.'"

"I love what the Brits said about Americans," Rich added. "And I quote, 'Americans are over-fed, over-paid, over-sexed, and over here.' To which the response was, 'The Brits are under-fed, under-paid, under-sexed, and under Eisenhower.'"

We laughed loud enough to compete with the incessant downpour.

"Did my father ever discuss politics?" I asked.

"Dr. Tom wasn't vocally political but he knew, as did we, that there had to be a better way to fight the Vietnam War," Rich said. "That is, do we or do we not fight it. President Johnson deployed troops in numbers but since Vietnam was an undeclared war, the U.S. military battled with restrictive parameters. We, the younger officer corps questioned, 'How are we going to win?' The answer, 'You're not expected to win. You're here to pressure the communists to back off, not to quote, un-quote, "be defeated in a war."' Vietnam was a no-win war of attrition; a one-year war fought eleven times over. No one can deny that Vietnam was truly a terrible war."

Annoyed, Rich fisted both hands. "That reminds me of the jerk I met in Pennsylvania while receiving my Master's Degree from Shippensburg University. There's a VFW in Shippensburg my contemporaries and I thought would be our haven until the first visit. This big, fat slob sitting at the damn bar who hadn't seen his belt in twenty-five years because of his protruding gut says, 'You boys aren't welcome.'"

> "Why?"
>
> "Because you lost the only war ever lost in American history."
>
> "I assume you're talking about the Vietnam War. Do you know anything about the Vietnam War? From a military standpoint, what do you know about the Vietnam War?"
>
> "I don't care about your military standpoint. You lost the Vietnam War. You're not welcome here."
>
> "Listen you great big, fat slob, unless you apologize to me and my comrades within the next few seconds, I'm going to sink this fist as far as I can into that belly of yours, and I guarantee it will hurt. My only fear is that I might not get my fist back."

Rich inhaled. "Several guys at that bar tried to reason with the idiot. 'Jack, apologize.' So this big, fat slob grudgingly apologized. We walked out of the VFW never to return."

"It took years for Americans to forgive Vietnam veterans for doing what our country asked us to do," Ken said.

"Without a doubt," Rich said, "ninety percent of my post traumatic stress can be attributed to the treatment from my fellow Americans post Vietnam."

I was taken aback by this admission. "Colonel, you've never said anything about PTSD."

"I realized I suffer from PTSD at a Marine memorial service," Rich said. "I stood consumed with anger, despite my tears. I've lasted no more than five minutes—twice—at The Wall. Names jump onto my face. I remember how they died, and I must leave. Those boys died in vain. I'm pissed at the politicians who put us in Vietnam and the Americans who didn't support us."

"Do you have flashbacks?" I asked.

"Yes. I'm sleeping one minute and the next I'm in Vietnam doing whatever hairy thing I did. Even awake I remember minute details as though I'm right back in the weeds. Sudden, explosive noises startle me. Last Saturday at a Mint Julep party, the host chose to loosen a bag of ice by dropping it on the deck behind me. I was over the rail in a heartbeat, dripping in Mint Julep. If I know it's coming, there's no problem. But when I don't, boy, it's a whole different ball game."

"Ah, the memories are what they are," Ken said. "Serving as a Marine ranks next to the birth of my kids. *Semper Fi* means everything to me."

"Civilians don't understand *Esprit de Corps* as love in the purest sense," Rich continued. "Marines love each other. Marines protect each other. We risk our lives for each other. No one dead or wounded is left behind. How's that for a sense of security?"

Ken nodded. "Marines rise to the occasion. We're a cult in the true sense of the word."

"Let me tell you about my radio operator, Leroy Green," Rich said. "During Operation Union II, a mortar fragment flew beneath my flak jacket and slashed my side. Leroy, tucked safely behind me in a paddy dike, charged through a hailstorm of bullets to rescue me. A bullet sliced his shoulder. I became furious at him for placing his life in jeopardy. 'Damn it, Leroy, I've trained you better than this, what the hell do you think you're doing?' Leroy would have none of it. 'Major, do you know why I came out to get you? Because I love you.' Civilians may not understand the bonds created by war, including the bond between an African-American radio operator and his German-Irish boss. We both ended up on the *USS Repose*."

"Add men like Dr. Viti and his corpsmen into the mix," Ken said.

"Without a doubt," Rich said. "Like Lou. I love Chief Hospital Corpsman Lou LeGarie. Here's a great Lou story. It was my last week in An Hoa, and I was showing my replacement Major Carew the terrain surrounding An Hoa. Lou was nervous."

"Major Esau, why do you have to do this?"
"I don't have a choice. Major Carew is relieving me. It's imperative I share my knowledge of the terrain."

"It wasn't long before a corpsman tailed us with his medical bag and a shot gun," Rich said. "Corpsmen didn't usually carry shotguns."

"Doc, what the hell are you doing here?"
"Sir, the chief sent me."
"What do you mean the chief sent you?"
"Sir, the chief ordered me to protect you for the next three days while you show Major Carew the terrain. He warned me that if anything happens to you I'm guaranteed to be put in a position never to get home."

"It was wonderful," Rich said. "To this day Lou LeGarie would do anything for his comrades. He was a jokester. 'I don't want to say I'm from a depressed area in Rhode Island but our rainbows are in black and white.' Dr. Tom Viti, Dr. Flip Gonder, Dr. Donnelly, and Chief Lou LeGarie were fine men of great example. Fifteen 2/5 corpsmen received Purple Hearts following their magnitude of courage and bravery."

"When a Marine's down a corpsman's up," Ken said. "We all witnessed corpsmen saving lives short of miracles."

"Got that right," Rich said. "I watched one corpsman save a life with the cellophane from a pack of cigarettes. This poor Marine had a sucking chest wound, and as strange as this may sound, it looked like his organs were moving because his pressure wasn't equalized. The corpsman removed the cellophane from the cigarettes and taped it to the wound to create a vacuum that protected his organs while equalizing the pressure. That's the kind of ingenuity they learned from Dr. Tom."

Rich became animated. "I threw another kid—conscious—on a medevac with his carotid artery cut by shrapnel. 'Stay with us, son. You'll be fine. Stay with us.' The corpsman reached a Kelly clamp inside the kid's neck and clipped that sucker off. I really never thought he'd survive. Twenty years later while getting a haircut at Marine Corps Headquarters I sat across from this smiling captain who says, 'Sir, do you know who I am?' No way, no how would I have remembered this kid. 'I'm afraid I don't remember where we may have met.' 'Colonel, we met in a rice paddy in Vietnam. You threw me on a helicopter with blood pouring from my neck.' He reached over to shake my hand. Now that's a small world. I wouldn't have given a nickel for that kid to see the next twenty minutes, never mind the next twenty years. Navy Hospital corpsmen were as courageous as the Marines they tended to. Navy corpsmen were and are, Marines who deserve to wear the eagle, globe, and anchor."

"Those stories are a far cry from ear necklaces," I said.

Frustrated, Ken raised his voice. "Not that it never happened, but ear necklaces were bullshit. You kill the enemy end of story. Picture the chaos of battle. You're in FEBA . . ."

Naomi gently laid her hand on Ken's shoulder. "What's FEBA?"

"The Forward Edge of the Battle Area, the point of enemy contact. You're a warrior killing the enemy. Is it logical that an infantryman—let alone a corpsman—would pause to cut an ear off? A dope in the rear or a guy roaming around after the battle is over may pull a stunt like that, but do you think these kids needed ear necklaces to prove themselves? Can you picture Colonel Esau tolerating such lewd behavior? C'mon, we're Marines, trained as professional military men."

Rich raised his Merlot to Ken. "Kenny, you're a good Marine."

"You were in Vietnam twice?" I asked Ken.

"Yes, I got wounded on point during my second tour for the *fourth* time and shipped back to St. Alban's Naval Hospital where I met your Dad. I met Rich years later through the Association of the Military Order of the Purple Heart."

"Kenny volunteered to be a point man," Rich said. "And he was a good one; intelligent and aware of his surroundings, with exceptional hearing and eyesight. Although most point men usually get . . . Ahhh."

Chief Hospital Corpsman Lou LeGarie and Dr. Viti outside of the BAS, An Hoa, RSVN, 1967.

Dr. Joseph Donnelly, USN, An Hoa, RSVN, 1967.

"Get what?" Naomi asked.

"Ah," Rich whispered. "They usually get dead."

"I was good on point although I almost drowned once," Ken said. "We couldn't ford this deep channel, and being the arrogant Marine, I volunteered to look for a passable line. I went down like a domino on the first step. I disappeared with my rifle, ammunition belt, and helmet, which twisted in front of my face. But I had absolute faith I would be rescued. In a heartbeat, my guys held hands and grabbed me. I hadn't even swallowed water yet. We found several spots—to avoid bunching—and walked across. It was tough. I'm six-two, and I strained to keep my chin out of the water. We carried one five-foot-five guy who couldn't swim a stroke on our rifles."

"That sounds like a scene from a movie," I said.

"Almost. Two guys hooked a rifle through their canteen belts and carried this kid sitting on the rifle. It wasn't easy, and he got dunked but we all made it across."

"Now that's true camaraderie," I said.

"Between Marines," Ken said with emphasis.

"What was the relationship between the Marines and the ARVN soldiers?" I asked.

"Most of them couldn't be trusted," Rich said. "But I couldn't say this ARVN is a traitor, arrest him. We knew that South Vietnamese government officials disseminated information to the VC to ensure that if the communists won, they wouldn't be beheaded. We also knew that one of An Hoa's engineers, a Mr. Han, was in cahoots with the bad guys because every time Mr. Han went to Da Nang to consult with his senior chain-of-command, we'd receive mortar fire."

I was shocked. "And you let him stay in An Hoa?"

"Hell yeah. Mr. Han was the perfect intelligence barometer."

"That's bold," I said. "Speaking of bold, did you ever disobey orders?"

"Like you did this morning?" Rich teased.

Naomi looked surprised. "You did?"

I shrugged. "Sort of. I thought an early morning out-and-back sprint to the beach would be easy."

"I told her that was the worst place to jog," Rich said.

"It can be dangerous during the summer because of beach traffic," Naomi agreed.

"I opted for fast and familiar," I said, "but after being swooshed, swiped, and almost pushed into a ditch by speeding cars—with absolute no respect for runners—I prayed for death before accident, thinking that it would be easier to face God than the dear colonel after running exactly where he told me not to run."

"Respect for runners?" Rich pointed to the window. "There along the side of the road would lay this pile of minutia."

Ken smiled. "Unbeknownst as man or beast. Or maybe rat. The rats in Vietnam were just about your size."

"Okay, boys, back to the stories," I said.

"Disobeying orders," Rich said. "Here's one. Flak jackets were Marine security blankets, despite the added weight. One senior officer ordered us to leave our flak gear behind during one operation, assuming we could move faster. Confident that I would have more hyperventilation and heat casualties *without* than with the flak jackets, I disregarded the order. For Marines, flak jackets were like binkies for babies."

> As we reassembled after the operation, one senior officer barked, "Esau, I told you to leave those flak jackets behind."
> "Sir, with all due respect, sir, I misunderstood you. I thought you said whatever you do, *don't* go out without your flak jackets. Sir, look at that wounded kid."
> "His leg is torn up."
> "Yes, sir, but look at the rather large piece of shrapnel protruding from his flak jacket. Thanks to you, sir, that flak jacket saved his life."
> "God damn you, Esau."

"End of story," Rich said.

"That's a good story," I said. "Very non-adversarial between ranks and the perfect segue to racial animosity. Did you deal with any racial animosity?"

"No. During combat, Marines rely on each other for their very being," Rich said. "There is no black white distinction. 'Can he keep me alive?' is the only concern. If he's black, that's wonderful. If he's white, that's wonderful. If he's polka dot, that's wonderful. It makes no damn difference."

"Hollywood perpetuates those ideas," Ken said.

"Hollywood," Rich grumbled. "Oliver Stone is a lying SOB who made a career out of selling grandiose falsehoods. *Platoon* wasn't a movie. *Platoon* was a bloated hallucination that really pissed me off. How could Mr. Stone, a Marine, purport that Vietnam military combatants were nothing but a bunch of degenerates killing civilians and saving ears? Mr. Stone should be ashamed of himself."

"What movie do you consider authentic?" I asked.

"*Hamburger Hill* depicted combat as combat in the Vietnam War," Rich said. "The others were jokes."

"*The Deer Hunter* is a bullshit story too," Ken said. "Americans in tiger cages playing Russian roulette, does anyone really believe that? Throw in *Full Metal Jacket*; a young corporal telling a bird colonel to go pound sand. Are you kidding me? The idea of not obeying an order was non-existent. Marines accused of disobeying a direct order disobey the 'don't go into the Okinawa after midnight' order. When nobody's looking they sneak out for, you know, whatever. It's never a command, 'Go charge that hill.' And he says, 'No, I'm tired.' Never happened. And *Apocalypse Now*'s a parody. No one could ever believe that to be true."

"*Apocalypse Now* is a comedy," Rich said.

"Yeah," Ken agreed. "Guys riding into battle balancing on the skid of the Huey. We held on for dear life in a Huey. Forget about sitting on the skid. Or better yet, Marlon Brando holding a jungle court. How ridiculous."

"Although I did like the line, 'I love the smell of napalm in the morning,'" Rich said. "Napalm saved my life."

Ken settled back in his chair. "Napalm was good. Terrifying, but good."

"Honey, explain how napalm worked," Naomi said.

"The enemy would fire from slit openings in tree-lined ground bunkers," Rich said. "Only bombs could penetrate the camouflaged spots; camouflaged being the operative word in the sentence. Napalm, however, spread through tree lines burning and asphyxiating everything in its path, including the camouflaged enemy. Like I said, napalm saved my life."

I flinched again. "Did either of you ever return to Vietnam?"

"No," Ken said emphatically.

"Yes," Rich said. "In 1974, with a Special Forces search team investigating POW's and the remains of those missing and dead. We combed crash sites in the southern end of North Vietnam and Laos. Although our efforts were sanctioned by the Paris Peace Accords, times were sketchy, especially in Laos. We weren't allowed to carry weapons."

"Now *that's* scary," Ken said.

"We wore camouflage utilities covered with international orange swatches as symbols of American non-combatants. Captain Rees, a Special Forces captain died protecting his men, even then."

"How?" I asked.

"The VC fired on Captain Rees and his men as they searched for a missing airman. Captain Rees ordered his men to evade and escape. He then stood up on the flank and pointed to his orange swatches to signal himself as an unarmed friendly. The VC shot him. He, like Captain James Graham, sacrificed his life to protect his men. General Kingston wanted to award Captain Rees the Medal of Honor which he richly deserved, but it wasn't politically correct."

"Politically correct?" I asked. "That sounds like a political spin."

Rich clenched his teeth. "North Vietnam had recently signed the Paris Peace Accords, and since the world couldn't know how the VC needlessly killed Captain Rees, they squashed it. It still angers me."

"Did you find any POW's?" I asked.

"No, but we did unearth American graves from the POW prison—the Hanoi Hilton—buried in a now flooded cemetery. Now here's a political spin. B52 crewmen were buried in the same cemetery but the Paris Peace Accords stated we could only retrieve the remains of those who died in captivity. And since the B52 crewmen were dead when they hit the deck, they had not died in captivity. Therefore we couldn't bring them home."

"That's such bullshit," Ken growled.

"We retrieved the bodies years later," Rich said.

Bullshit's a perfect word, I thought. "Within my repertoire of Vietnam readings, POW stories are truly the most heart-wrenching."

"While serving as the Assistant Naval Attaché in London, I spoke to several POW's about their experiences in the Hanoi Hilton," Rich said. "Not one, Stockdale included, held any animosity toward their enemy. I listened, wanting to inflict harm on their captors. Every POW was tortured. Did you hear that, Ms. Hanoi Jane Fonda? Everyone. One POW became an Ambassador to Vietnam, several retired from the military as generals, and John McCain, a once presidential candidate, still serves as a United States senator."

"Do you have any desire to visit Vietnam today?" I asked.

"No," Ken said.

"I could never return to South Vietnam," Rich said in a melancholy voice. "We convinced the anti-communist people of South Vietnam to trust us. America promised to protect South Vietnam from their northern communist counterparts. And one day we packed our gear and left. Tell me how I can look these people in the eye? I can't." He hung his head. "It's terrible really. Terrible."

An air of sadness and defeat permeated an uncomfortable silence. Determined to lighten the solemn mood, I wracked my brain for a Dr. Tom story guaranteed to make the colonel smile.

"Hey, is it true that Dr. Tom stole patients from St. Albans Hospital?" I asked.

"Very true," Rich said with a sigh that curved into a smile. "As expected, the young amputees at St. Albans were Dr. Tom's first concern. To overcome the psychological shock of losing limbs, Tom arranged parties through restaurant owners and boyhood friends Jimmy Devine and Marty Gilligan. With complete disregard for hospital bureaucracy—his field trip request had been denied—Tom ordered a bus to transport amputees to Jimmy's pub located in the Bronx. Tom made certain that Jimmy and Marty lined the pub with single, young women, knowing that it was essential for these boys to feel accepted and desired, despite the loss of legs or arms or in some cases, both."

"Now that's homeopathic medicine," Ken said.

I quickly stood and grabbed my plate.

"Naomi, let me clear the table so we can get ready for desert."

"Sounds good," Naomi said.

"Hey, let's go watch some baseball," Rich said to Ken.

"Sure thing, Colonel."

The rain hammered the windows as we walked out of the dining room together. I hugged Rich as hard as I could. "I love you, Colonel."

"I love you too. And I know you're dad is smiling down on your noble endeavor. This is no easy task, young lady, but I know you will let the world know our truth. Make us proud, Lucia. Make us proud."

"Yes, sir."

Major Richard H. Esau Jr., An Hoa, RSVN, 1967.

Major Richard H. Esau Jr., Hawaii, 1968.

❧ *Dear Daddy* ❧

I know that you considered it a privilege to lead Vietnam's Navy Hospital corpsmen; the breed that exemplified "above and beyond the call of duty." United States Navy corpsmen served in Vietnam as members of the Marine Corps; the Navy/Air Ground Forces; the Naval Support Hospitals in Saigon, Da Nang, Thailand, and Cambodia; the USS Repose; *the* USS Sanctuary; *and as advisors to Vietnamese Military Units also known as CAP Units. More than six hundred Navy corpsmen lost their lives in Vietnam. Three Navy corpsmen were Medal of Honor recipients; twenty-nine received the Navy Cross; one hundred and twenty-seven received Silver Stars; two were awarded the Legions of Merit; two hundred and ninety were awarded Bronze Stars and almost five thousand Navy corpsmen received Purple Hearts. And the numbers continue to rise.*

"Doc" Dennis Noah and I chatted while sailing aboard The Maine Course, his spectacular forty-five foot boat. As we spoke, I couldn't help but notice a sadness that transcended Dennis's recollections. I would soon learn that this soft-spoken, gentle man bears the burden shared by so many other Navy corpsmen. Dennis does not acknowledge the enormity of his accomplishments under the worst possible conditions. He does, however, share the reflective burden of wanting to have done more.

I saved an email from Dennis after admitting a fear of losing my Vietnam mind isolated on my Vietnam island. Some days I truly questioned the survival of **Dr. Tom's War.** *My determination was never the issue. My sanity was. But as the heavens would have it no other way, a cyberspace voice came to the rescue.*

He loved you Pops—they all did.

Dear Lucia:

Don't be so hard on yourself. You're not dispassionately writing a Tom Clancy fictional novel. This venture into the mind of the Vietnam combat veteran is not research one discovers in a library. Vietnam veterans are a unique breed. Our war was not only fought against a foreign enemy, but against and within hometown America. Like our forefathers, we were saving the world from the perils of Communism. But the Vietnam War was a far cry from World War II and Korea. America's lack of support left its veterans conflicted, with no moral imperatives, unlike our fathers of the "Greatest Generation." Harassed, we silently retreated, where most of us have remained for years. We don't discuss the Vietnam War, we simply share our experiences.

Now enters little you within this highly sensitive Vietnam world that elicits such powerful emotions. This interplays not only within your own mind, but in the minds of those you interview. Your perspective although uniquely distant—is extremely close. Your daily walk is a fine line. I know that being Italian makes it almost impossible for you not to get emotionally involved—I understand, 'cause my mom came from Milan, Italy—but step away when you need to breathe. Use your insight to allow these stories to unfold without becoming consumed by the horrors of Vietnam.

You're doing a great job with Dad's memory and with every Vietnam veteran who never had the chance to tell his story. Keep plugging. We're all behind you.

Dennis

BOATS AND BANDAGES
CHATTING WITH FMF CORPSMAN DENNIS NOAH

Marine Corps Museum Memorial brick, Quantico, VA, 2007.

*Captain Dennis Noah aboard
The Main Course, 2009.*

T*he Main Course* is an impressive boat moored on the Chesapeake Bay. *Not a bad place to spend the afternoon*, I thought as Dennis and I settled ourselves on board for a chat.

Dennis was my homerun in the "Who knew Dr. Tom" search on 2/5's website. Sheer luck and a wicked Maryland blizzard served as the catalyst for his response to my repeated attempts at a conversation via cyberspace or touch-tone. Almost six months passed and I was ready to throw in the towel. But on that frigid February day, alone in his office after bank employees had departed early, Dennis slowly, methodically, and meticulously unlocked his well-padlocked Vietnam

The Main Course, 2009.

vault. I knew immediately that a face-to-face discussion would furnish details far beyond a telephone chat. And I was more than happy to wait until the weather cooperated.

And today, although I sensed some trepidation, I knew that Dennis was anxious to articulate life as Vietnam corpsman. I also knew that I would ask little and listen much. The conversation would be delicate. I would not look or act official. I would not press hot buttons or pursue political issues. I would listen attentively. And then listen more. And Dennis would let me know when enough was enough.

"How did you find yourself in Vietnam?" I asked.

"I joined the U.S. Navy immediately following high school because America was engaged in a war. A Noah has fought in every war since the Revolutionary War, leaving me proud to continue the legacy. I volunteered for the Fleet Marine Force after Navy Boot Camp and Hospital Corps School because Vietnam sounded cool. Camp Pendleton's B school—a three-month-Reader's-Digest-Marine crash course—followed suit, although I honestly never felt adequately trained to be a combat Marine. I was a well-qualified corpsman with a basic knowledge of jungle warfare.

I landed in Da Nang, Republic of South Vietnam, via Okinawa in May of 1967. Da Nang was exciting, but what did I know? I was nineteen, idealizing war from TV's *Combat*. Five corpsmen and I boarded a C-123 bound for the Second Battalion Fifth Marine Regiment stationed in An Hoa. Our An Hoa introduction was to say the least *abrupt*. The pilot descended into his final approach to the distinct clank, clank, clank of sniper fire rattling the belly of the plane. *Man*, I thought, *it's time to kiss my ass goodbye*. But the pilot safely maneuvered the plane—*bam*—onto a metal runway. Safe but shaken we reported to the Battalion Aid Station, a group of old, beat-up, pale-yellow concrete French buildings to meet Dr. Viti and Chief Hospital Corpsman Jed Blackmore (not real name). Chief Blackmore turned out to be a real jackass. But Dr. Viti was pleasant and approachable. Chief Blackmore assigned me to Hotel Company, Third Platoon."

The name Blackmore genuinely surprised me. Chief Hospital Corpsman

Lou LeGarie dominated all prior conversations. I knew that Blackmore preceded Chief LeGarie but to date, Blackmore was never discussed.

"Blackmore has never been mentioned by anyone but you," I said. "What did he do that awarded him such a dubious honor?"

"Chief Blackmore read a poem about a *dead* corpsman during our initial orientation. Green and hungry for guidance, my comrades and I listened to prose foredooming our death. It was inappropriate. I hated that stupid ass son of a bitch from that day forward. Thank God Blackmore was replaced by Chief Lou LeGarie shortly thereafter."

I thought that was strange. "That's not a very comforting welcome. So let's talk about Dr. Viti and Chief LeGarie."

"Dr. Tom Viti was *revered*. Infamous for his risk taking and sense of humor, Dr. Tom was respected and admired by *everyone*. Dr. Viti was cordial, affable, and enjoyed the occasional practical joke. He wasn't a stuffy officer. The Battalion Aid Station doors were always open for discussion. We'd meet at the BAS and talk shop; hallway conversations about what field medicine tactics did and didn't work. Dr. Viti and Chief LeGarie ran a helluva Battalion Aid Station. But we couldn't joke with Chief LeGarie the way we could with Dr. Viti. Chief LeGarie was all business. Chief LeGarie and Dr. Viti shared a brother-like love and respect; although, Chief LeGarie was more Marine smart than Dr. Viti. Chief LeGarie understood his position in An Hoa while Dr. Tom sidestepped the role of the traditional battalion surgeon. Dr. Viti bore the heart a field corpsman. Battalion surgeons didn't normally accompany dangerous missions but Dr. Viti eagerly saddled up. Chief Lou, realizing Dr. Viti was too valuable to be parading through deep shit, reined him in to become a smarter Marine simply by keeping him at the BAS. But everyone knew Dr. Viti's presence in the weeds boosted morale. The Marines and their corpsmen were more comfortable and at times, more daring, knowing Dr. Viti was by their side."

"Did you rub elbows with Dr. Viti in the weeds?" I asked.

Dennis shook his head. "No, Dr. Viti usually traveled with the command group. It was essential he remain protected. Corpsmen accompanied their assigned platoons. But Dr. Viti went out on a limb to make certain the corpsmen were kept safe from undo harm in the field and back on base. Under Dr. Viti, corpsmen were relieved of radio watch and claymore mine duty as well as listening-post duty along An Hoa's airport runway. Corpsmen were also excluded from patrols lacking appropriate firepower. And no one ever questioned Dr. Viti's leadership."

I silently smiled. Dr. Tom never let anyone question his leadership role—ever.

"On occasion, however, the corpsmen, myself included, would poke fun at the good doctor's big-ass, damn-high, rubber-wading boots; the kind worn by fishermen and cow farmers. Honestly, Dr. Tom was the only American I ever saw wearing rubber waders to keep his feet dry in Vietnam. Marines and field corpsmen wore heavy combat boots with a metal-plated sole intended to impede punji sticks. Dr. Viti also carried a Ka-Bar, the baddest military knife on the block. And again, he's the only doctor I ever saw carrying a Ka-Bar in Vietnam. Marines used Ka-Bars in hand-to-hand combat. But we, Navy Medical, didn't have hand-to-hand combat training. It was a comical play in opposites, Dr. John Wayne Viti hoisting a Ka-Bar in his rubber boots."

"I'm sure Chief LeGarie teased the Brooklyn boy about his pig farmer boots."

Dennis grinned. "No doubt. And I can't say enough about Chief LeGarie. Everyone called him gunny because of his gung ho attitude. Chief LeGarie was more Marine than most of the Marines that I met. The guy was a meticulous perfectionist at the BAS. Attention to detail was the name of his game. He knew everything about every corpsman at a single glance. Corpsmen were listed on a huge, white, neatly-lined, erasable board posted at the BAS by name, arrival in country, assignment, status, comments, and dates. It read *Noah; HM3; 6 May 1967; 2/5 Hotel Third Platoon; Status-Active; Rotation Date Estimated: May 13, 1968.* Wounded and dead were written WIA: Da Nang; or KIA: Antenna Valley.

Chief LeGarie was tough but like your dad, compassionate. Both were genuinely concerned about the welfare of their corpsmen and the Marines. They'd agonize over the loss of each. It was truly like losing one of their own. Although demanding, Chief LeGarie gave his corpsmen the tools and expertise to expect the best. Beneath the coarse tough-guy façade lived a man who truly cared. Chief's World War II and Korean War experience was a shot in the arm for An Hoa's BAS. He gave engraved Zippo lighters to all corpsmen rotating out. I framed my Zippo lighter as a prized possession."

"Let's talk about the Battalion Aid Station," I said.

"The Battalion Aid Station served as a pipeline for triaging the wounded and treating minor illnesses and injuries. An Hoa's BAS was truly in a constant, constant flux of triage with incoming wounded. Medevac choppers landed on the helipad behind the old French buildings and able-bodied corpsmen hauled stretchers onto sawhorses. Dr. Viti, Chief LeGarie, corpsman Ware, and rotating BAS corpsmen did everything humanly possible to keep Marines alive. Major surgery was performed at the BAS, but it wasn't the proper facility for long-term care. Medevac choppers, designated by proximity, time, and the patient's necessity to be in the hands of a surgeon transported the additional wounded. If Charlie Med or Chu Lai's Battalion Aid Station was overloaded, patients were transported to the Navy hospital ships, the *USS Sanctuary*, or the *USS Repose*."

"Did corpsmen accompany the wounded on medevac choppers?" I asked.

"Not usually. Field and BAS corpsmen accompanied mine and booby trap casualties if there was no threat of enemy engagement. But field corpsmen couldn't take a spot on a medevac chopper with multiple casualties during a firefight."

"Did An Hoa have any American nurses?"

FMF Corpsman Dennis Noah, Nong Son outpost. "Doc" Noah weighed 110 pounds standing 6 feet tall in 1967.

FMF Corpsman Dennis Noah behind An Hoa's BAS, RSVN, 1967.

Lt. Viti in an open market outside of An Hoa—wearing his rubber boots.

*Medevac landing with
casualties behind the BAS,
An Hoa, RSVN, 1967.*

*Battalion Aid Station triage,
An Hoa, RSVN, 1967.*

*Litters inside the BAS, An Hoa,
RSVN, 1967.*

"No," Dennis said. "But I once requested additional medical aid for a Marine whose leg was severed by a land mine in the weeds. A white-uniformed nurse from the *USS Repose* landed in a hot LZ. I was shocked. I felt responsible for placing her in harm's way. It was my first and last request. Doctors and nurses were too valuable. American nurses were angels from God."

"What were the more common Marine ailments treated at the BAS?"

"Malaria and fevers of unknown origin were as common as they were deadly in Vietnam. A fever of unknown origin, a non-malaria fever that skyrocketed with no flu or cold like symptoms, was successfully treated with antibiotics if caught on time. Marines were also plagued with upper respiratory infections from Vietnam's chronic filth congesting their lungs. Add septicemia, a tetanus-like infection to the list as well as blood poisoning, septic cellulites, and trench foot. Trench foot was treated with a Betadine wash and wrapped in tough skin, today known as liquid bandages. Some Marines used trench foot as a ticket home but not without issue. Toes shriveled like rotten apples, causing lifelong problems. Severe cases required amputation. I insisted that Marines air and powder their wet feet in the field."

Dennis transfixed his eyes on the shoreline, lost in thought.

"God." He sighed. "We were always wet. And did I hate being wet. I still hate being wet. I hate wet feet, I hate wearing a bathing suit, I hate sandy beaches, and I hate swimming, even though I own this boat. I can't explain it, I just hate it. But I'm sure that wouldn't be considered an ailment; an aversion maybe, but not an ailment."

I nodded. "I don't think you'll find wetness categorized as an illness on Web MD."

Dennis smiled. "I saved one Marine from completely ruining his feet. Stateside couldn't find size fourteen jungle boots so the platoon sergeant called me in. 'Doc, please find Martin (not real name) jungle boots to replace his no use stateside leather boots or you'll be stuck taking care of his forever

A Nook Beau —"The Boss of the Rice Paddy," 1967.

wet, screwed-up feet.' Sure enough I bought two pairs of size fourteen jungle boots on the Vietnamese black market."

"How?" I asked.

"I pointed at my feet. 'Boots, boots, boots.'"

"Dear Lord," I said. "What size is size fourteen?"

Dennis stretched his arms across his chest in jest. "As big as a Vietnam rat. Vietnam rats scared Marines. Rats the size of cats would nibble the exposed hands and head of a sleeping Marine. Rat bites required a painful two-week treatment at the BAS."

FMF Corpsman Dennis Noah riding atop the water buffalo that almost took his life, 1967.

"How funny that a rat could scare a Marine," I said.

"Oh not just rats," Dennis said. "Let's not forget hairy, ghastly, vile, horrible, leggy, crawling centipedes. Ugh, Vietnam centipedes could make any man shudder. To this day I shake, rattle, and roll my boots upside down before putting them on."

"Did centipedes bite?" I asked.

"Not with any real harm. But insect, snake, scorpion, monkey, and animal bites could become infectious. Reactions could become septic, which varied treatments between the BAS and the field. And monkeys, man they were nasty. I've seen monkeys meaner than hell sink their teeth into flesh of any kind. Speaking of animals, this is a good story. During one patrol, we crossed a rice-paddy island village that was encompassed by a six-foot, solid hedgerow. Two small doorways, serving as both entrance and exit, aligned each side. Well the hedgerow blocked my view of an ol' mammasan grandma tethered by a rope to her water buffalo. As we unexpectedly met, I unfortunately scared the crap out of her. She threw the rope at me and tore ass. I tugged the rope unaware that I was pissing off this water buffalo tied on the opposite end. The monstrosity became enraged, pivoted, snorted, and stampeded straight toward me. I froze. Steve Irwin screamed, 'Doc, hit the deck.' I did. Irwin nailed the water buffalo between the eyes. It dropped like a rock. We paid the family for the devastating loss of the animal, but no one, least of all me, minded."

"One shot?" I asked in disbelief.

"Yeah, could you believe it? One lucky shot, and the monster was done. Okay, where were we?"

"Common Marine ailments," I said.

"Okay. We treated painful skin infections caused by eyeglasses. Remember, contacts weren't invented yet so rain, steam, and mud wreaked havoc on glasses.

Guard straps caused skin surrounding the ears to slit and fill with pus. Abscess were lanced and treated with antibiotics."

"How odd to think of wearing glasses during combat," I said.

"You'd be surprised at how painful it could be. I know from firsthand experience. Other ailments included severe cases of heat exhaustion, which required immediate evacuation from anywhere to the Battalion Aid Station. Saline IV's and cold water dousing were vital to lower body temperatures. Death or recovery could be quick. Here's a story that I'm proud of; I initiated the termination of a massive battalion operation because of the deadly heat."

I shifted closer. "Oh, I don't want to miss a bit of this story."

"An Hoa's battalion commander coordinated a Battle-of-the-Bulge sweep through the Arizona Valley. Tanks, amtracs, Dr. Viti, the BAS corpsmen, even the H & S Post Office, were included. General Patton would've been proud. But it was beyond hot. The heat was overwhelming. Eight thermometers cracked within hours. I requested medevacs for several Marines suffering from heat exhaustion, but the CO denied my request and ordered casualties to recoup on tanks. The tanks sizzled like frying pans. I hounded the platoon commander after laying several unconscious Marines on amtracs.

> "We've got to stop. We're in trouble."
>
> "Doc," he said, "my hands are tied. See the captain."
>
> So I did. "Captain, sir, it's too hot. This heat's deadly. We must evacuate these fallen Marines. If we don't stop, we'll lose half of the battalion."
>
> The captain simply shrugged. "I can't do anything about it. Orders are orders."
>
> "No way," I said. "I must do something. I'll talk to the battalion commander."
>
> He looked at me cockeyed and said, "Son, you don't want to do that."
>
> I was incensed. "The hell I don't."
>
> "Well go ahead but don't say that I knew anything about it."

"So I walked to the battalion commander looking like shit, saluting every neatly starched officer along the way. I stared at the bird colonel's silver birds nervous but confidant and said, 'Sir, with all due respect, sir, we have casualties lying on amtracs that will die in this heat. These men require medevacs, saline IV's, and rest. We cannot proceed under these conditions. This heat will kill someone.'

"He hesitated. I fixated on his eagles. E3 grunts are blinded by eagles. A full bird colonel is one rank short of a general. A full bird colonel is a god; a god grunts never meet, much less request to terminate an operation. I showed the god my broken thermometers, and much to his credit, he was neither rude nor nasty. 'Son, are you sure these men aren't suffering from heat exhaustion?'

"'Sir,' I responded with the utmost confidence, 'I have several Marines suffering from heat exhaustion bordering on heat stroke.' Now heat stroke is a complete neurological breakdown of the body. This deadly runaway heat cooks the brain. Without realizing it one becomes hot, clammy, *stops* sweating, and passes out. Heat stroke kills. I was adamant. 'Sir, we must evacuate these men or they will die. We must cease this operation. This heat will kill our men.'

"I was nervous but I thought, *Screw this, what are they going to do, send me to Vietnam?* The bird colonel called your dad. 'Dr. Viti.' Lucia, your dad's response was stellar. 'Corpsman Noah is right, Colonel. Heat stroke is extremely dangerous. Patients must be stripped, hosed, and pumped with saline and adrenaline IV's. Patients require shade and water. If their bodies shut down, they'll die.' The bird colonel stared me down and said, 'Thank you, son.' 'Thank you, sir,' I said relieved beyond words. All movement was terminated. Shocked, my captain, warned me, 'Doc, don't ever do that again.' Medevac choppers retrieved the heat casualties, and we headed back to An Hoa within the hour."

"That's an impressive story," I said. "You should be proud."

"I'll admit, I was really nervous," Dennis said. "But I knew we could not continue in that oppressive heat. Heat exhaustion, dehydration, and dysentery were not to be taken lightly. *Severe* cases of dysentery were treated at the BAS. I cured dysentery with peanut butter, handing out cans of C-rat peanut butter like they were M&M's. Vietnam's peanut butter was saved from the Korean War and resembled more hard-cookie than soft-butter. But it corked you up like the Dutch boy with his finger in the dike."

"Now that's resourceful," I said.

"I had to be creative, especially in the field," Dennis said. "I shriveled leeches with salt because it was faster than burning them with lit cigarettes. I also used chlorine instead of Halazone tablets to sanitize drinking water dispensed from rice paddies fertilized with human waste. Halazone tablets gave the water a bitter, acidic iodine taste, and chlorine didn't affect the taste. Kool-Aid was used—unsuccessfully if you ask me—to mask the tablets acrid aftertaste. Yuk. The smell of Kool-Aid still makes me nauseous.

The ducks that caused food poisoning, 1967.

"Here's a funny story. During one lengthy outpost stay, I requested chlorine in typical military fashion. And in typical military fashion, a helicopter delivered one hundred pounds of highly-concentrated chlorine, enough to treat the waters of St. Louis for a week. I burnt my arms lugging the barrel up the hill. I doled out a dab—just enough to sterilize the water—every morning into Marine canteens. Of course we didn't put a dent in the barrel. It's probably still sitting on that mountain."

"How long were you out in the field?" I asked.

"Days, weeks, sometimes long enough for our uniforms and boots to rot off and to run out of C rats. We'd forage bananas. I ate a *lot* of bananas in Vietnam; a lot of bananas. And you won't hear me complain about C rats. I was just happy to eat. Although I will say, chopped ham and eggs were green. Ham and mothers—ham and lima beans—floated beneath an inch of grease. But like I said, we were just happy to eat.

"You'll like this story. During one particularly long, hot day we patrolled through a village filled with ducks. C rats were virtually nonexistent so the guys killed six ducks plucked, cleaned, and asked me—the hunter—to cook them. I cooked a duck stew with local greens and rice in a villager's black pot on the communal mud stove. It tasted pretty damn good but for some reason I couldn't eat it. Maybe because I was the cook, I'm not sure, but I just couldn't eat it. Well, all twelve Marines got food poisoning. The entire squad puked from both ends for days. Ho Chi Minh's revenge hit them hard. Who knows why, but I was grateful not to have eaten any duck stew. Would you believe I have a picture of those ducks?"

"I'd like to see that picture," I said. "What happened when food and medical supplies ran low?"

"Medical re-supply choppers were dispatched to us if we couldn't get back to An Hoa. One pilot, who couldn't land because of the dense jungle canopy, dropped medical supplies, C rats and believe it or not, beer cans over a two-block area. One beer can hit me in the head. Thank God I was wearing my helmet."

"Oh. That would have been tragic," I said. "Let's switch gears and talk about combat field medicine."

Dennis hesitated. "That's a tough subject. Gory. Corpsmen in Vietnam were medically well-prepared. We had the knowledge and the access to use a wide spectrum of drugs against Vietnam's natural, hostile environment which was, at times, just as debilitating as the enemy. Common field ailments included boils; lacerations and abrasions; trench foot; lock-jaw; eye and ear infections; insect bites; razor grass burns; heat stroke; dehydration; dysentery; and the stomach flu. Combat injuries included sprains and breaks; white phosphorous and napalm burns; mortar and shrapnel removal; and field amputations. I treated whatever I could with whatever came out of my B1-bag."

"Excuse me, Dennis, but can you describe your B1-bag?" I asked.

"A B1-bag is a corpsman's medical tool kit filled with battle dressings of various sizes; a cut down set—scalpels, forceps, bandage scissors that cut skin and muscle but not bone for minor surgeries; a suture kit; morphine syrettes; ointment for White Phosphorous also known as Willy Peter; and atropine sulphate, which counteracts the effects of mustard gas and other chemicals; ACE wraps; tourniquets; slings; anti-bacterial ointments; antibiotics and pills—Pen VK, penicillin, Darvon, aspirin, antihistamines, Thorazine, malaria pills and salt tablets; tongue depressors; thermometers; gauze; and as time went on, whatever I could grab from the BAS. I also packed my C4 bag with supplies. Swollen B1-bags flagged corpsmen as instant enemy targets. The enemy would often demoralize Marines by killing their corpsmen."

"Did you carry a fire arm?" I asked.

"I carried a 12-gauge sawed-off pump shotgun on night ambushes, a rifle during sketchy patrols, my trusty, rusty .45, and sometimes its magazine."

I scrunched my face in disapproval. "Sometimes?"

"Lucia, if *I* had to shoot we were all dead, so a magazine was worthless. Besides, the magazine pouch blocked my Serum Albumin cans."

"Serum . . ."

"Serum Albumin," Dennis said. "It was a blood serum that was used as a blood volume expander for field amputations or injuries sustaining a significant loss of blood. I taped the protective metal green cans to my canteen belt and since I couldn't carry it *and* a magazine pouch, I ditched the pouch. I never had enough of the stuff."

"Were field amputations common?"

"Field amputations were as common as the relentless bombardment of booby traps, bouncing Betty's, land mines, and command-detonated mines," Dennis said. "If I couldn't immediately evacuate Marines with limbs dangling from their sinews, muscles, or nerve endings, amputation saved their lives. And whenever possible, I wrapped severed legs with ACE bandages instead of tying a tourniquet because tourniquets killed healthy tissue three to four *more* inches below its tie. And since limbs never severed neatly, a straight-line amputation sliced an even greater portion of the healthy leg. Well, ACE wraps preserved more of the viable limb so post amputation, a prosthetic would fit at the articulation of the joint and allow the knee to bend. Amputees could then walk with a normal gait instead of the stiff, peg-leg pirate walk from a prosthetic that couldn't bend."

"How did the ACE wraps work?" I asked.

"I covered severed stomps with battle dressings, wrapped ACE bandages over the end and applied pressure to stop the bleeding. The blood would coagulate—clot—and ultimately save a greater portion of the limb.

I also layered chest wounds with ACE bandages and their cellophane wrappings. The ACE wrap and plastic casing prevented further blood loss and the plastic's elasticity allowed the patient to breathe while blocking air from entering and collapsing the lungs."

Dennis paused. "Chest wounds were *horrendous*. The NVA used AK-47's, a fire power that could severely incapacitate without necessarily killing. Bullets could be heard rat-rat rat-tat-tattling as they mushroomed, punctured, and splintered, tearing one's insides to hell. If lungs were lacerated, blood would ooze from the nose and mouth. *Without* heart damage, death could be painstakingly slow. If medevac choppers couldn't land, it could take hours for someone to die. I remember one eighteen-year-old conscious kid with a sucking chest wound. Blood poured from his nose and mouth. I knew that death was imminent. The bullet had sliced through his arm pit, ripped into his chest, and shred the crap out of his lungs. I cradled him, and we talked like two guys drinking beer. I nodded off; when I woke up he lay in my arms, dead."

I remained silent.

"Head wounds were equally horrible," Dennis said. "Bullets punctured the skull and often left a softball-size hole in its exit path."

"What did you do for pain?" I asked.

"I was conservative with morphine. I refused to turn the mobile into stretcher cases. Besides, morphine can kill. It suppresses breath and the body's ability to function when it's important not to. Amazingly enough, the body compensates for pain. Patients sometimes don't feel a thing, particularly with horrendous wounds.

"During one patrol, Corpsman Cobb grabbed me as I jumped to the sergeant's command. 'Squad leaders up.' 'Stay put,' he said. 'You don't need to know what's going on.' And good thing I did. Within seconds a resounding boom shook the ground. The squad leaders, the platoon commander, and the senior sergeant lay spewed by a claymore mine. It was horrid. One squad leader struck full force, resembled uncooked chopped meat. Holes perforated every inch of his body. And by God, he was still alive. I ran to him first but he refused treatment. 'Doc, save the other guys,' he said. 'Go. I'm not going to survive, you can't help me.' He died within minutes. But I'll be damned, I never, *ever* saw another wound like it; this Marine looked like uncooked hamburger."

I could not and did not attempt to hide a subtle moan.

"Yeah," Dennis said with a tempered resolve. "I often thought, 'What the fuck am I doing here?' Excuse me."

"No worries," I said. "I've heard the word before."

Dennis leaned forward, exhaled, and bounced his thumb off his chest. "I shouldered the burden for saving lives at age twenty. My decisions dictated who lived and who died. During combat, corpsmen tended to Marines capable of fighting *before* administering to the severely wounded. It's not that corpsmen didn't save lives. We did. But in choosing between a Marine with a severed leg or a through-and-through upper thigh gunshot wound—without bone intervention—the latter was patched up first and handed back his rifle to maximize fire power. And, officers and senior platoon sergeants were treated before *anyone*. A lack of leadership could be deadly.

"I remember helping Barnes (not real name) when someone yelled, 'corpsman up.' The lieutenant *and* the first sergeant had been hit. Barnes pleaded, 'Doc, please don't leave me.' But I had to. God, I felt guilty. But almost the entire platoon, including the squad leaders, was green. Our sergeants had been medevaced earlier, and a battle raged. Hell, I knew that it was selective and cruel but necessary. We were leaderless. Barnes was medevaced before I returned."

"Did you ever regret your decision to be in Vietnam?" I asked.

Dennis vigorously shook his head. "No, never. I wanted to save lives. My father, a World War II veteran, offered sound counsel before I left for boot camp. 'Son, give boot camp and Hospital Corps School your best. Learn everything you can. What you learn will someday keep you and those around you alive.'

"And I did. I graduated at the top of my class at Hospital Corps School. I loved medicine. I still do. Dr. Viti's kudos for bandaging severed legs and saving lives was an ego boost, but guilt accompanied my dead, maimed, and mangled. I'd stare at my hands dripping with blood, feeling defeated. 'Why couldn't you save this guy?' Yes, I was proficient. But Vietnam field surgery was meatball surgery. I'm forever ridden with the guilt of not having accomplished enough. I eventually unglued. I became incapable of treating the mutilated and lifeless. I could no longer decide who boarded the chopper and who bled to death. My days were measured by casualties. I purposely didn't remember names. I had no interest in tracking the dead. I wanted to burrow my way to China. Corpsman Cobb and I dug trenches the size of Volkswagen's. I went home the *day* I received my clearance. I couldn't spend another *second* in Vietnam. I have photos of Corpsman Cobb wearing the dead-pan expression of the infamous thousand-yard stare. To this day, I can finger a bullshit thousand-yard stare a mile away. Shuffle six combat Marines with six Marines who never stepped foot on foreign soil, and I'll know who's who by their eyes."

I debated whether or not to continue with this line of questioning, but Dennis decided it for me.

"And I, like many combat veterans, have an emotional attachment to Vietnam that is as difficult to understand as it is to explain," Dennis said. "For me, life in Vietnam existed as a dramatic twilight warp that erased past and future realities. I couldn't imagine another world or comprehend my former life during Vietnam. I understood that another world existed and that I would return to it, but Vietnam was an existence of purgatory and hell that obliterated all other realities. Some Marines couldn't differentiate between the two worlds. Although I never understood why, Stutes was a perfect example. Here was a married man with a baby girl that he'd never met. And when asked why he wanted to stay in Vietnam, he'd say, 'I belong here.' I knew Stutes would exit Vietnam in a body bag, and he did."

"Do you have any flashbacks?" I asked.

"*I think about Vietnam everyday; every day of my life; every hour of my day; twenty-four hours a day; seven days a week.* Nightmares still persist. I toss and turn, slumbering into a trance, neither asleep nor awake. I try to scream, but I can't. I try to wake up, but I can't. I try to remember, but I can't. I do, however, remember the fear. But fear was nothing to be ashamed of, especially among the corpsmen. Corpsmen stood between life and death. Some corpsmen couldn't handle Vietnam. The Marines medevaced one truly unreliable corpsman after threatening to shoot him. But green corpsmen knew crap about Vietnam combat. They didn't train for combat with Marine infantry units. Corpsmen would step out of choppers and freeze. We'd scream, 'Get down, get the fuck down,' and bam, they were gone. I don't credit myself for being brave. I was scared shitless. We all were. I credit Sergeant Gibson for taking me under his wing and keeping me alive early in my tour. He'd bark, 'Follow me, do everything I do, when I tell you, how I tell you, and do it immediately. Don't ask questions.' During my first patrol, Sergeant Gibson ordered me by his side. 'Doc, you stay with me. The rest of you go.' Everyone jammed across this rice paddy while we stood there in no man's land. Seemingly out of nowhere, a sniper started popping rounds. Crack, crack, crack. I burrowed myself head first in the dirt. Gibson defiantly grinned.

> "Doc, what in the fuck are you doing? Did I tell you to do that? Am I doing that?"
>
> I was pissed. "What, you can't hear that guy shooting us?"
>
> "Of course I can! But didn't I tell you to do what I do and only what I do, when I do it? Do you see me lying in the mud like some pig? Get your skinny ass the hell up. That sniper couldn't hit the broad side of the barn from ten feet. We couldn't be any safer. Now get up."

And of course we were fine. Shortly thereafter Gibson yanked me down to the command, 'Corpsman up, corpsman up.'

> "Doc, stop."
> "What do you mean stop, Sarge. Someone's hurt."
> "Do what I say. Count to one hundred."

So I did. I looked at him and he nodded. 'Now go.' When it was over I asked, 'Why the hell did you do that?' 'Secondary explosions; make counting a habit.' Secondary explosions often occurred within minutes. The enemy knew one wounded Marine attracted twelve conscientious ones to the rescue. Do you know what you call twelve Marines hovering over one of their wounded?"

"I wouldn't bet a guess," I said.

"A Marine Corps cluster fuck," Dennis said with a smirk. "Life in Vietnam was nothing more than a series of harrowing events rated by the pucker factor."

"The what factor?" I asked.

"The pucker factor," Dennis said. "It's a euphuism that expresses fear. You're so scared your asshole puckers. Go Noi Island adventures were rated by the pucker factor. The Marines appropriately named it No Go Island. Thank God we—Hotel Company—ventured only once, playing John Wayne and the Normandy Invasion. We trudged across the river in amtracs, dropped our front ramp, and got clobbered. The rounds bounced bam-bam-bam-bam like marbles spinning in a bucket. It sounded like a million guys were shooting at us. We closed the ramp and left."

"Weren't amtracs and tanks safe?" I asked.

"Yes and no. I saw one two-hundred-and-fifty pound command-detonated bomb split a tank's hull—a *tank's* hull in half. The driver soared from the turret like a mortar bursting from its tube. The guy broke three-quarters of his bones. And tanks were worthless during the rainy season; the damn things sank in the rains. We guarded one stupid-ass-sunken tank in an open rice paddy under sniper fire for two days. And of course the tank crew returned to An Hoa. We knew the instant the tank rolled from the road to the rice paddy it would sink. And it did. Tank number two, larger and sporting a hook, arrived to drag out tank number one. And tank number two sunk. Tank number three arrived, hooked bridles to both tanks and saved the day."

"What was the purpose of your tank adventure?" I asked.

Dennis shrugged. "I was a grunt, and grunts weren't privy to the purpose of any Vietnam enemy encounters. The brass knew, while we stood steadfast, ready to save the world. Vietnam combat Marines conquered hills, established positions, and left. A week later, Marines traded lives for enemy dead on the same goddamn hill. It was a senseless command from Washington, DC's political majority waging a war that disregarded the loss of American lives. For me, Vietnam quickly transitioned into a quagmire of disillusionment and frustration. Survival and medicine superseded saving the world."

"Was there any such thing as rest?" I asked.

"During those rare celebrations of downtime, we were boozing teenagers talking shit and drinking beer and rum. Our Vietnamese beer, Ba M'Ba was better known as 33. Vietnamese Manila Rum was crowned with an inch of alcohol that resembled STP Oil and smelled even worse. We'd flip coins, and the loser had to drink the first inch. The winner never reached the bottom. It was gross but it was alcohol. Here's a good story; picture this. Twelve disgusting, grimy, filthy, grubby, muddy, soiled Marines and my ugly skinny-ass knocking on the door of the air conditioned Air Force chow hall in Da Nang—a really nice chow hall with tables, tablecloths, real forks, knives, ceramic plates, glasses, hot meals, and freshly-brewed coffee. The Air Force officer eyeballed us and shook his head. 'You can't come in.' The Marines were indignant. 'What do you mean we can't come in?' The officer just kept shaking his head no. 'You're all a filthy rotten mess, and you'll make my chow hall a filthy rotten mess, so you can't come in!'

"I then heard the *click, click, click* of M16s. These Marines were ready to fight their way in. I walked to the door. 'Guys, this isn't worth it, let's go.' And we did. Several weeks later a 122mm rocket blasted the chow hall. We thought that was just wonderful. But today, if I introduce myself as a corpsman attached to a Marine unit at a VFW Bar the Jack Daniel's flows."

"Did you ever catch Marines dabbling with drugs?" I asked.

"No, but I made myself quite clear. 'If I ever see you with drugs I haven't given you, I'll write you up.' Most of the Vietnam drug stories cropped up during the latter part of the war. Besides, Marines were damned disciplined. My Army buddies share horror stories of disobedience, with and without drugs. But that behavior was non-existent with Marines. I *never* heard, 'No, I refuse.' It was *always*, 'Yes, sir, how fast, how high, and when.' Marines followed orders without question, and I gave medical opinions. Platoon sergeants would ask me, 'Doc, do they have another two miles left in them?' And I would say yes or no. If I ordered emergency medevacs, the commanding officer may have asked, 'Doc, medevacs will stop this operation, are they really necessary?' And again I would confirm or deny; end of conversation. *I* sometimes bantered with figureheads as the one who didn't. But Mickey Mouse crap in the middle of a war zone really pissed me off. My morning company muster story's a perfect example."

"I must ask," I said. "What is a morning muster?"

"Morning mustard." Dennis grinned. "No really, muster is a company lineup for a named head count and inspection. Since I attended muster for the BAS, I blew off company inspection. Well, for some ungodly reason, my first sergeant demanded that I stand company muster. I refused, and he insisted. So I quickly discovered the first sergeant's shot card was missing. 'If I can't find it, Sergeant, I'll have to administer every shot again. Excuse me, sir, I've got to get to company muster.' That threat included thirty shots. The sarge got my message. 'Hey, Doc, you don't have to attend company muster twice.' 'Thank you, Sergeant. Guess what? Your shot records were misfiled.'"

"Ouch on the thirty shots," I said.

"My fellow BAS corpsman joined me on another rebellious occasion. Dr. Viti's replacement hounded the BAS corpsmen to practice bandaging. We ignored him. Hell, we'd been in country for over six months, we didn't need training. But this guy's nagging annoyed the crap out of us so we acquiesced. During practice, we taped him to a stretcher and left him on An Hoa's runway. We simply walked away. We didn't give a damn. Would they have sent us to a stateside brig? Hell, yeah, let's go. This doctor left An Hoa shortly thereafter. Rumor had it, he couldn't hack it. Dr. Viti was a tough act to follow."

"That's funny," I said. "Do you have any other stories from the lighter side?"

"One crazy Seabee would bulldoze the jungle along Liberty Road and Liberty Bridge *alone*. Marine patrols and sweeps included twelve men, machine guns, and air support, and this Seabee's riding a big green caterpillar tractor *alone* with nothing more than his M14. I thought that he was nuttier than hell."

Dennis eased back into his chair. "I'll never forget this incredibly naïve and funny kid we nicknamed Whiskey from Piggett, Arkansas who sounded like Gomer Pyle. 'Goooooolly, well would you look at that!'" he said with a perfect Gomer Pyle drawl.

"Whisky went to Bangkok on R & R, fell in love with a whore, and convinced himself that he'd marry her. We suspected that this gal was just trying to gain access into the U.S. and warned, 'Whiskey, this woman will disappear the second she's in California.' Whiskey insisted. 'No, she loves me, and I love her.' A million dollar wound sent him home before anyone could ever find out.

"Another time we almost had a Wild West shootout in An Hoa. Two Marines argued over a poker game, took out their M16s, and paced each other outside their hootch, ready to shoot and kill. We stopped the fiasco in the nick of time."

"That's crazy," I said.

"On a sadder note, one brokenhearted Marine shot his M16 into the back of his mouth after reading a Dear John letter. But since the kid shot the back and *not* the roof of his mouth, the bullet pierced his brain stem instead of his brain cavity, so he didn't die instantly. He was conscious for hours. We tried everything to keep him alive, but we couldn't save him. We'd find Dear John letters next to dead bodies with M16s on the floor. Although it didn't happen often, it happened often enough."

"How sad," I said. "Let's switch gears and talk about the media."

"I'll tell you sad," Dennis said. "I sadly watched one female *Life* photographer bogged down by camera equipment get shot as we assaulted a tree line. And I shamelessly told several reporters they were crazier than shit for joining us on Operation Essex. One reporter screamed bloody murder after getting frayed by shrapnel. I yelled to the Marine next to him, 'How bad is he?' 'It's a flesh wound.' I threw the guy a battle dressing. I'd be damned before running through mortar fire to band aid a flesh wound. The reporter was fine; the wound a tiny reminder of why he shouldn't have been there.

"For us, the media was a useless vessel for exposing untruths. Families sent hometown newspapers filled with anti-war marches, peace rallies, and hippies spitting on the military while we read the *Stars and Stripes*, a morale boosting rah-rah-rah-Marines-kick-ass-and-President-Johnson-awards-medals-because-everyone-loves-us-rah-rah-rah newspaper. We didn't understand. We'd read about Tom Hayden and Jane Fonda and wonder why they weren't shot for treason."

"I assure you," I unabashedly admitted, "I can say nothing in Jane Fonda's defense. Nothing. Those who choose to defend her Vietnam antics are clueless as to the gravity of her actions."

"Hanoi Jane Fonda decorates urinals as target practice in my VA Home Chapter building. Now what does that say?"

"Not much," I said. "Okay, let's switch gears again and talk about medical treatment for the Vietnamese."

"Infections were common among these peasant field farmers. Villagers responded well to penicillin, Pen VK, and amoxicillin because they didn't have any medicine. Not even aspirin. Open wounds and sores were covered with water buffalo feces as the medicinal and spiritual cure-all. I found an NVA medical bag that was pathetic. The contents were crude—a glass syringe packed in a little tin box, sewing needles, battle dressings made from strips of shirts rolled up and tied with a bow, mammasan's scissors, and American stolen meds.

"Kids were treated for a myriad of infections, worms, parasites, burns, bruises, breaks, sprains, you name it. They'd wave their fingers for band-aids. '*Bac-si, Bac-si, bouco dow, bouco dow*,' meaning, 'doctor, doctor, it hurts.' One six-year-old Vietnamese-French girl from the river village adopted me after I treated her arm wound. She'd jump in my arms. '*Bac-si, Bac-si, boucu dow*,' and I gave her band-aids, gum, candy, and C rats. We all did. One afternoon we passed through what had now become a lifeless village. The NVA captured every breathing creature. I've often wondered about the fate of that little girl."

"Did you go on many MedCAPs?" I asked.

"Yes, although it didn't take long to resent providing aid during unofficial MedCAPs. Of course, MedCAPs successfully changed the hearts and minds of the Vietnamese villagers, but how many times can you provide unofficial aid and comfort and witness four Marines blown to smithereens in mammasan's front yard? And why did the explosions and ambushes occur on our exit, never our entrance? Young Marines would see a knife and think, 'cool souvenir.' Well guess what lay beneath the knife? *Boom.* Boys would kick cans—as boys do— and blow their feet off. It really pissed me off. Villagers knew where every mine, booby trap, and Viet Cong tunnel lay. Vietnam's tunnels were intricate mazes of *death* for Marines. Thank God for napalm. Napalm saved my life and the lives of many military men. This may sound morbid but the more crispy critters we fried, the longer we survived."

"Truthfully," I said, "everyone I've spoken to so far describes napalm as a lifesaver. How did napalm work?"

"Jellied gasoline-cylinder bombs would airburst one hundred and fifty feet overhead, steam, flip end-over-end, and explode. *Whoosh, whoosh, whoosh.* Napalm detonated a hurricane wind that sucked *in* toward its fire. As the blaze dwindled the napalm would boomerang, burn, and suffocate everything in its path."

"Whew," I said. "Let's talk about the Vietnamese children."

"Oh, boy! At times nothing could be more lethal than a toddler. I've seen Marines run like chickens from a four-year-old strapped with a grenade. Marines incapable of shooting children ran *into* ambushes. These were the people that I treated. I became one angry, embittered son of a bitch. I avoided all memorial services and Purple Heart ceremonies including my own. Dr. Viti handed me my Purple Heart in a box at the BAS."

"If you don't mind me asking, how did you earn your Purple Heart?"

FMF Corpsman Dennis Noah recuperating in An Hoa after falling into a punji pit, 1967.

Dennis pointed his finger at me and glared. "I'm no hero so don't make me out to be one. I didn't want a Purple Heart. A corpsman tagged me, without my knowledge."

Dennis's humility threw me off guard. "Okay," I said. "Rest assured, no hero accolades. But you had to sustain an injury to get a Purple Heart, didn't you?"

"Yes. Pellets of shrapnel literally grated my back and left shoulder. Dr. Viti removed the larger fragments and remnants of black metal surface to this day. On yet another rather lethal outing, shrapnel superficially embedded in my left eye. But I destroyed that Purple Heart tag. I wouldn't dare accept a Purple Heart for Mickey Mouse shit surrounded by such seriously injured Marines. I wouldn't *dare*. I wouldn't even accept a Purple Heart for my right knee going to hell in a punji pit. I could've really bitten the dust that day but an apprentice dug the hole."

"Okay, so now I'm confused," I said.

"I plunged into a punji pit, hauling a sixty-pound backpack, my piss pot, B-1 bag, and weapon, convinced that I was soon to be a dead man. But my right foot caught a jagged, protruding root that broke the fall. A punji trap normally had smooth walls. That root saved my life. I hung upside down as my knee snapped, crackled, popped and cracked again. Sergeant Bucky, who weighed all of one hundred and fifteen pounds hauled me out. I was writhing in pain. Sargeant Bucky hoisted me piggy-back to An Hoa.

"Chief LeGarie kept me on light duty at the BAS. My recuperation was a vacation with three squares a day. An Hoa's combat base was relatively safe compared to the jungle laden with booby traps, claymore mines, and VC slithering like snakes on the earthen floor to slit your throat. Sappers, mortars, and sniper fire were An Hoa's main threats." Dennis paused with a slight smirk. "Sappers were very, very, very tiny, like you."

I smiled. "That's a lot of verys."

"Well, it's true. They were minute, like you. Wearing nothing more than a sumo wrestler's diaper and holding a satchel charge, the Kamikazes would crawl—at night—through incredible mud to knife the concertina wire behind the BAS. We'd find them dead from random grenade and H&I fire in the morning. But at least we knew the sappers were the enemy. We were convinced half of the Popular Forces—the Vietnamese soldiers supposedly on our side—were NVA. Here's an interesting story. A group of PF soldiers joined us as we protected a ville surrounded by NVA. Lieutenant Bond (not real name) assigned everyone *but me*, a non-combatant, a PF soldier. If overrun, the Marines were ordered to protect themselves from the PF's. Lieutenant Bond hedged his bet on the PF's shooting Marines as part of the enemy ambush. Thankfully, we didn't get overrun.

"Another time, Vietnamese Rangers carrying American weapons leisurely strolled by our squad on patrol. Our squad leader chatted in English with the lead Ranger before bidding him farewell. We nodded and waved. Ten feet after the last one passed I turned around. The Rangers had disappeared. I saw nothing but the trail going back to the firebase. I tapped the guy ahead and said, 'Look behind you.' And he did. 'Doc, I don't see anything.' 'I know,' I said. 'That's my point.' The Rangers carrying American weapons were NVA guerillas.

"Another lethal afternoon we passed Marines, or so we thought, in full uniform—flak jackets, helmets, canteens, gas masks—while patrolling through Antenna Valley. We waved and by God, they waved back. As we crossed a rice paddy, the ground erupted with combat fire. Marines, my ass; the imposters were an NVA heavy weapons platoon. These sharp shooters nailed Stutes between the eyes. Hours passed before another company arrived. The bombing and mortar fire was so intense our own men thought we were goners. Marines, crawling to retrieve the dead, were shocked to find us alive. Marines were found dead lying on their jammed M16s. It was horrible."

I could sense Dennis's uneasiness bordering on agitation. I thought it best to wrap up the conversation. "When did you leave Vietnam?"

"I rotated out shortly after the first TET offensive and the Battle for Hué City. I was in the forward Battalion Aid Station outside of Hué City. Do you know the Marines proved victorious at the battle for Hué City, but American newspapers declared the battle as a loss? We didn't understand. We didn't lose the Battle for Hué City."

Dennis sighed. "Leaving Vietnam was like flying on the Starship Enterprise into the rings of another dimension. Stepping into a civilian airliner in Da Nang was like stepping through a time portal, a reality warp into the twilight zone. I heard distant explosions, boom-boom-boom, thinking it was all some dream. There I sat, drinking booze in air-conditioned comfort surrounded by round-eyed stewardesses on a commercial airline while my guys were dying. That was incredibly tough. The lack of combat decompression caused total shock. Three nights after a deadly ambush, I was in my living room watching TV. It was all surreal.

"And there was no such thing as a welcomed homecoming. People threw garbage and held signs emblazoned with 'baby-killers' and 'rapists' at the gates of El Toro Marine Base. I harbored a hollow-gut fury. My father received free movie admission wearing his military uniform. I changed clothes in the airport men's room. I wasn't ashamed of my uniform or of my service. I just didn't want the hassle. America shunned anyone looking remotely military—tan, filthy, sporting a crew cut, and wearing funny black shoes.

"Very few Americans understood the plight of the Vietnam combat veteran. High school buddies made comments about killing babies and raping women. I've never been nor do I plan on ever attending a high school reunion. I'm even tight-lipped about Vietnam with my wife, Susan. Vietnam was never a desired topic of conversation. Decades passed before I told anyone, including my job, that I served as a medical corpsman. Only my immediate family knew. My career transitioned from medicine to banking because I never wanted to touch another band-aid for as long as I lived. It took me years to realize I should've been a doctor."

"You would have been a wonderful physician," I said. "I'm sorry that my fellow Americans politically thwarted you from the pursuit of your dreams."

"America disgraced the Vietnam veteran with little conscience. Today, America supports her troops, regardless of their opinion on war. I've been in airports as Marines and soldiers walk through and people stand aside and clap. Americans pay tribute to the combat veteran *because* of our legacy—the Vietnam combat veteran's legacy. We, as combat Vietnam veterans, left an indelible mark on American history. We, as combat Vietnam veterans didn't lose the Vietnam War. We lost the politics. We didn't let America down. America let us down."

Dennis sat stoically. I fidgeted. My heart ached for words that would not come. Enough was enough had arrived.

"Hey," I said determined to dissipate the black Vietnam cloud hovering over *The Main Course*. "Let's take a break. I'm boldly going to request a sample of your one-of-a-kind-Noah Bloody Marys."

Dennis relaxed into a smile that assured me we were done for the day. "Sure thing. You drink while I steer this baby around the bay."

"Deal," I said.

Dennis hesitated. "Lucia?"

"Yes."

"Thanks. Thank you for listening. Thank you for caring. Thank you for sharing your father with me all over again. Thank you."

Unsuccessfully fighting back tears, I hugged Dennis as hard as I could. I could not speak.

An Old Corpsman's Dream
by Dennis L. Noah

They were his Marines to heal and to save
But due to the terrible craft of the NVA
Their going home birds were chartered by Graves*
And their fellow travelers were also silent and cold.
They come to him during the night in military style
They march out of the mist, surrounded by the dark
With lifeless bodies garbed all in green
Slowly and silently these Marines seek their corpsman.
Their eyes are sunken and stare straight ahead
Their cheeks are hollow and skin without glow
With ageless faces that remain for all time
And outstretched arms pleadingly fixed.
They've come from beyond to inquire into their fates
With haunting voices they ask the old corpsman
"Doc why didn't we live like many of the rest?
We were so young and filled with desire."
He tells them that he tried and he tried and he tried
"I wanted you so much to survive and return to the world
But your wounds were so beyond the limits of my skill
That nothing I could do would avoid another NVA kill."
They did not respond and lower their arms

From his mind they fade silently as they have come
The old Corpsman awakens to the rising sun
But in the darkness of other countless nights
His Marines, they will return again and again.

*Graves registration recorded and transported the dead home

A Grunt Corpsman's Prayer
by Dennis L. Noah

Oh God, as I kneel over this grievously wounded Marine
Trying to maintain his sacred life with my human frailty
I know that without divine intervention I will fail
Please blow your healing breath into his body
And bestow upon me a tiny fraction of your infinite knowledge so my skills
will be equal to my worldly task.
Oh Saint Michael, warrior and gallant patron of the Corps
Lower your shield above this Marine's failing body
To protect him from further harm on this field of battle
Swing your sword to deflect our enemy's bullets
And gain me the time to render him whatever assistance
Is needed to stem his terrible crimson flow.
Oh Blessed Mary, Mother Divine, warm him with your love
A mother's love that will restore his desire for life
And let him know that a mother's hope is his for the taking
So he will awaken to the dawn of a new morn' and future
From the darkness and pain of such a terrible ordeal
Because the mother of the one has made it right.
Oh Saint Joseph, patient, gentle and wise father
Be at his side as he lingers between existences
Teach him that he must now fight his biggest battle
Speak to him with the soft firmness of a devoted father
Guiding him down this crooked and torturous path
So he may find his way back to his physical self.
Oh God, if it is truly your divine will that he not survive
Open your gates for him and forgive him of any wrong doings
Saint Michael, carry his spirit on your shield to his maker
Saint Joseph, Shepherd him through his heavenly beginning
Blessed Mother, help this Marine to a place near your son
And God, please do not let him die from any failing of mine.

❧ Dear Daddy ❧

Jim Meyers and I spent an afternoon reading his letters written to his mom—Jim's dad died when he was eight years old—from An Hoa. The treasure trove was found in the attic after Mom's passing. Mom, unbeknownst to all, had saved every one. I instantly requested the opportunity to share them with the world. Jim and I spoke openly and honestly about your Vietnam.

"These letters are amazing," I said.

"Yes," Jim said. "They're like old friends stirring dimmed recollections."

"What goes through your mind as you read them more than forty years post fact?" I asked.

"I reacquaint with the young author, thinking, you were a fine Marine. I wouldn't have minded knowing you myself."

I smiled. "These letters are an eloquent legacy from a man determined to change the world."

"Indeed. These letters speak of opportunities and successes which prove the value of America's presence in South Vietnam. My words depict with conviction and purpose the constructive difference Marines made in the lives of the South Vietnamese. We committed ourselves by extending America's best hand to assist those in need. Left to communistic influences, the people of South Vietnam were mere victims, juggled and manipulated as pawns, within the clutches of her Northern aggressors. But we stood in harm's way to say, 'No, you're not going to bully, torment, and harm the citizens of South Vietnam on our watch.'"

"They're also the perfect historical narrative of the 2/5's role in An Hoa," I said.

"Indeed. They highlight how 2/5 protected An Hoa's Industrial Complex so it could become a distinct microcosm of the nation South Vietnam could be. We guarded Nong Son's coal mine so that the Industrial Complex could utilize its resources to up start the engines and independently run South Vietnam; perhaps efficiently for the first time in its history. Our accomplishments were commendable. America's military built medical clinics, schools, roads, and bridges, and enhanced irrigation systems. My hometown church donations—Operation Concern—clothed local village children. And, as we helped South Vietnam resist the throes of communism, doctors and corpsmen transformed local ideology by administering to the wounded, sick, and the elderly. And no one did so with more passion than your father. These letters reflect the attitude that history should bear witness to. I reflect as a man satisfied by my Vietnam memories."

"But a change occurs as time draws near to your homecoming," I said.

"Yes. Combat's a proving ground—a baptism by fire with consequences that take their toll," Jim said. "But by the same token, I belonged to a band of brothers that made a positive difference in people's lives. And along the way I learned how to appreciate and celebrate life's simple pleasures. And I do mean simple."

"That's a far cry from what most people remember about the Vietnam War."

"Sadly, these pages belong to a war that disgusted America, a time often described as a dark horror in our nation's history. The Vietnam War as seen through the eyes of this young Marine returned to an America that aided and abetted the enemy through political theatrics and the media's poetic license. I shared the common baby-killer cloak when nothing could have been further from the truth. This young Marine suffered—along with America's Vietnam combat Marine veteran—a grave injustice.

"Take the letters, Lucia. Let **Dr.** **Tom's War** give my children, my grandchildren, and my great grandchildren a bird's eye view into the heart of a dedicated Marine that stood among the multitudes of men like Doctors Viti and Gonder, Chief LeGarie, Richard Esau, Tony Marengo, and John Newton. Let this letter-diary honor the memory of Captain James Graham as a true American hero. Allow America to understand that the Vietnam War was not lost by the heart of America's military."

Letters Home

Dear Folks,
Today...
wonderful da...
I received 3...
really Christ...
I receiv...
things just co...
after lost...
First, for me pay...
and luckily so. At approxim...

26 FEB 67
...to be a
...good Lord for.
...d it was
...uch!
...wife, so
...ved it though
...d unmarried

Captain James L. Meyers, USMC, 1968, Quantico.

Lt. James Meyers, USMC, An Hoa, 1967, *after Union II.*

January 28, 1967
Dear Folks,

I've just returned from a combat outpost on "Operation Tuscaloosa." I never thought I would be so glad to see An Hoa. Seventy-six Marines and I were dug in on a hill called My Luc (2) in the heart of VC land. The battalion minus swept the outer edge of our tactical area. Two 105 howitzers were fired into our position in direct support of the operation. The operation was a success. The battalion inflicted heavy casualties on the VC 20th Battalion—an estimated company size force engaged north of this small outpost position. LTC Airhart had faith in me—the new lieutenant in-country—to man this outpost with a provisional platoon of Marines. His decision lends itself to the training of every Marine officer. Thank

God for Marine training! I am confident, even when so new in a combat zone.

Today my feelings are mixed. I tried not to let my emotions get the best of me in front of my men. We came upon litter bearers carrying wounded VC away from the heart of the day's previous battle; three wounded women, an old man and a small boy with napalm and shrapnel wounds, all confirmed VC, now prisoners. They were sniping and laying booby traps around the area. My heart couldn't help but go out to these people, even though they were the enemy. They have a stench about them. The women have black teeth with deep eyes and a prevalent fear in their eyes. The Communists tell these loyal local farmers that Americans will burn homes, kill men, eat children and rape their women. It's why they fight us. We are not of their land, even this continent, and so they believe the VC.

The small boy was younger than David [nephew] and the corpsman treated him for a neck wound. As I passed them, I stooped down to examine and give the boy some water. I felt his bandage and said, "Owie, Owie." He was really scared for a second because he must have thought I would kill him. I took my towel, cut it in half, poured water over it and placed it on his forehead. He immediately calmed down. When I saw him calm, I smiled and winked. He said, "Owie, owie" and proceeded to guide me to a scalp wound, an elbow wound, a shoulder and side wound—all small cuts from mortar shrapnel but none bleeding. The corpsman patched him up and I gave him some gum. He never smiled but I could see something in his eyes—perhaps bewilderment and surprise at the care and treatment. The women were patched up, questioned and medevaced to Da Nang. The intel sergeant told me that an old man bit off the tip of his tongue rather than risk talking to us. Their fear is unwarranted, misdirected. I hope that we can change this. It's difficult to realize that this civilization was here two thousand years before us. The Vietnamese farmers and peasantry want nothing more than to be left alone by all—to live as they have lived for thousands of years. The communists tell them of the worldly dangers of capitalism and the American war machine, pointing to our presence in Vietnam as a "for instance." These peasants seem to lack an understanding that the instigators are the Northern invaders from the other side of the DMZ, who look like them.

The small and I do mean *small*, upper Vietnamese class is intelligent and anti-communist. If only *they*, could work with their own people, problems would cease and life would go on as it has years previous. However, if the communists are allowed to spread the turmoil and distrust to the South Vietnamese people via the Viet Cong and North Vietnamese Regular Army, the immense members of Southeast Asia—millions of people—will be mere pawns in their hands and a direct threat to the rest of the free world. You must see what it's like to really understand, empathize and witness the atrocities pressed upon these poor people to believe that we must remain in Vietnam. We should've been here long ago.

My prayers of forgiveness are many. I hope in destroying what evil lurks in the villages known to possess VC that the innocent be spared. But I know, because I have seen, that this may not be. I liken it to a doctor cutting away a malignant growth and the surrounding healthy tissue. I see only life and death. The in between is sometimes more grotesque than any one could ever imagine. I see the face of that little boy, knowing it may have been our artillery and mortars that left him parentless and bleeding—but with no other alternative. The enemy unit was dealt a heavy blow, but unfortunately, with innocent civilian loss. I hope the good Lord understands and helps me sleep at night.

I think of you all and home often. The days remaining are still too long to count, but my hopes and desires carry me through these days with "This too shall pass."

Stay well and God Bless,

Jim

Saturday, February 11, 1967

Dear Friends,

It was truly a pleasure to receive your letters written while you were at your arts & crafts meeting. To a service man away from home, any news is good news and a Godsend. I was particularly impressed with the letter from my church people.

I'm stationed in An Hoa, South Vietnam with the Second Battalion, Fifth Marine Regiment of the First Marine Division, an infantry battalion attempting to safeguard and clear a 144 square-mile area. The goal is mammoth for a mere battalion, but we take on a typical "John Wayne" Marine pride and consider it routine. It's "our watch."

The situation here is not well at hand, let no one be mistaken. We control only certain facets of the vast terrain and govern what we can of the people's movement. But the country knows only too well that the VC are present. Our strides have come a long way and our control for safeguarding certain areas grows, but the guerilla war is one of no front, no lines and with great infiltration. Our hope presents itself in the form of the people whom we protect. It lies in their ability to distinguish between life as the free world would contribute from the education of its leaders or life under Communist Viet Cong, Ho Chi Minh's North Vietnamese Government and the Communist world as it's known to us.

One thing is certain—*any* educated course of action that would change the living conditions for the whole of the people would be for the better. The poverty, disease, filth, and the lack of plain and simple hygiene practices run rampant in Vietnam. Of course, you'll always find one person to say, "those people have never known any different, they're content and happy with life and have been for thousands of years—who are we to tell them how to live?" Yes, we could turn our backs and walk away unconcerned. This civilization was here two thousand years before our own. It hasn't changed much since then and it's still here. That manner of thinking however, is absurd. These are people just as you and I. They have a great desire as well as a need to improve their conditions. If they do not go along with the VC or NVA, it's atrocity-ville. If we bear witness to Christ, we cannot turn away from this great darkness. It is our *moral obligation* to help them help themselves; to stand in harm's way. And, we can do it better and faster than anyone else in the world.

Our second obligation and reason for being here is political. It's in our country's best interest. If aggressors could organize this nation as a pawn army, such as the VC, our sons and daughters would be turning them away from our homeland, not from across the sea. It would be the free world's turn to fight for survival against an enemy that started as a small malignant growth and went unchecked until the essence of life was threatened. The price we would pay would be far greater than the small price we are paying now. I often ask myself what our nation needs as a national disaster to spur her against an enemy. We are a land built by thinking men. We must realize that the threat in Southeast Asia is just as dangerous to our national security as the Japanese bombers who bombed Pearl Harbor.

Needless to say, I firmly believe in our military and economic commitment to South Vietnam. I also believe that there should be a greater effort from a nation with a common goal. I realize the criers for peace in Vietnam—for withdrawal sake only—are few. But with the play of our present day press even the minorities have a big "voice." Sometimes the "voice" is out of proportion to the actual size of the owner.

To the advocators of a cease fire on North Vietnam, I would like to extend a guided tour of the South. To my battalion's north east position, there is a reinforced company of the North Vietnamese Army. Another regiment of the NVA is located in the mountains behind us. Company-sized NVA units are now attached to company-sized VC units, such as the V-20 and the R-25 units to our west and north. That sounds like we are surrounded, doesn't it? Well you're right!!!! We are. We run sweeps and patrols, maintain combat outposts, plus a few of our own innovations to keep the enemy off-guard. My baptism under fire came on my second day in Vietnam as a small VC unit tried to over run our outpost on My Luc (2). That same night, a one-hundred-and-twenty man Special Forces Camp to our west was over run by the same unit. Under the NVA leaders, twelve- and fourteen-year-old boys are indoctrinated as "sappers," the modern day version of the old Japanese "Kamikaze," suicide fanatics bent on mutual destruction. The stamp of NVA arms, supplies, uniforms, flak jackets, helmets and gear is better or equal to those of our Marines. The supplies from the North increase as does NVA activity in the south. If we cease bombing the manufacturing centers, the supply routes, the storage bins, the targets of the North, who do we aid? I would take personal offense to a fellow American that would better equip or encourage our common enemy, especially when I'm on the other end of that enemy's delivering arm!

The Australian and Korean commitment to this war effort is greatly appreciated. I see the entire situation as one for the United Nations and hope that they recognize it as they did in Korea.

Our morale is high. Our battle Marines are those with whom you would be proud to serve. Their aggressiveness in the field is only outdone by their humanitarian work on civil affairs and environmental development with the young and old. Our position is tenable, our effort determined, our strides forward and our progress mounting. At this rate, we'll be here for quite a while. You can liken it to the building of a pyramid in a sandstorm. It will take a lot of people, time, work and prayers. But it can be done.

I would like to offer you a challenge to help. An Hoa Civil Affairs can use bars of soap, children's clothing, aspirin, cold tablets, blankets and the likes. On Operation Independence and Tuscaloosa, hundreds of refugees fell in behind our American forces pressing the enemy during VC and NVA sweeps. Here, on the outskirts of An Hoa, Vietnamese people, now refugees, have their first real exposure to what the American is truly like. They learn that he does not burn their homes unnecessarily, kill men, rape women or eat the children as the VC say. If you will meet the challenge, no matter how slight, you can join us in making a difference here. I can send a delivery address.

Once again, let me say how much I enjoyed hearing from you. Arts & crafts night sounds like fun!

Our spirits *are* up!

We're glad you're with us and may God bless you.

Sincerely,

Jim Meyers

February 13, 1967

Dear Mom,

The new chaplain has asked me be the battalion lay leader and take over for him in his absence from a Wednesday evening Bible study class. I was tickled at the invitation and look forward to becoming active again. My past "church" passiveness concerns me. This is just what I need.

Dr. Pyke [a retired missionary from my home church] wrote me two letters. It will take time to choose my words before I answer. He thinks strongly about my ministerial calling and my lack of that recognition. I truly enjoy his letters. I will answer but not just yet. I must find a certain something before I'm able to do so.

Today I flew to Nong Son with another small security team to re-con the area and report if it's physically capable of vehicular traffic. There were a great number of VC and NVA troops which could be observed from our position and the recon unit perched on a hilltop that sits at the entrance to Antenna Valley across from Nong Son. You see very little of the enemy and when you do it's usually in groups no larger than five or six. This was a real temptation!

We are hampered by the South Vietnamese leaking intelligence so if we decided to mount a battalion force to sweep after them, they wouldn't be there. Same old story—they'll know that we're coming.

The top gunnery sergeant lifted my pride today by telling me that I received more volunteer offers for the security team drops than any other non-line company lieutenant. He said, "You must be tactically sound for these buggers to go after you've only been here a month."

I just smiled and said, "It must be my aftershave."

I'm proud to know that, however. I am good with Marines!

Love,

Jim

February 26, 1967

Dear Folks,

Today, Sunday has turned into a wonderful day—with much to thank the good Lord for—I received three packages mailed on the 11th and it was Christmas in February. Thanks so much.

First, let me say that I'm healthy, strong and unmarred. And luckily so! At approximately eleven-thirty last night I was in the rack when I heard whistling about three-hundred meters in the distance. I lay silent and heard another one closer walking towards us. By the time I determined that the second mortar landed closer, one foot was in my boot, my helmet was on and I was screaming at my gunnery sergeant to sound the word that we were under mortar attack. I ordered the men to crawl into their bomb shelters. Mortars, small fire arms and machine guns broke the sounds of night.

Everything went smoothly. I have men to be proud of. It's understood that we look out for each other. It's a good feeling for an officer to have of his men. The mortars lifted and we dashed to our defensive perimeter positions for which I am responsible to see held at all cost in this panhandle of the battalion.

Let me put your mind at ease. *My* bunkers have the strongest roofs (old rails from the railroad) plus an extra layer of sandbags and the deepest trench line in An Hoa. Lieutenant Colonel Mal Jackson used our bunkers to show General Nickerson on his visit to An Hoa. Nobody, but nobody, without an Air Force could over run our position around the Motor Pool! We maintain the southern most tip of the perimeter which looks like this:

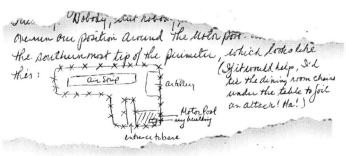

Also, last night the humorous anecdotes flew as we crawled into the bunkers and trenches. As we were scrambling outside of the hootch, the gunny said that the VC would pay if they hit his rolled courtyard of freshly planted tomato plants. Another sergeant had shrapnel pierce his fiancé's picture and boy was he teed-off at ol' Charlie. They laughed at me because shrapnel had ruptured a can of Dinty Moore Beef Stew that splattered all over my flak jacket. Several of my men asked if they could snack off my back. Losing that stew can become my own little "Remember the Alamo" cry!

We were ready and loaded for bear if they came our way. No breach attempts were made, however, and the VC were hit by our artillery and mortars—as well as small arms fire before their mortars quieted down. Our Marines acted quickly and efficiently, returning a maximum rate of fire as the twentieth VC mortar hit the camp. We feel this dispelled any thought they had to over run us. It was probably just a probe at the defenses.

Enough excitement for now. Let me assure you again that I'm alright. We are perfectly capable of taking care of ourselves.

God bless and keep you.

Love,

Jim

March 7, 1967

Dear Folks,

Hi again! I'm alright, just back from the field and safe in An Hoa. We supported the later phase of Operation Stone. I reconnaissance-ed VC trails to the east—nothing. I will remain in An Hoa for a little while.

Your packages arrive in droves. I have the lollipops for the kids—they really love them! You've been so outstanding in correspondence and goody packages that I think that I am the envy of my men. I do share and the men think that I'm "A O.K." in their book!

Today, General Krulak, head of the III Marine Amphibious Forces in Vietnam, visited An Hoa. He was impressed and encouraged with the battalion's performance despite the pouring rain.

The people here are delighted with your response [Operation Concern]. I promise to take pictures.

Love,

Jim

March 14, 1967

Dear Folks,

Today the Division Inspection Team arrived to inspect the Battalion Motor Transport Section of which I am in charge. Eight battalions and units attached were inspected to date and, thank goodness, we were one of the two units that received a stamp of approval.

*Lt. James Meyers,
An Hoa children sporting
their "Operation Concern"
clothes and Dr. Viti,
An Hoa, RSVN,
1967.*

*Lt. James Meyers holding a
Vietnamese girl sporting an
outfit from Operation Concern;
a hometown clothing-aid effort
spear-headed by Jim's mother,
Dora Amelia Herbert and sister,
Jean Meyers Herbert from St.
John's of Hamilton Methodist
Church located in Baltimore,
MD.*

*An Hoa village children and their
mamma-san escort sporting 'new
threads' courtesy of Operation
Concern.*

*Lt. Gen. Victor "Brute" Krulak,
USMC, Lt. Col. McNaughton
(2/5 CO), Chief Hospital Corpsman
Lou LeGarie, and Dr. Viti. An Hoa's
BAS and field triage unit, touted as
the best, was frequently used for VIP
site visits.*

Panhandle behind An Hoa's airstrip occupied by amtracs, supply, motor transport and the BAS. This dirt compound was often smoothed out by pallets dragged along the surface by Mighty Might Vehicles. The area was often used as a basketball court.

Using corrugated sheeting provided by the Seabees, The Motor Transport Platoon constructed a secured and shaded service area to maintain motor transport vehicles. Fighting holes and sleeping quarters are in the forefront.

Looking Southwest from An Hoa's Observation Tower, 2/5 Marines march in form to 'chow.' An Hoa village in the distant perimeter; foreground the in-ground COC. An Hoa, RSVN, 1967.

Lt. James Meyers posing in front of the Dispatcher for the Motor Transport with an "inherited" WWII Army grease gun. Avis-Rent-A-Car, Lt. Meyers' former employee outfitted Motor Transport with camouflage "We try harder" buttons.

Since my arrival, I've established a quality control point, a double check on vehicles coming in and leaving the battalion area. This received high praise and will be considered as a new suggestion into the Marine Corps Motor Transport System as to whether it's worthy of Corps-wide adoption. I call it "Speed-Shop," an idea which I credit to my Avis Operational Training.

Love,

Jim

March 23, 1967

Dear Folks,

In addition to being the Battalion Motor Transport officer, for a short while I will be the Sparrow Hawk platoon commander. It is an alert platoon called out—at anytime—as a relief force to areas engaged by an enemy of considerable greater size. This is a large responsibility for me. The platoon is reinforced by a lot of fire power and larger weapons than normal, making it small but deadly—hence the "Sparrow Hawk" code name. There seems to be an increase of enemy activity in our area.

The men and officers are not pleased with the new colonel. He appears to lack the tactical know-how or guts to pursue the VC. He seems content sitting back and defending our perimeter. In order to safeguard our Tactical Area of Operation, we must go to the VC and the NVA. They won't come to us until they are assured of a minor victory or a telling blow. Perhaps the new colonel is learning this, but some people are getting bitter in the process. Our battalion has a reputation for being aggressive and he has one for being a paper worker. The two just aren't mixing! We've had only one real operation in two months since his arrival. I had three beneath my belt in the first four weeks with the old 2/5 colonel. I guess I shouldn't complain but if you let ol' "Victor Charlie" run around the countryside without fear, they build their arms and ambush sites and erect defensive positions—all proving twice as hard to vacate. The new executive officer and operations officer look fine. Perhaps the two of them can convince the colonel of his shortcomings. By the way, this is for your information and for me to get off my chest—not for publication or talk of any kind—OK?

I got an infra-red sniper scope from the intelligence officer to see if we can detect who or what has been cutting our electronic sensors and claymore mine lines at night. The scope enables one to see in pitch black darkness as if it were daylight without being detected. An ideal enemy approach site is in front of our position—a drainage ditch thru rice paddies—that enables one to come directly into our wire. The scope will help immediately. That's about all the news for now.

Hope you're all well.

Love,

Jim

March 31, 1967

Dear Folks,

I'm well, healthy and trying to adjust to the increase in temperature which seems to grow with each day. I hope your spring {Maryland} has finally reared its head and you're enjoying fair weather for a change.

Some changes have happened since I last wrote. I have been appointed as the command group platoon commander. The command group consists of the colonel (the battalion CO), the executive officer (a major), the S3 or operations officer (another major), a surgeon, several radio operators, civic affairs officers (Army and Marine captains and their groups), and two corpsmen. An "operation" is any action over twenty-four hours in which two or more companies participate. I provide battlefield security to the command group, moving when they move, setting the men in place when they stop and intervening in any action directed at them. With our large protruding whip antennas, the command group is evident and security becomes challenging. The billet should prove an interesting one. I volunteered for it. Don't become too worried, I'll feel safer there than sitting in old vulnerable An Hoa. And the time goes much quicker in the field. I will get to see every battalion operation—so if you hear of our operations, I'll be the body guard to the battalion commander. Our next operation is called "Dixie."

I'm taking my command group platoon on several daylight patrols in order to familiarize them with the terrain. They're all volunteers. I feel good about that. We should work well together.

The North Vietnamese Army is certainly on a large infiltration move to the south. They seem to be all over. They're entering the south in regimental strength as our last major battle, "Operation Newcastle" has now confirmed. I hope we keep the pressure on Hanoi. I'd hate to see them up-to-par on supplies. They could give us a bigger fit if that happened.

I've met an interesting group of German Peace Corps workers. They're young—twenty-two to thirty-five years of age and quite well read. When time permits and I can get away, we have good conversations. I've invited one husband-wife team to visit us in the U.S. I worry about them outside our defensive perimeter. Although the VC have no qualms with Germany, I wouldn't trust them an inch. And if we were attacked, the Germans—due to the nearness of their location would have as much to fear from our defensive fire as the attacking VC or NVA.

Tomorrow General Buse will be here to present Purple Hearts and a Silver Star award. I will be one of the two platoon commanders standing with my platoon as honor guard.

I've never seen so many crazy insects in my life. The flies and mosquitoes use me for a dart board! Thank goodness for the mosquito nets. The insect repellent is just an aperitif to the bugs!

Please take care and thank you for your faithfulness in writing. It's the best morale booster in the world, honestly. And the most dependable!

My love,

Jim

April 13, 1967

Dear Mom and Folks,

Operation Dixie is now complete. I've returned to An Hoa safe in good health. It's good to be back, we took a few casualties, most of them due to mines and booby traps. I lost a few close friends on this one, but whether it be callous or a "thy will be done" attitude, it isn't quite as hard to accept. That must seem horrible but it's true. I guess one has to reach a certain threshold of resistance and perhaps I have reached mine. I hope so.

Miss you.

My love,

Jim

April 15, 1967

Dear Folks,

I feel rested now and I'm ready to go again. There's a rumor that we may be moving—where I don't know. The battalion has done a tremendous job holding this mammoth-sized area. I understand that we're up for a Presidential Unit Citation. The men have more than earned it—and the price they've paid could never be compensated by any award.

Best to all.

Love,

Jim

April 24, 1967

Dear Mom and All,

Operation Concern contributions will be greatly received. I'm glad you're getting so much cooperation from the Marine Reserve Unit, my thanks to Sergeant Major Bean.

I passed the colonel's battalion inspection which always makes me feel good. I'm short-handed in the Motor Transport Section as individual demands increase day-to-day. The men work hard and have so little reward. I had a "cookout" for them the other night—hamburgers and hot dogs that I made a deal for. We sliced a large oil drum in half from top-to-bottom, placed it on its side and welded rods to set as a grill. I got mustard, ketchup and pickles from the mess sergeant and my "light fingered" driver who works on mess hall runs. All seemed to enjoy it and I hope it can become a monthly affair. I miss you all.

My love,

Jim

May 2 1967

Dear Folks,

I'm writing from the field while participating on a large operation called Union. The Marines from Chu Lai (north) have joined us in a united effort to clear a large NVA force operating in the hills and valleys in our eastern area of responsibility. It's one of the largest operations in numbers of forces committed. I wonder if you're receiving reports at home.

These mountains and valleys with their many streams are conducive to a vacation resort. I could just as easily be in Cumberland, Maryland. Sounds carry and the clouds cover the mountain peaks—a beautiful sight for an artist to paint. The only regret is the condition under which I am now seeing this part of the world.

I know you'd enjoy the myriad number of multi-colored birds and flowers which frequent the land. All of Southeast Asia is not ugly. To the contrary, it can be really beautiful if you let yourself see through the present setting. I guess that's the secret to life everywhere, however, isn't it?

The summer weather is sizzling. I never knew the sun's rays could be so hot. Heat stroke and heat exhaustion have become common. The only solution is to gobble salt tablets as you would M&M's, drink plenty of water and keep your head covered. I can see why the Vietnamese wear straw hats and sleep from noon to three in the sizzling hours of the mid-day sun.

It will take some time to get your letters as it always does in the field. *Don't* worry if you don't hear from me for a while—we plan to be gone a long time on this one and I won't have much chance to write. I just couldn't sleep and I thought I'd drop a line in the dawn's breaking light.

Love,

Jim

May 12, 1967

Dear Mom,

Operation Concern deserves much praise. Lieutenant Colonel Jackson will see that an official thanks is given. I will request to go along on the distribution of goods so that I might send pictures depicting the results of your efforts. Your work on Operation Concern will be rewarded when you see the faces on these little tots. They're cute as can be and must be taught like any other children. It's hard to make them understand that they shouldn't beg. I've cured Ba [local Vietnamese girl] as the little pixie can get downright choosy as to what I give her now. It's a strange relationship—like having my own before I really do. When I leave An Hoa, Ba runs the gambit of emotion. Leaving her will present a problem, but her mother is still alive and I think more harm than good would come if I think of keeping her.

God Bless.

Jim

May 13, 1967

Dear Mom,

Hi again! I'm sick as a dog—from a flu or virus from bad water that my Halazone tabs didn't affect from Nong Son—an area that seems to take its toll on men's health. We've temporarily lost men to malaria and this virus bug. I'm sure it will pass in good time. Two of my very best friends are Flip Gonder and Tom Viti, both surgeons assigned to the 2/5. We sleep next door to each other in An Hoa. They take a personal interest in me which makes me feel pretty good. Except, they've threatened to move the outhouse tonight so I can't find it. They are the practical jokers of the battalion! They also take good care of Ba. A good friend when you are sick is a Godsend.

Just lying here, propped up, so many things come to mind. The war and our efforts as an infantry battalion haven't given me a chance to rest. I've been given yet another duty as embarkation officer—my fifth billet to fill. It's a good thing to pass time, but lately I'm worried. Being on the western edge, the frontier of what is considered "secure" (if any may be called so), an endless stream of agony and terror is wrought on innocent Vietnamese by the VC to persuade support. My platoon is the reactionary force that scatters the VC when such an intelligence report comes from the surrounding village. We cannot afford the manpower to man each village and work with the native forces. Without good leadership, the native forces, if threatened, will give away their arms in terror to the VC. The key is to work closely with these people so that they may develop

An Hoa's favorite little Vietnamese pixie-girl, "Ba," An Hoa, RSVN, 1967.

Lt. James Meyers with "Bo," a young son of the local handyman, George. Described as a smart, great kid, "Bo" swept the quarters and helped the Marine mechanics work on the engines.

a pride in themselves. A servile attitude is resultant in gory sights if the VC so chooses.

I thought I was becoming hardened to the dismembering of the human body but it still wretches my insides. My fear of needles and blood is gone and I can watch field expedient surgery without swallowing too hard. But I'm affected by anything abdominal. I don't think I'll ever get used to the sight of human intestines.

My temperature is coming down—only 101.3 at present. I hope it drops to normal by morning. I still have a backache plus an aching in both legs, so it's time to sleep. I haven't been able to sleep in over two weeks. I'm sure my weight will come back up with an appetite. I just can't eat in the field.

Take care, Mom. I'm glad to hear that you're better. Your letters are wonderful. God Bless you all.

Love,
Jim

May 18, 1967
[To the people of St. John's of Hamilton Methodist Church, Baltimore, Maryland.]
Dear All,

Your interest and response to the needs of the Vietnamese people is overwhelming. It's a tremendous boost to receive mail. It's such a good feeling that people realize the truth instead of the distortion that the large voice but small minority declare so widely. I'll let you see via slide pictures the reception of the goods [Operation Concern] so that you may pass it on. I know that we are often asked to contribute and we never see the end results. We'll try to change that by showing the contributors that their donations were utilized.

There's so much to tell of the happenings here, but time is little and it would take so many words to put on paper. I'm accumulating good pictures with which to capture the surface story of the land. Thank you all.

Many Blessings,
Jim

May 26, 1967
Dear Mom,

I've recovered my health and am active once again.

An emergency staff meeting was called tonight. We were placed on a one-hour regimental alert. We have an estimated six hundred North Vietnamese Army Regulars trapped in an entrenched bunker area to our east. Tomorrow we'll move to reinforce the first battalion in a search and destroy of the area. It should prove interesting. The troops are psyched at the thought of closing with an enemy who will not vanish. I believe that this will be a continuation of the Regimental Operation Union II, unless given another operational name. I will serve as the provisional platoon commander that provides security to our command group on Nong Son—the large hill at the mouth of Antenna Valley. Going into the valley will fall to the line companies. Don't worry about us. This is what we're best trained to do and my Marines have never been so eager or so ready.

Onward!!!!

Please give my love to all.

Jim

June 9, 1967

Dear Mom,

Hi! All is fine and I'm all right after the Union II encounter. It has taken me a few days to shake the depressive pang that accompanies the loss of close friends. I lost three good friends and fellow officers, all from our 2/5 battalion.

Captain Jim Graham was from Frostburg, MD and is now up for the Medal of Honor. He was a devout Christian and husband—and much admired by his men and fellow officers. He will be greatly missed. Before his departure, Captain Graham shared a Christian witness with me such as I've never heard. Scripture became real and prophecy took on a new meaning for me. There's something truly unexplainable about Captain James Graham; this man died saving Marines. His Christ-like example was as real as it gets. I must now examine my own faith in light of such a fine man.

Captain Graham sparked my desire to search the scriptures during our walk along my defensive positions on the lower hillside of Nong Son. We spoke in non-military terms, as personal as any faith-based conversation can be. I will never forget Captain James Graham.

My two fellow lieutenants were newcomers, although I went through Basic School with one. I must lean on the premise of "God's will be done" and accept what has happened. At times as such, this is an extremely bitter pill. Forgive my somber thoughts, if only we could have gone into that valley to give Fox Company some relief but we were not committed to the operation. Jim Graham's Foxtrot was in support of another battalion getting hammered by the Second NVA Division. We need to pray for the families of those who were lost. I miss you all.

Love and prayers,

Jim

June 23, 1967

Dear Mother and All,

How's my family today? I'd sure like to walk in the front door right now and find you all there. Or, better yet, I'd like to slip in beside you in the family pew at church. I always liked doing that.

Today is the third day of summer and I wonder if the heat is as unbearable there. It is certainly a critical factor in the field.

Operation Calhoun was announced to kick off on the 25th and last five days. It will be across mountains and jungle. No matter how horribly I hated the forced marches at Quantico, I'm thankful for what they've taught me now.

We will rest for the next two days. I'll go with the artillery liaison officer tomorrow to call in practice artillery missions. I've learned that in Vietnam you can never practice or train too much.

As of July 1, I will officially be a first lieutenant and my name will be turned in to the captain's Selection Board on July 6.

That's most of my news for now, hope all is well. Please take care and God bless,

Jim

July 3, 1967

Dear Mom and Folks,

Dr. Tom Viti and I have started a weightlifting program. Tom's a really funny guy. He's Italian and his uncle is a big wheel in the Mafia in New York which gives many of us a laugh. Captain Pat Blessing (the CO of Echo Company and a big Irish weightlifter), gave us his two hundred pound weight set before returning to the States. Tom gives me an untold amount of medical advice and has become quite a counsel. I now call him "coach." He tells me, "Whenever you think of home or sex, run out and use your weights!"

Well that's just what we've been doing and I'm pooped. Believe me, it's a poor substitute for both. And we've shared an untold amount of laughter from this program in the last week-and-a-half. What one does with time to make the time pass!

My love always,

Jim

July 9, 1967

Dear Mom & All,

Here we are further into the summer months and the heat is progressing. It's just plain uncomfortable. The past few nights have been fairly cool which has been a blessing.

With the escalated effort we've come under attack the last four nights. Casualties have been light and morale remains high. There appears to be an overwhelming amount of enemy troops in our tactical area but I believe that we can handle any threat they might impose at the present time.

Nong Son, to our south, was almost overrun on July 4th. The Marines captured a Chicom flamethrower that could shoot a flame farther than what we have. The enemy climbed an inverted cliff and snuck over the hilltop's lower LZ. Had they not lit everything up, they may have been successful.

We were sent the following day to extract damaged vehicles. The division brass was also there to access what had transpired. Our battalion S-3, Major Dick Esau, threatened to throw a bird colonel off the mountain after the "numb-nut" colonel made inappropriate remarks about the brave Marines who sustained the action. The major endeared himself to every one of us. Those Marines fought a good fight there against a significant enemy force. The colonel was an idiot! Dick Esau (a boyhood friend of Tom Viti; their dads work together at Madison Square Garden) is a tough New Yorker who speaks his mind. He's a field Marine leader that I'd follow to the gates of hell.

I miss you all.

God bless,

Jim

July 18, 1967

Dear Mom,

I had to pick up some construction material in Da Nang. I'm building a new shop system for the Motor Transport area—complete with cement slab flooring and sheltered area. I'm arc welding one-hundred-and-five canisters together for main supports and have pulled more "McHale's Navy" deals than you can shake a stick at. I've become the battalion scrounger. I now have more contacts in Da Nang than I ever knew in business. I'll send pictures to report how construction goes. I only hope that we don't catch mortars on all our direct fruits of labor.

Blessings,

Jim

August 3, 1967

Dear Folks,

Here it is, August!

I owe you an apology for not writing. I've lost one of my closest friends, Lieutenant Paul Bertolozzi. I think that the circumstances surrounding his death have had a large effect upon me. I guess I'm really soft inside. I've tried to become conditioned to the goriest sights of this war. I do pretty well, that is if anyone *can* do well in observing one's fellow man cut down in the prime of life in some desolate rice paddy thousands of miles away from his home. "Bert" volunteered as Paymaster (instead of yours truly) to say good-bye to his Marines on My Loc (2). He, along with a fifteen man mine-sweep, was ambushed by a VC-NVA advised group of approximately sixty to seventy men. It was a professional encounter executed with tactical proficiency. Fifteen Marines were killed. One miraculously lived. The whole thing was over in two minutes. The compassionate pangs in my heart are strong at the end of any battle when I observe fallen Marines, but losing a close friend is a traumatic experience when conditions such as these lay claim to them. I still believe that our rightful place is here, though our military might is greatly hampered by the rules of engagement.

I now introduce Ham, the son of my laundry woman. He has brought us considerable VC intelligence. He locates booby traps by "showing up" on our patrol routes. He is very bright and extremely proud of his cut down Marine uniform (utilities).

I've told Bill Nixon, the civil affairs officer, to hold the Operation Concern gear received from the church folks until I can get pictures of its distribution. Right now my platoon remains on a 10-minute alert status and I can't yet accompany him on his village units. If I switch places to provide his platoon security, I'll take some snap shots.

Mom, believe me, I'm all right, physically and mentally. Tom Viti and his chief corpsman, Lou LeGarie, a decorated Korean "Frozen Chosin" more-Marine-than-corpsman, keep me healthy. I'm glad that we run security for the Battalion Aid Station. The corpsmen are a great breed! How could one not love a man who runs without hesitation to the aid of fallen Marine in the midst of battle.

Home will never seem so good, so warm, nor faces so dear when I "return to the world" as my troops say.

God bless,

Jim

August 5, 1967

Dear Mom,

The cake and cupcakes were out of this world!!!! The red ants did not get to the goods this time and since the battalion has a new generator supplying electricity to the area, we're using a refrigerator (a new purchase) to preserve the big cake.

I was sent a copy of the Navy Times which included an educational supplement. I have written for career information and home study courses—of the correspondence variety—which I believe will help some of my young men. I see so many that merely need someone to take an interest and point them in a direction. I'm on a big "completion of high school" drive for my troops. I'll channel the more promising ones into college. This endeavor makes me feel like I'm helping my men. I have many high school dropouts, several graduates and relatively little education past high school. Most come from broken homes, with no purpose or intention in life and thus volunteered for the Marine Corps as it was their only challenge towards a sense of accomplishment. I feel that I'm getting to a great many of them. I hope that I can make a difference in their lives.

Much love,

Jim

August 15, 1967

Dear Mom,

Hope all is well at home and you're enjoying the summer. I've enjoyed the snap shots and cards from all.

This evening as I returned from my routine battalion staff meeting, my men had my old wooden chair outside of the hut with a "For Sale" sign on it. When I went into the room I was surprised with a regular aluminum and vinyl chaise lounge chair. It had a large sign on it—"Happy Birthday Lieutenant" from "The Men." It was certainly a nice gesture. I'll see that it gets continuous use!

Time is going by quickly. I've been so busy that the days blend into one another. The seven-day routine with chapel marking the only notch of a new week is a grind, but if there was a pause, I'd be more mindful of the days than I am right now. The only solution is to keep busy.

At present we're trying to beat the monsoon with all types of preparations for the rainy season. If it's not heat, it's something else. We seem more adequately prepared now.

God bless. My love,

Jim

August 25, 1967

Here it is, the 25th of August already! Why pretty soon I'll be climbing the big bird home! Here's hoping the lyrics to September Song are true, "the days grow short when you reach September."

I recall the days leading into autumn with a great deal of sentiment as back-to-school excitement permeated the air. I enjoyed Gettysburg College and wish I could take the drive there this Sunday. We often joke by stopping a buddy and asking, "Would you like to be one of my riders north this weekend?" At Camp Lejuene that was a frequent occurrence. You heard plans made on Thursday evenings—from driving to New York or going to the Falls for a picnic. It's a recall of things pleasant in the past and the hopes of the time to come.

Much love,

Jim

August 28, 1967

Dear Mom & All,

I took the devil's food cupcakes next door to the doctors' quarters and Dr. Joe Whalen (Flip's replacement), Tom Keating (the dentist) and Tom Viti (the surgeon) and I enjoyed them while playing monopoly. It's good to get back after being out several days. I particularly enjoy the doctors because their conversation is always better than some of the others. I don't like to talk shop all of the time—and a Marine is a Marine is a Marine, even at the dinner table.

Give my love to all.

Many blessings,

Jim

September 9, 1967

Dear Folks,

Here we are in the month of September already! I've been extremely busy with Operation Swift and much too preoccupied to find a pen long enough to write to anyone.

I feel badly but believe me it couldn't be helped. We were called to help Kilo or "K" Company in a horrendous battle with the NVA. They were on our left flank and receiving heavy fire the first few days. The colonel and our command group for whom I command the 46-men security platoon came back to An Hoa. "Swift" is still in progress but main contact was broken early evening, yesterday. To date it was one of the bloodiest sustained battles of the war. Three NVA regiments and the CP of the NVA Second Division were encountered en masse in fully entrenched ideal positions. The North Vietnamese fought hard and long and deserve professional credit as soldiers. I believe our tactics employed were in question. Support on several fronts was too slow due to a "political red-tape" hindrance. Why the richest nation in the world makes her so called "pride" Marine fight with so little and on limited terms is agonizing. Especially when I see that lack measured in the face of the "anything goes" professional Northern soldier. They don't belong here in the South. Times like this make me bitter and proud. Bitter at the politics played while lives are on the line and proud at the repeated displays of courage these young Marines give. Our kill ratio measures approximately 2 to 1 which is poor when you aim for 10 to 1. I get so exasperated that I think I should get into politics myself. I've seen too many "acts" for dignitaries, rehearsed answers to known questions of concern and a multitude of facades masquerading as the truth.

I truly believe that we should be here. But we tread water long and swim with so very little strokes. The military needs a free hand and less political interference and visitation. I sometimes wonder what happened to the "Honest John's" and question their existence. I think of Captain Jim Graham and Bert Bertolozzi. They were great men. I fight for the ideal in hopes of making a better tomorrow. I guess I shouldn't expound like this but I get so doggoned provoked I could scream. I revel in my command. I demand and receive that which I know is right and must be done without hesitation. That's why I like the field; the search and destroys get me away from the paper war entanglement and desk jockeys who try to convince me that things should be done the way they were in World War II and Korea. We need more Major Esau's, Captain Graham's and staff sergeants like Tony Marengo. We need more lieutenants like Bert and Bill Harvey and John Newton. Not more Bundy's or McNamara's! Our men need support to do their jobs without having to wear gloves. The political couching and muting of our warriors has got to stop!

Some fight the battle on two fronts—one of persuasion to our own and the one we carry to the NVA and VC guerillas. We fight harder in hope that we will endure and then lead again into tomorrow.

Tomorrow is the 10th and Sunday. We hold a memorial service during which men never stand more erect nor bow so low. No one has to be told to come to these and yet the attendance is astonishing.

I've read your many letters upon my return. I am blessed with a truly remarkable family. I could never configure the words to match my feelings. You all hold a very special place in my heart. Even here I feel our nearness is unsurpassed. I wish I had the time to write more but my commitment has nearly doubled and the opportunity to write isn't what it used to be.

I hope the coming months go quickly. I become more eager each day to return home; next October, then November, and December. I think I'll pack an item a day to prepare for departure. It will sure be nice to walk across Glenmore Avenue and see the home front.

My love,

Jim

September 28, 1967

Dear Mom & All,

Today I helped distribute Operation Concern clothing at a "County Fair." I hope to send pictures of the wonderful contributions and the good use we have made of your expanded efforts. My love,

Jim

October 4, 1967

Dear Mom & folks,

It's another rainy day in An Hoa with the ground now six to eight inches of mud. Amidst it all I've been alerted to make sure we have a fording capacity on all battalion vehicles and must re-submit a new embarkation plan. It looks as if the Fifth Marines are destined to go to the DMZ. The 3/5, I believe, is already en-route although it will take several weeks for them to re-position. The 1/5 has been alerted to pull out in trace of them and the Army will assume our old positions.

Exact positions of the relocations are unknown at the present time. The North Vietnamese artillery has caused quite a concern to Marine units along the DMZ. Consequently help is needed in re-bolstering our positions along the de-militarized front.

I don't believe that we will be moving before November or early December. This is my personal opinion. We are not up to snuff in equipment or organization since our last operation of heavy contact, so it should take a little time to prepare. Of course one never knows how badly you're needed or the condition of our fellow Marine units to the North.

Love,

Jim

October 10, 1967

Dear Mom & Family,

After a severe storm that just about had me grabbing my ears and sucking my thumb, everything is calm once again. I'm back from another four-day jaunt. Coming back to letters from home is the best part of returning from the field. Thanks for the Q-tips. I now have the cleanest ears in An Hoa. What a great feeling!!!! I can hear you all laughing now but it's the simple joys that are missed so!

The river is 45' above normal level and the valley floor is flooded. Several villages were wooshed—not washed, wooshed away! We had 11 inches of rain in three-and-a-half hours. I don't care if I never see another drop of rain.

My good friend Tom Viti, the battalion surgeon has been told he will be going home around November 15th. He lives in New York City. I'll miss Tom quite a bit. He's one of the most levelheaded down to earth people I have met in the service. When I received my "Dear John Letter," Tom Viti saved me from the wound that consumed me. I was preparing to take a provisional platoon to Nong Son when Tom came over to tell me to take care of myself. He saw my face after reading THAT letter and reminded me of my Marines and of their family's dependence that I get them home safely. Truly, his words, his concern re-focused me more than I can say. I'll always cherish him as a dear friend. He has a big heart, almost as big as his smile. My love to all,

Jim

November 22, 1967

Dear Mom & All,

I've just returned from a logistical support mission trying to procure enough gear for our movement north. It will be a large one. No one knows the exact area.

Please forgive my lack of writing. My days have been from six a.m. to ten p.m. minus pen and writing time. To complicate matters our air strip is out and news from home is sporadic. It will be at least ten days before that is improved. By then we may be in deep in the throes of movement. However, I don't estimate the move until mid-December.

I hope you've all had an enjoyable Thanksgiving. We received an air drop of Turkey loaf which made the day somewhat recognizable. It's not the same but past memories certainly live on. Even here, there's so much to which to thank the good Lord.

Lt. Pete Peterson, Lt. Martin Dunbar, Lt. Paul Bertolozzi and
Lt. Mike Long, An Hoa, RSVN, June 1967.

The holidays are rapidly approaching. I don't know how I'll react when I hear the first Christmas carol. Christmas day may be spent in the mountain jungles. But no matter where my thoughts, I will turn homestead to the many unforgettable events and beautiful decorations that have always accompanied our holiday season.

Blessings,

Jim

December 3, 1967

Dear All,

The kiddies in the snap shots are outfitted in Operation Concern clothes. I hope to get more pictures but my schedule never seems to coincide with Civil Affairs. I will soon write a thank you letter to the church members in appreciation for all that they have done.

These particular children were adopted by a group of us, including Tom Viti (the surgeon) and I. The children live with a Vietnamese nurse who runs a small orphanage-like place. They're really dear. Suiting them up makes me want to cart them all home. Dom and his brother Noah are my favorites. Ba and her mother moved into Da Nang so I don't see her anymore. Noah is as quiet as a church mouse and says, "Sorry 'bout that" every other sentence. The two little tykes belong to my mammasan who sweeps and does laundry for us occasionally in An Hoa.

Tom Viti left today. He will surely be missed. Dr. Tom affected this command. His MedCAPS—villagers are treated medically—have done so much good in "winning the hearts and minds" of the locals. Tom has had a great impact on the physical health of the Vietnamese not just our Marines. Tom may have done more with his medicine and caring heart than we have done with our might. I'll miss his smile and sense of humor. Just knowing he's not here with us, leaves a real "hole" in my heart.

Love,

Jim

December 5, 1967

Dear All,

Today has been a hectic one. I have been asked by the CO to investigate the death of a Vietnamese mother and infant. The doctor was called to the local village as I had provided his security. Childbirth, though one of the messier chores in life is still most fascinating.

The mother went into convulsions. It was thought that some of the embryonic fluid passed into her bloodstream. The doc tried external heart massage and an adrenaline injection into the heart but nothing worked. Both mother and child died. You wonder about the success of life in Vietnam. The absence of medicine, of sanitary procedures, the disregard for hygienic practice and yet, those who do survive are innately strong. Truly only the strong survive here.

I must run. Thank you again for the packages and the loving thoughts behind them.

God bless you all.

Love,

Jim

December 13, 1967

Dear Mom,

The weather has been chilly due to the frequent rains. At night there's a constant breeze along the valley floor. You can see the vapor from your breath, quite a different picture from those of sun-baked Vietnam, huh? I don't think the temperature dips below sixty degrees but the variation from the daytime heat and extreme dampness makes it more severe.

Our move north is expected in one week. We've been ready but the weather rains have hampered both road and air traffic in this northern part of South Vietnam. At any rate, we're ready to go at a moment's notice. The colonel said that in all probability we'll spend Christmas en route to our new area, Phu Bai and Huế City.

I'm beginning to send gear home as to not be burdened by the move. It's a good feeling because it makes the time seem so much closer. By January 12th I should know my arrival time in the States based on my flight date out of Da Nang. Of course there's a variable called Okinawa through which all Marines must pass en route to the States, but I shouldn't be there longer than thirty-six hours.

My orders to Marine Corps Schools, Quantico are now official. I've received a naval speed letter verifying my appointment that will also be published in the Navy Times. I don't know what my billet will be but most likely will include instructing the candidates or new lieutenants in OCS. By April-June, I should pin on captain's bars, providing my nomination to captain is accepted by the January board of promotion. Love,

Jim

December 20, 1967

Dear Folks,

I was in Da Nang for a conference and managed to sneak into the Bob Hope's Christmas Show. It was a gas! I say sneak because I hopped into the midst of a colonel's party and got a fifth row seat. It was a nice taste of home. My battalion commander gave me the mission of "procuring" Christmas decorations for An Hoa since our move has been delayed twelve days. He suggested that I change my name to "McHale" since it seems to apply. I could only answer with a grin, knowing what a master scrounger I've become. Sgt. Wes McCabe (Arizona) and

I would get "pinched" in the states for some of these "borrowing" or "procuring" practices from some of the other "wealthier" branches of military service.

We brought back red, white and yellow paint, a giant wreath from an Air Force Squadron commander's quarters, several small wreaths from the windows of The Gunslinger's Club (AF Officer's Club) and a long strand of Christmas lights from the roof of a USO Club. We may be an infantry battalion, but we have some spots that will remind us of Christmas, even in An Hoa.

Please know that you're thought of much and sorely missed. Truly, my heart will return home this Christmas and New Year. Distance will be meaningless.

God bless you all.

Love,

Jim

✈ *January 27, 1968*

Dear Mom,

Things have progressed and the move north has many interesting points. My replacement has reported for duty. Now there's little to do but wait for a flight date. I don't expect to leave before the second week in February. Flight dates are received according to quota. I must wait my turn.

The rainy season has passed bringing heat and dust wherever you turn. I'm trying to keep busy. An even newer move looks like it will help. There's an extreme build-up of North Vietnamese units prompting our sudden move further north towards Huế City. Hopefully, the first few days in February will have me in the rear admin area to process coming home. Believe me, I'm all for it. This is my 377th day in Vietnam and my 13th month, but who's counting? That's long enough to be away from home, isn't it?

Tell Jeannie [older sister] I appreciate her trying to maintain the Christmas tree for me (I understand it is still up), but it looks like the time will be too long even for the heartiest of trees [Jeannie kept a very brown Christmas tree standing until Jim's returned in March of '68]. I look forward to gathering around the piano with my family. I'm also eager to sit at the family table to eat, talk and laugh as we have always done. I miss laughing and the sound of music as these simple things were denied in Vietnam. I see life in a greater perspective now. Although we tried to make bright moments for each other, the contented laughter amidst the civil society that I've known, just isn't here. I long for it. There's much to recapture and enjoy as I've never enjoyed before. What a lesson in appreciation this tour has been in spite of the darkest of times. This life lesson has enabled me to look with a discerning eye to see what wisps of light shine through even the darkest moments. Mom, you've always imparted that lesson to us. My father, God rest him, would have been so proud of you. I know what you have taught me has enabled me to pass through the most trying times in my life this past year. "Thanks" doesn't touch my appreciation of you for all that you have taught and sacrificed in raising Miriam, Al, Jean and I. I only hope to pass it on to a son or daughter of my own as you have done. Passing through the crucible of life is a great test. We need each other. With the love of God, family and friends, we are able to emerge from the Refiner's Fire of life's most potentially consuming moments nobler than when we entered. The fire isn't enjoyable. I have left large parts of me on this battlefield of life. We all have. Looking back, however, I've gained a sense of victory and an increase in the value and worthy encouragement to go on, again, into tomorrow.

Hope you're faring well in the winter weather. I won't know how to act when I see snow. Save a big hug for me. God bless.

My love,
Jim

On June 20, 2010, James Meyers shared an email from his son, Captain Dan Meyers, USMC, in recognition of Father's Day. "For some reason," James said via cyberspace, "I felt as if I could share Dan's note with you as you have read and shared my personal, family letters written from Vietnam. I would have shared Dan's sentiments with your dad, were he alive, wanting him to know the strong character and loving heart of my son. As his daughter, I share them with you. XXOO, Jim."

Dad,

Growing up it was never hard for me to answer the question, "Who is your hero? Who do you look up to the most? Who has been the most influential person in your life?" For me, it was always my dad. I was always so proud of having my father rooting for me on the sidelines, pushing me to always do better and always convincing me there was nothing I couldn't do. Your example of spiritual discipline, Christ's love and your true love with mom is still a resounding presence in my life. I have always been so proud of your accomplishments and service to our country. There are many times I think of what it would be like serving together and I often ask myself, "What would dad do in this situation?" In many ways, you were with me overseas. You were a resounding voice that helped consciously guide me through trying times and times of moral and ethical decision making. There were many nights I would sit around a fire with my Marines and we would reflect on home and family. As you've heard from my Marines, many of my stories were about you and your endeavors in Vietnam; insights shared of a rather comical family adventure. I would look at an empty MRE box (our seat of choice) and wonder what it would be like if you were there.

I often think about your life, your struggles and the tumultuous times that you were raised in. I can't imagine where I would be if I lost you at a young age. Grandma was a truly amazing person to be both mom and dad as you were growing up. Growing up, it was strange never having any grandfathers. I can only imagine being young and not having a father. You have meant so much to me. I want my sons to know you. I want you to influence their life. I don't want them to just hear stories of you, I want them to actually know you. I need you to stay healthy and strong so you can tell them stories about your life well into your 80s. You and mom are such incredible people. Your lives have brought light into so many lives. God willing, you will continue to do so well into the lives of my children. I love you dad, there is not enough paper or ink to write you how much you mean to me. Please take care of yourself. I need you to be there when we bring James Daniel Meyers into the world. Whenever that may be, I need you there.

Your Adoring Son,
Dan
Captain Daniel James Meyers, USMC
Father's Day 2010

❧ Dear Daddy ❧

John Newton was one of the many 2/5 Marines who responded to my request for "anyone who knew Dr. Tom Viti" posted on the Second Battalion Fifth Marines website. John's response also extended an invitation to Chatham, Massachusetts to share his admiration for you.

John Newton's interview took place in John and Janet Newton's ice cream shop, Short 'n' Sweet—a quaint, historical gem you would have loved. Built in 1903, this once little, red school house now offers sixty-two creamy ice cream flavors including Blue Crunchasourus, Moose Tracks, Main Black Bear, and, of course, your favorite, Rocky Road. John and I chatted in between scooping, although I was eventually fired—something about not scooping fast enough.

John is a humble gent and a talented writer. Most Newton Vietnam quips and quotes were sprinkled with a dry humor that lightened up the foreign land. I had to beg for an official Vietnam photo for the longest time because John insisted this picture of Superman was as official as it got.

Daddy, John's blithe—yet logical and introspective—view added levity to this Catch-22 on the other side of the world. Written memories range from the witty . . .

I often spoke to my rehab students about my Vietnam experience. Lectures included a question-and-answer period. My favorite question came from a young Chatham lady who asked, "Is it true that the Viet Cong stuck candy bars up the butts of American prisoners?"

"You need to repeat that question because it sounded like you said something about candy bars and butts."

"I asked if it was true that the Viet Cong stuck candy bars up the butts of American prisoners."

"Hmm, I'm pretty certain that the VC wouldn't have wasted a candy bar like that."

. . . to the melancholy . . .

"Death was instant old age in the shape of broken metal, oozing years through a hole in your head or your guts. It didn't take long to ooze at nineteen years of age, and it's easier for the one engaged in it, straining, breathing, slowly and languidly until done. That was death."

Short 'n' Sweet
Conversations and Ice Cream

Captain John W. Newton, USMC, (Ret.) 1966-1969, standing in front of Short 'n' Sweet Ice Cream Shop, Chatham, MA, 2009.

Lt. John Newton, USMC, Quantico, VA, 1966.

John and I nestled into the back office of Short 'n' Sweet, a comfortable distance away from the ceaseless barrage of customers seeking a cool treat from Cape Cod's blazing summer heat. I welcomed John's eagerness to chat.

Jet lag had begun to take its toll on my patience and psyche. Fatigue and determination collided. Today, *Dr. Tom's War* felt like a massive undertaking; a responsibility of immeasurable proportions. "Going the distance" in honor of Dr. Tom lacked even the slightest bit of solace to the overwhelming grief penetrating every inch of my being. I felt as isolated as the barren baseball diamond built between Iowa's cornstalks. My

Field of Dreams was beginning to wear me down. I missed Pops something fierce. I yearned to hear Dr. Tom's voice console the tragic and add levity to a summer of Vietnam War speak.

And yet I knew, as if guided by divine intervention, that I was exactly where I was supposed to be. John's cyberspace conversations hinted at a casual amiability that promised to lace slapstick descriptions into Vietnam's more absurd moments. And at the moment, I needed absurd to alleviate my funk.

"So talk to me about Dr. Tom," I said.

"No doubt your father was highly-regarded, respected, well-liked, and a good sport with a quick wit," John said. "Throw in gutsy and fearless. Dr. Tom thought nothing of scampering around, alone, under a barrage of mortar fire administering to the wounded, seemingly unconcerned for his welfare. That's courageous, especially during enemy

Lt. John Newton, USMC, and "Captain" the evening prior to his An Hoa departure, Quantico, VA, 1966.

engagement. Doctors *don't* get body guards. In An Hoa's Battalion Aid Station, Dr. Viti was the consummate professional as were all of the doctors— Gonder, Tom's counterpart, Donnelly our dentist, and Chief Hospital Corpsman Lou LeGarie. The doctors, corpsmen, and battalion aid station crew cared for the Marines and provided aid and comfort to the Vietnamese. Their efforts in changing hearts and minds were extraordinary, especially during County Fairs."

"Can you elaborate on the purpose of County Fairs?" I asked.

"County Fairs offered medical aid, gathered intelligence, and gave civil affairs assistance in fixing the obvious and educating the Vietnamese. Marines would cordon off each village prior to first light to block enemy entrance or exit."

I understood the concept of entering but the exit confused me. "Exit?"

"Yes, the occasional Viet Cong asleep with mammasan. Now even *he* was stuck."

I smiled. "Got it."

"Dr. Viti and his corpsmen treated hundreds of Vietnamese with ailments ranging from infections to cancer. Corpsmen hung health and hygiene posters that illustrated simple, hygienic rules and daily cleansing practices to ward off infections. Donald Duck cartoons were shown—in Vietnamese—on a sheet screen that was viewed from both sides. Toothpaste and toothbrushes were also distributed although those, along with most paraphernalia, weaseled their way to the black market. Almost everything American turned into dollars somewhere. Even U.S. greenbacks were sold on the black market."

"How was American money sold on the black market?" I asked.

"I'm not sure," John said. "And as far as County Fairs were concerned, there was a downside. Sadly, villagers were often terrorized by the Viet Cong after County Fairs. The VC was family, so it was a difficult, no-win situation for everyone."

"Couldn't anything be done to stop the brutality?"

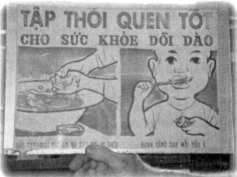

Medical Corps Health & Hygiene posters displayed during MedCAPS and County Fairs, RSVN, 1967.

Corpsman handing out candy during a County Fair, RSVN, 1967.

Children lined up for medical treatment dispersed at a County Fair, RSVN, 1967.

Dr. Viti, dispensing meds during a County Fair, RSVN, 1967.

"Nothing that worked for an extended period of time," John said.

I inhaled deeply. *Keep it light for now. Focus on dad.*

"Do you have any favorite Dr. Viti stories?" I asked.

"God, Dr. Viti just loved to *tell* stories."

John hunched forward and lowered his voice. "I can still visualize Tom leaning forward, giving the listener a confidential air, smiling, narrating a tale that's just between men."

"Yes, Dad had an uncanny ability to rein you in on many a tall tale," I said.

"Dr. Viti was also a great practical joker who, like most of my comrades, enjoyed teasing. Here's a great story."

John folded his posture and voice as he transformed himself into a Marine from the pages of An Hoa, Republic of South Vietnam during 1967. The now familiar transformation back to the war had begun.

"An Hoa's forward air controllers, Mark and Guy, publicly proclaimed themselves above the silliness of being involved with an infantry unit. Their sissy attitude pissed us off and warranted our revenge. Since Mark woefully suffered from premature baldness we decided to mix a cure-for-baldness concoction of every conceivable, pour-able junk—including gun oil and Tabasco sauce—that fit into a medicine bottle. The liquid looked as foul as it smelled. I carried the bottle into Mark's hootch, touting America's latest and greatest baldness cure. 'Hey, Mark, check this out. This medicinal solution grows hair. Pour it on your scalp, lower your head below your heart to increase circulation, wrap your head with a towel to keep it warm, and *voilà*, hair.'"

John scrutinized an imaginary bottle as he held it up to the light. "Mark scrunched his nose as he carefully examined the bottle."

> "Oh man, this looks and smells nasty," Mark said. "I'm not going to use that."
>
> "Man, this is good shit. Dr. Viti gave it to us. It's medicine, proven to grow hair and stop receding hair lines."
>
> "C'mon," Mark whined. "You have to be crazy to put that on your head, look at it."
>
> "You'll be sorry. This stuff is one step short of a miracle."
>
> "What's it called?"
>
> "Who cares? It's a secret. Dr. Viti doesn't even know. Rub a little in your scalp, what's the worst that could happen?"
>
> "Are you sure?"
>
> "Yeah, try it. Take the bottle."

"Within days, this character wore a towel wrapped around his head," John said. "Convinced that this magic potion grew hair, he was about to ask Dr. Viti for more. We forewarned the good doctor eager for him to play along. Dr. Viti however, was less than enthusiastic."

"Jesus, guys, are you nuts? You could've burned his scalp."

"Really, Doc?"

"Yes really, this is dangerous not medicinal."

"Oh?"

"Don't worry, fellas. I'll handle it, but no more magic hair potions."

A disappointed Mark left the BAS after Dr. Viti shared the news the tonic had been discontinued."

"That is a great story," I said. "Tell me more."

"Okay, here's a story that I'll never forget," John said. "Dr. Viti and I once shared a tent during a two-company operation that traversed an area known as Christmas Village. After settling in, the company operations officer decided that he, I, and the radio operator should link with another company about four hundred meters away. This officer, who enlisted *after* the Korean War, made rank without combat experience and yearned for action. Reluctantly, off we went, trudging through incredible thicket, flooded rice paddies, and a small village hearing nada—human, animal, bird, or otherwise—not one single sound. As yet another enormous rice paddy lay ahead I knew we had to turnaround.

I was adamant. "Sir, meaning no disrespect, sir, but that kid and I are going back."

"What?"

"This is dangerous. You don't know where you are and you don't know where you're going. I didn't stay alive the past ten months doing this nonsense. We're out of here."

"Well . . ."

"Sir, do what you want, but we're going back."

"Lieutenant Newton, are you scared?"

"Absolutely, sir, absolutely."

"Okay, okay, we'll go back."

"We shuffled back showered by sheets of monsoon rains," John said. "A rice paddy once knee deep with water was now chest deep. It was unbelievable. Halfway across the paddy the operations officer slid out of sight, much to our delight, but quickly bobbed up, water-logged, and muttering obscenities. We arrived at camp wet but safe. But the ending is the best part of my story. Back in our poncho-laced hootch, Dr. Tom had brewed his famous one part C-ration coffee and six-part medicinal Brandy in his steel helmet. It was absolutely superb; the perfect finale to a rotten night."

"Brandy served to soothe many a long Dr. Viti day," I said, wishing I could take a tiny sip strong enough to appease my angst. "Do you have a *favorite* Dr. Viti story?"

John thought but for a second. "My favorite Dr. Viti story occurred during Operation Newcastle."

"Did you know Dr. Tom was awarded the Vietnamese Cross of Gallantry for his work during Operation Newcastle?" I asked.

"As it should be," John said. "Dr. Viti exemplified courage, bravery, fortitude, and comedic grace during Operation Newcastle."

"I sense that your favorite story will explain the comedic grace component," I said.

John nodded. "Lieutenant White had landed two shots in the groin on day two of Operation Newcastle. I remember staring at his utilities thinking, 'Geez, what do you say to a guy who's just been shot in the nuts?'"

I cleared my throat. "That is a good question."

"That remains to this day, unanswered," John said. "As we scrambled around under exploding mortars, an amtrac appeared and lowered its ramp to, lo and behold, good ol' Dr. Viti. Two kids shouldered Lieutenant White into the amtrac until he shook both off and screamed for each to find cover. White steamed his way solo to Dr. Viti and collapsed on a sandbag. A corpsman offered the wounded lieutenant a lit cigarette and medicinal brandy. Doctor Tom was a madman. 'Those sons of bitches, those sons of bitches.'"

John paused. "You know, Dr. Viti began and ended every sentence with 'sons of bitches' when the shit hit the fan."

"Let's just say it was his favorite expression under duress," I said.

"A sea of bullets ricocheted wildly in and around the amtrac as Dr. Viti began to slice White's scrotum. I froze, mesmerized by this Pieta of Lieutenant White leaning back, calmly smoking a cigarette, sipping his two ounce dram under a nativity of rounds erratically bouncing in and around the vehicle. Dr. Tom's Brooklyn accent transcended the gunfire. 'Those sons of bitches. Close the fucking door.' Oddly enough, a young Marine thought it best to correct the good doctor. 'It's a ramp, Doc, not a door.' Neck down, your father was cool-hand Luke, steady Eddy as he performed this very delicate surgery. But above the Adam's apple he was a raging maniac. 'Son of a bitch. Okay, shut the fucking ramp. Those sons of bitches.' The ramp closed, sealing them in. The visual of Dr. Viti operating under intense enemy fire will be a lasting tableau."

"That is a wild one," I said.

"Operation Newcastle was wild," John agreed. "Post battle on day three, Dr. Tom spotted a dead VC in the enemy-dead quarantined perimeter wearing a U.S. battle dressing. And with his characteristic, 'those sons of bitches,' he explained he had dressed the cadre's wounds a day earlier, assuming him to be a civilian farmer.

"Son of a bitch! Yesterday that little bastard cried about Marines trying to kill him. I cleaned and bandaged the little shit so he could pin me down in the rice paddy like an afternoon rat. The little bastard took pot shots at me."

"Maybe your fee's too expensive, Doc," I said.

"Ahhh . . . Those sons of bitches."

I swallowed hard as Dr. Tom's voice echoed in my brain, slicing fissures through my heart. "Can you highlight the more colorful stories from Operation Newcastle?"

"Operation Newcastle was a one-of-a-kind military experience," John said. "We, being Echo Company, left An Hoa at dusk on foot during a horrific thunderstorm destined for a debarkation site previously secured by an additional unit. Conversation and movement remained ghost-like and hush hush. I stumbled into Major Howard (not real name) our commanding officer, furious at the sight of his lit cigar."

John's voice became barely audible.

"What the hell are you doing? Put that goddamn cigar out."

"Lieutenant Newton, do you know who you are speaking to?"

"Oh, okay, Major, put that damn cigar out, sir."

"He did, much to his credit," John said.

"And yours," I quickly added.

John shrugged. "Entrenched in darkness and secrecy, we radioed An Hoa to crank up the six-by trucks waiting with our LCRs ready to transport us across the river."

"Excuse me," I interrupted. "But what are LCR's?"

"Inflatable landing-craft rubbers," John said. "We had secretly practiced the dip-cut-and-stroke paddle of these rubber babies hidden under tents in An Hoa."

"Are you talking about inflatable rubber boats used by divers? Isn't that a bit out of the ordinary?"

"Yes," John said. "The LCR's were an unusual and top-secret tactic intended to catch the enemy off-guard. And the element of surprise was never in doubt until the six-bys roared in gunning and jamming gears on a junky road with a kid shouting, 'Hey, lieutenant is this where you want the rubber boats?'"

John smacked his forehead with his palm. "I slapped my forehead in disbelief. Two weeks of clandestine undone in an instant. The enemy and the dead knew that we had arrived. The band, the band, someone strike up the band. 'Yeah,' I grumbled. 'I want the rubber boats here.' We set up accordingly and forged on . . ."

John stood, stomped one foot in front of the other, and rolled his eyes. "I stepped into a rubber boat filled with six inches of water thinking, 'Oh, great, I'll be soaking wet this entire event. There's nothing I hate more than being wet. Anything that starts out wet isn't going to get any better.' We snuck across the river very George Washington-like, but I didn't paddle, I was George."

I made no attempt to hide my smile.

"On shore we trekked in queues through at least five miles of twisting tributaries and creeks that sliced deep gullies into mud-trenched banks."

> At yet another hellish washboard site, the guys lamented, "Oh shit, Lieutenant."
> "What are you balking at, you're wet already," I barked.
> "This one looks bad, real bad."

"After inspection I said with complete Newton authority, 'Let's go. We've been walking through this crap all night, what's the big deal about this one?' So with a great air of leadership and step-off-and-follow-me-men-bravado, I plunged into waist-high, oozing, horrible mud. I was now wedged in sludge. 'Holy smokes.' I was nervous but for a moment. 'Oh man, you're not going to leave me here, fellows, are you? Okay. Shit. Shit. We have no choice, let's go.' So we did. Struggling to catch the guy ahead, we dropped like flies in this incredible muck. As the column became disjointed I whispered, 'Pass the word up, hold the column, pass the word up, hold the column.' It ended two guys up. Those boys had vanished. So I mumbled behind, 'Pass the word back, close it up. Pass the word back, close it up.' And it stopped two men back. Isn't this just swell? I was now leading segments of a chopped-up snake. My boys, now disintegrated into twos and threes, were lost in a dark place called bad. Easier said than done, I lined my staggered men back together. I remember thinking, 'Marines owned the night. But do you suppose it's because the enemy simply didn't want it? Maybe they found it less than good. Maybe by a peculiar preference, they wished to stay at home, asleep with mammasan.'"

"You're funny," I said.

"Exhausted, we continued until first light, shredding jungle by the hack-and-slash of our machetes until our hands burned with blisters. As we continued north through more slush, a radio transmission warned of a VC unit—probably kicked out of mammasan's bed—passing parallel in the opposite direction."

John whistled as he guided both hands to side swipe each other without crashing.

"Great. We were just two ships simply passing in the night. We established a blocking position as Fox Company blitzkrieged across the river and swept to us by first light. Other than a lone sniper, the sweep occurred without incident. A command post frag order then moved us further from the river, forcing us to trudge *back* through the same muck from the night before."

John stood again, stomped one foot in front of the other, and dramatically rolled his eyes. "It was god awful, but we made it. Lieutenant Fuller forged the left flank, and I stayed on the right. Once set in, we didn't budge for hours. The next day we moved five hundred meters around three o'clock when all hell broke loose. A tremendous fire fight raged until sunset. Lieutenant Bill Eads, Echo's artillery officer, saved the day by discharging sixteen, seventeen hundred rounds of artillery within twenty-five meters of us. I lost most of my hearing that day. Several Marines were killed, including Lieutenant John Fuller who was posthumously awarded the Navy Cross. Lieutenant Fuller had given his helmet to a kid who dropped his during the previous night's river crossing. Unfortunately being helmetless during battle sadly led to his demise. After Fuller's death, his platoon sergeant, a Korean Vet, became so distraught, so hysterical, and inconsolable he was evacuated to Da Nang. 'Oh my God, he's dead, he's dead. Jesus, John's dead. I can't believe it, he's just a kid. Oh my God, no.' The sight of John Fuller, this baby-faced kid, *dead*, caused the veteran's experience cup to runneth over. Although next to command, he was choppered to An Hoa. He later returned, losing no respect.

"Our corpsman, however, gave us a lighter moment. Peppered with shrapnel, including one that lodged in his throat, this kid wore over a hundred battle dressings. This character looked like a mummy."

John held his throat and whispered hoarsely.

> "Hey, Lieutenant Newton, take my picture."
>
> "Why, you look like a mummy."
>
> "I want to send it to my mom so she'll know that I'm okay."
>
> "And you think she's going to get that message with this picture?"
>
> "Yes, she'll know that I'm alive."
>
> "Doc, you're wrapped with over a hundred battle dressings with a piece of shrapnel sticking out of your throat. Are you sure about this?"
>
> "I'm sure, please, Lieutenant, take my picture."

So I took his picture."

"And that was day one?" I asked.

"Yes. And day two was a chapter from the keystone cops. As Jesse Pender, my radio operator, and I walked through a potato field, we were barreled over by a resounding *boom*."

John shielded his head with both arms and curled his torso onto his lap.

"*Boom*. We bolted into a narrow, dusty, ditch within the patches of dirt too dry for rice and too small for graves. Pender maneuvered behind, using me as his shield. Pummeled by bullets, I burrowed as low as I could. Fortunately the gook shooting couldn't aim. Someone yelled, 'Hey, I think the lieutenant's dead. He's not moving.' I howled. 'No, God damn it, I'm not dead, but I will be if you don't get some fire over here sooner than now.' They blasted an M79 into the area, and I bid a hasty retreat, thanking Pender very much. 'Pender, the next time you use my body for cover, I'll shoot your ass myself.' We pressed forward to Lieutenant White's platoon, now heavily engaged in a horseshoe-shaped ambush, and dug into the trench line that connected to the battle zone. A resounding *boom* exploded within seconds of my ordering a squad of my Marines to follow suit on higher ground. *Boom.* A small black-orange cloud now separated Jesse, me, and my squad. *Boom.*"

> "Pender, give me the radio. Captain, what the hell are you shooting at?"
> "We're not shooting, Lieutenant."
> "You're not?"
> "No."
> "God damn it!"
> *Boom.*

John paused.

> *Boom.*
> "Pender, get down."

"Mortars pounded us. I had two choices, take cover or die. Pender and I somersaulted again into an even tighter channel. I landed flat on my back thinking, 'Man I'm too pretty to take one of these in the face.'"

> I radioed Blessing. "Captain, we're catching shit."
> "Well, good luck to you and the Red Sox, Lieutenant Newton, but I've got my own problems. The CP's pinned, and everyone's heavily engaged."
> *Boom.*

"At that, Pender wasted no time lassoing down the line with me in tow. Radio in hand, I rolled over, entangled in belts and straps and got stuck. The radio cord stretched to its capacity as Pender continued plowing through this incredibly narrow gutter. I scrambled, attempting to talk war to Blessing while shouting, 'God damn it, Pender, stop, stop, stop.' But no matter how fast I hustled, Pender moved faster, until we were nothing more than a phone-line accordion act corralling down this skinny ditch. Blessing was frenzied. 'Lieutenant, Lieutenant. What the fuck is going on?' I couldn't help but laugh despite the danger. And suddenly, the fire ceased."

"Just like that?" I asked.

"Good thing, wouldn't you say?" John said.

I nodded. "Very good."

"And the battle ensued. Here's an interesting note about Operation Newcastle. Post our five-day battle, there were no signs of battle or carnage; no broken twigs, blood trails, brass or shell casings. The Viet Cong policed every vestige, a not-so-unusual-psych-op tactic that left an unsettling holy mackerel effect on our troops. Gooks were sometimes like ghosts that disappeared without a trace, without a print; without leaving even a piece of shit. Legend had Vietnamese women canvassing the battle field with meat hooks that snagged and dragged bodies from beneath the clavicle. I say legend because I never saw a mammasan carrying a meat hook."

"Mammasans and their collar meat hooks were well documented in my Vietnam research," I said. "In print, however, not pictures."

"Here's another interesting story about a nineteen-year-old Vietnamese detainee from Operation Newcastle," John said. "Early on, squad leader Hamilton (not real name) found a Vietnamese teenager who would have been a VC soldier save for his flaw as a spastic, cerebral palsy victim. This kid smacked his hands like flippers and wobbled from side to side when he walked. And even though he was clean and well-fed, he was without an ID card—cardinal sins that mandated detention. So Hamilton dragged the gimp by his collar like a limp rag doll, occasionally prodding him along with his rifle, under enemy engagement for almost five hours. By day's end, although unhurt, the guy was battered and bruised."

Hamilton proudly delivered him to the S2 sergeant. "He's all yours."

"What the hell is this?"

"A Vietnamese detainee."

"A what? This is nothing but a dumb spastic Vietnamese kid. What do I need him for? Let him go."

"So Hamilton let his captive loose. The next morning we stumbled upon him badly beaten by the VC because of his Marine adventure; no doubt unable to explain that life with us hadn't been a bowl of cherries either. The gimp seemed ordained to be interrogated by Marines during the day and thrashed by the Viet Cong at night; his unfortunate crime being a spastic, clean, and well-fed kid."

"All because of an ID card?" I asked.

"Absolutely. Males between the ages of twelve and thirty—military age—in a village without an ID were deemed criminals. Those of military age and not in the military were bad guys and therefore detained or imprisoned."

"Detainees were sent to prison?"

"Well, portable Vietnam jails," John said. "Detainees and POWs were housed in twelve-by-eight, three-foot high prison cages laced with barbed-wire and bamboo erected over an earthen mud floor. The cages were never out of the sun or rain and had no limits to the number of people imprisoned. The bamboo boxes served as sleeping quarters, cafeteria, and latrine. Detainees were later sorted and dispersed for re-education."

"Political re-education?"

"Yes."

"Did you ever discuss the politics of American presence in Vietnam?" I asked.

John shook his head. "Negative. Politically, I kept Marines alive while completing the mission. Although I dare say, Marine Corps Parlance is the opposite, nothing is more important than the mission. But I was a reserve officer. 'Take away my bar but don't take away my R.' I focused on my duties with an attitude that said, 'Hey, let's get out of here alive with as many people as we can. Let's do the job, without doing anything stupid so we can find ourselves one day *dead* in a book.'"

Front side of a safe conduct pass, RSVN—1967.

Back side of a safe conduct pass, RSVN—1967.

"That sounds safe and sound," I said.

"It was sound advice for saving lives. Lucia, in the latter part of the 1960s, Washington, DC's politicians and some career military men represented a confused system. As a consequence in Vietnam, military lives were not only lost to battlefield bullets, but to bad decisions or lack thereof, from those drowning in a mire of sinking careers. From my perspective, careers were short and bullets were real."

"Was your company commander, Lieutenant Colonel Jackson a part of this confused system?" I asked.

"Not really. Lieutenant Colonel Jackson was a mustang with a tendency to micromanage. This story is a perfect example. We held daily, evening staff meetings for the S Shops, otherwise known as intelligence and operations. The meeting room was a narrow hootch with low tiers and a screen roof. The low eaves obstructed the view in but one could easily see out. The room had a PA system with a microphone and huge speakers. One night a poor, slap-happy PFC strolled by whistling and swinging his arms in only a t-shirt. Now Lieutenant Colonel Jackson had recently ordered post five o'clock, Marines must wear uniform blouses, not t-shirts. So Lieutenant Colonel Jackson halted mid-sentence and blared through the PA, 'You there.' The kid froze. 'Yes, you.'"

John twisted his head in every direction, mimicking the great voice hunt. "Now the kid's searching for the mysterious voice. 'Yes, you,' continues Jackson. 'Do you know you should be wearing a blouse after five o'clock, not a t-shirt?' The kid was beyond confused. 'Yes, sir.' 'Get one on.' The kid bolted like a flash of lightning never knowing Jackson was the culprit."

"I've been told by several 2/5 Marines that Lieutenant Colonel Jackson sparked mixed emotions," I said.

"That's true. Lieutenant Colonel Jackson and Captain Blessing, my company commander, shared an uncomfortable dynamic. They didn't see eye-to-eye on anything. Lieutenant Colonel Jackson lectured Blessing, and Blessing raged about Jackson."

John lifted both hands and wrote with an imaginary pencil in the palm of his left hand. "It looks like I'm taking notes during these interrogations," John said with an Irish brogue, "but I'm really scribbling how many days I've got left with this miserable asshole."

"Colonel Esau spoke highly of Jackson," I said.

"Esau and Jackson worked well together. But here's a typical Jackson-Blessing encounter. We were milling around a village when a family of pigs strolled by Captain Blessing. The wormy sow, trailed by her seven suckling babies, dragged her pink-white, over-used teats in the dirt. Captain Blessing bucked to attention, saluted rigidly, and said, 'Make way for the command group. Good morning, Colonel.' Blessing rocked forward on the balls of his feet, bended slightly at the waist, and continued his salute until they passed.

Unbeknownst to Blessing, a frowning Lieutenant Colonel Jackson stood directly behind him. Captain Blessing turned around and puffed his cheeks into a second less hearty, 'Good morning, Colonel.' Blessing quickly vanished."

"That's Hollywood timing," I said.

"Another time, two of my young lads got drunk in the village outside the wire and bullied the villagers by twirling their knives. Of course, they were hastily policed back to An Hoa. Lieutenant Colonel Jackson went nuts trying to determine who they were, but Blessing refused to rat them out. The kids received an article fifteen, a non-judicial punishment."

"Translated?"

"You're chewed out and fined. The incident remained hushed. Scaring the Vietnamese was their only crime."

"How did the troops react to Captain Blessing?"

"The troops loved Blessing with his out drink, out cuss, and out fight any man on the planet persona," John said. "Everything was the worst it could possibly be, and everyone was a girl. One night Captain Blessing caused such a ruckus in An Hoa's EM club he was thrown out, cursing and laughing, surrounded by the thunderous clamor of his boys. Blessing never conducted himself quietly, so it was quite a scene. And Blessing often made Dr. Donnelly miserable. He'd get drunk in Donnelly's hootch, fill his outside bunker with foul liquids, shout 'incoming,' and watch Donnelly leap into the quagmire. Blessing did this night after night after night, and Donnelly fell for it night after night after night. But Captain Blessing was special, and I'm grateful chance cast me his way. Blessing understood that Vietnam wasn't about ranks and rising stars but about the young Marines entrusted to his care. The troops knew this and loved him for it."

John paused. "Likewise, Colonel Esau was an excellent leader who held his company grade officers—including yours truly—in high regard. Few compared to Esau's level of Marine. I consider myself fortunate to have worked for Esau in An Hoa's command post."

"That doesn't surprise," I said. "Colonel Esau is as they say, a Marine's Marine."

"You betcha," John said. "Colonel Esau was good friends with Dr. Tom."

"Colonel Esau and my dad remained the best of friends," I said. "Colonel Esau delivered the eulogy at Dad's funeral. Needless to say, there wasn't a dry eye in the house."

I exhaled, shifted in my chair, and stared at the memory of the worst day of my life—Dad's funeral. John remained quiet. I silently berated myself. *Get back on track.* "Describe the combat base in An Hoa."

"In addition to the Marines, An Hoa housed four U.S. military organizations—the Air Force, the Seabees, the Navy, and the Army. The Air Force operated the Air Tower; the Seabees managed all construction projects; the Navy directed medical and spiritual services; and the Army supervised Vietnamese Pacification

Lt. John Newton outside of his bunker in An Hoa, RSVN, 1967.

Lt. Col. Mallet Jackson, USMC, An Hoa, RSVN, 1967.

Lt. Col. Mallet Jackson and Major Richard H. Esau Jr., RSVN, 1967.

and Civil Affairs. And since An Hoa hosted the extra handful, the higher brass, in their omnipotent wisdom, built a Staff and Officers Club that sold hard liquor."

"Why would selling hard liquor be unusual in an officer's club?"

"Infantry battalions were usually awarded two beers, per man, per day as staff, and officers bought warm San Miguel Beer from the Enlisted Men's Club back door. But 2/5 was awarded hard liquor from the military chiefs because of caring for the additional military facets. Therefore, An Hoa's 2/5 was the only infantry battalion in South Vietnam that hosted a thriving bar. One enterprising gunnery sergeant who shall remain nameless claimed ownership of running the Club. I'm sure his real job went undone."

I welcomed John's seamless transition in keeping the conversation on the lighter side. "Okay, let's hear some funny club stories."

"The Staff and Officers Club served as the nightly rendezvous. Chivas Regal cost twenty-five cents, beer ten cents, and mixed drinks cost fifteen cents. So a couple of bucks went a long way. Alcoholism posed a serious threat because we drank ferociously. And drinking was part of the deal. But we didn't booze for the drink-till-I-stumble-down drunk. We drank for the you-can't-hurt-me-now drunk."

"There's nothing wrong with a shot of courage," I said.

John smiled. "Here's a good club story. Marines dispelled low trajectory artillery missions over the club. Periodically, a bore riding pin would loosen from the artillery round and fly solo, causing it to sound like a low-flying, flying saucer. One night while I walked to my table fisted with drinks, three of those babies flew over. Someone hollered, 'Incoming.' The place emptied in a flash. That was the closest I came to death because I was literally trampled and hoisted from that hootch. Several weeks later, a young Lieutenant Eads and I joined the usual gang of thieves enjoying the bar. The flying saucers began again. Only this time, I told Eads not to move. The bar emptied. Eads and I lingered among a sea of drinks, leisurely downing as many as we could. Two hours later, we gathered more cocktails and jingled across the base, soon confronted by a Marine in full flak gear."

> The kid looked as confused as I. "Lieutenant?"
> "Son, why are you in full gear?"
> "Sir, we're in condition red."

"Now condition red is high alert," Johns said. "I was shocked."

> "Really? We're being mortared?"
> "Yes, sir. There's been an attempt to hit the ammo dump, sir."

"Remember, at this point we've been in condition red for over two hours. 'Well, carry on Marine.' So Eads and I briskly sprinted into an airstrip bunker, guzzled even more juice, and watched a fantastic fire show."

"True story?" I asked.

John nodded. "War is hell. Here's another good bar story from Da Nang. I forget why we were in Da Nang, but several of us rambled into the Stone Elephant, a MAC V Navy Bar. We were quickly confronted by a civilian bellowing, 'You need to check your weapons, boys. They're not allowed in town.' Yes, we were a bunch of untidy, rough, and tough sombreros hoisting our .45's in our shoulder holsters, but check our weapons? Never."

"Fat chance," Sarge said. "We never check our weapons."

The civilian produced his ID as an Army colonel and sneered. "Well, now that we've straightened that out, you sissies can put your weapons down or you can stand there while I call the MPs."

"A cooler head prevailed, and we checked our weapons," John said. "Inside, we were the only military in uniform in what felt like a stateside bar."

"I would safely bet you didn't drink while on patrol," I kidded.

"Of course not," John said. "But we did make up for it every chance we got. Speaking of patrols, this is a memorable patrol story. Lieutenant Eads and I came to a fork in the road during one two-man patrol. Since Eads was a far superior guide than I, little right/left discussion took place before I said, 'Fine, you're the man, if you say left then let's go left.' Within the first ten feet Eads stepped into a foot trap that pierced through his boot and miraculously missed his foot. Eads muttered several choice words. We stripped the trap and continued maybe fifteen yards before he fell into a man trap. He caught himself, hoisted up, and rolled out unscathed. The trap was lined with bamboo stakes. Four bottom spikes connected to twenty-pounds of explosives. The slightest trigger would have hemorrhaged us both into a dusty crater."

John fixed his eyes on the floor. "Eads stared into the hole. 'This is the wrong way. The other path is most definitely the right way to go.' I said, 'Yeah, I think you're right.'"

I dramatically wiped my hand across my forehead. "Whew."

"Indeed," John said. "But that was a two-man patrol. Patrolling with a platoon in tow was different but just as dangerous. Patrolling dikes had a Disney-World-waiting-in-line-snaking-back-and-forth affect. The dikes were heavily lined with well-concealed punji pits and booby traps. It took the enemy less than thirty seconds to realize that dry, cool, and shade were favorite American spots. Platoon leaders hassled Marines into the sun and water. And you wouldn't believe what these kids lugged around. I'll never forget one corpsman and the things he carried."

"Another good story?" I asked.

"Yes. At first the green medicine man carried no weapon, just his Unit-1 bag plus a canvas bag bloated with so much medical paraphernalia, his arms couldn't hang along his sides.

"Nervous, Doc?" I asked.

"A little."

"Doc, Doc, man what the hell is all of this shit?"

"Things I need, sir."

"For what, we've got hospitals that stay in one place for Christ's sake."

"These things will make them better, sir."

"These things will make you slow. Where's your weapon?"

"I'm a corpsman, sir. I'm here to help people, not hurt them. I don't need a gun."

"You should live so goddamn long! The enemy doesn't give a shit about who you are or what you want, be it unless you're dead. Hey, somebody stop the war and get this screwball a gun."

"Within days," John continued, "the corpsman's throat snarled a piece of shrapnel. It wasn't serious but it counted. He included a weapon and ammo on his next venture. Shortly thereafter he tripped a booby trap causing a wound severe enough for evacuation. He returned with a heart of darkness transition that required my attention."

"Doc, where the hell's your Unit-1?"

"Sir, with all due respect, sir, I'm going to get me some gooks. I've got to protect myself."

"I can see that. But that's all I see, grenades, weapons, and ammo. You're a corpsman, goddamn it, where the hell's your Unit-1?"

"Sir."

"Doc, go get your Unit-1."

A bullet pierced his knee within weeks, and he was shipped home, no doubt a happy camper."

"What did you carry?" I asked.

"Not much," John said. "I carried a rifle, deluding myself into thinking I wouldn't be spotted as an officer. I balled my poncho into my cartridge belt and jammed C-rat fruit in a sock tied bandolier-style slung over my shoulder. I shed whatever I could. I even quit wearing socks. And I never had problems with leeches or immersion foot. God, immersion foot, a.k.a. trench rot, was ugly and dangerous. Capillaries shut down, circulation ceased, and gangrene set in. Once nailed, it spread rapidly. But trench rot was hard to avoid. Marines got trench rot from being wet, and we were always wet. Boy did I hate being wet. To this day I have a strong aversion to anything clammy, damp, or soggy. I was truly miserable during monsoon season, humping through mud up to our armpits. And in the summer, that muck transformed into very red, very dusty, dusty dust."

John became quiet and pensive. "We really did."

"Did what?" I asked.

"We patrolled constantly and built new defensive perimeters in every unestablished base location before settling in. We filled sandbags and dug foxholes. One time I loaded and piled sandbags on top of a split-level bunker much to the delight of a young, exasperated Huck Finn Marine.

> "God, Lieutenant, don't they teach officers anything? You're doing it all wrong."
>
> "Doing what wrong?" I asked.
>
> "Your sandbags. They're all wrong. They're too round and won't stack well."
>
> "Oh?"
>
> "Stuff 'em three-quarters full so they mold to lay flat. They have to lay flat to make a compact wall."
>
> "Oh, okay. I knew that; sort of. But why don't you show me anyway?"

"And of course he was right," John said. "The grunts knew sandbags. Not from any particular Marine Corps boot camp exercise but from Vietnam's on-the-job-forever-moving-and-filling-sandbag training. I studied sandbags in an air-conditioned, well-lit room in Officer Candidate School, minus the training."

"Does one Marine in particular stand out in your mind?" I asked.

"Yes," John said. "Carole Smith (not real name). His misfortune began as a Marine Corps draftee. Smith had a girl's first name and looked like Pigpen, the character from Peanuts who trailed dust wherever he went. With nothing but a third grade education, this poor kid was beyond inarticulate and couldn't add two and two. And for that, his fellow Marines tormented him. And if life hadn't dealt him a bad hand already, Smith suffered from premature baldness. The Vietnamese barber would shave stubble and fuzz from his receding hairline, and Smith would later agonize for hours. And although Smith could trip standing absolutely still, he was John Wayne magnificent in the heat of battle. Private First Class Smith was unbelievably spectacular with a weapon. He was the guy you wanted next to you during a gun-fire exchange.

"During one night patrol—as Smith carried the radio, a Marine from Smith's squad tripped a booby trap that pummeled five Marines. In the confusion of scrambling for help, Smith handed his squad leader a pack of cigarettes, frustrating the squad leader to no end."

"I don't want a cigarette now, for God's sake. Put those away and get back on the radio."

"Oh, okay."

"Smith replaced the pack in his flak jacket and continued calling for medevacs. But Smith became incomprehensible, even for Smith."

Frustrated on the other end of the net I demanded, "Smith, put the squad leader back on the phone."

"Okay, Lieutenant."

"What's wrong with Smith? I can't understand a word he's saying. Check him out."

"The squad leader quickly realized that Smith had been hit," John said. "Shrapnel had pierced the cigarette pack in his flak jacket and lodged into his chest. Smith was showing the squad leader the hole in the cigarette package because he couldn't articulate a proper explanation. He was immediately medevaced."

"Do you know what happened to him?" I asked.

"No," John said. "We never knew what happened to these kids unless they came back. I'll never forget another scrawny PFC who looked just like Wally Cox with thick, black, horn-rimmed glasses. I assigned him to stand watch but discovered this nitwit sleeping soundly, rifle in hand. Incensed, I grabbed the rifle and gave Wally's noggin a knock which of course, woke him up. I was pissed. 'Private, just what the hell do you think you're doing?'"

John sat erect in his chair.

"Lieutenant, sir," Wally said. "Can I have my rifle back?"

"No, now it's mine. But here's what I'll do for you."

I handed Wally two grenades with both pins pulled. "Now fall asleep."

"Sir?"

"At least now I'll know if you nod off and I'll send Murphy (not real name) to stand watch. I'm not going to let you snooze so I can have my throat slit."

"Several minutes passed before I heard boom. I stormed over, still pissed."

"Yeah, it took you a few to figure out that you could just chuck 'em."

"With all due respect, Lieutenant, I heard something, now can I have my rifle back?"

"No, you have your bayonet. Stand watch with that."

"Now that's tough love," I said.

John leaned forward. "Sleeping on watch was a big, bad deal. Yes, it was easy to nod off after a nineteen hour day, but sleeping on post was a court martial offense. The sleepy PFC endured an unusual punishment that evening in An Hoa. Donning full combat regalia—helmet, flak jacket, backpack, canteens, magazines, and rifle—he guided and guarded officers to the piss tube installed thirty yards from the officer's quarters."

I must have looked confused because John grinned. "The piss tube was an artillery shell casing dug into the ground that served as the local urinal."

"Oh. Did you ever catch any of these sleepy PFC's cutting off ears?" I asked.

"If ears were severed on my watch it was a well-guarded, un-paraded secret because they knew if caught, I would've shot whoever did it," John said without hesitation. "I made it quite clear. 'If I catch any of you doing that kind of crap, I'll shoot you myself and send you home in a body bag. Don't worry, I'll write your mom a nice note, telling her what a hero you were. We're not going to sink to that level. We're here to elevate people, not to become animals.'"

John hesitated.

"Posing a dead head was the worst scenario. One badly decomposed body got stuck in the wire at Nong Son. The head rolled off as we pulled the corpse out of the wire. The head became a photo op complete with cigarettes. But truly, such scenarios were few and far between."

"Were the Viet Cong and the North Vietnamese Army worthy adversaries?" I asked.

"Yes. And the VC would add decades of practice by monitoring and rehearsing Marine jungle drills. Christ, if you left your ass hanging out, they'd chop it off and serve it to Ho Chi Minh on a silver platter. They would patiently sit and watch you because they knew you were going to fuck up. They'd come out of their huts and holes and bingo . . ."

John raised his right hand, lifted his thumb straight up, extended his forefinger forward, and pulled an air trigger.

"You're dead," John said. "All it takes is time and the Vietnamese had time. Time was all they had. There was no such thing as going home. They were home."

"What about the ARVN soldiers?"

"ARVN's were barometers for gauging enemy contact, especially on patrol. If they were aggressive and stayed close, all was right with the world, enjoy the scenery. But if a great display of puffery accompanied their banishment into the countryside, shit-howdy, look out! Parris Island would have done marvels for these kids. They'd juggle hand grenades to entertain the ladies."

"How loyal were the Vietnamese villagers to Marines?" I asked.

"Sketchy," John said. "And when a trip wire detonated a U.S. grenade in mammasan's front yard, the idea that villagers were terrorized by no-win situations vanished. More Marines were slaughtered by booby traps and mines than killed in action during 1967. I remember one front-yard booby trap that killed one Marine and wounded four others. Frustrated, one of our squad leaders—let's call him Watson (not real name)—dragged out an elder mammasan and clicked his Zippo lighter against the eaves of her tiny hootch."

John stood and clicked an imaginary Zippo high in the air.

"Mammasan yanked and snuffed the smoking straw," John said as he flamboyantly patted the air with both hands while blowing hard into the air.

"Watson clicked his Zippo again, only this time, he held the frail, thrashing woman back as even more straw burned. Watson loosened his grip, and mammasan retrieved the straw and stamped the flames. He then shoved mammasan ahead of the squad of onlooking Marines to safely guide us through the village. Once out of harm's way, Watson flicked his Zippo across the eaves of the last hootch; a small vengeance for the death and mutilation of our own."

I sighed. "That's sad, but I've heard stories along the same vein."

John sat stoic, seemingly resigned to do what needed to be done. "On a less lethal outing PFC Sanchez (not real name) quietly walked up to ol' mammasan feeding her chickens. Sanchez bent forward, picked up a squawker, and snapped its neck. The chicken dangled limply in his hand, and mammasan whimpered. I could see the bird twitching as Sanchez tucked its legs beneath his web belt. Sanchez snatched another chicken neck and held it in mammasan's face. Mammasan spoke rapidly while fanning the folds of her skirt and kicking the other chickens away. Sanchez removed his helmet and dropped it between their feet. The old woman stopped, headed into her hootch, and returned with a large wicker basket. Trembling, she placed several thin-shelled eggs from the basket into the steel helmet. Sanchez released the chicken and bowed a thank you. Mammasan smiled nervously, but I really don't think she understood."

I stayed quiet.

"One corpsman accused me of being callous upon the death of a young female VC cadre," John said.

"Callous would be the last word I would use to describe you," I said.

"Well, during this particular incident, as we cautiously entered a hostile-fire ville quieted from our artillery strikes, we collided with two mammasans bucking a litter with a badly wounded Vietnamese girl. Shrapnel had disemboweled her."

I shuddered at the gruesome image.

"I examined her closely. Her full set of white teeth clearly indicated that she was an urbanite and not a local yocal. I thought, *She's pretty, the wound is not, but she is. She won't be soon though. She's dying. She's young, as young as the men, and they are men now, who work for me.* My corpsman requested an emergency medevac. I denied his request, knowing she wasn't going to survive. I approved a routine medevac. Minutes differentiated the two. Doc insisted, demanding that I act more humane. We argued. She died during the debate. The mammasans squawked. We moved on. She was later identified as the Viet Cong responsible for the initial gunfire onto my Marines; my men. It was a righteous kill.

"I tried to convince another mammasan to retrieve a VC hiding in a tunnel outside a village that battered us with sniper fire. I drilled her as she defiantly spat her beetle-nut, 'Where are they, mammasan?'" John vigorously shook his head and altered the inflection in his voice. "'No, no. No see VC.' Mammasan knew what I wanted, and I knew she wouldn't say. So Sergeant Riley (not real name) shoved his rifle butt into her shoulders. She wailed, 'No, no. No see VC.' Riley then grabbed her by the collar and shoved her head into the cave. Mammasan remained defiant, 'No, no. No see VC.' 'Fine,' Riley said. 'We'll just blow it up.' And much to mammasan's horror, Riley threw in a grenade. Mammasan wept as the cave collapsed. Her short, shrill sobs filtered throughout the village as we left. But we—as did she—knew the VC who fired at us were in that cave."

"Oh, John," I said for lack of having anything profound to say. "If you don't mind me asking, were you scared?"

John nodded. "Yes, of course. The life expectancy of a second lieutenant during a firefight was seven seconds. Lieutenant Rogers (not real name), a brand new second lieutenant with no combat experience sprang to his feet during Operation Tuscaloosa with a resounding 'follow me men,' and fortunately no one did because he was instantly stitched.

"But I psychologically insulated myself in Vietnam. Early in my tour I worried about my weak stomach, especially at the sight of the grossly wounded. I pictured—and feared—my men asking, 'Hey where's the lieutenant?' 'Oh, he's throwing up all over the bushes.' But that didn't happen. I compared my experience to walking through the meat department at the supermarket. I didn't retch at the entrails and viscera of little creatures on display. My reflective thoughts were self-centered. The longer I stayed unwounded, the more I thought, *when and how bad?* But in some ways, it was easier for the Marines in Vietnam than for their families waiting at home. My wife, Janet, remembers the military car slowly driving down Lincoln Street thinking, *please don't stop here.* That would have driven me really crazy."

John shuffled through his Vietnam scrapbooks overflowing with papers and photographs. He pulled a paper from the middle book. "This poem expresses how I felt. Read it while I get a coffee refill. Would you like anything?"

"No thanks." John left, and I silently read the words written on paper yellowed with age.

> If I think perhaps it will be.
> When I'm out of this and with my wife and son we will live
> in Cape Cod. There it is only crowded during the summer. My
> wife, my son, and I will drive Route 28 on a glorious Indian
> summer day. We'll find ourselves alone like ants on a strip of

ribbon lying loosely in folds on the coast's ragged arm. We'll stroll on the beach, over the dunes, and by the lighthouse. There will be a fresh and clean stiff breeze. My wife and child will be the silhouettes that move ahead of me. My son will discover hermit crabs and starfish among things that are alive and good. My hands will grow cold. I'll slide them in my pockets where I can feel them. They will feel rough because I work outdoors. I work with my hands because my mind will not yet be whole. Memories will bleed. The wind burning my cheeks won't bother me. We'll walk home in the dark and meet no one. My son will ride on my shoulders with his small hands wrapped around my head. He'll hold my ears so that I may not hear. I will say thank you. Thank you. Thank you.

If I think it perhaps it will be.

The lump in my throat that since had subsided began to swell. John returned with his coffee and a small cup of frozen yogurt for me. *Perfect*, I thought.

"Thank you," I said gratefully.

"It'll cost you," John said.

"Your poem is poignant."

"Thanks. I was just thinking about another kid who reached his tolerance threshold and granted himself a ticket home ten months into his tour."

"How so?" I asked.

"By repeatedly smashing his fingers in the breach machine gun and sharing the tall tale of a horrific tumble. Dr. Viti immobilized his digits by attaching wires to his forearms before sending him stateside. His A-gunner later admitted the truth. The Marine was done. But I understood. Courage and humanity remained intact early in one's tour. But time, terror, and horror affected even the toughest; and some more than others. We roped off a section in our hootch because it felt like whoever slept there—we quit counting after four—was destined for death or destruction. That corner evoked evil-bearing spirits. So we hung a red, white, and blue sign over our door that proudly cheered, 'Fuck Communism.'"

"If you don't mind me asking, do you suffer from any PTSD?" I asked.

"Not really," John said. "But I was an older officer, sporting a college degree and job experience, not a fresh, unshaven eighteen-year-old high school graduate. If a kid didn't have a strong family scaffolding to nurture him back into society after his two-year commitment, damage was plausible. America was hostile to her boys for going to Vietnam. That more than anything was the telling blow. Once home, I eased back into society while working on a military-base cocoon in Quantico. I wasn't entrenched in the anti-war rallies and marches, so it didn't matter. But, and this is a big but, when looking for employment there was a reluctance to hire a Vietnam combat Marine veteran. That label flagged trouble. People talked about combat Marines because they *were* combat Marines. You never read about a former coast guardsman scaling a tower to shoot people; or a former Navy, Air Force, or Army man. But a former combat Marine veteran often becomes the story's lead title. That not only pissed me off, it cost me my first job."

I was taken aback by John's admission. "How so?"

"I was the successful business man sporting a Marine field jacket. People would ask, 'Hey, John, why you're wearing a field jacket to a conference?' My response was full of bravado. 'Well, if it was good enough to die in, it's good enough to wear at meetings with clowns like you.' A succession of these ill-natured remarks didn't impress the corporate environment. In retrospect, I wouldn't want me working for me either. You don't need that in business. But I learned a lot about John Newton in the Marine Corps, specifically in Vietnam. Left to my own devices I never would've tapped into my psychological resources. I've never endured anything more challenging, and I don't think I ever will. I say I'm the same slap-happy, wild and crazy guy I was before Nam, but some say I'm quieter. I won't argue. But remember, this is the gospel according to Saint John Newton."

"If I may be so bold to ask, do you believe in God?"

"I absolutely believe in a higher power but how do you define a spiritual man? Is divine intervention my reason for waking up in An Hoa before the July 4th attack? My rubber lady became a honeycomb of shrapnel without me in it. I never arbitrarily woke up before or after that night. Wow."

"That's more than a wow," I said. "That's downright scary."

"Oh I had many close-call wows. Once while patrolling across a rice paddy island I stopped to diddle and dither with my map and binoculars. I quickly noticed that Doc Cunningham and I were standing too close together. Having thought the mere words, I turned and dodged a bullet intended to pierce me between the eyes. I should've been killed but remained unmarked. Doc, however, got shot through his knee cap, awarding him his third Purple Heart and a ticket home."

"Did you pray?" I asked.

"Wows led to many wild promises to God beginning with the if-you-get-me-out-of-here-I-will-never prayer."

John sorted through his Vietnam scrapbooks before pulling out another sheet of aged paper. "Here's another Newton quote."

"Minutes go by; minutes when I think; minutes when I don't," John said at a deliberate pace. "Why am I not dead? There's prayer but to whom? More lead; long, long, short, long, inches right, inches left, down two clicks. I must not die here lying on my stomach in the dirt. I pray, 'this is my rifle. There are many others like it but this one is mine. I know it's mine because I landed on it, and it now massages my groin. I don't feel the pain. More minutes pass by. Why in the name of God don't you hit me? I know it will come, and when it does I'll relax. The passing minutes grow monotonous. Jesus, will I ever understand the difference between the quick, the dead, and the living?'"

"Kudos on your writing," I said. "How often do you think about Vietnam?"

"Every day," John said. "Every single day. But thinking about Vietnam doesn't bother me. I have many good memories. Why just the other day, two World War II vets came in for ice cream. So we sat as three old warriors—eating ice cream and swapping war stories. One guy asked me if I had read Tom Brokaw's *The Greatest Generation.*"

> "It's on my list but I haven't gotten to it yet," I said.
>
> "Well, as far as I'm concerned, Vietnam veterans are the greatest generation," the guy said. "Yeah, we went through the depression—but we came home from the war as heroes. We marched in parades while girls hugged and kissed us. People loved us everywhere we went. But when you came home everybody hated you. And you went about your business, quietly working and raising families with only negative fanfare. So as far as I'm concerned, the label, "The Greatest Generation" belongs to you."
>
> I was really taken aback. "Wow those are very kind words."
>
> "I mean every one of them."
>
> His buddy, listening to the whole yarn, chimed in, "I agree."

"That's a good memory that will forever reside beneath the surface. Today the warrior is honored, despite one's opinion on war. But Vietnam veterans were betrayed by their own countrymen.

"One night a home-made mortar—a five-gallon pail filled with explosives and debris—landed in An Hoa. A hand grenade fuse was screwed into the top, and a pin-ring string was tethered to a rock. The can was supposed to land while the rock continued flying, causing the rock to pull the string and detonate the grenade. Ironically, the explosive contraption didn't work. I say ironically because the five-gallon soy sauce can sported a logo from USAID—two clasped hands with a caption, 'From Your Friends In America.' As far as we were concerned, the irony was lost on no one.

"But again, I will tell you Vietnam was exciting. Excitement keeps war going. The worst part of war is waiting for it to begin. Once it starts, it's 'Yahoo.'"

"Let's switch gears and talk about the outpost at the coal mine, Nong Son," I said.

"The 2/5 was stationed in An Hoa to provide security for Nong Son, South Vietnam's only coal mine. Nong Son's anthracite was transported to An Hoa's Industrial Complex, one of three complexes built in South Vietnam designed to illuminate Southeast Asia and manufacture fertilizer as a by-product. An Hoa's Industrial Complex also promised South Vietnam a hydroelectric plant and a water purification system. But coal mining was more symbolism than realism. Workers mined a teaspoon a day, just enough to say, 'you can't stop us.' And since funds never reached the project level because of government corruption, Nong Son became a someday mine."

John leaned back in his chair with a distant expression in his eyes and seemed to forget about me as he spoke. "Nong Son will someday produce coal that will someday fire the turbines in the someday industrial complex that will someday generate electricity to someday afford this country industry. The coal from this someday mine couldn't fit on a spoon. So while Marines wander the someday coal mine getting shot, gooks work in the empty someday mine in safety.

"One of Nong Son's two supervisory engineers, a Mr. Han, was assumed to be VC because he'd magically disappear before An Hoa received mortar fire. He'd board a chopper and we'd know, 'tonight's the night.' The other engineer, a South Vietnamese businessman whose name escapes me, personally financed the project. He was a true patriot with a vision of South Vietnam as a free democratic society."

"Several 2/5 Marines have mentioned a Mr. Han," I said. "The idea of keeping him around makes me nervous."

"Then this story will make you really nervous. During my tenure, the An Hoa air strip was secure enough to jog around. At one end a VC screwball sniped as we trotted around the corner, which was a little unnerving and caused an increase in pace. But he always shot high. We considered an ambush but decided he might be replaced by a better shot so we left him alone and briskly rounded the corner on subsequent runs. It was all very Mash-like."

"You're right. My running sneakers would have collected dust. Describe the village outside of the combat base."

"You'll like this," John said. "There was a sprawling flower field by the refugee center outside the wire filled with thousands of lovely, tiny white flowers. I'd stare through the wire silently mulling, 'Within such terrible warfare, anguish, and pain, a flower field thrives.' Weeks later while patrolling through the field I discovered it was really a community shit house. The miniscule white flowers were shredded pieces of toilet paper hanging on bushes. The field was alive with flies so every step was buzz, buzz, buzz, and buzz. Thus, this became my metaphor for the Vietnam War: 'While it may resemble a field of flowers, it's really just a shit house.'"

"You're right," I said. "I do like that."

"Phu Da (2) was a crowded refugee village outside of An Hoa. I remember the town's tinker who made tin pots from metal scrapings and the dress shop with its local tailors. I bought Janet a Vietnamese Aodai, the traditional split dress. Conversing in bits-and-pieces of French, Vietnamese, and English was quite amusing. I gestured the shape of a woman for sizing which caused an outbreak of giggles. Of course the garment was sewn to the stature of a Vietnamese woman so it didn't fit Janet. But I do remember the tinker and the tailor. I wonder if there was a Marine and a spy, sounds like a good name for a book, doesn't it?"

"Yes," I agreed with an easy smile. "It does. How about the Vietnamese children?"

"I didn't get particularly close to the kids; the tiny devils could be lethal. We'd often find the charming little urchins either laying booby traps or being used as one. They were filthy, and scampered around in tattered, threaded shirts. Their bellies bulged with worms which added a grotesque burden to their already too-tiny waistlines. The babies seldom wore pants. The Vietnamese theorized that they would simply dirty them. And both Vietnamese adults and children squatted on the side of the road to urinate whenever and wherever. I remember one three-year-old boy with a leg wound doctored by water buffalo dung, the Vietnamese band-aid thought to scab and ultimately heal wounds. His eyes were loaded with conjunctivitis pus and his belly extended a mile out, most likely from worms. A troop of flies loudly commuted between the mucous and the pus deposits in the corner of his eye. The expressionless child made no effort to swat the flies away. It was as though he learned to live quietly behind them offering nothing more to us than a thousand-yard stare."

John stared.

"I remember another young girl, burnt by napalm. Her conscious eyes glittered against her charred flesh without shedding a single tear. It was as though she felt no pain. Napalm saved many American lives, but not without consequence."

"Every 2/5 Marine that I've spoken to describes napalm as saving lives but not without consequence," I said.

John silently nodded.

"Let's switch gears again," I said eagerly. "Pops shed quite a few pounds in Vietnam. Did you?"

"I weighed a whopping one hundred and thirty pounds in Vietnam. I ate two cans of C-rat fruit per day and the occasional, wonderful French bread or pastry, a legacy of Vietnam's past. I declined Vietnamese food, and was leery about their pork. 'Is that the pig I saw running around an hour ago?' Besides, the Vietnamese drowned their food in Nuc Mum, a potent smelling fish sauce squeezed from dead fish bloating in the sun."

"Yuk," I said. "Were you hungry?"

"One gets past the hungry point. I did, however, smoke many a Marlboro, and thanks to Janet, I was the king of An Hoa. I could buy almost anything with a pack of Marlboros. Phillip Morris had a deal for combat warriors—ten cartons mailed directly for ten bucks. C-rat cigarettes, Chesterfields, and Camels were

An Hoa's Industrial Complex, RSVN, monsoon season, 1967.

Vietnamese children outside of An Hoa, RSVN, 1967.

Vietnamese Store, An Hoa, RSVN, 1967.

Popular Forces, An Hoa, RSVN, 1967.

Lt. John Newton operating the radios inside of An Hoa's COC, 1967.

stale. 'Not to be Sold' was stamped on the five-pack for good reason. You know, officers paid thirty bucks a month for hot chow and C rats."

"You paid for food? That's odd."

"Yes, it's true, an officer and a gentleman gave back half of their sixty dollar hostile-fire, combat pay—extra pay for being in a war zone—for food. The grunts ate for free, although hard liquor was off limits."

"Did you ever drink Vietnamese sake?"

"I didn't touch it, since it was unstrained and filled with nasty floating animals. Here's a good rice wine story. Marines routinely called in at specific checkpoints during patrols. One group heading to Nong Son vanished at their last village checkpoint before crossing the river. We tried repeatedly and in vain to reach the Marines. While gathering a rescue mission we heard a voice mutter over the net."

> "Help. Help. Someone help us."
> "Where are you?"
> "At the bottom of the beach."
> "What? What beach, why? Are you at Nong Son? "
> "No, we never made it across the river."

"What do you mean you never made it across, what's wrong?"

"I don't know, but we're sick, we can't move. You've got to come and get us?"

"Who's we?"

"Us."

"Us?"

"Yes, all of us."

"The village chief had invited the entire group, including the platoon commander, to a rice wine toast as they waited for the barge. Although unintentional, the rice wine had poisoned them. Every Marine was flown to Da Nang to have his stomach pumped. Even though it about did the big tough Marines in, nothing happened to the five-foot, ninety-pound village chief."

"Do you have any colorful animal stories?" I asked.

"Vietnam animals were interesting to say the least. Water buffalos were the size of small condos. They were housed in the muck, shit, and piss of underground corrals. The fifteen hundred pound mammal nervously trampled, stank of stagnation, and could smell an American a mile away. Rats infested static bunker positions garnished with empty, discarded C-rat cans. Phu Lac (6) and Nong Son were home to some as big as cats. Tigers roamed Antenna Valley, a one-time French Game Preserve and hunting paradise. And leeches looked like little eels. You couldn't feel them sucking blood, but the greasy worms dressed themselves on you during river crossings. One leech latched himself onto a kid's penis, causing the lad to bolt. We had to tackle him to remove the slimy creature. Scorpions were decent-sized, dangerous, and often found in your boots. Centipedes were six inches long and hairy. And cobras occasionally slithered into bunkers to escape the blazing sun. Here's a great snake story. One tunnel rat—do you know what a tunnel rat is?"

"Yes, I do," I said enthusiastically. "Tunnel rats were volunteers who stripped down to their boots and trousers, protected only by a .45 and a flashlight, to check a complex system of VC underground tunnels. Pretty brave I dare say."

"Very good. Well this kid ventured—unknowingly—into a cobra booby-trapped tunnel, head first. One minute I was looking at his feet, the next second he was upright, breathing heavily, cobra in hot pursuit. Gunfire. The cobra, now dispatched to snake heaven, lay tail-tied by a trip wire. The Marine released the unhappy fellow who fortunately moved with less alacrity than the Marine. This incident caused me to adopt a seal-with-gas-grenade-and-blow-up-tunnel approach for the remainder of my tour.

"This was another strange story. We found a huge box six inches underground on Operation Independence. The tunnel rat scraped the dirt, lifted the lid, and found layers of banana leaves. He probed the layers with his

Thumbing a boat ride

Marines take advantage of Vietnamese fisherman's offer to row them across the river during a search and destroy operation southwest of Da Nang. The Marines are members of "E" Co., 2d Bn., Fifth Marines, 1st Marine Division.   (Photo by LCpl. J. E. Russell)

Sea Tiger newspaper clipping "Thumbing a boat ride." "Marines take advantage of Vietnamese Fisherman's offer to row them across the river during a search and destroy operation southwest of Da Nang. The Marines are members of 'E' Co., 2d Bn., 5th Marines, 1st Marine Division."

bayonet until he realized he was scraping a face in a coffin. That ended that project."

I bit my lip. "That is spooky. I have but a few more questions, do you need a break?"

"No, I'm fine."

"How often did friendly fire occur?"

"Friendly fire occurred on occasion. This friendly fire story just ruined Lieutenant Colonel Jackson's day. Post the July 4th attack on Nong Son, Marines cleared highly-sensitized, unexploded 106 rounds lining the mountain road. Marines removed the live ammo by blowing it up halfway down the mountain. After gingerly accumulating enough ordinances to discharge, they signaled up the mountain to close the road. One unfortunate communication confirmed an explosion as a truck passed through its middle, unfortunately blowing it and its driver, *Dwight David Eisenhower*—the fourth or fifth cousin of General Eisenhower—*the* General Eisenhower, off the cliff. This was the culmination of a bad week for Lieutenant Colonel Jackson. An Hoa had been badly mortared; Nong Son, the spot that every U.S. general proclaimed as impenetrable was penetrated, diminishing the already diminished Foxtrot Company decimated less than a month prior by Operation Union II; and now General Eisenhower's relative was killed by friendly fire. Lieutenant Colonel Jackson did, however, weather the storm."

"Yikes," I said, genuinely surprised.

"Another time, a company from a different battalion dumped us with 60mm mortars. Blessing was beyond insane, trying to get the CO to cease fire. Much to Blessing's dismay, the guilty CO fluffed it off. 'No casualties, just a little boo-boo on our part sorry. Oh gee, silly us. Ha ha.' Blessing was outraged. 'Are you out of your fuckin' mind? You're trying to kill my troops, and you think it's funny?' If Blessing could have crawled through the radio, he would've killed that CO.

"It was frightening to witness Marines exchange bullets and mortars. And for the most part, when all was said and done, no one was hurt. Well, if we can't harm ourselves are we killing the enemy? Did Marines just fire blindly? We're supposed to aim and shoot. Before the M16s only one in four weapons was an automatic. Firing occurred as an aim and squeeze, aim and squeeze. But with the M16s, Marines flipped on the automatic and fired erratically. Contact was questionable. Scaring the enemy to death with extraordinary noise was not."

Yes, I thought. A perfect segue to discuss the controversial M16s. "Let's discuss the M16s."

John whistled. "The M16s were extremely controversial. The M16s jammed. The M16 prototype was fine. But the production model eliminated the prototype's chrome bolt which reduced the strength of its buffer spring. The prototype had a chrome bolt and strong stock buffer spring that easily slid the bolt home. And the M16s high rate of automatic fire caused a rapid carbon buildup. Since the lack of bolt chroming made it porous, the rapid carbon buildup didn't allow the bolt to easily slide in. A weakened spring exacerbated the problem, which ultimately caused the gun to jam. It simply wouldn't fire. Not good. During Operation Union II several Marines were discovered shot execution style, laying on their jammed M16s. But a bright, young Lieutenant Jones (not real name) changed the course of the M16s while destroying his own career. Jones, a career Marine on the fast track, wrote a letter to the Marine Corps commandant outlining his M16 concerns, which in itself, was fine. Jones, however, cc'd the *New York Times*. Weeks later, The *New York Times* printed his letter in the Sunday edition. Lieutenant Jones's phone rang on Monday. 'Lieutenant Jones, this is the Marine Corps commandant.' Now it was highly unusual to receive a direct call from the commandant. 'You're on your way to the Philippines to participate in a news conference. You'll be briefed prior to the conference.' And Jones spoke briefly about the M16s at a news conference in the Philippines. But he was never to be heard from again. Although there was no official reprimand, Jones's Marine Corps career ended. He was snubbed for promotion with nothing in his OQR—Officer Qualification Record—to indicate why. According to the higher brass, Jones was a whistle-blower and therefore a goner. Before the incident Jones considered himself a career Marine on the fast track. But he absolutely changed the course of the M16. Colt, the weapons manufacturer recalled and rebuilt them."

"Why did Jones cc the *New York Times*?"

"I'm not sure. Maybe he thought his complaints would get lost climbing the chain of command."

"So he wasn't court-martialed or punished, he was just never promoted."

"Correct," John said.

"Did you have any court-martials in An Hoa?"

"There was an attempt to court-martial a radio operator in An Hoa for marijuana. To convene a general court in An Hoa was a big event that included attorneys to defend and prosecute. And this was a general court-martial, so the general and his legal beagles flew in from Da Nang. But thirty seconds into the big hullabaloo the general declared it a frivolous charge. The accusation was based on a cigarette wrapper found underneath this kid's rack, a rack surrounded by twenty others. Court lasted seconds."

"Who accused the poor chap?"

"A first lieutenant assigned in the rear with the gear. Coming from my infantry perspective, behind the scene, rear-gear officers were little marionettes. Not to disparage anyone, but no matter how hard an infantryman tried not to, he felt above his non-infantry fellows. We were all in harm's way, but there was a sentiment that infantry Marines were real Marines; especially lieutenants, corpsmen, and radio operators, who roamed as small clusters of instant enemy bush targets."

"Radio operators?" I asked.

"Sure. Radio operators tended to be even more Marine because their radio antennas pointed high in the air and shouted, 'Here I am, here I am.'"

I knew it was time to wrap up as the ice cream shop became almost disruptive with voices. "When did you leave Vietnam?"

"I left Vietnam right before the first TET offensive. The 2/5 had since left An Hoa and settled into Phu Bai, an area that was rocketed on a regular basis. And my departure did not fail to meet excitement expectations. While waiting on the airstrip, a rocket slammed onto the tarmac which caused me and twelve other Marines to bolt into one of the zigzagging above-ground bunkers. A second boom blanketed us with dust, lumber, corrugated metal, and shrapnel. And when the smoke cleared and the dust settled I was the only Marine not drenched in blood. 'Holy mackerel,' I thought. 'Another save! I'm leaving Dodge at all costs.'

"Within minutes, a C-130 destined for Da Nang arrived. I ran onto the airstrip as the bird carved a wide circle overhead before touching down. *Boom.* The pilot quickly ascended, unmarked, as I, along with the same twelve Marines beelined back into the bunker. *Boom!* The PA screeched, 'He'll try one more touch and go. If you don't get on, I don't know when he'll be back.'

"Now touch and go means they don't stop. They touch down, drop the rear ramp, taxi, and elevate. Boarding's a bit chancy. And since I was scheduled to leave Da Nang for El Toro the next day, as the bird became a speck on the horizon, I sprinted down the airstrip. As the pilot dropped the ramp, I cut through the middle of five other determined Marines, abandoned my bags on the tarmac, and scrambled on. Off we flew.

"We landed in Da Nang, a city in complete turmoil. Dog Patch was screwed by gunfire, and Freedom Hill had been over run. Around eleven o'clock that night, M16s were issued straight from their cases to all viable bodies, including the wounded, now formed as reactionary companies. So I spent my last night in Vietnam in the R & R Motel, drinking San Miguel Beer, smoking Marlboros, loading M16 magazines, and watching a fantastic firefight."

I grinned. "And you safely made it home."

"Yes. And home in the beginning felt like being in the land of Oz. A car backfired at a stoplight the first day I drove. I opened the door and hurled myself onto the ground. Everyone stared. Janet grabbed me. 'John, it's okay, you don't have to do that anymore.' Another night while drinking hot toddies on the roof of a four-story building with friends a jet jockey broke the sound barrier." John stood and flew his right hand over the top of his head. "Vaaaaarooooooom, Varoom, Varoom. I galloped down four flights of stairs, holding my drink, *without*, may I say, spilling a single drop, before reality clicked."

"Without spilling a single drop," I said. "I'm impressed."

And as if by divine intervention—again—Janet poked her head into the room.

"Hey you two," Janet said. "It's getting pretty crazy out there. All hands on deck."

"Sure thing," John said.

"Thanks, John," I said as the lump in my throat began to swell.

John smiled with ease and grace. "My pleasure, Lucia. My pleasure."

John Newton and Jesse Pender,
Carlsbad, CA, 2009.

Parking insignia posted outside of
Short 'n' Sweet, Chatham, MA, 2007.

🌺 *Dear Daddy* 🌺

Who were you, this beautiful man who touched the hearts of so many? I see your face so completely energized and vibrantly alive in your Vietnam photos, you're almost unfamiliar. How did you so effortlessly imprint the life of every 2/5 veteran that I spoke to? And your orders, official documents, and Navy Personnel Records list such outstanding achievements:

- *Bronze Star Medal with Combat Distinguishing Device—and Citation*
- *Vietnamese Cross of Gallantry/Operation Newcastle*
- *Vietnamese Medal of Honor*
- *Presidential Unit Citations (2)*
- *National Defense Service Medal*
- *Vietnam Service Medal with FMF Combat Insignia*
- *Republic of Vietnam Campaign Medal*
- *Conspicuous Service Medal from the State of New York*
- *Congressional Record—Proceedings and Debate of the 97th Congress, Second Session, April 20, 1982*

Exceptional. I remember that you credited Vietnam as the "one place you could practice medicine for the sheer sake of medicine," but you omitted the "I was brave" tag. Listening to tales of treachery against the nameless, faceless, and senseless circumstances that surrounded An Hoa's Dr. Tom shamed me for never making the opportunity to know more. Daddy, these men—your colleagues and brothers-in-arms spoke freely. These men—the esteemed members of 2/5 radiated with respect and reverence for you, Doc Tom, for you, Daddy. Pride accompanies the sharing of each vignette.

"Operating Room Nurses Share With Readers Inspiring Reports From Vietnam"
Letter by Mrs. Susan L. Dzubak to *The Herald Statesman*, 1967.

As secretary of the operating room at St. John's Riverside Hospital, I want to tell you first our strong feelings on behalf of those who are fighting to protect our freedoms in Vietnam, second our disgust and distress over those who oppose our United States effort and are even willing to assist the enemy, and third, to share with you a report from the fighting front in Da Nang from one of our former hospital associates, Lt. Gaetano Thomas Viti, a physician who worked with us as an intern before he entered the Marine Corps last November.

We nurses feel that what he has to say is extremely important, and that his experiences carry a serious message that our husbands, sons and friends need the support of the American public as they fight for our freedom—yes, including the freedom that this protestors use when they carry signs or raise their voices in Vietnam demonstrations!

We feel strongly about the need to support our troops, the more so after hearing from Dr. Viti within the last few days.

He tells us about an operation completed by the battalion, "and I was out with them for eight days," he reports. He says the boys did a fine job, and he describes the devastation left behind by the Viet Cong.

"It was really something going through those villages," he relates. "The only people left were children and old women—the men were all gone. But on the third day out they found us.

"You know I am used to getting shot at now, but something happened that left a really bad taste in my mouth.

"We came to this one village and there was this sixteen-year-old boy who was shot up in the leg. So I patched him up.

"Then, in the same village, the battalion ran into a force of Viet Cong. I set up my 'hospital,' and started to work on the wounded. We called in a couple of helicopters to get out the wounded.

"While I was carrying this wounded Marine, someone opens up on my and my casualty—with a carbine. I hit the dirt and carried—or dragged—this boy to the helicopter. I put him on an it took off.

"After about 30 minutes of lying in a rice paddy and saying every prayer I knew, they got the sniper. When I went to look at him, I found he was the sixteen-year-old boy that I had patched up in the morning. If he didn't like my kind of medicine, he could have told me instead of SHOOTING at me!"

"The Viet Cong had all the women and children in front of them, using them as a shield," he informs us, "and the enemy were shooting at the Marines from behind the human barrier."

In such a moment, we can well realize of the indignities heaped upon our fighting men overseas by the antiwar demonstrators here can be really demoralizing!

Lt. Viti puts his reaction in these words:

"Boy it really hurts the morale of our boys to read and hear about the protestors and their marching. Some cannot wait until they get home to begin college.

"I am really waiting to see the change that will take place on our college campuses when these young patriotic boys go back to school!"

We in St. John's operating room are so inspired by Dr. Viti's words that we just could not resist sharing them with you and your readers.

DR. TOM'S WAR

Dr. Viti, his crew of corpsmen and the BAS staff outside of the
An Hoa's BAS, RSVN, 1967.

Dr. Viti in An Hoa, RSVN, 1967.

*Chief Hospital Corpsman Lou
LeGarie:*

Dr. Viti served America, the
Navy, and the Marine Corps with
distinction and valor. He personified
leadership, integrity, and knowledge, while courageously caring
for the young Marines fighting
to defend America. His presence
boosted Marine morale. Hell, they'd
ask for him. Much to the dismay of
the command post, he insisted on
joining as many operations and
patrols as possible. This crazy
battalion surgeon loved to get his
hands in shit. But the CP understood

that his habit of exposing himself while treating combat casualties was a bad idea.

Slackers, although scared of Dr. Viti, whined for no duty chips. "Doc, I have this, I have that, I don't feel well," etc. . . . Marines weren't crazy about operations. Vietnam was a back-and-forth war. Marines held or lost ground and geared up to win or lose it again. It was frustrating. So Dr. Viti held sick call super early—almost too early—on operation day, so if the sick, lame, and lazy didn't make it, too bad.

Dr. Viti boosted corpsmen morale with his bravery and confidence while making his expectations clear. "Don't worry, I'm right here. And I don't want to hear any bitching and moaning. We're here to do a job."

Out of respect, I always called him Dr. Viti. I also made sure he knew everything I did. He was appreciative and told me so. "I appreciate that, Lou. But I'm confident and comfortable with everything that you do for me, the corpsmen, and my Marines."

Dr. Viti had an uncanny talent for triaging casualties. But he'd swear and throw stuff as the wounded and KIA's flooded the BAS. "Those sons of bitches. Those sons of bitches. What did they do to my boys?"

Everyone became a son of a bitch when Dr. Viti got mad.

But Dr. Viti could easily flip his switch. One night under mortar fire, he massaged the heart of a young Marine. He sweated and cursed over this kid for almost an hour before he stopped and cried. Not saving this kid devastated him.

Dr. Viti was tough and *always* ahead of the game. Hell, he'd line Marines up to watch them *swallow* their malaria pills. We, including me, hated the pills because they made us nauseous. He also made sure the BAS was stocked with supplies and support on every level. He even implemented a soup kitchen for Marines recuperating at the BAS.

Dr. Viti assured the Vietnamese villagers that Americans were dedicated to helping *them*. Even the bounty on his head didn't stop him. The Vietnamese dressed in their finest clothes and waited hours to see the "*Bac-si Bac-si*, number-one." The kids would run up to him, rubbing their bellies. "Da Boom, da boom," meaning stomachache, to get the candy and gum lining Dr. Viti's pockets.

Vietnam was Dr. Viti's pig glory. He made decisions without questions. He didn't answer to any son of a bitch; only God. He practiced his love of medicine to save lives, not for political bureaucracy. St. Albans Naval Hospital in Queens, New York, wasn't his cup of tea. I knew he'd tear those people up. And he did. He had to be where the action was, he didn't wait for things to happen, he *made* things happen. Truthfully, he didn't want to leave Vietnam, and we didn't want him to go.

Dr. Viti got so goddamn mad after losing *his* Marines and Lieutenant Paul Bertolozzi on a road sweep, he wouldn't allow *any* Vietnamese into the BAS for days. Nothing would upset him more than losing his "sons." He was beyond sad when he learned that his dear friend, Captain James Graham was killed on Operation Union II.

Dr. Viti got mad, but I only saw him tear ass and scream like a son of a bitch once at his Marines. A blunder could've gotten him, me, and a corpsman killed. He was so goddamn mad I bet they heard him yelling all over Vietnam.

You see, Dr. Viti, me, and a corpsman went to care for Marines reportedly wounded in an ambush. But evidently someone blew the report and the coordinates and sent us on a wild goose chase. We drove, knowing the further we drove, the better our chances were of getting killed or captured. I finally said, "Goddamn it, Dr. Viti, what's going on here? We better pull this jeep around before someone blows our ass out of the sky."

Our own guys saw our vehicle in the middle of nowhere and, thank God, called the COC to check before they shot us. But even the COC didn't know who we were. One Marine finally recognized us. Good thing because friendly fire kills people.

Dr. Viti blew a friggin' fit. He flailed around, ready to deck somebody. There was no chance of calming him down. He kept screaming. "You assholes almost got us killed." I stayed behind when he sought out Major Esau.

A Vietnamese family visited the BAS with a sick infant wrapped with a frog, grass, mud, and rocks. Dr. Viti couldn't believe it. He asked me, "Chief, why is this baby wrapped with a frog?"

"Vietnamese medicine. China has snakes, Vietnam has frogs."

"Medicine? What do they think they're doing?"

"Drawing out toxins and bringing his fever down. You should be grateful, this could be worse."

Dr. Viti didn't understand. So I continued to tease him. "Seriously, it could be chicken manure and bones from who knows where and what." Dr. Viti patiently probed the belching frog lying spread-eagle on the boy. He stared at the frog. I couldn't resist saying, "He likes you, maybe that's why they came, the frog wanted to see you."

"Lou, this frog is goofy, even for a frog."

"These people think this frog will heal this child."

"That's bullshit, this baby's sick with pneumonia."

Dr. Viti tried to grab the slimy creature, but it leapt. He tried and missed again. Now losing his cool, he ran after the leaping frog. "Son of a bitch!"

"Hey, Doctor Viti,' I said. "Be careful, I think they want their frog back."

Dr. Viti kept going. "Son of a bitch. Chief, get this god damn frog out of here. Son of a bitch." Pissed as hell, he chased the frog. The Vietnamese family wailed. He finally caught and threw that son of a bitchin' frog like it was a football. The god damn thing just splat. The family bawled.

"Chief, get these people out of here so we can take care of this kid."

"Sure thing, Doc, but I think they're mad."

"About what?"

"Their frog, sir. They want money for their frog."

"You're kidding me, right?"

"No, Doc, you just killed their medicine."

"Let Civil Affairs take care of this."

Dr. Viti saved the kid, and Civil Affairs paid for the frog. The corpsmen would croak like frogs around the BAS, and Dr. Viti would laugh. I don't think he ever got over that frog. He threw it like a son of a bitch!

On another occasion, a cross-eyed Vietnamese sergeant major complaining of stomach trouble came into the BAS. This guy was so cross-eyed I thought he had a disease. Dr. Viti examined him, diagnosed constipation and ordered him to drink a black-and-white—a mineral oil and herbal root laxative. Since the guy felt so lousy, I dispensed half a canteen instead of the usual one ounce measurement. Dr. Viti thought I was trying to kill the guy, but I wasn't. I knew that quick would work best. Well, believe it or not, this sergeant major came back for more that very afternoon. Dr. Viti was surprised.

"Lou, what are you doing? You can't give him any more, you'll kill him."

"No, no, this stuff's working. It's getting rid of whatever was bothering his stomach. He said he feels great."

This guy came back for the next two days for his medicine. On day three, I walked into the BAS and found him lying on a stretcher, hooked to an IV, dehydrated from using the head. But the best part of my story is that his eyes were straight. Seriously, they weren't crossed. This guy shit his eyes straight!

Dr. Viti promised to put my story in *Reader's Digest* as a new cure for the cross-eyed. Dr. Viti and I laughed and laughed for days.

An Hoa hosted Saigon's high-class engineers who often visited the BAS. Doctor's Viti, Gonder, and Donnelly attended their parties, but I didn't go. After being in China and Korea, I wasn't interested in eating Vietnamese food. Dr. Viti brought bread back.

"Hey, Dr. Viti, what the hell is in this bread?"

"Sesame seeds."

"Hell, I've never seen sesame seeds with legs."

And we'd laugh like hell.

Dr. Viti was famous for cooking spaghetti feasts from canned dehydrated shrimp and tomato gravy in pots and pans he conned from the Vietnamese. He even hung a salami over his little portable stove.

Dr. Viti liked to throw dice in a game called Ships, Captain, and Crew and play baseball and volleyball. The colonel would raise hell because I used volleyball trick shots to confuse the gook engineers. Dr. Viti and Dr. Gonder would laugh like hell. Shit, we had a great time.

Battalion Surgeon Floyd Gonder, MD:

Tom and I worked side by side treating some truly hairy, horrific wounds. He was a skilled and competent physician with a zest for life. That's what it takes to be a good surgeon.

One night, Recon Ranges stationed behind the BAS requested an artillery strike. Soon thereafter choppers arrived with several injured Rangers. One kid's leg was blown open. Blood squirted everywhere. Tom and I jumped on him, clipping hemostats on the arteries to control the bleeding. We started IV's, secured the hemostats, and immediately choppered him to Da Nang. Charlie Med saved the kid's leg. We were surprised because we really thought he'd bleed to death. We learned that friendly fire caused the wound. The wrong coordinates were called in. Damn, that was horrible news.

I emphasize Tom and me as Marines but we were Navy Medical. We were both so honored to serve with the Marine Corps. In Vietnam, Marines worked together as a beautiful symphony to ensure that efficiency overcame stress in the heat of combat. Every Marine had a specific job. They didn't worry about their safety, they just did their jobs. The presence of a battalion surgeon during enemy engagement boosted morale. Marines relished the fact that Tom or I would be on hand, doing everything possible to save lives.

Flying was risky. Dr. Viti and I were very, very cautious. Danger was ever present. We worried about jumping in and out of choppers or just getting blown out of the sky. Since helicopters didn't have armor, some were shot up like Swiss cheese. Tom and I were on several medevacs that got hit but, thank God, no one ever got hurt. It was frightening to see the rounds flying right through the chopper.

On a lighter note, Tom, Dr. Donnelly (the dentist), and I were invited to dinner by the village chief after a MedCAP/DentCAP. Vietnamese dining was an experience. Mammasan would catch a chicken, cut its throat, and let it bleed into a cup until the animal bled to death. The chicken was roasted over an open fire, and the blood was served as sauce. Although it was always a bit raw, we weren't about to not eat their food or drink their homemade rice wine. An invitation was such an honor. Tom and Joe didn't know how they made their rice wine, but I did.

"Do you know how they make their rice wine?" I asked. "The Vietnamese women sit in a circle, chew the rice to a pulp, and spit it into a container that is passed around. The spit pulp is mixed with water and special ingredients to raise the sugar content and left to ferment in a vat. That mixture is then grounded and filtered to clear excess debris."

Joe was shocked. "You're making that up."

I assured him, "No, I'm not."

"Shit, Flip, I extract their teeth—their dirty, rotten teeth filled with bacteria and fungus. They can't just spit it out like that. Do they clean their mouths before they chew it?"

"*You* extract their dirty, rotten teeth. Do you think they clean their mouths? Look at it this way . . ."

Joe couldn't help it. "That's disgusting and that's the only way to look at it."

Joe cringed. We were invited to dinner because Joe extracted the teeth of several people living in the house. Tom couldn't resist. He stood, boisterously toasting Joe, which forced Joe to lift his glass and drink. I thought Joe was going to die drinking that wine.

Fleet Marine Force Corpsman Roger Ware:
Dr. Viti walked in the footsteps of 2/5, the most decorated battalion in Marine Corps history. He was vigorous, tireless, enthusiastic, and willing to go the extra mile for everyone. Add funny, warm, friendly, compassionate, and interesting to that list. Every 2/5 corpsman would have followed Dr. Viti *anywhere.*

Dr. Viti and Chief Lou LeGarie—Dr. Viti's shot in the arm—streamlined the BAS standard operating procedures to offer the best care, regardless of the illness or injury. Anything less was unacceptable. They counseled newbies one-on-one to prepare them for their impending, hair-raising combat experience while raising the morale of experienced corpsmen who questioned their qualifications. It was hard to stay upbeat when corpsmen were maimed and blown to pieces, but Dr. Viti's door was always open for discussion. He told every corpsman, "Guys, when you're in An Hoa come to medical, let's talk, let's see what's going on and how we can help."

Although Dr. Viti stressed over the atrocious nature of war wounds—one can't imagine the flesh devastation from gunshots, heavy artillery, mines, or booby traps—he never criticized the system; never. We'd be torn apart, surrounded by chaos, with no equipment and short on supplies, and good ol' Dr. Viti worked without complaining.

Vietnam was real and immediate. Corpsmen instinctively reacted.

Dr. Viti and I would share a smoke while discussing the WIA's and KIA's and the devastation it would cause generations of families; or the amputees, now wards of the government, and how their injuries would forever affect them. These guys would never be the same. We hoped we made a difference.

Dr. Viti was a private person who controlled his fear. Heck, he knew if he lost control, panic would spread like wildfire among the corpsmen. His dignity and levelheadedness instilled confidence. He led by example despite his overwhelming responsibilities. Dr. Viti was truly loved.

One night a helo dropped off a corpse devastated by a heavy artillery shell. The head, limbs, and half of the chest wall were gone. The body was a half a trunk and a rib cage. It looked like a flak jacket stuffed with straw and shreds of flesh. I placed him on the ground and waited for a litter. Dr. Viti ran from the BAS mad as heck, screaming, "Get him off the ground, get him the fuck off the ground! Goddamn it, get him up!"

But I had nothing to put him on. It wasn't my intention to be cold or bitter. But Dr. Viti refused the excuse; we were to respect our men, our boys.

We held him up and placed him gently on the litter into a body bag and sent him to Graves.

Dr. Viti screamed out of frustration. This Marine was our son, and Dr. Viti couldn't help him, despite his medical knowledge and training. He, as we, felt so utterly helpless.

Dr. Viti interjected humor into his daily routine, telling stories about New York, spaghetti, and the mafia. He'd play basketball that was more tackle than basketball and threw horseshoes with the corpsmen to relieve stress. It didn't matter that he cheated. We loved playing with him. It was a great way to unwind. Since I was a one-hundred-and-fifteen-pound, skinny, bowlegged runt, the go-to guy, Dr. Viti and I lifted weights to get buff. He arrived chunky but like many of us, lost weight and muscled-up.

Dr. Viti often said that the Mafia could come to Vietnam and take care of the enemy in no time.

Dr. Viti taught me how to suture with my hands instead of using instruments. He'd laugh. "Someday, Country, you'll be as fast as me." It's a really nice memory.

Dr. Viti chain smoked; cigarette after cigarette after cigarette. I hid mine because he'd bum them. "Hey, Roger, give me a smoke."

"Sorry, Doc, I ain't got none. Smoked the last one about an hour ago."

"Country, you're lying. Give me a smoke."

"All right, Doc. Here you go."

Lucia, include this in your book.

An Hoa's Battalion Aid Station was infamous for being the most squared away medical aid station in the Marine Corps' First Division. An Hoa's BAS set the gold standards as the dog and pony show for visiting generals, dignitaries, and VIP's. The BAS was always tidy, manicured, and raked. Our I's were dotted and our T's were crossed.

The regimental and division surgeon used 2/5's BAS as a model for other Battalion Aid Stations. Lt. General Krulak, the commanding general of the Marine Fleet Force Pacific, toured medical with staff officers, the colonel, Dr. Viti, and Chief LeGarie.

Lt. General Krulak shook Chief Lou's hand, laughing. "Hey, Doc, what the hell are you doing down here?"

"Well, General, I'm keeping An Hoa's medical squared away."

"It certainly looks like that."

Chief LeGarie warned us that Lt. General Krulak, nicknamed the "Brute" was short, so we had to look up to him, otherwise he'd have our ass. The Brute always wore sunglasses, but he'd know how high our eyes were. Dr. Viti and Lt. General Krulak chit-chatted. "General, this is what we use for, this is our ward."

The general would nod his head in approval. "Very impressive, nice location, good flow."

Other visiting generals and VIP's included the Marine Corps commandant,

General Wallace Greene; the Navy surgeon general, Vice Admiral Brown; Lt. General Lew Walt; Lt. General McMasters; Major General Robertson; and Generals Nickerson and Masterson. That's quite an impressive list.

Lance Corporal Brenton MacKinnon:

An Hoa's BAS was my first stop from the medevac chopper due to a rat bite at Phu Lac (6). The BAS was Dr. Viti's kingdom. Dr. Viti's official persona inspired confidence and relief to those minutes away from his magic fingers.

I was relieved to know the painful intramuscular, rabies injections were replaced by a duck embryo, a subcutaneous serum that didn't hurt. I had a two-week protocol of daily circular stomach injections patterned from noon to six o'clock and nine o'clock to three o'clock. Dr. Viti gave me the first code of injections while showing a corpsman, who then assumed the job. For the day's remaining twenty-three hours and forty-five minutes, I was assigned to the BAS to carry litters from helicopters; escort the wounded from the perimeter and the rocket pad; and to aid Dr. Viti and his corpsmen during triage and surgery.

I watched Dr. Viti administer to dozens of ill and wounded Marines and Vietnamese. Ailments varied from a simple stitching to death. In every instance, regardless of whom, an officer, a hysterical seventeen-year-old enlisted Marine, a Vietnamese villager, an ARVN soldier, or a POW, Dr. Viti treated each with compassionate energy and authority.

While standing perimeter guard duty one night, a commotion erupted in the adjacent fighting hole. The animal-like howling shrieked so incredibly, I thought a Marine had been set on fire. NCO Masterson (not real name) asked me to escort this hysterical PFC as a *hostile* prisoner to the BAS. I obliged. We were all cynics by then.

The nineteen-year-old unwounded Marine was thought to be having a mental breakdown or fabricating one to relieve himself from combat duty. This kid wailed, "I can't take it anymore; all of my friends are dead. I'm not going to make it to the end of my rotation. I won't make it home alive. My mother will be left alone. I'm going to kill myself . . ." and on and on *and* on.

Although we interrupted Dr. Viti's rare opportunity to sleep, he was unruffled and cheerful, which I found amazing at two a.m. He ordered the young Marine released to his custody. But Masterson was afraid to leave Dr. Viti alone in a potentially violent situation. We not only needed Dr. Viti, we worshipped him. So we stood while Dr. Viti transitioned from medical physician to psychiatrist as he assured the Marine that he'd be re-assigned to the BAS for proper evaluation so he could appropriately deal with his concerns. Watching Dr. Viti alleviated our prejudice. He demonstrated compassionate grace, helping this broken man regain his equilibrium in the midst of chaos. Masterson and I resumed our assigned tasks, grateful we weren't falling apart or so stressed we needed to pretend.

Coconut wireless was immediate and spontaneous. By morning, An Hoa Marines knew this PFC had endured or faked a breakdown. Responses varied. This kid shrieked our private thoughts. Was he authentically seeking help or pretending? We never found out.

But that didn't matter to Dr. Viti. He demonstrated the same respect and compassion to that Marine he would have given to one wounded by shrapnel.

Navy Chaplain Delbert Von Almen:

I was the Protestant chaplain. Dr. Tom Viti, a Catholic, often led mass as a lay leader in the absence of a chaplain. Tom's dedication to God was admirable.

Dr. Tom Viti and I both administered to the wounded at the BAS. After one massive and lengthy operation, Dr. Tom examined a fatally wounded eighteen-year-old Marine and with a heavy heart said, "Chaplain, he's for you." I held the boy's hand as Tom continued to the next stretcher. This young Marine whispered, "Chaplain, I'm too young to die." He said nothing else. He breathed no more. I lifted the boy up to God. I asked the good Lord to be with his mother and father who not yet knew of their son's death in Vietnam.

Lieutenant James Meyers:

Children walked up to Dr. Viti with both hands amputated wearing signs that read, "This too will happen to you if you cooperate with Marines." Dr. Viti understood the atrocities perpetuated by the enemy.

I lay witness to Dr. Tom's passionate efforts at saving the life of a young Marine crushed under a truck. He screamed, cursed, and smacked this kid. "Don't leave me, don't leave me. C'mon, big guy, stay with me, don't you leave me. Son of a bitch. C'mon, son, *don't leave me.*"

Dr. Viti rampaged through a gambit of emotions when he lost that Marine. His battles were fought between the life and death of the wounded. Tom Viti was the director in keeping these men, his Marine sons, on the road to life.

I'd tease Dr. Viti about hairy tarantellas living in banana trees. He was all over bananas because they helped with dysentery but we really made him nervous.

We built an open shower with a cement deck behind An Hoa's M building. Although the water was cold, it was nonetheless a *shower.* One afternoon as three of us scrubbed and sang our hearts out we heard, *karpow!*

We froze at the familiar sound. Could a sniper really be lying belly-flat, taking pot shots while we showered?

Karpow!

I tried to determine the genesis of bullet's direction but as the next one hit the building I yelled, "Fellas, shower's over!"

Dr. Tom's retort. "Well, obviously the enemy doesn't like your singing."

Tom spoke of his family in revered tones. Oftentimes, we'd read passages from letters aloud and laugh or listen quietly to the reverberation of the comment, allowing our minds to complete vivid pictures portrayed by the spoken word.

Doctor Tom never missed the opportunity to make us laugh. During a Christmastime firefight, his round face popped up with the biggest grin. "Merry F_____g Christmas!" Tom shifted tense moments to the lighter side, reminding us that, "This was but for the moment, because joy comes in the morning."

Private First Class Gary Hilt:
I woke up one evening violently ill, stumbled to the outhouse, and passed out. I spent four days at the BAS suffering from a severe bout of dysentery. Dr. Viti administered Compazine shots to stop the vomiting, meds to plug my bowels plus a shot glass filled with a wonderful brown liquid that tasted like Brandy. I was too weak to walk to the crapper so the corpsmen carried me. I painfully cried for my mother to their jeers. "Oh, the big Marine is crying for his mommy."

Dr. Viti would never have tolerated such behavior—had he known. Dr. Tom, a kind and compassionate officer, treated *everyone* with respect and integrity. His efforts at the BAS were interesting, wonderful, and heart-wrenching.

Dr. Viti was always cool and collected despite the constant commotion at the BAS. I watched him care for a little, bitty six-month-old baby that had been shot in the ankle. I could see the ankle socket dangling from the baby's leg. Dr. Viti gingerly picked up the baby's calf, and his foot all but fell off. Although the parents were hysterical, Dr. Viti didn't freak out. He saved the baby but not his foot.

Lieutenant William Harvey:
The lethal sharp edges of elephant grass lacerated my arms from the top of my flak jacket to my finger tips. The lacerations became infections that wouldn't scab. Dr. Viti poured antiseptic on a steel brush and scrubbed the sores until I bled. I was grateful he joked during this draconian cleansing process because it hurt. He wrapped both arms with gauze and sent me walking. I healed within days. It *was* strange, but it worked. I still have the scars.

Dr. Viti was a man of quick reaction. The corpsmen thought the world of him. A battalion surgeon in a war environment is a leader *and* a practitioner. Between the BAS staff and his field corpsmen, He commanded over one hundred Navy personnel. That's not a little job.

Although I complained to Dr. Viti about several new and terrified corpsmen, he didn't agree with me about shit-canning these guys. And since I was a snotnosed second lieutenant, and Dr. Viti was a higher-ranking, well-respected Navy lieutenant it was, "Yes, sir, no, sir." I expected corpsmen to perform accordingly as Marines but Dr. Viti knew to give them time. And after time, most of them came around.

Private First Class Bill Patton:

Dr. Viti treated me for immersion foot. After the medicated salve and shots of penicillin—administered three times a day—failed, he scrubbed and polished my open sores with a scrub brush saturated in Clorox. Yes, it was painful but it healed in days.

Captain Michael Downs:

Dr. Viti and Chief LeGarie treated Marines affected by Vietnam's heat and humidity by running them—when they were healthy—around the airstrip in flak jackets and helmets to acclimatize them. Dr. Viti and Chief LeGarie also established a collecting and clearing surgical shock trauma center in An Hoa that provided the wounded a greater chance of living. Here, Dr. Viti slit open the chest of a wounded Marine, massaged his heart and as far as I know, saved his life.

One physically impressive Marine lieutenant medevaced himself to An Hoa during a raging outpost field battle. Dr. Viti questioned the visibly unwounded officer strolling off the medevac. His response to the lieutenant's floozy excuse was everything but congratulatory. Dr. Viti didn't fare well with malingerers or stalwarts.

Foxtrot Company had endured several tough engagements before my arrival in the fall of 1967. Dr. Tom requested that Colonel McNaughton remove Fox Company from the active list with an addendum that stated, "If necessary, a medical declaration will preclude the colonel from sending Fox Company." According to Dr. Viti, Fox Company was not physically or psychologically ready for another active engagement. Navy doctors didn't confront battalion commanders. And Dr. Viti didn't consult with me, the company captain, before doing so. I wasn't privy to this information until after all was said and done. Foxtrot remained in An Hoa as the security company during the next operation. Dr. Viti was a man of conviction.

We respected Dr. Viti not only for his medical competence but for his compassion for the well-being of every Marine. He repeatedly sacrificed his own security to administer to the wounded.

Staff Sergeant Tony Marengo:

I watched a bullet spin the helmet of a young Marine three hundred and sixty degrees around his head. I crawled to retrieve him, convinced that when I removed the helmet, the kid's head would be in it. Incredibly, the injury consisted of nothing more than a welt and some broken skin.

While serving as my rear security during an ambush soon thereafter, this kid, fearing it would give away his position, refused to shoot the enemy. He became so nervous, he'd wet his bed. I sent him to Dr. Viti who assured the eighteen-year-old that he had both reason and right to be scared. It was not long before he returned to me and confidently said, "Sarge, I'm all right now. I can go

Dr. Viti outside of An Hoa's BAS, RSVN, January 1967.

Dr. Viti hoisting surgical supplies, An Hoa, RSVN, 1967.

Dr. Viti and his men gearing up for a MedCAP, An Hoa, RSVN, 1967.

Dr. Viti treating children on a MedCAP, RSVN, 1967.

Dr. Viti treating children on a MedCAP, RSVN, 1967.

Newspaper clipping, The Sea Tiger — "Taste it . . . it's good." "Brave but doubtful, this Vietnamese boy closes his eyes as Lt. Gaetano T. Viti spoons out vitamins during a County Fair in Ben Dau hamlet, southwest of Da Nang."

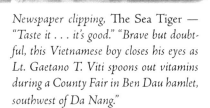

Taste it . . . it's good

Dr. Viti holding a Vietnamese baby suffering from a head fungus common during monsoon season, An Hoa, RSVN, 1967.

Dr. Viti; USN, HM3 Corpsman Roger Ware; USN, HM3 Corpsman Charles Theodovich; and Chief Corpsman Lou Legarie at a MedCAP, 1967.

Medical supplies in an Amtrac. Note the Addam's Family sign on top of the amtrac.

back with my infantry platoon." This kid gallantly distinguished himself as a tremendous and heroic Marine during Operation Union II.

Another Marine kept fainting prior to Operation Newcastle. I called Dr. Viti. "Doc, there's something wrong with this kid, he keeps fainting."

After a quick exam, Dr. Viti bounced him against an amtrac—made of homogenous steel, and let him know under no uncertain terms, "The next time I see you, you better have two bullets in you—not one but two."

The guy froze, nodded, and walked away.

"Geez, Doc, he looked pretty sick to me," I said. "But you're the doc, what's wrong with him?"

"He's scared, but he'll be fine. I told him I'll see him again when he's wounded twice, not once, but twice."

The Marine looked more frightened of Dr. Viti than the enemy. Dr. Viti was as much psychiatrist as he was medical doctor.

Dr. Viti had several run-ins at New York's St. Albans Naval Hospital. Bureaucracy bothered him. Not his patients, certainly not his Marines. Imagine his frustration when dealing with doctors unwilling to extend themselves within the comfortable walls of a Veteran's Hospital. He cold-cocked one doc for complaining about his poor financial compensation after operating on a wounded Marine. Dr. Viti lacked patience for the ignorant who never stepped foot on foreign soil. His life as a battalion surgeon was based on his dedication for the wounded, not for money or show.

During Operation Newcastle as we moved along the Song Thu Bon, an enemy sniper shot knocked three Marines down. We immediately took cover and returned fire. As I lay behind a small hill with my forward observer, Dr. Viti crawled up from the amtrac and peaked over the lid of his helmet with a chirpy, "Hey, Tony, Ya' got the machinetta? Lou sent me some coffee and we can make some Expresso."

We're surrounded by sheer chaos, the shit's hitting the fan, and Dr. Viti's smiling, peering up through the helmet that's covering the better part of his face, talking coffee. I laughed. Dr. Viti's ability to ease tensions under enemy fire was admirable. Of course he was exactly where he wasn't supposed to be at the onset of a full-fledged battle. But he knew that I had wounded.

"Yeah, I have the coffee pot. But Doc, man, you've got to stay back, we'll bring the wounded to you."

Dr. Viti stayed until my wounded were safely evacuated.

On another occasion, Foxtrot Company was stationed at the Nong Son Mountain outpost with Captain Graham. Dr. Viti arrived from An Hoa to check Marines for cysts, sores, cuts, and open wounds. He carried a case of C rations off the helo.

Captain Graham asked, "Hey, Doc, we have plenty of food up here, why did you bring C rats?"

"Oh, this is just a little extra for my Marines."

"Well, I'll get someone to carry that for you."

"Oh that's okay, I'll take care of it."

"Hey, no problem, I'll call one of the boys."

"No thank you. I'm fine. Please, don't let me interrupt you."

"Okay, Doc, it's all yours."

Dr. Viti was really carrying a case of beer. He knew Captain Graham was a religious man who didn't smoke, drink, or curse. Tom knew the beer would be a real treat for us without Captain Graham having to know a thing.

Dr. Viti knew that Fox Company didn't get much relief from never-ending patrols, operations, or defensive positions established in An Hoa or Con Thien. So he worked with Lt. Colonel Jackson to make sure we went to China Beach on R & R. I was shocked when he said, "Hey, Tony, you're going to China Beach for a little R & R."

"What do you mean, Doc?"

"You're on your way to China Beach for a little rest and relaxation."

"Should I assume you had something to do with it?"

"I showed Lt. Colonel Jackson I meant business with my salt and pepper shakers at the chow hall."

"You did what?"

"I asked Lt. Colonel Jackson if he thought I was a better tactician or physician by using the salt and pepper shakers as my props."

"You've lost me," I said. "I'm not sure how salt and pepper shakers follow tactics and medicine."

"Funny, that's what Jackson said," Dr. Viti said. "I shuffled the shakers around the table in dramatic display of moving Hotel Company here, Golf here, throw in Echo and Fox over here, and confused the crap out of him. 'Okay, Lt. Colonel Jackson, I won't pretend tactics, so don't pretend medicine. Fox Company needs a break, send them to China Beach.'"

I couldn't believe what Tom was saying. "Is this some kind of a joke?"

"No. Go enjoy and don't get into too much trouble."

Captain Patrick Blessing:

Dr. Viti endured many horrifying incidents. One of my lieutenants tripped a booby trap and lost both legs and one arm. Dr. Viti saved his life. This Marine, my friend, is alive today because of Dr. Viti.

Captain Dan Powers:

Dr. Viti was a congenial Brooklyn New Yorker who knew how to separate the cheap shit from the cream. He was easygoing, unpretentious, and well-respected as both an officer and a physician. He joined the companies on many battalion-sized operations. A battalion surgeon was crucial. He took risks that other surgeons didn't simply by exposing himself. The boys loved the fact that he rubbed elbows with them in the weeds. his presence was a great comfort to us all.

Name Withheld:

Dr. Viti and I were the real players. The Vietnam War separated the haves and have nots. If you didn't have the passion for a gig like Dr. Viti's, it showed. I have many bright, articulate, wealthy, professional friends that could've gone to Vietnam but didn't. Most feigned medical shortcomings. They're not worth shit as people. I wouldn't count on them for anything. The firemen who died on the stairwell in the Towers on 9/11 were the real deal. Dr. Viti would have done that. The Marines were his family.

Sergeant John Culbertson:

Dr. Viti was a true patriot who worked triple overtime under an incredible amount of stress, passionately caring for Marines as though they were his children. Helicopters retrieved bodies like meat delivery trucks and dumped them on Dr. Viti at the BAS. He worked tirelessly to keep those guys alive. No other medical practice is more traumatic, demanding, painful, or difficult. It's just a fact. Dr. Viti was remarkable.

During Operation Tuscaloosa, seventeen Marines were KIA and fifty-two were WIA. The dead and wounded were choppered to the BAS. And pardon my expression, but there wasn't time to fuck around. Everything was horrific and immediate. How can anyone expect someone to function under such incredible burden and ravage without having a piece of your soul torn out? And yet, Dr. Viti patched up young Marines thrown into the meat grinder of battle day after day after day; *and* treated Vietnamese civilians and soldiers. Although there was never a doubt of whom Dr. Viti worked for and who his boys were.

Dr. Viti chose the harsh reality of war to live on the dark side of critical care medicine and perform a thankless job in the brutal pit of necessity. And he didn't pussy foot around with fakers. He knew the difference between the truth and horseshit.

I wrote several books on the Vietnam War because of America's misconception of the Vietnam veteran as a drug addict, rapist, and baby killer. Vietnam was filled with heroes like Dr. Viti, men genuinely concerned with the welfare of others. I'm proud to be a Marine. I was surrounded by good men who shared a brotherhood. I received three Purple Hearts in seven months. And yet, women in the U.S. spat on me. I became disillusioned with Americans. I hated many civilians. I believed and fought for America's ideal of freedom, and America turned her back on me, on us. A majority of Vietnam's conscientious objectors sidestepped Vietnam because of cowardice, not lofty principles. I never believed that the hippies and dope smokers were legitimately concerned with the loss of American lives. These hoodlums picked a Vietnam moral high ground because their ass was on the line.

Dr. Viti was ever present during hurricane forces and uncontrollable sandstorms of tragedy, fixing what he couldn't prevent. What hollow place did he have to make sure his skin wasn't torn off? The good that came from the

Vietnam War did so from men like Dr. Viti whose heroism is characterized by their display of love for their fellow man. He practiced medicine for the love of humanity, not for the love of money. He couldn't prevent tragedy, he could only save lives. It's absolutely heroic that he maintained his sanity to care, nurture, and love his patients in the chaos of war. He aspired to a higher calling, and so must we.

Think about it, Lucia. Your father dealt with a mix from the blender of death and destruction. It wasn't pretty. His psychological imprint was negative and painful. It's like having a starfish grasp your face until you can't breathe. So you pry off each leg, one by one, until you *can* breathe. Dr. Viti did just that by giving his Marines and the people of South Vietnam his very best. Isn't that the best anyone can ever do?

I'm proud of your dad, Lucia. And I'm proud of you.

Private First Class Bill Gavin:

Lucia, your father saved more Marines than you'll ever know. Dr. Viti was revered because of his daily, merciful care given to his wounded. He treated my knee, infected and swollen like a basketball, from rusty, barbed wire scratches. Above all, I remember his kindness and courtesy.

Lucia, include this in your book. Dr. Viti, Vietnam's battalion surgeons, and Navy corpsmen dealt with the utmost horrors of war. These heroes tended to every conceivable wound, from fingers sliced by jungle brush to a deadly sucking chest wound. Marines revered doctors and corpsmen. A Marine would do anything—*anything* for Dr. Viti and their platoon corpsmen. I'm sure if he was alive today, you'd see firsthand the reverence bestowed upon him as one of the finest men to ever wear jungle boots.

Major Luke Youngman:

The corpsmen held Dr. Viti in high regard. Dr. Viti and Chief LeGarie built an impressive collecting and clearing triage area on the LZ behind the BAS.

Dr. Viti was a force to deal with for those instances deemed inappropriate.

Dr. Vita was a great storyteller, and this is my favorite story. Naval corpsmen established village aid stations to attend to the basic medical and dental needs of the Vietnamese. One enterprising corpsman told Dr. Viti that he removed a frog and leech draped around the throat of an elder village woman.

"You did what?" Dr. Vita asked. "How could you—that was the only thing saving her life. Great, she's probably dead now. You removed her life support!" He pretended to have a complete fit and gave the corpsman quite a scare.

Private First Class Dick Beauchaine:

Dr. Viti examined a pot-stoned Marine complaining of a headache. Disgusted, he ordered the skipper on him. Dr. Viti thought it strange—as we all did—that anyone would feign an illness for a no-duty chip when he just smoked some marijuana.

Dr. Viti did an unbelievable job in chaos you can't imagine.

Captain Gene Bowers and Fleet Marine Force Corpsman Roger Ware:

Late one evening a six-by traveling on a muddy, narrow, and precipitous road along the Song Thu Bon, slipped and overturned down a ravine. As the truck's rear wheels made a shallow turn on the man-made switchback, it flipped and crushed several Marines. Those not ejected couldn't avoid the truck landing on their chests. We lifted the truck, crawled under, and pulled them out. Since we were less than two miles from medical, Dr. Viti and his staff quickly arrived.

Captain Gene Bowers:

I watched Dr. Viti foot from one Marine to another, wiping mud, vomit, blood, and pink froth from their faces before administering mouth-to-mouth resuscitation. His demeanor was one of total concentration and mild panic, although I could see the tears streaming down his cheeks. Those young Marines suffocated under that truck. Dr. Viti couldn't save a single soul.

Fleet Marine Force Corpsman Roger Ware:

Dr. Viti, Chief LeGarie, me, and three corpsmen tended to everyone, including the dead. These Marines were so badly mangled. Dr. Viti was frustrated and overwhelmed by the traumatic crush injuries. His Italian blood was boiling mad so he cussed and cussed and cussed. I know. I was next to him. It was horrible. Everyone injured died. The ejected Marines weren't even hurt.

Captain Gene Bowers:

Dr. Viti wasn't afraid to put his hand on your shoulder and look you square in the eye. On one occasion, as I carried casualties into the BAS, I witnessed him stick his finger into a bullet hole in the chest of a young wounded Marine to stop the bleeding. And he did just that.

Dr. Tom dealt with tragedy day after day after day.

I was in the BAS when he cared for a female Vietnamese laborer whose legs were shredded by a tractor blade. A bulldozer working next to the fence got caught in the wire. The driver backed the dozer—unknowingly—over the Vietnamese lady's legs and crushed them below the femurs. As Tom reached for a compress, she raised her legs and I could see her horror at the sight of nothing but ivory bones. It was terrible.

Dr. Viti with Vietnamese children, An Hoa, RSVN, 1967.

Dr. Viti with Vietnamese children, An Hoa, RSVN, 1967.

Dr. Viti, and 'Ba' in An Hoa, RSVN, 1967.

Fleet Marine Force Corpsman Roger Ware:

Dr. Viti and I ultimately had to amputate her legs below the femurs. Dr. Viti was adamant she go to Da Nang. So the woman's family brought everyone and everything—animals and baskets of their belongings—to the BAS to go with her. Dr. Viti ordered, "Only one person goes and no belongings." The family argued until a decision was made. The scene was super stressful.

S1 Adjunct Lou Orlando:

I watched Dr. Viti open up a Marine wounded by shrapnel and massage his heart. Dr. Viti, a Marine's Marine, was an incredible surgeon; just incredible.

There's a famous story about several Marines complaining of night blindness for a no-duty chip. So Dr. Viti lined them up in front of the BAS, ordered them drop their draws, and kicked their asses as their medical treatment.

Name Withheld:

My greatest memory of Dr. Viti comes from a time I thought my world had fallen apart. I opened a Dear John letter, the rue of many military men whose wives, unable to cope with war, needed to live a normal life in a relationship with someone else. Dr. Viti wrestled me from my pity party. He focused me on God's purpose of being the best I could be in this place, at this time. Tom Viti rendered me back to life to lead, fight, and survive another day. I believe that God used Tom Viti as His instrument to save this Marine who walked among the wounded.

I cherished Dr. Viti. We all did. Now remember, Lucia, a great part of him lives on in you.

Fleet Marine Force Corpsman Dennis Noah:

Captain James Graham's death, Foxtrot's company commander during Operation Union II, was a tough blow. I met Captain Graham—all Marine and genuinely kind—at the BAS. Hotel Company helped retrieve the dead for Operation Union II. The horrific loss of life was unimaginable. Dr. Viti was devastated by the loss of Captain Graham. Everyone knew the two were friends.

Boyhood Friend Ronald Bushemi:

During one hellish episode, sniper fire wounded a corpsman as he boarded a chopper. The kid was down. Under fire, Tom jumped from the helicopter and dragged him back. God only knows how many lives Tom saved. But that was Dr. Tom. He spoke of his Vietnam adventures that amounted to nothing more than risky behavior to rescue wounded Marines. I thought he was nuts. I would write to him and ask, "Why are you doing this?"

His response. "Ronnie, I'm responsible for the welfare of these men. I'm committed to saving their lives."

Gunnery Sergeant Sam Jones, USMC, Dr. Viti, and Dr. Floyd, 'Flip' Gonder, USN.

Tom was a hero in every sense of the word.

Tom dove head first into a crowded foxhole during his first mortar attack and casually lit a cigarette as the others stared in disbelief. When the fire ceased one officer commented, "Geez, Doc, you are the coolest individual I've ever met."

"Oh yeah, thanks."

He later told me, "Cool nothing, I was shitting in my pants. I lit a cigarette because I was so nervous, I didn't know what else to do."

Tom happened to be sitting in the shitter during one mortar attack. Afraid to expose himself, he stayed there peering through the wall cracks. But since there was nothing he could do, he sat until the attack ended. And of course, he made a joke out of the entire scene.

Lt. General Victor H. "Brute" Krulak:

Dr. Viti was warm, professional, and concerned with his business. He was surrounded by children in An Hoa—the Vietnamese kids loved him. American doctors and corpsmen did more than America ever gave them credit for. Their many acts of compassion have never been recorded. Did you know surgeons even repaired cleft lips and disfigurements during County Fairs? Not only was this a tremendous contribution to that individual's adult life, but that individual was totally committed thereafter. When you made a child well, not only did the child love you, so did the parents.

Marines and sailors didn't say, "I'm here to change their hearts and minds."

They said, "I'm here to do what's right."

Dr. Viti looks good in these pictures, but I don't think anybody enjoyed their work in Vietnam. Anybody, anybody, anybody. Remember it was dangerous twenty-four hours a day. And it was a full-time job for Dr. Viti.

*Dr. Viti and the Engineers
of An Hoa's Industrial Complex,
An Hoa, RSVN, 1967.*

*Staff Sergeant Anthony Marango
and Dr. Viti, enjoying spaghetti in
An Hoa, RSVN, 1967.*

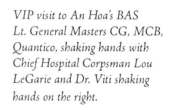

*VIP visit to An Hoa's BAS
Lt. General Masters CG, MCB,
Quantico, shaking hands with
Chief Hospital Corpsman Lou
LeGarie and Dr. Viti shaking
hands on the right.*

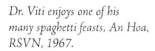

*Dr. Viti enjoys one of his
many spaghetti feasts, An Hoa,
RSVN, 1967.*

Outside of the BAS standing left—name unknown, Dr. J. Donnelly, Dr. Viti, name unknown, Dr. F. Gonder, An Hoa, RSVN, 1967.

FMF Corpsman R. Watson Jr., Dr. Viti, FMF Corpsman Mike Lentz, Dr. Floyd Gonder, FMF Corpsman Frank Heil, FMF Corpsman Charles Theodovich after award ceremony, An Hoa, RSVN, 1967.

Dr. Viti reading the World Journal Tribune with name unknown, RSVN, 1967.

Gunnery Sergeant Sam Jones:

Dr. Viti didn't tolerate bullshit; he was a no BS guy; no BS at all.

One malingerer insisted on constantly reporting to the BAS for sick bay. Excuse the expression, but this PFC deadbeat was a general fuckup that wasn't worth the powder it would take to blow him to hell. Malingering is a court-martial offense.

Well, one time, Dr. Viti sat at his desk in a t-shirt, so this character thought he was talking to a corpsman. But not only was this the battalion surgeon, this was *Dr. Viti*. And he had the gall to ask, "Hey, Doc, how 'bout a no-duty chip so I don't have to go to the field?"

No duty or light duty chips kept Marines from patrols or operations. The jerk-off named the entire list as Dr. Viti calmly rejected every excuse. "No, No, No . . ."

So the kid, thinking he could outsmart the corpsman, said, "Hey, look, I want to see the real doctor."

"I think that's a good idea," Dr. Viti said. "Let me get him, he's sitting at the other desk."

Dr. Viti walked behind a partition separating the two office desks, put on his jacket that showed his bars and medical insignia and yelled for the kid to come in. You can imagine his look of surprise when Dr. Viti yelled, "Get out of here."

This character later played Dr. Viti for night blindness.

Dr. Viti was boiling mad. "Son, what are you doing here?"

"Sir, I can't see."

"What do you mean you can't see?"

"I can't see."

Dr. Viti grabbed him and shoved his fist in his face.

"Oh yeah, can you see that? Gunny Jones, throw this kid on the damn amtrac."

Major Richard H. Esau, Jr., Dr. Viti, Communications Operator Phil Perozzio, USMC, the First LT, S-2 Intel Officer (name unknown), out in the weeds.

We'd be in the field for thirty days at a time with absolutely nothin' so we enjoyed kickin' back in An Hoa; drinkin' and eatin' because tomorrow we could be dead. We bought as much booze as we could from the Da Nang's Air Force Base and An Hoa's Officer's Club. One night, Tony Marengo invited Major Esau and Dr. Viti to his hootch for a spaghetti feast after an official order declared that liquor was not allowed in hootches.

Sergeant Marengo was Mr. Hospitality. "Major, Doctor, would you like a drink?"

"Damn right we'd like a drink."

"Well, get off that footlocker."

"My God, that's quite a stash."

Dr. Viti got so polluted that night they laid him on a stretcher, placed it on a mule, and drove him back to the BAS.

Dr. Viti's father, Dr. Felice Viti wasn't one to fool with. Dr. Viti didn't get no sheltered life of a doctor's son. Dr. Viti senior threatened Tom—before he became a doctor—by making him work as a longshoreman in Brooklyn's dockyard where the facts of life were real plain.

Communications Operator Phil Perozzio:

Dr. Viti was easy to tease. One night when things weren't so hairy the command post conversation had Dr. Viti jittery as Major Esau asked, "Hey, Tom, do you know how the command structure works?"

"Yeah, you are the man in charge."

"That's right, but if I'm wounded or need to leave, you're in charge."

"Me? That can't be right."

"Yes, you, Lieutenant Viti, are second in command and the man in charge."

"C'mon, Rich, I can't be in charge just because I'm a lieutenant."

"If anything happens to me what happens next is your responsibility."

"What if I don't want to be in charge?"

"You have no choice."

Dr. Viti became very serious as Major Esau continued. "Hey, Phil, who's in charge if I'm hurt?"

"Doctor Viti. In fact the last guy to climb the ranks was awarded the Medal of Honor for his bravery. But he unfortunately lost his life. Ahh, life in the service. A company clerk could be the man in charge if there are two privates below him."

"But I'm not a . . . I've never been trained in infantry . . ." Dr. Viti stuttered.

"You don't have a choice," Major Esau said. "You're in charge until someone relieves you. Besides, Phil will help you."

"Sure will." Phil turned to Tom. "Don't worry, the guys know what to do."

"Yeah, Tom, I'm not sure my men will even listen to you," Major Esau said.

"Why?" Dr. Viti asked.

"Because you don't know what the hell you're talking about, that's why."

Dr. Viti was frazzled.

"The officer of the day in the COC could be a lowly-ranking second lieutenant," Major Esau continued, "but he's still in charge. However, if a captain walks in, then he's in charge. If a major walks in, then he's in charge."

"I think I understand."

Major Esau couldn't resist. "I'll give you another example. A ship's captain is sometimes not a captain. Say you have a tug boat, the captain of that ship could be a lieutenant, right?"

Dr. Viti wore this exhausted, priceless stare. "I'm just a country bumpkin doctor, what am I doing here?"

An Hoa's H&S and Communications Personnel always busted chops. Dr. Viti often played along with practical jokes. When Joe went to sick bay for treatment of an infection, we'd give Dr. Viti a heads up. Dr. Viti played the grim reaper well. The kid returned—chin down to his chest—with the devastating news that his infection required immediate evacuation and possible amputation. We faked our sorrow for as long as we could.

MGY Sergeant Delbert E. Turner:

I manned a portion of An Hoa's two-men day, four-men night defensive positions. One early morning sweep I waded through waist-high muddy, muddy mud. It was awful. I was a mess. Returning to my hootch, I cut through the BAS and bumped into Dr. Viti. He eyeballed me and yelled, "Hey, corpsman, up! I need help with this green/red thing. I don't know whether to give him an injection or cut this mud man away with my surgical kit."

From the waist down I was a statue of red, wet, mud, and clay. I couldn't help but smile. "I'm done, Doc. Done." Dr. Viti always found a way to take the edge off.

Commanding Officer H&S Company Al Boccutti:

Dr. Viti was a jolly guy who joked around, finding humor in almost every situation.

Private First Class Steve Zeck:

I met Dr. Viti in An Hoa's BAS because of a through-and-through gunshot wound in my right thigh. He cut, cleaned, and sewed the wound. I spent almost two weeks in An Hoa. He was always jovial. He and the corpsmen took good care of me and kept the beer flowing. The corpsmen loved Dr. Viti, and so did I.

Forward Observer David Wall:

Dr. Viti was as quick with his jokes and wise ass remarks as he was with his smile. We could talk to him *about anything*. I was so terrified once, my heart pounded so fast, I almost passed out. He examined me and literally whacked my ass. "You're more than fine! Get out of here and back with your unit. I have more serious people to deal with than you."

I was truly humbled.

Captain Gene Bowers:

Dr. Viti was the denizen of an Italian opera; boisterous, friendly, full-of-life, and easy to tease. He was not above a sipping of strong spirit. Although this would no longer be politically correct, a black sign of the time read, "POWs never have a nice day." We cut it so it read, "WOPs never have a nice day" and hung it over his bed.

He gloried in that sign.

Private First Class Roger McDowell:

Dr. Viti never had a break. Spare moments didn't exist. Marines were hustled into the BAS with arms and legs blown to pieces or intestines hanging out of their stomachs. His hands were always covered with blood. And through it all, he was so likeable, so down-to-earth.

Dr. Viti was our lifeline. Pure and simple.

A conversation between Lieutenant James Meyers and Battalion Surgeon Floyd Gonder, MD:

"Tom was a fearless and likeable go-getter," Flip said. "I was slightly jealous of him because he was so well-loved, but it was hard not to love him."

"Tom made everyone smile, even under dire circumstances," Jim added.

"Although we never went to the field together—one doctor remained in An Hoa at all times—we worked as a team at the BAS," Flip said. "Everyone, including the enlisted men, was on a first-name basis. Medicine in Vietnam was a rewarding dedication of working together as a family caring for Marines and the Vietnamese. The Vietnamese were *so* appreciative of their medical care."

"Tom built multiple area clinics which swayed public opinion and directly related to a decrease in booby traps," Jim said.

"Because of the care medics provided, the Vietnamese were willing to work with Americans and provide intelligence," Flip added.

"The Marines nicknamed Tom and Flip I and O because of their physical stature," Jim said. "Tom and Flip standing side by side looked like and I and an O. We'd say, 'I and O won many Vietnamese hearts and minds.'"

"Hearts and souls, you might say," Flip said.

"MedCAPs and DentCAPs also worked well," Jim said. "The Vietnamese were cognizant of enemy presence, but since they were going to see the *Bac-si*, *Bac-si* Number One, Americans were forewarned, so we never received fire."

"The Vietnamese walked endless miles to be treated on MedCAPs and DentCAPs," Flip said. "God, a hundred people lined up. It was so rewarding.

"The Vietnamese didn't age well. Fifty-year-old elders looked like they were one hundred years old. Endemically, the middle-age village women had black teeth, horrible abscesses, and gum disease. I don't know if it was related to beetle nut or a lack of dental care. They sat stoically as Joe Donnelly, our dentist, extracted their rotten teeth. Joe taught Tom and me how to extract rotten teeth. Patients were so grateful afterwards, they'd bow. God, their mouths had to be sore."

"Extracted teeth were viewed as badges of honor," Jim added.

"Patients could eat again and live a normal, pain free life," Flip said. "But Dr. Donnelly couldn't hide his expression. Tom and I often teased Joe—who was already jittery, but a great sport."

"Indeed," Jim said. "Joe's expression gave away his poker hand. We'd imitate Joe examining these horrible abscesses. 'Oh . . . ughh, what's going on in here?'"

"Fear was nothing to be ashamed of," Flip said. "Although Tom and I traveled with the security of the command group, the group least likely to get killed, Marines and their M16s couldn't protect us from mortars. I often questioned my survival, especially as my tour geared down. Before operations, I wrote letters to my dad, my mother had passed away while I was in college, and several girlfriends. I would ask Tom or Chief LeGarie to mail them if I happened to be killed. When safely back in An Hoa, I'd get my letters back. Jim, do you remember the medicinal Brandy celebrations after the near escapes and harrowing experiences?"

Jim nodded. "Yes. We'd race to the BAS. Do you remember Tom's Bronze Star ceremony?"

"I had already rotated," Flip said.

"Tom's bronze star ceremony was a day where truth was stranger than fiction and twice as funny," Jim said. "My motor transport Marines escorted Tom as honor guards under fixed bayonets. It was an absolute hoot. And of course he loved it; and marched in wearing a big ol' grin. But truthfully, Tom was embarrassed by his Bronze Star ceremony, humbled by *his* never recognized wounded and dead Marines. But we were proud of him and encouraged him to, 'Stand and step forward to receive this honor because of your men. You need not be embarrassed, you only need to think about what's to follow.'

"A cookout and a priceless tongue and cheek awards ceremony followed the real thing. Chief Lou blew up latex gloves as balloons and our awards ranged from the ridiculous to the sublime. We had pills for old age, dysentery, incontinence, and gave him a beautiful briefcase we bought in Da Nang to use as his lunchbox."

"I bet he loved that," Flip said. "I can just picture his smile."

First Platoon Sergeant Sam Henderson:

Dr. Viti was the most unusual battalion surgeon I'd ever met during my twenty-nine-year Marine Corps career. He accompanied the men in actual combat when he could have stayed at the BAS. One time, he joined Fox Company chasing a regiment of VC. He stopped to examine a Marine and assessed, "Son, you're fine."

"But, sir, my head and stomach hurt. I'm afraid I'm really sick."

"Son, there's nothing wrong with you."

So Dr. Viti threw the kid on top of the amtrac, climbed up with him, and off they went. He stayed by this scared kid, on the amtrac, chasing the bad guys. I have nothing but the utmost respect for Dr. Viti.

Lieutenant Gene Minors:

An Hoa's officer's club saloon was a long hootch with a one-way, L-shaped entry door. The bar sat at the corner end. One night as I sat drinking beer at the table by the door, I saw Dr. Viti sitting at the bar. Suddenly, a friendly artillery round pre-detonated just outside the wire. But we thought it was incoming, so we bolted to the outside bunker. Now remember, Dr. Viti was sitting at the bar—*at the corner end of the saloon*—and I sat by the door. And I guarantee that I bolted through the door, around the corner, and into the bunker without a single soul passing me. But miraculously, there was Dr. Viti drinking his beer. I was shocked.

"Dr. Viti, how did you do that?"

"Experience, son, experience."

To this day, I don't know how he landed in that bunker before me. I even checked for holes in the saloon walls because I couldn't believe it. Dr. Viti *materialized* himself in the wall of the bunker.

Dr. Viti was featured in a New York Times article by Bernard Weinraub entitled "Navy Doctor From the Bronx Is 'No.1' to South Vietnamese Village Children" and published November 27, 1967.

Weinraub followed Dr. Viti to the tiny villages in the fringe of the Marine base camp on his daily rounds. The children scampered after them yelling, ""Bacsi No. 1! Bacsi No. 1!" Dr. Viti, in turn, checked "a child with worms, an old woman with a gashed leg, an infant suffering from malnutrition."

Dr. Viti and a team of medical corpsman "built a series of clinics in nearby villages and constructed a medical-care station for the Second Battalion, Fifth Marine Regiment, about 15 miles south of Danang."

According to Dr. Viti, "We scrounged for everything. Well frankly, we stole."

Dr. Viti and his medical team the women of the village how to suture, take care of wounds and other medical treatments.

Dr. Viti remembered treating a bad gash on the leg of a young Vietnamese man. He worked on the leg for thirty minutes. "An hour later, as the doctor left the village, he came under heavy fire from two snipers, Marine reinforcements rushed into the village and shot the snipers, wounding one and killing the other." Dr. Viti couldn't believe it. "I saw the dead guy and he was the same one I treated."

In a brief moment of peace, Dr. Viti looked back on his time in Vietnam. "In the field the frustration is terrible. A lot of times you can't get them out. Out there you have your two hands and that's it and you just have to work like hell with what you have."

Dr. Viti escorted by honor guard to his Bronze Star with a Combat "V" ceremony An Hoa, RSVN, 1967.

General McNaughton reading Dr. Viti's citation during Bronze Star with a Combat "V" ceremony, An Hoa, RSVN, 1967.

Dr. Viti accepting his Bronze Star with a Combat "V" award in An Hoa, RSVN, 1967.

Dr. Viti's Bronze Star with a Combat "V" party. Gloves were blown up in lieu of balloons. An Hoa, RSVN, 1967.

*Dr. Viti's Bronze Star
with a Combat "V" party.
An Hoa, RSVN, 1967*

*Dr. Viti's Bronze Star with
a Combat "V" party. Chief
Hospital Lou Legarie on right.
An Hoa, RSVN, 1967*

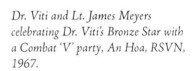

*Dr. Viti and Lt. James Meyers
celebrating Dr. Viti's Bronze Star with
a Combat 'V' party, An Hoa, RSVN,
1967.*

*General McNaughton and Dr.
Viti celebrating Dr. Viti's Bronze
Star with a Combat "V" party,
RSVN, An Hoa, 1967.*

Dr. Viti, RSVN, 1967.

Louise Viti in Hawaii, 1967 posing in a dress purchased in Viet Nam.

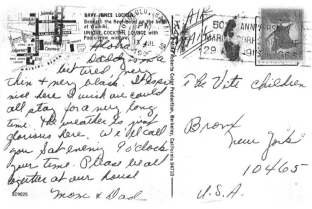

Postcard from Dr. Viti on R & R in Hawaii, July 1967.

Postcard from Louise Viti during R & R in Hawaii, July 1967.

Tom and Louise Viti enjoying
R & R in Hawaii 1967.

Dr. Viti enjoys some R &
R in Hawaii. Note the
exhaustion in his eyes.

THE NEW YORK TIMES, FRIDAY, NOVEMBER 24, 1967

Navy Doctor From the Bronx Is 'No. 1' to South Vietnamese Village Children

By BERNARD WEINRAUB
Special to The New York Times

ANHOA, South Vietnam, Nov. 22—As the jeep crawls through the tiny villages on the fringe of this Marine base camp, the children scamper around the driver and shout: "Bacsi No. 1! Bacsi No. 1!" In their jargon that means the doctor is tops.

The bacsi or doctor, Lieut. Gaetano Thomas Viti of the Bronx, climbs out of the jeep and makes his daily rounds, checking a child with worms, an old woman with a gashed leg, an infant suffering from malnutrition.

"Most of these villages are VC [Vietcong]," the slight, ebullient doctor said, trudging through a dusty street and waving to several old women. "Their sons, their husbands, their fathers are in the VC."

"You learn here that these people have the same fears as anyone else," he said. "They don't want to die either."

Within the last year, the 33-year-old Navy doctor and a team of medical corpsmen, serving with the Marines, have built a series of clinics in nearby villages and constructed a medical-care station for the Second Battalion, Fifth Marine Regiment, about 15 miles south of Danang.

"We scrounged for everything," said Lieutenant Viti

with a smile. "Well, frankly, we stole."

With the help of the Navy Seabees, the doctor and his medics converted a sandbagged amphibious tractor into an operating room for the marines, built a helicopter landing pad for medical evacuees and constructed six wooden buildings that are used for emergency care.

In the villages, the medics taught suturing, the care of wounds and emergency treatment to a dozen women who attend to the women and infants who line up each morning outside thatched-roof shacks built by the Americans.

"I ask them why their husbands are in the VC," said Lieutenant Viti, the father of four children, who was drafted two years ago. "I tell them I don't understand it."

"They always say the same thing," he said. "They always say that we are here to take over their country, to take their rice. I don't get it."

An Incident Last March

Lieutenant Viti's most poignant—and perhaps most poignant—memory of the war arose from an incident last March, when he met a youth whose leg was badly cut. The doctor treated the gash for 30 minutes.

An hour later, as the doctor left the village, he came under heavy fire from two snipers.

Marine reinforcements rushed into the village and shot the snipers, wounding one and killing the other. "I saw the dead guy and he was the same one I treated," said Lieutenant Viti.

The doctor, who will return to his home at 3066 Otis Avenue, in three weeks, sat in front of the battalion aid station and lit one cigarette after another as he quietly discussed his year with the Marines. "In the field the frustration is terrible," he

said. "A lot of times you can't get them out. Out there you have your two hands and that's it and you just work like hell with what you have."

As he spoke, the senior enlisted man among the corpsmen, Chief Lou LeGarie, rushed over to report that helicopters were bringing in casualties—marines who had been riding on a truck that hit a mine.

When they arrived, covered with woolen blankets, the wounded men were carried into the emergency room. Several

winced in pain. Others lay, breathing heavily, with their eyes shut.

"When I take off your shoe, just hold on," Lieutenant Viti told one youth, who bit his lip and stared at the ceiling in silence. "Just hold on. It won't hurt. Walter, write down he had morphine."

Outside, the helicopters continued to bounce onto the landing pad, bringing more wounded. As one moved down, a hospital corpsman, Sam Jacobs of Philadelphia, said angrily: "It

always happens on that same damned road. I got a piece of shrapnel in my ear on that road. I'm deaf in one ear for the rest of my life because I went on that damned road."

The New York Times Newspaper Article, "Navy
Doctor from the Bronx is No.1," by Bernard
Weinraub. Published November 24, 1967.

HEADQUARTERS
2nd Battalion, 5th Marines
1st Marine Division (Rein), FMF
FPO, San Francisco, California, 96602

1/JJH/jjp
20 Jun 1967

From: Commanding Officer
To: Lt G. T. A. VITI 712765/2105 (H&SCo) (12Jul67) USN

Subj: Temporary Additional Duty; orders to

Ref: (a) MARCORMAN, par 1320
        (b) ICCI 1710.3_
        (c) 1710.10_

1. Pursuant to the authority contained in reference (a) and in accordance
with the instructions contained in reference (b) and (c), you are authorized
to proceed to HAWAII on the date indicated opposite your name on temporary
additional duty for a period of about six (6) days in connection with R&R.
YOU WILL NOT LEAVE THE STATE OF HAWAII WHILE IN HAWAII.

2. Upon arrival on R&R, you will check in with the R&R Processing Team which
will meet you as you debark from the aircraft.

3. The uniform for travel aboard R&R aircraft will be the appropriate Summer
Service uniform. Civilian clothing will be worn at all R&R sites except that
the wearing of the military uniform is optional in HAWAII and at Camp Zama, JAPAN.

4. Upon completion of the above temporary additional duty, you will return
to your present station and resume your regular duties.

5. These orders are issued with the understanding that no expense to the
government for travel and or per diem is authorized in the execution of these
orders. If you do not desire to execute these orders without expense to the
government for travel and or per diem, this authorization is revoked and you
will immediately return these orders to this Headquarters.

6. You will have sufficient funds in your possession to defray your expenses
while on R&R. Prior to departing on R&R, you must convert all MPC's to U. S.
dollars or dollar instruments.

7. You will ensure that your Immunization Record is current and carried on
your person at all times. Providing Cholera shots are due, they must be
taken at least six (6) days prior to departing on R&R.

J. J. HORNAK
By direction

Copy to:
Force R&R Section, Danang
CO, 5thMar

CERTIFIED TRUE COPY

USMC

```
HEADQUARTERS
2nd Battalion, 5th Marine
1st Marine Division, REIN, FMF
FPO, San Francisco, Calif. 96602
13, July 1967

FROM: Commanding Officer, 2nd Battalion, 5th Marines
TO:  LT  Gaetano  Thomas  Anthony  VITI,  MC,  USNR,
712765/2105

Subj: Operations; participated in:

Participated in Operation LINCOLN in the Quan Nam
Province, Republic of Vietnam from 5 Jan to 9 Jan 67.

Participated in Operation TUSCALOOSA in the Quan Nam
Province, Republic of Vietnam from 24 Jan to 28 Jan 67.

Participated in Operation INDEPENDENCE in the Quan Nam
Province, Republic of Vietnam from 1 Feb to 9 Feb 67.

Participated in Operation LANOKE from 26 Feb to 28 Feb 67
in the Quan Nam Province, Republic of Vietnam.

Participated in Operation DIXIE from 7 April to 10 April
67 in the Quan Nam Province, Republic of Vietnam.

Participated in Operation NEW CASTLE from 22 March to 25
March 67, in the Quan Nam Province, Republic of Vietnam.

Participated in Operation UNION I from 2 May to 12 May 67
in the Thang Binn Province, Republic of Vietnam.

Participated in Operation UNION II in the Quang Tin
Province, Republic of Vietnam from 2 June to 4 June 67.

Participated in Operation ARIZONA from 14 June to 18 June
67 in the Quan Nam Province, Republic of Vietnam.

Participated in Operation CALHOUN from 24 June to 29 June
67 in the Quan Nam Province, Republic of Vietnam.

Participated in Operation ESSEX from 6 Nov 67 to 17 Nov
67 in the Quan Nam Province, Republic of Vietnam.

Participated in Operation BADGER HUNT/FOSTER from 13 Nov
67 to 28 Nov 67 in the Quan Nam Province, Republic of
Vietnam.

General McNaughton
```

The Sea Tiger, USMC, November 11, 1967

Fifth Regiment Aid Station Aiding Marines and Villagers, Da Nang

The Battalion Aid Station of the 2nd Battalion Fifth Marine Regiment, First Marine Division, is in itself a mammoth operation with practically unlimited capabilities.

Not only is the Aid Station responsible for the medical care and treatment of the battalion's 1200 Marines, but also for the treatment of the local Vietnamese.

In addition, the sanitary conditions of the An Hoa complex and surrounding villa fall under the jurisdiction of the Battalion Aid Station.

The Aid Station's staff also runs six MedCAPs a week in the villages surrounding the Marine Base at An Hoa. Approximately 150 Vietnamese patients are treated on each MedCAP.

When Dr. Gaetano T.A. Viti Lt., USNR, (Bronx, NY) reported to the Second Battalion Fifth Marine Regiment as their Battalion Surgeon, hospital facilities were virtually non-existent.

Originally there were only two buildings; one small one which currently houses the battalions medical records and a sandbagged amphibious tractor which has now been converted into an operating room.

Since Dr. Viti's arrival to the Second Battalion Fifth Marine Regiment, he and his staff have built the Aid Station into a professional medical entity.

The medical complex now contains seven buildings, a helicopter landing pad, and is almost as well equipped as a "stateside" hospital.

The Aid Station has been developed to such a high level of proficiency that it now harbors the facilities to do any type of emergency work that is necessary.

The staff of the Battalion Aid has shown many times how great their capabilities are to treat patients, and what a high degree of thoroughness and professional ability they are able to exert in an emergency situation.

On July 3, 1967, the Marine combat base at An Hoa and the Marine Outpost at Nong Son were attacked simultaneously by the Communists.

Forty-five resulting casualties were treated by the Aid Station. Of these, only one man was lost; a quadruple amputee.

The staff of the BAS works ceaselessly in projects to provide extra comforts for their patients.

Not only do hospitalized Marines receive excellent medical care, but three hot meals daily, cold drinks, and beds with mattresses and clean linen as well.

Chief Hospital-man W.G. LeGarie (Los Angeles, CA) is presently making attempts to get movies and hot water shower for the patients.

Chief LeGarie has served 23 consecutive years with the Marine Corps as a Navy Hospital-man.

In addition to their work in garrison, the BAS also provides medical corpsman to the infantry company of the battalion.

🌺 *Dear Daddy* 🌺

Dr. Tom's War wasn't just our skip down memory lane. It was the walk of every combat Marine veteran that I spoke to. Void of political agenda, unofficial, and attentive, I was trusted from those who expected nothing yet offered everything. There were no illusions, trick questions, or cutesy anecdotes. Raw words filled timeless vignettes reminiscent of harrowing episodes and larger-than-life escapades. Sacred truths blended with spectacle, both celebratory and horrific. Distant memories refusing to fade, cast their shadows across tethered souls. These men, destined by fate, often stripped of their humanity, suffered, sacrificed, and willingly prepared to die for each other. I know of no greater love or nobility. These men won their war. America lost hers.

Daddy, I dare not embrace the remorse shadings to think I understand. And I wish I could tell you that wounds have healed. But I can't. But I can credit America's proper recognition of your brothers-in-arms. America's confused home front matured from hating the war to honoring the warrior. The Vietnam combat veteran once scorched into the American consciousness as the wanderlust drunkard or addict void of ambition has now emerged into a realm of respect. Vietnam combat vets are so cool, men lie just to be one. For those betrayed, a lot too little and even more too late; lives have been forever tainted. This violated silent majority admitted to sharing with me as they do only with other vets; some even shedding light on that which had not been discussed for more than forty years. And every day, it was you, Daddy, that lent his healing hand. The mere mention of your name gave me access to unlock and unfold the reality of survival in a world where the rules forever changed, for little was as it was supposed to be.

Daddy, if you were here to share your tales from this faraway land, oh how I would beg to ask, "How the hell did you, as a physician, maintain your faith in light of its carnage?"

And what do I sense your answer to be?

"Baby doll, shit happens in life. And in war, bad shit happens."

THE FINAL INSPECTION

The soldier stood and faced God,
Which must always come to pass.
He hoped his shoes were shining,
Just as brightly as his brass.

"Step forward now you soldier,
How shall I deal with you?
Have you always turned the other cheek?
To my church have you been true?"

The soldier squared his shoulders and said,
"No, Lord, I guess I ain't.
Because those of us who carry guns
Can't always be a saint.

I've had to work most Sundays,
And at times my talk was tough.
And sometimes I've been violent,
Because the world is awfully rough.

But I never took a penny,
That wasn't mine to keep.
Though I worked a lot of overtime
When the bills just got to steep.

And I never passed a cry for help,
Though at times I shook with fear.
And sometimes, God forgive me,
I've wept unmanly tears.

I know I don't deserve a place,
Among the people here.
They never wanted me around,
Except to calm their fears.

If you've a place for me here, Lord,
It needn't be so grand.
I never expected or had too much,
But if you don't I'll understand."

There was silence all around the throne,
Where the saints had often trod.
And the soldier waited quietly,
For the judgment of his God.
"Step forward now you soldier,
You've borne your burdens well.
Walk peacefully on heavenly streets,
You've done your time in hell."

—Author Unknown

Voices

First To Fight: An Inside View of the U.S. Marine Corps
Lt. General Victor H. "Brute" Krulak

Between 1962 and 1968, I went to Vietnam fifty-four times for periods of five to twenty days. I saw a lot of the country, from the DMZ in the north to the Ca Mau Peninsula in the south. And I saw a lot of the people, from French-speaking dilettantes in Saigon to Moslems at Phan Rang on the seacoast to Montagnards in the hills near the Laos border. As far back as 1963, I went on operations with the Vietnamese Army and the Vietnamese Marines and saw how easily sizeable enemy forces could melt into a countryside willing to support, or at least tolerate, them. Everything I saw kept bringing me back to the basic proposition that the war could be won when the people were protected. If the people were for you, you would triumph in the end. If they were against you, the war would bleed you dry, and you would be defeated.

Sound and logical as it appeared, the Marines' strategy had two defects: General Westmoreland did not agree with it; and it was unable to address the reality that the enemy enjoyed a privileged sanctuary in the ports of North Vietnam and in Laos, through which a growing cascade of deadly munitions was flowing.

But then there was Vietnam. Vietnam, where a whole procession of circumstances stood stubbornly in the way of victory. There were weighty political restraints, problems with our ally, grave, almost decisive, problems with the privileged sanctuary, and broad internal disagreements at home as to strategy and in the field as to tactics. All of these things challenged not just the ability to win but even the will that has so characterized the Marines over the years. It slowly became plain to me that everything that had ever been said about Marines as fighters found its validation there—innovativeness, resolution, obedience, patience, endurance, and the ultimate in raw courage.

How Shakespeare Saved My Life
Lance Corporal Brenton MacKinnon

I found my identity while scanning my editorial assignment on the thematic parallels between the Shakespeare's *Hamlet* and *Julius Caesar*'s Brutus—a draftee for the wrong cause. As I flipped through *Julius Caesar*, I noted Shakespeare's portrayal of ambitious politicians and officers *de corps* whining about who fragged Caesar as honest legionnaires—whose names were never recorded—prepared to die in battle. Shakespeare sure got that part right.

The battle began. Poor intelligence, lousy communications, and tactical blunders coupled with the usual combat chaos had a familiar ring. Shit rolled down the hill for my guy Brutus. Nobody wanted to be taken prisoner. General Cassius—on the verge of being overrun—committed suicide.

Act Five Scene Five Julius Caesar.

The armies of Mark Anthony and Octavius have defeated the legions commanded by the conspirators who assassinated Caesar. Capture is worse than death.

Brutus to Strato: "Thou art a fellow of good respect, thy life hath some smatch of honor in it. Hold then my sword and turn thy face while I do run upon it. Wilt thou Strato?"

Strato to Brutus: "Give me your hand first. Fare you well my lord."

Brutus to Strato: "Farewell good Strato. Caesar now be still. I killed not thee with half so good a will."

Brutus dies.

I froze; thinking of solders aiding the death of friends as an act of love. Could this disjointed reality truly be classic literature read in a suburban classroom? As my eyes surveyed the schoolroom, the circle of desks faded into a dense fog that floated through South Vietnam's Central Highlands. Beneath my feet, the coffee linoleum transformed itself into earthen rice paddies. Maimed and twisted bodies lay scattered like rag dolls, painfully whispering for help.

Final Scene Operation Union II June 2, 1967.

Foxtrot Company 2/5 had been mutilated by NVA superior forces in an open rice paddy. Andy lay shot in the gut. His chance of survival was nil.

Andy to Joe: "Do it, Joe! Please do it! I'm dead anyway. Don't let them hurt me anymore. Please, you must go. If you stay, you will die."

Joe to Andy: "Jesus, Andy, Jesus. Are you crazy? Do you realize what you're asking me to do? Jesuuuuuus, Andy!"

Andy to Joe: "Please, Joe, please."

The enemy could be heard torturing the wounded prior to execution.

Andy to Joe: "Please, Joe. For the love of God, you must do this for me."

Joe to Andy: "Jesus, Andy! Jesus!"

Joe aimed, weeping silently.

Andy to Joe: "Thank you."

One shot is fired.

Joe flees.

The teacher's voice beckoned me back to suburbia. I stumbled through the remainder of the day. I did however sleep that night, uninterrupted, for the first time in years.

⛿

A rat bite saved my life.

I slept solo in a bunker with my radio at Phu Lac (6), an outpost infamous for its rats. Every night, I placed an open can of C rations on the edge of my bunk so the rats could eat their fill and leave me alone. Well, the night before Operation Dixie, exhausted from the day's preparations, I forgot to feed my rats. The pain from a rat biting my left bicep woke me up. Early the next morning, I was medevaced to An Hoa, relieved of my duty as a radio operator assigned to an amtrac flamethrower team. That afternoon, that amtrac hit a mine. Everyone, including the radio operator, was killed. The rat has since become my totem.

Vietnam taught me that life *was* worth living.

While laying hostage to VC sniper fire, certain that death was imminent, I prayed, "Okay, dear whatever and whoever, if there's any meaning to this collective incarnation, let me hear the roar of thunder or see the beauty of a hummingbird. Send me a sign." And of course nothing happened. Freedom soon took hold of my senses. I realized there was nothing but me, lying in a rice paddy dodging bullets. No longer cursed to solve this mystery, I smiled thinking, "Only a fool would've traveled ten thousand miles to get it. It's really what you make it; it's what you think it is." I laughed. And as I did, the firing ceased. I safely walked back to the tree line, feeling lighter than ever. I wanted the big lesson but I got exactly what I needed.

Even though Smith (not real name) and I disliked each other, we always met Fox Company's newbies *together*. Our mutual disdain was as obvious as our differences. I was from California, college-read, articulate, and friendly. Smith was from Alabama with an eighth-grade education, monosyllabic, and moody. But we stood side by side to examine the green Vietnam Marines. We could surmise through body language, gestures, and presence, those who would die quickly, get wounded, or cause another to be wounded or killed. I watched one red-head and asked Smith, "Do you see what I see?"

"Yep."

"Is there anything we can do about this?"

"Nope."

The kid was shot three days later. Smith and I also stuck together during firefights because we were survivors. Two variations of extreme energy attracted enemy chaos. The first was the aggressive, Vietnam-is-my-super-hero-comic-book Marine, who lacked the calm and centered state of mind necessary to assess appropriate behavior. Marines surrounding Joe-hero were collateral damage. His focus to move forward stunted his ability to protect anyone.

The second extreme was the Marine too frightened to return fire or handle crises. Survivors stayed in the middle; nothing too heroic and nothing too cowardly.

Marines surrounded Vietnam's chaos and destruction in black humor which insulated them to the grim reality of being in hell. The expression, "What are they going to do, send me to Nam?" stemmed from any behavior that grunts could be punished for.

Early in my tour, I was a flippant, loquacious, happy-go-lucky, joker. Sergeant Klebert (not real name) disliked me immensely and often verbally confronted me as a phony, incompetent, kiss-ass, college boy. During one patrol, Klebert was positioned fifty yards to my left as we lay seventy-five yards away from our platoon. A bullet tore through a leaf hanging in front of my helmet. The next morning, Klebert's glare assured me that I was the intended target. Divine intervention and the VC interrupted Klebert's plan. A week later he was killed in an ambush.

Rear pogues, indulged with amenities and privileges, were simple squires on another planet to us, the knights. Several days after Operation Union II, I received cookies and bourbon from a California buddy. That night, while watching the radio in the admin shack, I passed out after two sips of bourbon. I was discovered, covered, and left to sleep. I woke up grateful to have *finally* slept a night. The next morning a young, newbie first sergeant called me into the office. "MacKinnon, you missed radio watch last night. Somebody found you asleep. I know you're probably exhausted, especially after what you've been through. Everyone tells me you're a good Marine who's contributed a lot. But I see you as the little kid who stole a watermelon from its patch. The farmer would have given you one, had you asked. But you stole the watermelon because you thought it would taste better."

Despite the obvious, I was more significant in the company than he was. I didn't have to ask him for anything. I could see the clerks trying to contain their laughter.

He continued, "Mac, do you understand what I'm saying?"

My response drew the line between us forever.

"No, Steve (not real name), I don't. I don't even like watermelon."

This boot camp kid knew shit about Vietnam. I knew more than I cared to, so I walked away.

One night as we lay side by side in the bush, filthy and paranoid, a Marine three Marines to my left began howling like an animal set on fire. The kid was suffering a grand mal seizure. We dropped our guards and carried him into the BAS. It surprised me that between boot camp and his Vietnam tenure this ailment wasn't detected.

A sad Vietnam memory is connected to the Mamma's and Pappa's song, "California Dreamin'." I shared my An Hoa hootch with two seventeen-year-old, best-friend Marines assigned to 40mm mortars. They had a battery operated record player and four records, including "California Dreamin'" they played *repeatedly*. It drove me absolutely nuts. Both were killed on Union II. My first day back after Union II, I turned the player on without looking at the record and heard "California Dreamin'." The song reminds me of the friendship and death of the best friends.

As an interpreter for Vietnam's Kit Carson Scouts and Cheiu Hois, I shared many late night conversations. I always asked, "Where are you from, why did you defect, do you think you'll ever go back?" The Vietnamese defected for two reasons, food and intelligence. They were starving and they wanted to survive. Vietnam was stuck in a never-ending war. Many villagers didn't understand communism, and most of the ARVNS were caught in a vertical, political environment fighting for power, money, and control.

I'll never forget this story.

My foot fell through a hollow section of a paddy dyke. Hoisting the radio, I weighed more than the average Marine, so I couldn't pull my leg out. I had to be lifted. Nervous but unscathed, I brushed away muddy soil and leeches. I grubbed a cigarette to burn a leech sucking on my leg, and as I bent down, bullets zoomed through the space that seconds before housed my head. An enemy machine gun lining the ridge, invisible and well-protected, opened his rampage. We bolted to the tree line and called for air strikes. Two A-4's flew in. I stood next to the forward observer as he radioed the fighter jockey on call for the target. "You're all lined up. Pull out of the ridge lines above it." We watched, confident the fighter jock would demolish the enemy machine gun. The plane flew into the machine gun position, but because the pilot was so fixated on his target, he didn't pull the plane up and out and thus crashed and exploded into a huge fireball. It was horrible. Just horrible.

Name Withheld:

There was an unwritten code with medals. "The guys who deserve them don't get them." In Vietnam, a Marine's courageous, daily sacrifice and devotion to his brother-in-arms was ordinary behavior simply unreported up the chain of command.

Corporal Bruce Eells:

Returning to America post-Vietnam was a huge letdown. Although I felt good about protecting my country, I was treated badly. To associate with the military labeled me a "baby killer," fighting an undesired war. The country was sadly, diametrically opposed. There was neither pride nor honor returning from a job America gave me. The Vietnam combat veteran was the red-headed stepchild found in the wrong place, at the wrong time, doing the wrong thing. It was disheartening. Once proud to wear straight utilities as my *only* wardrobe, I was now spat upon and turned away in combat boots and green. It didn't take long to switch to tie-dyes and hippie pants. My fellow Marines and family appreciated me but everyone else cared less.

I harbored psychological wounds. I withdrew, stuffing my emotions deep, deep down. I pursued civilian life as best as I could. I drank to fall sleep. Memories and nightmares became distorted.

I never talk about Vietnam. Everything I've lived these past forty years is about where I stand among my Vietnam memories. That was then and this is now. Nothing I can say or do will change it. I've accepted my past. If I had to do it again, I would. I wouldn't trade the experiences gained from the life I've witnessed. Vietnam gave me an appreciation and understanding of life in all of its hell and glory.

I made a difference in the lives of the Vietnamese people.

One seasoned, invincible, and fearless Marine risked the security of his tree-line position to retrieve water from a nearby well. We laughed, watching him attach his canteen to the well's rope, convinced that the well water was no different from the shit-filled rice paddy water. Within seconds, sniper fire severed his knee. This kid spun like a top to the ground. One limb blew twenty-five yards behind him. We dragged him back to safety. He looked like Jell-O from his hip to his stump. He died within minutes.

Name Withheld:

I returned to a nation deeply divided as neither hero nor patriot. There were no thank you's, homecomings, or celebrations. Many viewed us with loathing and contempt as baby killers, murderers, and rapists. Pride was non-existent. I wasn't even welcome at my local VFW. I launched a lifetime of heavy drinking to suppress feelings of guilt, fear, anger, and loneliness. Vietnam was shared *only* with my fellow Marines. The honor of being a United States Marine was all that I had left.

The chaplain, the rev, ho boy *there* was a study. I'm happy to hear he's still alive. I didn't think he'd survive Vietnam. If he wasn't an alcoholic, I'll eat this table, but if he's ninety-something, that's a strong case for hoisting a highball on a regular basis. The good Reverand served in Korea and volunteered for active duty in Vietnam because he felt it was his calling. His idealism quickly evolved into inconsolable grief at the sight of wounded Marines. He became depressed, often lamenting, "I can't do anything. These choppers come in with terribly wounded kids, and I can't do anything to help them. This is the most terrible thing I've ever seen."

The chaplain visited the XO club early and stayed late every night, drinking hard. It was sad. Here's a guy who's supposed to lift people's spirits but his own were simply shattered. He really made me feel bad.

MGY Sergeant Delbert E. Turner:

The Vietnamese were humble people who lived in war for decades. Homes lacked even the minimum creature comforts. Dirt floor huts lay covered with beds of straw mats. Stoves hoisted an old kettle over an open fire. They ate what they raised—rice, meager vegetables, fish, chicken, and pigs. Owning a water buffalo was like owning a Cadillac.

We evacuated a village in the VC-infiltrated Antenna Valley. The Vietnamese were searched before boarding choppers to ensure that they weren't harboring grenades or weapons. One small elderly Vietnamese woman carried a stick that hoisted a cloth satchel filled with her life's belongings. Within the tiny, frayed purse lay an empty perfume bottle. This minute memory of her worldly possessions as she left the only place she's ever known; this tiny, tiny, empty perfume bottle became my reality. We transformed communities threatened and abused by their own people into refugees.

Combat *is* a sobering reality. It's impossible to deal with the reality of war without experiencing war. If you lose a loved one, you're against the war no matter how justified its purpose may be. To witness the death of your friends is to experience hate, anger, sadness, and frustration. Revenge becomes violence engaged at the enemy. People think that Marines fight for their country, flag, and apple pie, but in the heat of battle, Marines fight for their brothers lining their sides.

I understood Vietnam as a war against communism and the villains of China and Russia. But separating what I know now from what I knew then is a hard dynamic. There was a terrible loss of precious life on both sides. Did we do the right thing?

My flashbacks and dreams are abstract. I visualize Americans and Vietnamese blown apart. Sometimes it's even worse than the actual horror of combat. Different incidences manifest into a single flashback. Drama escalates into chaos. I think I'm going to die. The feeling of not surviving awakens me.

I deal with survivor's remorse, why am I alive? Why them and not me? Why did I come back with both arms and legs? Have I achieved my life's purpose? Have I contributed to society? Have I shown my wife and children enough love?

Boot camp is the paramount gel for molding Marines. Surviving Marine Corps boot camp distinguishes one to wear the eagle, globe, and anchor. The

Marine Corps leadership is standoffish and stern. There's a distinct line between the enlisted, non-commissioned officers, staff non-commissioned officers, and office services. To mature in knowledge and rank and achieve NCO status is a true accomplishment. Marines assume a legacy of tradition and success that becomes a part of who they are. I'm a Marine with a job to do. My mission comes first and then my men. I am the father, and the troops are my sons. Father strives to teach and care for the welfare of his sons. It's the foundation of being a Marine. I am a Marine. I'm not an ex-Marine and never will be. I *am* and always will be a Marine.

The monsoon rains were horrendous. One night I was so drenched and cold, I zipped into a body bag to maintain what little body heat I had left. One battalion sergeant major decided my actions were unprofessional and sent the chaplain to provide guidance. "Son, is this really necessary?"

"With all due respect, chaplain, I'm the guy in the rain all night long while you sleep inside a warm hootch. This may sound callous but the guy who uses this is never going to know I was here."

"Well, son, you have a point."

Name Withheld:

During my first night patrol, my confidence transformed into sheer terror, anger, hatred, and the confusion of what has become a recurring nightmare.

NVA troops were moving through our area. Our platoon was to deploy a strategic ambush or establish an observation location and act accordingly. The intelligence and the orders were vague. "Prepare, advance, see what happens, and do what's necessary."

I had a bad feeling. Everything was pitch black and deathly quiet. Every sound seemed amplified. We reached our checkpoint and discussed who would scout and reconnoiter our final position. The sergeant and corporal decided that since I was too green, I would establish a perimeter and await their return. Passwords were finalized. Within minutes there was a burst of automatic weapons fire followed by pleas for help. Silence. One Marine lay dead; the other severely fucked up. I was ordered to move the men from the hill and hunker down in a secure nearby location. We moved to a lower, concealed position along a rice paddy bank. Within minutes I heard troop movement. The rattling of heavy equipment assured me that those approaching were not friendlies. I hugged the ground, acutely aware of all smells—my sweat, the plants, the shitty paddy water, the equipment, and the enemy. I knew I wasn't going home. Radio orders advised to maintain a defensive position and "Fire only if necessary. Stay hunkered down." Flares illuminated the NVA running for positions between Marine squads. All hell broke loose. The battle lasted all night. Flares, mortars, automatic weapons and "Puff the Magic Dragon" rained hellfire and destruction.

We regrouped at dawn and searched for dead gooks. We found nothing but body parts and blood. Going forward, I felt no fear. I raged to fuck up a gook in my kill zone. Revenge became my mission; killing and mutilation my pleasure; death my satisfaction. I refused friendships. I merely worked with my comrades to accomplish our mission.

We were later informed that the sergeant and corporal were killed by friendly fire from a newbie. I was numb.

On one mission, a point fire team detonated a fatal booby trap. But the explosion didn't just kill, it tore flesh to shreds and left intestines hanging from trees and body parts strewn over a large area. Not much was said as we collected body parts.

On another mission, we were designated as rear echelon clean-up and stepped into a world of shit, which forced us to run for cover through total chaos. We huddled behind a paddy dike along a short, wooded tree line. Clueless and in deep, disorganized trouble, we fired blindly into jungle, mud, dirt, and water as the world detonated around us. I shivered, acutely aware of the sights and smells of what I assumed to be my last day alive. I tried to think of home. I couldn't. I prepared to meet my Maker.

A brand-new-John-Wayne-second-lieutenant-two-weeks-fresh-from-OCS stood, drew his pistol, and insanely ordered us to charge forward. No one did. Within seconds he exploded into the twisted heap of a lifeless body. One Marine bolted forward, firing his M16 over the embankment. Enemy bullets instantly ripped his helmet. Shreds of his face and brains sprayed all over me. Another Marine, now berserk, ranted and fired wildly in all directions including mine. There was no time to think. I shot him.

The battle subsided at dusk. We regrouped, set up a perimeter, and cautiously retrieved our dead. The smell of blood thickened the air. We couldn't reach two Marines due to heavy fire under a lack of concealment. We shot flares and M72 rounds to protect ourselves and the bodies throughout the night. Hidden, the gooks laughed and taunted us. "Marines, you die." I had yet to see a gook much less shoot one. I had shot a fellow Marine. I watched my comrades die. My mind was scrambled. I was only sure I was still alive.

After eating nothing but C rats for weeks, we killed a village duck and cooked it with some rice over a pile of heat tabs. We didn't care that the duck was under-cooked. It was *real* food. I had severe dysentery by the time we reached An Hoa. I couldn't even keep water down. Disregarding my health, I joined a patrol to Liberty Bridge. Needing to shit, yet exhausted, I threw fear and caution to the wind to squat in nearby grass. I felt the wire as I tripped it and heard the dreaded pop. I screamed, "Grenade."

Despite my best efforts to run and drop, I flew through the air. I don't remember landing. I woke up face down with dirt in my eyes, ears, nose, and mouth. I couldn't feel or move, but I wasn't dead. I seared with pain. The corpsman rolled me over. "Don't move." He cut my pants to pinpoint the source of blood flowing in my crotch. I was terrified. Were my male organs blown off? What then would be the purpose of living? Was I crippled? I cried for morphine. Although the corpsman screamed at me, I barely heard him. Was I now deaf? Slowly and painfully I understood; no morphine because of my head wound. My male organs were intact. I could no longer think.

I sat to rest and unknowingly threw my backpack on top of a bouncing Betty. I froze at the sound of its pop. It didn't detonate. I wet my pants.

Gunnery Sergeant Sam Jones:
I'll tell you what I think about Vietnam. I'm a professional Marine. The Marine Corps sent me there to do a job, and I done it. The political part was not my department. I was in Vietnam to be a Marine and take care of my Marines.

Name Withheld:
One Marine committed suicide. Barely five-foot-four, he had trouble keeping up on our humps, marches, and patrols. The NCO's constantly chewed him out, hoping to get him squared away. One afternoon at Nong Son, he placed his M14 on the sling arm, angled it back, and shot himself in the head. It was sad.

Private First Class Gary Hilt:
In An Hoa, fifty-gallon garbage cans were dumped off the back of a truck. Dozens of kids draped whatever they could hold over their heads to catch the poured slop. One day the driver unknowingly backed over and killed a kid. The parents were paid five hundred dollars.

The South Vietnamese Army split when the shit-hit-the-fan.

One multi-vehicle convoy from Nong Son to An Hoa carried four-duece ammo and bad explosives. Because the gooks seemed to have Marines laid out in a sandbox, we wrapped this gorgeous ammo in a tarp. This run was more than familiar. The road cut through a steep, thirty-foot incline with a sheer cliff descent on the mountain's opposite side. We knew it well.

It was hotter than hinges that day. As I leaned on my M14, *boom*. The six-by ahead of us had detonated a mine that blasted a force powerful enough to snap the truck *in half*. Guys flew, rounds spilled, and the truck was on fire. I watched one Marine blown off the stake rack literally burning alive. We didn't know if the four-deuce would explode because of the incredible heat generated by the explosion. I thought, *Geez if any gooks are up that hill, we'll be fragged. Or if there's a gun across the river, we're ruined.*

We had no radio and we had wounded. I knew we had to get to the bottom of this hill. Although the truck was in flames, there was enough room to run between the split, so we did. We ran *through* the burning chassis to the bottom of the hill to get people up and out of the way. We just did what had to be done.

Name Withheld:

War is about killing people and breaking things. The Bible says give to Caesar what belongs to Caesar. Do what the leadership of your country tells you. I never rationalized orders. I followed my orders.

Private First Class Keith Keating:

John Kerry became a Vietnam veteran when it became fashionable for him to do so.

Name Withheld:

The Vietnam War was an honorable cause stifled by Washington, DC politicians and worthless pieces of shit like John Kerry. John Kerry called us war criminals, abandoned his command for pussy wounds of the butt, and claimed himself a hero. I hate John Kerry more than I hate Jane Fonda. And I hate Jane Fonda, Kerry, and his French buddies.

I'm a registered Democrat, but the party of FDR and JFK no longer exists. Democrats are now the bomb-throwing, name-calling, void-of-idea party. Liberal Democrats make me sick. The liberals who say, "I support the warrior but not the war," may as well say, "I support teachers, I just don't like what they teach." It's all so ridiculous.

Private First Class Roger McDowell:

I was awarded a bunch of medals that wouldn't buy a cup of coffee when I landed in San Francisco's airport in December of 1967. Americans demonstrated against everything and anything military. I still harbor resentment. I came home to nothing. Dr. Viti and his corpsmen witnessed so much death and destruction, I don't know how they ever lived a normal life. I still have nightmares. My wife wrestles me awake too many times to count.

I'm proud to be a Marine. I answered America's call to service. I would do the same today.

Private First Class Bill Patton:

I was a nineteen-year-old, ten-foot-tall, bullet-proof, by God U.S. Marine!

When I came back? Oh boy, now I can fill up your tape recorder. I was shocked at the rejection given to Vietnam vets. I returned to a Texas university filled the draft dodgers, peaceniks, and protestors. Hardly a day went by that somebody didn't call me a baby killer. I got kicked out of a government class simply because I was a Vietnam combat veteran.

Early in the second week of a freshman-level government class, while discussing federal aid to education, a grad-student instructor with hair down to his wazoo says, "Mr. Patton, you're a veteran going to school on the GI Bill?"

"Yes, that's correct."

"What makes you think the government should pay for you to go to school? Are you any better than the rest of us?"

"Well, I spent two of the last and best years of my life overseas fighting for this country so the people hiding behind their student deferments—you know the guys with back trouble—the ones with the yellow stripe down it—don't have to go. What's your story?"

"I never served."

"That's what I figured."

"Mr. Patton, this class will be you waste of your time."

"Yes, at least we can both agree on that."

I didn't want to be near that scumbag.

One day while walking across campus with two other veterans—we hung together simply because nobody else wanted to be around us—I passed a long-haired, peace-beaded, hippie-tricky trotting down the sidewalk in a Marine Corps dress blouse with a big peace sign on the back. That outfit lit me like a coal of fire. I snatched him up by the stacking swivel and pressed hard into his face. "Were you in the Marine Corps?"

"Do I look like I kill women and children?"

"You're disgracing the uniform of the United States Marine Corps; my Marine Corps. Take it off!"

"Yeah, yeah."

"You have about five seconds to take it off or I will take it off of you."

"Yeah, right, man! Whatever you say, man, you no good baby killer, murderer . . ."

I beat the living shit out of him. I would've done more damage if my buddies had not yanked me away. But I can assure you, I got that shirt off.

⚑

Lieutenant Mauro (not real name), pardon the expression, was a real shit bird; a basic crap officer nobody liked, including his fellow officers. One miserable monsoon afternoon this idiot called a rifle inspection for Marines recovering in sick bay or those coming and going on R & R. And of course, he jumped down my throat. "Marine, you've got water in the bow of your rifle."

"With all due respect, sir, it's raining."

Dave Moore, our first sergeant, a helluva-guy, went ballistic. Without saying a word he steamed, hauled his freight out the door, and returned with the battalion executive officer who tore Lieutenant Mauro a new you-know-what right in front of the troops. "What in the hell do you mean holding a rifle inspection in the rain with men recovering from battle wounds?"

Lieutenant Mauro was transferred out of An Hoa not soon enough for us.

Lance Corporal Daniel Day:

My Vietnam tour was nothing like Oliver Stone's *Platoon*. I never saw dope. And other than a warm beer in An Hoa, we never drank. We didn't have time for drugs and booze. We were humping in the weeds. And we didn't have any morale problems. We didn't. We just didn't.

Surreal best describes one An Hoa mortar attack. As we hunkered down in slit trenches, a record player blared Sam Cook's "Cupid Draw Back Your Bow" between the silence of the booms.

One explosion burned my USMC bulldog tattoo down to just the "U."

A label sewn into one very well outfitted NVA medical bag read, "From Berkeley California's Peace and Freedom Committee."

Vietnam taught me that I can handle what comes my way. Nothing in civilian life bears resemblance to the sacrifice, endurance, or heart of combat. If I think I'm having a bad day, I remember Vietnam. I volunteered for Vietnam. It *was* the right thing to do. I wasn't bitter about the war. I was upset with the protestors. Finding enemy medical supplies with the notes from Berkeley College sewn on the inside label was disheartening. Marines went through great care and efforts to change the hearts and minds of Vietnamese civilians. And we did. We did.

Staff Sergeant Tony Marengo:

My Marines didn't rape Vietnamese women, smoke heroin, frag officers, or wear ear necklaces. I never lost control of my men. My comrades were true patriotic heroes. How much can one man love another without sexuality? Enough to sacrifice his life for them. And Marines did, regardless of race or creed. Prejudicial animosity didn't exist among my troops. Marines risked their lives for each other. Marines didn't retrieve a black man or a white man, a Mexican, an Indian, a Jew, or a Catholic. Marines retrieved a person.

ANTHONY H. MARENGO
Sergeant Major
U. S. Marine Corps
Vietnam

Silver Star

Other MEDALS-CITATIONS: Bronze Star w/Combat "V", Purple Heart w/2 Stars, Combat Action Ribbon, Navy President Unit w/2 Stars, Good Conduct w/5 Stars, National Defense Service, Vietnam Service w/10 Stars, Vietnam Gallantry Cross Unit w/Palm, Republic of Vietnam Campaign w/Bar, Meritorious Unit Commendation w/4 Stars, Republic of Vietnam Civil Action Unit.

Highly decorated for his bravery in battle, Anthony led his men valiantly.
With respect and love, your family.

Battalion Surgeon Floyd Gonder, MD:

The White Horse Division of the South Korean Army—the ROK's—was fearless and ruthless. During one amtrac patrol we received enemy fire from a distant local village. Despite the AK47 bullets flying *way* over our heads, the ROK's leveled the village. Our CO went nuts but he couldn't stop them.

One ROK, who accidentally shot himself through the foot, came to an afternoon sick bay. I cleaned the wound and administered a penicillin shot. His CO took him out of the back of the BAS and shot him in the head as a lesson to his comrades. "ROK's don't leave Vietnam by shooting themselves in the foot."

🖈

Steaks were served as lunch on my R & R flight to Hong Kong. I couldn't believe it. "Oh my God, steak." One civilian complained to the stewardess that his meat wasn't properly cooked. I wasn't the only one ready to sock this pansy-ass. A bunch of strange-looking, no-haired, black-tanned Marines bolted upright, ready to slug him for complaining about his steak. To this day I don't complain in restaurants.

🖈

A Protestant chaplain, a Catholic priest, and a rabbi were flown into An Hoa's airstrip before risky, high exposure operations or Bald Eagle Missions. Their presence was a clear indicator that we may never see An Hoa again.

Communications Operator Phil Perozzio:

War *is* psychological. Some couldn't handle the loneliness while others feared the unknown or dreaded the rear routine boredom. Some Marines liked the boonies because it kept their minds alert. Other Marines flipped out in base camp. They'd shoot their guns in the air or throw grenades to ward off anything and everything, afraid that something would happen simply because it should.

🖈

The Vietnamese would fight ten years to move half a block. Time meant absolutely nothing to them because they would eventually take that block.

🖈

Colonel Mallet Jackson used Major Esau wisely. Colonel Jackson was a mild-mannered man who kept his P's and Q's. Major Esau was a good commander who knew everyone's strengths and weaknesses. Rumor had it, Major Esau was added to Mallet's mix to make sure what needed to get done, did. Major Esau had the knowledge, the drive, the pride and the presence. So Major Esau was the man in charge, but Major Esau was not the man in charge.

🖈

I made a deal with my father that I would write home everyday. And I did. But I never told him anything that I did. And I made sure that no one else did either.

Lt. General Victor H. "Brute" Krulak:

Operations were all the same—rough. During one operation a young Marine asked, "Sir, aren't you scared?"

"Sure I'm scared. Everybody's scared. You have to be scared. If you're not scared you shouldn't be here." He was killed shortly thereafter. The bullet went right through his helmet. He was lying as close as you and I are sitting here.

The Vietnamese always looked puzzled. They lived under a dictatorship they didn't understand and an authority they feared. They wanted to be left alone. But the war wouldn't leave them alone. The VC stole their rice and children and told them that Americans were bad.

The Vietnamese had funny health habits. They covered festering lesions with mud and dung. They didn't know how to properly splint broken arms and legs so children grew up deformed. They lived in un-sanitary conditions without bathing. We taught a Vietnamese group how to shower. They stood beneath our fifty-five gallon gas drums filled with water, fully-clothed, and tried to eat the soap.

Cpl. John P. Petersen, An Hoa, RSVN, 1967.

Name Withheld:

Two young Marines stuck their M16s in their mouths and blew their brains out after receiving Dear John letters.

Lance Corporal John Peterson:

My favorite combat cliché describes combat as ninety-nine percent boredom and one percent sheer terror. Although more the exception than the rule, some couldn't deal with the anxiety of boredom. One kid accused me of peeing in his canteen. Our corpsman sent him to An Hoa. Another Marine babbled paranoid accusations of his squad plotting against him. He too was sent back. Marines who couldn't cope endangered their fellow Marines. I controlled my fear. Running away was not an option. I sucked it up and prayed that I would endure, alive.

Name Withheld:

Everyone talks about being scared all of the time and we were, but sometimes I think we were more bored than scared.

Lieutenant James Meyers:

The Marine Corps teaches a perspective of heritage and a code of ethics; God, Country, and Corps. Marines understand that our bodies endure what the mind may not conceive possible. Our training vernacular disregards self-imposed limitations. "I don't care how much it hurts I will persevere. I don't care how big it is; I can take it."

The Marine Corps is a fraternity of resolute determination, engrained with a philosophy that draws not only from within, but from the core of each other. Marines *never* discussed Vietnam as a war that shouldn't have been. Never.

I was grateful to America for sending her finest sons and daughters to protect the innocent from the barbarians. America's ideology was undermined by the anti-war protestors and the ill-conceived political strategists usurping America's military by politically fighting a war that should have been fought by the military.

Thus raged the battle within the fighting Marine; America's expectations to protect her homeland; our efforts in dealing with those expectations and how we were treated because of it.

⚜

Jane Fonda?

Recall the words Carl Limbacher reporting, "For the story behind the story . . ." (Saturday, May 1, 2004 10:57 a.m. EDT)

> Celebrating the 29th anniversary of the fall of Saigon, the North Vietnamese general who led his forces to victory said Friday that *he was grateful to leaders of the U.S. anti-war movement* . . . "I would like to thank them," said Gen. Vo Nguyen Giap, now 93.
>
> North Vietnamese Col. Bui Tin, who served under Gen. Giap on the general staff of the North Vietnamese army, received South Vietnam's unconditional surrender on April 30, 1975. In an interview with the *Wall Street Journal* after his retirement, Col. Tin explicitly credited leaders of the U.S. anti-war movement, saying they were "essential to our strategy. Every day our leadership would listen to world news over the radio at 9AM to follow the growth of the anti-war movement," Col. Tin told the Journal. Visits to Hanoi . . . by *Jane Fonda* and former Attorney General Ramsey Clark and others, he said, "*gave us confidence that we should hold on in the face of battlefield reverses.*"

To understand the Vietnam veteran's continued disdain of Jane Fonda is to understand the following:

> • The consequences of Jane Fonda's visit to North Vietnam and the infamous photograph. The Jane Fonda, laughing and clapping on

the seat of an enemy anti-aircraft gun, wearing an NVA helmet Kodak moment as American military forces remained battle locked with the NVA.

• America's Jane was North Vietnam's photo op. America cannot ignore or *justify* the *reality* of the repercussions suffered by Ms. Fonda's behavior on *enemy* soil. North Vietnamese government officials used Jane Fonda as psychological warfare against American POW's to boost their country's failing resolve.

• Jane Fonda described her North Vietnam visit as a humanitarian effort aimed at disclosing America's alleged bombing of non-military dikes. Ms. Fonda maintains that she requested *not* to visit NVA military installations, but did so upon the insistence of her North Vietnamese hosts. Ms. Jane Fonda begs the Vietnam veteran to *understand* that she complied with the enemy's wishes—smiling and cooing on an enemy gun—because her North Vietnamese hosts, serenaded her.

• Jane Fonda's North Vietnamese hosts *killed* Americans fighting to protect South Vietnam from *them.* Jane Fonda chose to ignore the havoc VC guerillas and the NVA wreaked on South Vietnam's communities in the name of Communism. Jane Fonda failed to acknowledge the NVA's butchery of the innocent citizens in Huế City.

• Jane Fonda's 1972 visit to North Vietnam's had NVA leaders salivating. Her anti-war sentiments were used in a radio address disseminated to U.S. POW pilots via Radio Hanoi; thus birthing Hanoi Jane—the American!

• Jane Fonda contributed to the death and destruction of *American lives*, South Vietnam, its people, America's allies, and America's families. Although Jane Fonda was not the sole U.S. notable civilian to visit North Vietnam, only *she* sat on an enemy gun, dressed in enemy garb, and lectured American troops over Radio Hanoi.

• Jane Fonda, a young, naïve, Tinsel Town gal marched to the beat of her own drum; a tempo outside of that which defined our homeland cause. Jane Fonda perceived herself as a global citizen. Jane Fonda used the enemy's homeland as her sandbox, playing with the hearts, minds, and lives of her fellow Americans.

• Jane Fonda's presence in North Vietnam remains to this day an act of betrayal.

• Jane Fonda should have been tried for treason.

That's why the Vietnam veteran so disdains Jane Fonda.

Second Battalion Fifth Marine Regiment, First Marine Division, United States Marine Corps; An Hoa, Republic of South Vietnam; 1967:
There is no way to define an idiot like Jane Fonda.

Fleet Marine Force Corpsman JP Higgins:

On one of our many MedCAPS we met a ten-year-old Vietnamese girl born with her heart on the *right* side, barely covered by skin. I could see her heart beating. I couldn't understand how she had survived in such primitive living conditions. A medevac transported her to Da Nang. We did everything we could for the Vietnamese children.

FMF Corpsman JP Higgins.

I recently asked Bill Rogers, my first platoon leader, the name of the blue-eyed, black Marine whose legs had been blown off. I did my best to save his life, and it was really important to name the face etched in my mind for the past forty years. His name was Thomas Leslie Ward.

Thomas Leslie Ward was a brave Marine who faced death with calm and prayer. Thomas Leslie Ward died serving his country. And his color mattered not, for we all bleed red.

One time, Headquarters and Services choppered a Catholic priest into the weeds to say mass and dispense Holy Communion. Unfortunately, the bird couldn't retrieve the dear Father so he nervously spent the evening with us. During the night, the metal casings of spent artillery illumination rounds *thunked* around us. Those metal casings could kill. The priest questioned the safety of the rounds. "Don't worry, Padre, the casings would leave nothing more than a nasty bruise." I felt awful lying to a holy man but he was so nervous I thought that God would forgive me.

I sat with the priest and several Marines in a small hootch outside a surrounded NVA village. An AK-47 round smashed the floor by the priest's foot. Everybody but the priest dove down head first. Padre leisurely commented, "That was pretty close, huh." And oddly enough, he refused to move. I could only think, "Man, this dude really believes what he preaches."

Chief Lou LeGarie instructed corpsmen at Camp Pendleton's Field Medical School. Nicknamed "Gunny" for being so gung-ho, Chief LeGarie was a legend. He even starred in the corpsmen's Field Medical School training film.

I walked into An Hoa's BAS to report to 2/5's Chief Hospital Corpsman, Gunny LeGarie. I couldn't believe it. My heart dropped. *Oh no*, I thought, *I'm doomed*. But after spending time in the field with my Marines, I realized that

Gunny LeGarie understood the relationship between a corpsman and his Marines. He trained his corpsmen to be better at saving lives.

Chief LeGarie did right by all of his corpsmen. He gave his field corpsman 4.0 ratings and promoted us when he could. Like him, I stopped being Navy and became a Marine at heart.

I went back to Vietnam in February. It was rewarding to see that wounds have healed. The Vietnamese are happy to see Americans. I tell family and friends it was time to return. But the reason for my visit stems from my heart. I needed to experience as an adult, the place where I lost that innocent boy. Did I think I would find him? No, not really, but I had to give it a shot. Did I find him? No, but hope is eternal and maybe, just maybe, someday I'll catch a glimpse him in the mirror. These heavy thoughts aren't easy to explain to others. But those, like you, Lucia, understand where many of us come from.

Hold those you love close.

Here's a story that I've shared with but a handful. It's not about Vietnam. It's about a man forever changed by Vietnam.

While serving as a lab tech at the Naval Hospital in Pensacola, Florida, the brass assigned me to autopsies, thinking that after Vietnam, it wouldn't bother me. What they didn't know was I recovered from my evenings of beer and women by working in the morgue. I'd nap on the autopsy table.

Because I had a knack for retrieving blood, I was often called by other techs for the difficult patients. Guess starting IV's in the dark of Vietnam—under fire—paid off.

Six-year-old David Turner became one those patients. The first time I met David, I asked his parents to leave the room and said, "David, I could draw blood from your arm, causing nothing more than a sting or I could use the biff method, otherwise known as a punch in the nose method. The biff method will give me lots of blood from your bloody nose."

David, like most, preferred to be stung. I examined David's blood and discovered that he had leukemia. David became a regular on the pediatric ward. This poor kid was stuck so often a tech's blue lab coat drove him into hiding. I was the only tech that he would allow to draw blood. David responded to chemo and eventually went home.

Several weeks later a Turner required an autopsy. I didn't make the connection and pulled out the tray. I knew that a child lay beneath the sheet. *Damn*, I thought, *I hate doing autopsies on kids*. I lifted the sheet, stunned to see David. I didn't know what to do. I felt like someone blasted my head with a baseball bat. David Turner dug a hole through my Vietnam wall. Vietnam was filled with the dead, severed, and mangled but I couldn't process David's death. In Nam, I marched on knowing that I did my best. But David was different.

I found David's leukemia. This towheaded kid sat on my lap as I drew blood.

I held him when he cried. Now he lay dead, and there was nothing I could do. I tasted salty tears streaming down my cheeks. The pathologist offered to perform the autopsy. I accepted his offer. I went home and got trashed. I didn't know how to grieve David. To this day, I've never felt as crushed as I did when I lost David.

I hope this didn't upset you, Lucia, but there's a link between this hard core Nam vet and how a little boy forever affected his life.

Lieutenant James Kirschke:

In the mid-1980s I lived with my family in Northern Italy. While there, at a café in Milan, I had just finished writing a postcard to a California friend, retired Marine Sergeant, Vincent Rios. Vince had also served with the Fifth Marines in Vietnam, where he had lost three limbs: almost all of both legs and one arm. I signed the postcard SEMPER FIDELIS near the end, and underlined those words.

An Italian engineer friend had noticed this, and kindly asked me if I had underlined *Semper Fidelis* because it was a foreign term. When I nodded, "*Si*," he responded in the finest Italian accent and demeanor, "Surely by their actions the U.S. Marines have made *Semper Fidelis* an American term." This comment brought tears to my eyes.

We always trusted more in courage and discipline than in sheer numbers, and we always had the necessary confidence in whatever ground contacts we had with the enemy. Yet the Vietnam War was one that, for the Marine infantry, had no front lines with secure areas behind them and very little slack. With the possible exception of one five day R&R, our Marines were in potentially or definitely dangerous situations throughout their entire of duty in Vietnam. If they survived long enough, the Marines, the small number of Navy corpsmen and the even smaller number of Navy doctors serving with the Marines had standard tours of duty in Vietnam that was supposed to be thirteen months, in contrast with the standard twelve month U.S. Navy, Army, and Air Force tours overseas.

In our Company, Hotel, Company, Second Battalion, Fifth Marines, we had a policy that our enlisted men and corpsmen did not have to go on patrol during their last month, but could stay at the successive company command posts—none of which were too secure at that time—during their last month, and could help with administrative details. But for the entire thirteen months, while our Marines were not always actively engaged with the enemy, they were always at least potentially so. We were at all times, therefore, heavily committed—combat operations, day and night reconnaissance, search and destroy and rescue patrols, day and night, a minimum of fifty percent alert every night, listening posts after dark, observation posts during daylight hours, innumerable work duties, and even informal classes when time permitted—all combined to make for a very tired, under-strength Third Platoon. This platoon was nonetheless expected to do—and always did—just as much as fully manned and rested rifle platoons in training were expected to do.

All of the Marines I served with in Vietnam continually shared whatever food and other supplies they had with the local villagers. Around My Loc (2), for instance, so many of the men from my platoon, Third Platoon, H-2-5, gave so much of their food away to the surrounding villagers, that they seemed to be damaging their own health. I therefore had to give special orders, several times, to all three of our rifle squad leaders to prevent this situation from becoming a major problem.

Fleet Marine Force Corpsman Roger Lansbury:

Vietnam gave me an understanding of true hunger and a desire for meat. After eating nothing but C rations for several weeks, my teeth and jaw actually ached for a firm piece of meat to tear and chew.

Vietnam also gave me an understanding of true thirst. We were pinned down in a large, dry rice paddy by mortar and machine gun fire. Although we silenced the enemy we were ordered to stay put for the night. I fell into an exhausted sleep and woke up to a thirst so profound, my tongue was swollen. Every cell in my body was thirsty.

Vietnam forced me to adopt severe rationing practices. I learned that my requirements for the basics were not as great as I had imagined. It's amazing how the body can survive out of necessity on what many consider deprivation.

Fleet Marine Force Corpsman Ray Knispel:

During Operation Colorado, I hauled a wounded 2/5 staff sergeant into the medevac chopper. We met playing poker on Hill 35 at the Regimental Aid Station. Days before the operation, this staff sergeant told us that he sent his two boys a Vietnamese jacket with a silhouette of Vietnam embroidered on the back. The boys were bullied by their classmates as the sons of a baby killer. He spoke with anguish. I remembered this as I watched him writhing in pain from the dangling shreds of flesh and bones from stumps that had once been legs. As he froze into a death mask, I prayed for his boys.

One night a major ran into the Aid Station screaming for help with a distraught Marine. Earlier, in the process of heroically saving his comrades, this Marine had killed several civilians. As the evening unfolded the Marine went ballistic, throwing things and people like toys. The major and I entered the tent to see the young Marine crying, surrounded by Marines, "Take my uniform, my stripes, the nine years I've given my country and set me free with a discharge that will honor my wife and children." The major nodded, and his comrades jumped. The tackle didn't stop the Marine from flinging one guy across the room. I sat on his legs and began cutting his utilities to administer a clean shot of Thorazine.

The major yelled, "Doc, we don't have time for this, he's busting loose."

"Sir, it should be sterile."

"Don't worry I'll take full responsibility, just give him the damn shot."

The Thorazine worked immediately. The Marine was transferred to the Aid Station and immediately evacuated. I thought about that Marine for days.

As I feverishly removed seventeen wounded from a burning LVT, a Marine standing by took pictures.

The platoon sergeant roared, "What the hell do you think you're doing?"

"I'm going to show the people back home what's really going on here."

The sergeant advanced. raging. "Fuck the people back home."

I stood between the sergeant and the Marine. "I understand how you feel, Sarge, but right now this won't help."

The sergeant stopped and stared as though in a trance. He didn't blink even when I waved my hand in his face. I tagged him as battle fatigued, set him aside, and worked among the remaining wounded. I later found out that this was the sergeant's third platoon lost in combat.

Once, as I stood frozen in shock and disbelief while scanning a grotesque assortment of wounded and dead, I heard someone scream, "God damn it, Doc, get those men out of there!"

"Is anyone alive?"

"Yes, get moving!"

I triaged the dead and wounded, marveling at the care and empathy of these big, tough Marines. They carried one kid with his kidney's dangling out of his back in a double-chair-hold-carry. The fatal wound did not deter their gentle compassion.

Private First Class Steve Zeck:

One radio man hit a box mine. Chunks of flesh and bone scattered all over the trees. Despite an all-out search we only found pieces—no body parts—and a radio-handset. I wasn't callous but I was grateful to have been walking on the other side. I regretted the incident but I was glad that it wasn't me. I thought, *It's not going to happen to me, I'll be fine.* I think most Marines thought this way.

I wouldn't trade my Vietnam experience. Being a Marine was probably the one thing I was best at. Killing the enemy and throwing grenades didn't instigate personal stress or horror. I was good at combat. Vietnam was them against us, the bad guys versus the good guys so whatever it took, so be it, and whatever happened, happened.

FMF Corpsman HM2 Raymond W. Knispel, USN, 1965-1967.

Vietnam became my only reality. No other place existed while I was there. I didn't think about anywhere or anything other than what I was doing. I checked off my calendar just like everyone else but I didn't dwell. "Oh boy, I should be home."

I didn't hate being in Vietnam. And I wasn't the only one. I was brave in Vietnam. I think we all were. Marines are proud to be Marines.

Vietnam didn't exist on an eight-to-four, four-to-noon, and noon-to-eight time schedule. We had breakfast at six a.m., re-supplied, and moved to our objective. We were in the field without sleep for almost a year. We napped for ten minutes here, fifteen minutes there, maybe an hour if we were lucky. Guys switched naps during night watch. But since every shadow sparked artillery and sniper fire, everybody was awake most of the night.

Falling asleep on watch was the worst thing a Marine could ever do. One night while serving as a fire team leader on a four-man listening post, I woke up to the watch Marine asleep. I manned the remaining time. At five a.m. I tapped the other two guys and brought them the hundred yards back to our lines. When the sleeping Marine woke up—he did so alone. I thought he deserved it. I knew he was safe from getting captured or killed. He survived—a bit upset.

During one patrol as I brought up the rear, I signaled the guy ahead of me to stop while I checked something. When I came back I realized he didn't see my signal. I was alone. *Great*, I thought. *I don't know where I am, I don't know where I'm going, I don't know where I came from, and now I have to find these guys.* Yelling would only attract attention, and *I was alone.* I stayed put, not knowing what direction—in the middle of the woods—to go. A few minutes later the guy realized I wasn't there and sent the fire team back. It was my most frightening Vietnam moment. I waited only a few minutes, but it seemed like an eternity. A million scary things went through my mind. The more time I had to think, the more I was afraid.

During one particularly hot summer's day while crossing a rice paddy, I was so tired, I became delusional. I thought, *I'm tired. I'm really tired. I want to stop. I don't want to get hurt. I don't want to get hurt bad enough to have to go home. But I wish the enemy could wound me enough to medevac me anywhere for a few days because I'm too exhausted to take one more step. Not one more step.*

An Hoa's wire was the extent of our lives; and beyond the wires lay nothing but a clearing. During perimeter duty, Marines would turn the lines into World War III at the slightest sound. And most often, the impending attack was either wind or shadow. Sometimes, we'd find sappers and snipers dead in the wire. But I'll bet most Marines shot without really knowing if anyone was there.

Getting into the wire at night after a patrol or ambush was tough. We shot flares, blared over the net, hollered, "Yankees, Dodgers" and sang "Yankee Doodle Dandy." Trust me, no one carrying a rifle wanted to ruffle exhausted Marines carrying rifles.

One night we were embroiled in a twenty-minute fire fight before the command post realized we were fighting another Marine platoon. Both platoons had called in artillery on each other.

The following scenario happened more than once. A Marine would sit in the middle of the field and sob, "I don't care what you do to me. I'm not doing this anymore. I'm not taking another step. I'm tired, I don't want to get shot and I can't stand the heat." So we'd drag him by the neck as he continued sobbing until a medevac choppered him out.

One well-respected Marine shot himself in the foot to go home. And he made no qualms about it. They took him to the BAS, and we never saw him again.

Name Withheld:

I've been startled from sleep walking through Vietnam's rice paddies too often to count. Powerful memories surface, and I harbor anger and resentment. It's mentally brutalizing to relive the pangs of loss. I wake up in a cold, terrifying sweat and run at three a.m. My chest will hurt so bad, I think I'm having an angina attack. But it's a panic attack. So I fall on my knees and pray. "God, get me through this night. Please relieve me of this pain and agony. I'll be a better man. I promise I'll do this and I won't do that and blah, blah, blah." The piercing pain is my spiritual bullet. It's a reality so real, I can taste it. And I don't feel sorry for myself. But I wonder when this trail of tears from this agonizing passage of humanity hurting humanity will ever end.

How does one deal with the knowledge that not only did the VC amputate the arms of those Vietnamese children inoculated by American medics during MedCAPs, they hung signs from their necks that said, "If you have anything to do with these Americans again we'll cut your head off."

Tell me, please, how do you deal with something like that?

Private First Class Dave Magnenat:

I was scared and apprehensive the first month or so in Vietnam. Months three to nine, I simply didn't care. I had to be there, so it didn't matter. As a short-timer, however, I was extremely careful. Extremely.

Name Withheld:

When I returned to America I didn't discuss Vietnam because no one understood. Friends thought I was being melancholy, and I wondered if they gave a damn. People remarked, "Something's different about you, man."

"You're fuckin' right something is different. You walk through Vietnam's rice paddies in one-hundred-and-twenty-degree weather and watch your buddy get his head blown off and tell me how to ever be the same again?"

So I buried what was in my heart and soul under lock and key. And I'll die with that key in my pocket.

Sergeant John Culbertson:

I'm not the only Vietnam veteran dealing with survivor's guilt. No one can rationalize, This is why I lived and this is why Joe Brown died. It's a mere toss of the dice. A mortar hit his hole instead of mine.

Let me tell you about William Cross and Luther Hamilton. Shrapnel pierced William's throat, and despite his buddy's best efforts, Luther couldn't stop the bleeding. So Luther Hamilton ran six miles through enemy territory—by himself—with nothing but a .45 to get help. By the time he returned—unharmed—William Cross had bled to death. That's a bunch of shit that you never forget. You think about it every night. It never goes away.

In 1967 Marines in Vietnam engaged in four thousand patrols and over one-hundred-and-fifty battalion-sized battles; unlike World War II when whole armies fought each other. Young Americans denouncing communism fought young Vietnamese in the name of democracy. Americans believed that communism was wrong and the Vietnamese were taught that America was an evil, aggressive, tyrannical force; a spider that crushed small countries with its legs. North Vietnam fought valiantly to stop America, and America sacrificed her youth and billions of dollars in resources fighting back.

The Vietnam War killed three-and-a-half million civilians, one million North Vietnamese, one million South Vietnamese and fifty-eight thousand Americans during its eleven-year span. The generals and the politicians were the only people that knew about Vietnam's strategy and logistics. And today we know of their divergence. There was no unified goal. So we ask ourselves, what did the Vietnam War solve?

Vietnamese kids ran alongside convoys, laughing and yelling, "Joe, give me chop-chop!" We'd throw C rations, candy, and gum. But I can't say that they were innocent. Little girls would hug you while trying to steal something. These eight- and nine-year-old kids understood war. At night, they lined trails with hand grenades and booby traps, intent and aware of the damage it would cause as we left the following morning.

And a fourteen-year-old girl would sell her body for a pack of cigarettes.

Private First Class Bill Gavin:

People ask me if my time in Nam was worth anything. Well, how long is a piece of string? What's anything worth? America fought in Vietnam intent on serving freedom to the Vietnamese on a silver platter. And yet, most Vietnamese chose not to accept freedom. So how many American lives should their freedom cost? I can't answer that. But I will say that during combat, Marines didn't fight for a country or a particular point of view. Marines fought to keep the Marines on their left and the Marines on their right alive. And that made the Vietnam War personal.

🪖

The corpsman who saved my life suffers from PTSD. Sadly, he doesn't remember the lives he saved, but he does remember the lives he lost.

One night, Doc Thorton (not real name) tended to a Marine, riddled with bullets, lying at the bottom of a fighting hole. It was pitch black. Doc Thorton removed the kid's utilities and felt for bullet holes in the dark because he couldn't turn on a flashlight. Working diligently and methodically, Thorton plugged every hole he could find. Doc left him to tend to another wounded Marine. When he returned, this Marine was dead. And that dead kid eats Doc Thorton's heart away day after day after day.

🪖

Every day was a different day and every day was a thousand years long.

The gooks would beat on drums and holler, "Marines you die."

🪖

The Three Rules of War:

1. Young men die.
2. Rule number one never changes.
3. Someone *will* walk point.

🪖

Marines marched in a column fifteen feet apart. Point men were either on point or tail end Charlie's. That is, if the point man hit something bad, the column did an about face so tail-end Charlie became point and point became tail-end Charlie. Under fire, everyone bolted to get the hell out. Point men hit more shit than anyone else in the column. And I liked walking point because I had a death wish. Here's why:

During one patrol, the point hit some real shit. As we hit the deck and faced outboard with our rifles, I saw two pajama-clad figures running thirty-five, forty yards away. I didn't get my rifle up in time to shoot the first one and watched the second one disappear behind a huge bush. I fired one round from my M16—a shot no bigger than a finger nail—into the bush. And somehow, this bullet made it through that bush. I inspected the bush after the firefight and discovered that the dead VC was a sixteen-year-old girl. Medical supplies were strewn all around her. I reasoned the other figure to be her mother, and the two women to be working together as a medic and nurse. I stared at the girl, void of any emotion. I felt nothing. Killing had so hardened me that if this girl would've gotten up, I would've shot her again. If necessary, I would've used my bayonet or knife. And then I made my grave mistake. I opened her clenched fingers and found a little clasp-top coin purse, the kind my grandmother carried. I opened it. I couldn't believe my eyes. Inside the purse lay Rosary Beads. Now I'm Catholic, she's Catholic, and I just killed her. And do you know what I felt? Nothing; absolutely nothing. I thought, *Gavin, look at what you did.*

But I also knew that when I pulled the trigger, I had no idea this VC was a woman, let alone a young girl. I thought I'd go Asiatic—a term used for kill-crazy Marines. I now had two choices; to continue to block my feelings with my firewall or to feel. I stared at this girl-child lying by my side. I knelt down, still staring. Another Marine came over. I told him to leave. I continued to stare and superimposed my girlfriend's face onto the dead girl. I forced myself to cry, knowing the minute I felt something, anything, I wasn't totally immersed in killing. But when the tears fell, I also knew, "Holy shit, now I'm in trouble. My wall's broken. When the time comes to pull my trigger, I might hesitate. And that hesitation could kill me."

That night, hunkered down on the perimeter, I vomited. The corpsman gave me pills but I couldn't stop vomiting. The sergeant yelled, "Hey, Gavin, since you've got the most kills in the company, we're going to get you a patch for your flak jacket."

"Sarge, today, I killed a sixteen-year-old girl."

Silence; no one said a thing. So I repeated, "Today I killed a girl." Silence.

I wanted someone to punish me, but nobody would. I was in Vietnam to do a job and I did my job. So, in an effort to reap vengeance on what I had become and give myself a sense of normalcy, I rebuilt my wall and punished myself into a death wish. I would leave Vietnam in a body bag. I was wounded on point and shipped stateside within a week. Had that not happened, I would've gone back to Nam as many times as necessary to get myself killed. That's what I wanted. I didn't want to be what I had become; what I had forced myself to become in order to survive. This is a difficult concept to convey to noncombatants.

To this day to a certain extent, I still have that death wish. I'm saved by knowing the instant I pulled the trigger on that particular day in Vietnam, I didn't know a young girl was behind that bush.

After Nam I moved to Alaska and became a big game hunting and fishing guide. I kill fish and bear. I'm comfortable knowing that I kill. I'm the guy standing in the photos with something dead next to him. I'm a warrior. It's what I'm meant to be until death. I keep things simple while waiting to share my next life with friends and foe.

I don't know what will happen—no one does. But at least I can say I never killed in cold blood, even when a sergeant ordered me to kill a wounded enemy. I told him if he wanted the VC dead, he could shoot him. He didn't shoot him either.

Name Withheld:

Second Lieutenant Jones (not real name) worked as an MP in Da Nang before joining our company. MP's had it easy. Being an MP was the perfect job for anyone who couldn't handle Vietnam's bush. And Jones fit the bill. The bush certainly didn't make the man.

The heat was particularly brutal during one, no-named operation. Jones, suffering from heat exhaustion, requested a medevac. His request was denied. We were ordered to douse him with our canteen water to lower his temperature but we refused. We weren't going to waste our water. So the NCO ordered us to surround him as he lay on the ground. We then peed on him. This foul act worked but not without alleviating every ounce of Jones's legitimacy as a leader.

The next day Jones, scared and confused, commanded his troops to withdraw during an ambush. We were heavily armed and should have belted the enemy with suppressing fire. Jones ordered us to retreat, to literally turn-around and haul ass. Our incompetent leader was going to desert our wounded. No one moved. These were wounded, not dying or dead men. The platoon sergeant stood and refused to obey the command. We stood. We were a bunch of interconnected amoeba's thinking, "That could be me lying out there—would I want me to run away from me?"

We ignored Jones and followed the platoon sergeant.

Private First Class Ron Powers:

Lucia, whoever tells you they weren't afraid in Vietnam wasn't there. Every day after Vietnam is a bonus because I never thought I'd leave Vietnam alive. And most Marines, including myself, didn't want to leave Vietnam. I complained, "I want to go home," but when I found myself wounded on a plane leaving Da Nang, I cried like a baby for leaving my brothers behind.

I can still see, hear, and smell my buddy dying in my arms. Blood gulped out of his head like pop pouring from a bottle turned upside down.

I inherited the nickname jinx during Operation Essex, but I now wonder if I was truly jinxed or incredibly lucky. Everything I'm about to tell you happened on Operation Essex.

I walked point, heading into a rice paddy to assault an enemy machine gun in absolute silence. I became uncomfortable. I had walked point long enough to acquire a sixth sense. I knew that we were going to hit the shit. But I also knew the Man upstairs was with me. We cautiously stepped into a trench. The Marine behind me passed within arms' reach, took three bullets in the face, and fell back. Another Marine got shot in the neck. Now cut off from the main body, I threw grenades at the enemy machine gun closing in. The enemy returned grenade fire, killing another Marine at the end of the trench. I climbed out and ran zigzag back to the main body under constant machine gun fire.

But here's the deal. I remember six Marines in the trench, and three of us getting out alive. I knew three guys died, but I also remembered that two guys helped me out of the trench. After meeting my squad leader at a reunion, he questioned the presence of the other two Marines. After a careful review, I realized I was one of four, not six Marines. I knew then the Man upstairs helped me get out of that trench, because the guys who did were as real as real could be.

Later that night, the enemy threw grenade after grenade into a foxhole I shared with my buddy. One fatal explosion hit and jerked him on top of me, unconscious but alive. A clean hole pierced his skull, and I watched his brains stream down the back of his head. I yelled, "Corpsman up," but Doc couldn't get close enough to drag the kid out. I was afraid. But I knew I couldn't let fear paralyze me or I too, would be dead. I remained unharmed.

During a search patrol the next day, I found a wicker suitcase wrapped with rope lying inside a hootch. I untied the rope and opened the case. A viper snake sprung out, bit my flak jacket, left a wet mark, and crawled away. I was fine.

Marine flak jackets were lined with little, curved, roof-like fiberglass, very uncomfortable shingles. Prior to the operation, being young and dumb, I sliced out the shingles with a razor and left the padded cloth. I removed every shingle but one that was stuck. When Essex was said and done, I removed a piece of shrapnel stuck in the one and only shingle that wouldn't budge; the shingle that covered my heart.

Fleet Marine Force Corpsman Ron White:

Here's a story about Jason Williams. A gook jumped from a bush and sliced Jason's belly open with a machete. The horizontal cut severed his stomach clear through to his backbone. I went into high gear. I protected him, stopped the bleeding by clamping the pumping bleeder, washed the intestines that hung outside of his body, and placed them back in. Dry intestines won't work, so it was important to have water, even muddy water, to wet and place the intestines inside the body. I laid him on a poncho and bolted to a medevac chopper. He lived. He has a helluva' scar, but he lived.

I carried four canteens because the wounded had two requests, morphine and water. I carried a .45 for awhile but ditched it for extra water. If I *really* needed a gun, I knew one would always be lying around.

We barely knew what was happening in the states in Vietnam. Families wrote about protests and marches but since we didn't read magazines or newspapers it didn't sink in. We didn't dwell on anything outside of our Vietnam world. Nothing else mattered. We never discussed politics. The Marines were in Vietnam to do their job and I was in Vietnam to take care of the Marines.

I never felt bad about Vietnam until I got back. I remembered my dad—a World War II vet—telling stories about World War II parades so I expected something, but we got nothin'. Some people were nice and others talked junk. They had the gall to ask, "Well, what did you do in Vietnam? What did you accomplish? How many people did you kill?" I never asked my daddy if he killed anybody. People *still* ask, and it *still* pisses me off. But I don't argue. Besides, opinions are like armpits—everybody's got two and everyone's entitled to their own.

Chief Hospital Corpsman Lou LeGarie:

One corpsman was deserted by his platoon in the boonies. Replaced after four hours of radio-watch duty, the corpsman went to sleep. The lieutenant moved the platoon without a thorough inspection and left this kid behind. The platoon realized the kid was missing at An Hoa's checkpoint head count. The lieutenant said, "Yeah, he had radio watch and went to sleep. That was the last I saw of him. Maybe he came back on his own." An Hoa was checked from top to bottom. No dice. The lieutenant was relieved on the spot.

The missing corpsman returned to An Hoa four days later. Luckily he knew his way back. Once alone, the guy moved only at night to avoid being seen by the enemy. During the day, he watched—and duly noted—VC and NVA movement. This poor kid barely slept. Why he even crossed the goddamn mine field bordering the An Hoa perimeter without getting blown up. Intelligence immediately snatched him for enemy info.

The lieutenant was history. Those Marines were entrusted to his care. It was his job to make sure that they were present, not even accounted for, but present in the field.

The NVA prisoners were tough; VC prisoners were like little rats. We'd interrogate and bribe Vietnamese POWs with cigarettes, food, and money, but we never knew if they were lying or telling the truth. We didn't treat POWs badly. Maybe an occasional whack on the head, but we weren't supposed to, so we didn't. We offered them a better life if they agreed to become Cheiu Hoi scouts.

Dr. Viti's replacements couldn't hack Vietnam. They couldn't step up to the plate or hold a candle to Dr. Viti. They were everywhere the action wasn't. The corpsmen would complain, "Geez, this doctor is not Dr. Viti."

I warned one guy, "Doctor, I don't give a shit what school you went to. None of us do. But I do care about my corpsmen. So you better have a meeting and tell them what you like and dislike. Don't chew their ass out for doing something they've been trained to do by another surgeon. If you keep this shit up, I'll go to the battalion commander and I will get rid of you."

And I did.

We had a crazy major *after* Major Esau that wanted Coca-Cola. And he'd order his Coke at the BAS. I finally put my foot down. "Excuse me, Major, I don't drink your Coca-Cola, and I'm not going to have these Marines pick up your goddamn soda. These men are wounded and battered. These Marines are healing so they can return to their companies. They don't need to do your shit."

Captain Gene Bowers:

The media, searching for bad and seldom reporting the good, were like Snoopy's buzzards hanging over the trees.

As we boarded choppers in An Hoa for Operation Essex, a *New York Times* reporter said, "I'd like to go with you."

I told him, "Man, you don't want to go with us, we're the lead assault company heading into an unsecured landing zone in Antenna Valley. We will have heavy contact."

This guy says, "Captain, what do you have to hide?"

I was incredulous. "Which helicopter would you like?"

WHY ?

Are you going 10.000 miles from home to live a helluva life and to die on this land?
This country is not yours.
We do no harm to your homeland.
Why have you come here to kill our men and women, and destroy our homeland?
We have fought for 20 years and we'll continue to fight until final victory — even if necessary for another 20 years — on our native soil, to defend our country our homes. This is only what your forefathers did about 200 years ago.
And you? What are you fighting for ?
Don't let yourselves be fooled by such lies as « to defend freedom and democracy », « to help on request of the South

Front side of a propaganda card described as non-radio "Hanoi-Hanna" techniques often found on the battlefields.

Vietnamese government »! The presence of hundreds of thousands of U.S. troops wantonly firing and killing in this little country, massive bombings destroying whole areas, the use of most atrocious weapons like napalm bombs, phosphorous shells, poison gas..., in themselves trample on the loftiest ideals of the American Revolution and besmear the honor of the American people. As for the so-called South-Vietnamese government, said Sen. W. Morse: « that government is just what we have rigged up ».
Are you resigned to playing the same role as those nazi soldiers who blindly obeyed Hitler's orders and committed crimes, or will you rise up and act according to your conscience, against this immoral US war, to be worthy of Washington, Lincoln, Jefferson...?
Do refuse to fight!
Demand your repatriation!
Get out of South Vietnam before it is too late!

Back side of a propaganda card described as non-radio "Hanoi-Hanna" techniques often found on the battlefields.

This foolish reporter dug himself in a small foxhole, *behind me*, stood, lit a cigarette and instantly took a round through his shoulder. Injured, he whined for morphine all night. We gave him as much as we could. He whined incessantly. I had to shut him up. "Sorry,' I said, "we're out." My morphine was for my Marines. It was pointless to talk to him, but I took great pleasure in telling him he was exactly where he shouldn't have been.

Generally reporters roamed freely, but if they endangered a mission or exposed us, I secured them with a Marine because I couldn't order them to leave. I made sure they knew they were not to move. "This Marine will keep you right here."

{It's important to note that Gene Bowers hesitated when sharing this story, respectful of how it would affect me—Lucia}

The VC and the NVA were terrible. The VC and the NVA disemboweled their victims. We returned to an enemy-ambushed friendly village and found the village chief and his family tied to stakes. The family members had their eyelids split and tacked up on their foreheads, forcing them to witness the torture inflicted upon their chief.

The VC had rammed a bamboo shaft, designed with flanges, up and out of the chief's rectum. The flaring, sharp flanges severed his rectum and intestines.

After one rather lethal ambush, we investigated a tree-line enemy machine gun outpost and found two enemy machine gunners chained to a tree so they couldn't surrender. They were chained by their officers.

And we're the guys who self-flagellate.

Going one more step in Vietnam was a matter of will. I never believed that I, this little speck on earth could say, "Jesus, please don't have me killed."

I don't believe God observes the follow of every sparrow or directs hurricanes and tornadoes. I think shit happens. So when the bullets were cracking and the mortars were landing, I repeated over and over and over again, "I will not die, I will not die, I will not die."

I feel that a self-projection of will power kept me alive.

Often we would uncover underground bunkers filled with tons and tons of dry, un-husked rice that wouldn't burn, so we creatively destroyed it by pouring oil, water, or urinating on it, to make it swell and turn sour. We also threw white phosphorous grenades in the bunkers just to screw it up. We never knew if the enemy could salvage it, but we couldn't leave this food source for the VC or the NVA.

We'd often run out of food in the middle of nowhere. Socked in by the weather, it could be days before we got re-supplied. One time, after successfully battling a group of NVA traveling along the Ho Chi Minh Trail, we rummaged through the belongings of the dead. We removed

Lt. Col. Gene W. Bowers, USMC (Ret.), 5 June 1960 - 1 July 1986.

their bologna-cloth shoulder bandoliers filled with dried rice, spread the contents, separated the blood-soaked rice, and boiled the rest.

Did you know that the Vietnamese were superstitious about the Ace of Spades? I wrote to a card-making company and requested as many as they could send. We stuck the Ace of Spades in the mouths of dead VC and NVA.

Things finally got quiet around four a.m. I was less than ten yards from the creek where Sergeant Kazmerski (not real name) lay shot. Shivering, he whispered, "Skipper, I'm hurt. I can't feel anything below my tits."

I knew then the bullet had severed his spine.

"Skipper," he said, "please come over here, please."

So I crawled to his trench. He asked me to get his wallet out of his pocket.

This kid didn't miss a beat. "Skipper, take the MPC and buy the platoon beer when you get back."

"No, Ski," I said. "You're going to need your money. You're going to a hospital in Japan. You're going to need money."

"No, no. Please, take it. Please."

There lay a man, either paralyzed or dying, worrying about buying his brothers beer.

Once while crawling through the shallow rows of a potato patch, I heard the snap of a pineapple grenade. I could see the flames and sparks from the spinning handle flying towards me. I thought, *Man, if the grenade lands close enough to my head that I can see the sparks, I'll have to roll into another row. If I can't see the sparks I'll be okay.*

The grenade exploded four rows away, knocked the dickens out of me, and popped my eardrum. I rolled over, ripped the tape off a grenade, threw it as hard as I could, and killed the enemy. But now I was as deaf as a post. A wheezing ring was my only audible sound. And I was crazy exhausted with a horrible headache from the grenade's concussion. Needless to say, I wasn't a happy camper. But I couldn't leave my men. I simply didn't have an officer I trusted enough as a company commander. So I didn't.

Dr. Viti later examined me in An Hoa and left me with no choice. "I can't do anything for you here. Your membranes are ruptured. I'm sending you to Da Nang."

{Gene Bowers reviewing photographs—Lucia} That's Doc Noah taking care of a little girl. We did everything we could for those children. Everything. We the baby killers.

Name Withheld:

Decomposing bodies stunk. I thought, *Man, Marines smell just like gooks when they die.*

Vietnam memories follow no particular order. Nightmares have random access. I'll rehash an incident and beat myself up. "If I went to the right instead of the left or if I called the artillery in here, could I have saved more lives, blah, blah, blah . . ."

Or I vividly remember a Marine stepping on a mine and lying splattered in his own guts. My hands and feet sweat, my heart races, and I think, *Oh shit, I don't want to think about this. I want to go to sleep.*

An Hoa downtime was about cleaning your weapons, getting your gear in order, and partying. Marijuana was cheap and easy to come by; a five-dollar bag stoned an entire squad. Manila rum tasted like burnt inner tubes and swallowed like razor blades. We were invincible.

Bruce Swander First Marine Air Wing:

Accidental deaths, suicides, even homicides occurred among Marines in Vietnam. A squad could be mistaken for the enemy at the perimeter, a doped up Marine could fire indiscriminately, or odd, lethal accidents with no eye-witnesses just happened. Each case required lengthy investigations, interviews, and depositions to determine the facts.

Vietnam was a helicopter war. Every 2/5 company was supported and transported by the First Marine Air Wing. Lucia, no matter how you overview the ground grunts, include among your facts that many Marines are alive today because of the air coverage provided by the Marine Air Wing. Yes, call me biased. But I can assure you that your Marines will remember Puff the Magic Dragon and the evacuation helos that supported them.

Name Withheld:

Look up the words war and atrocity in the dictionary. Now describe war. War is the worst thing that could happen to anyone, civilian or military. War is hell; total living hell.

Weapons Platoon Sergeant Harold Wadley:

I'm seventy-five years old. My Vietnam memory is good, but sometimes I can't remember what I'm doing in the barn until a horse snickers at me. I'll wake up at three a.m. with bits and pieces of stories. I don't think I suffer from post traumatic stress. I'm just an ordinary Marine. I went through Vietnam with such a fine bunch of guys. I hope I never forget it. Forgetting would be the worst thing that could ever happen to me. Some Marines are indelibly imprinted in my mind. Others, I still can't figure out how they became Marines, let alone landed in my outfit. Since I had the weapons platoon, I worked with all three platoons. I don't mean to blow my own horn, but this is quite an unforgettable compliment coming from this bunch of Marines. "Sarge, you don't have to tell us to clean our weapons." When I broke my rifle down to clean it, so did everyone else. I never once gave a direct order, other than, "No, stay behind tonight." I got on Byrne's case once—I had to—but other than that I just *suggested* something. Those Marines were always one step ahead of me.

We used to string concertina barbed wire around rice paddies as a perimeter line to protect Dr. Viti and his men during County Fairs, MedCAPs, and DentCAPs. One time, we tromped the wire right through a rice field. If you're halfway familiar with farming, you'll know that tromping through a grain field isn't good. The poor farmer begged us not to drag the wire through his paddy. The platoon sergeant was ready to club the guy. I argued, "For crying out loud, crap. This wire doesn't do us a bit of good anyway. If we have somebody or need to get somebody it will just be in our way."

We finally got permission to roll and stash the concertina wire. We apologized to the farmer. He understood but it didn't help his rice crop. It was a real sad day is what it was. We were sick over that. The ol' farmer went to Duc Duc for reimbursement.

There was a price for everything, including killing a water buffalo. Many of us were country boys raised with livestock, so we understood. It was big deal and a sad day for the entire village to lose a water buffalo in cross fire. The Vietnamese depended on those animals. Water buffalo's weren't purposely shot. We left one family weeping on a water buffalo shot in an enemy cross fire. It was a *bad day*, and I mean it was a bad day. We thought hard about how we could wrestle another water buffalo to them.

One time dinks ambushed us from the west side of the trail as we guarded our tall tanks. Did you know those tanks were a hazard to jump from with your ammo and weighted gear? Man, when you landed, particularly if it wasn't raining, the dirt was harder than bricks. You could easily break a leg.

So now we're being ambushed. And, boy, did we bail and hit the ground. But there was so much dust, we couldn't see. The tankers wheeled in toward the paddies but of course they didn't have any targets because they couldn't see.

When we finally opened up on the enemy, Branson (not real name) shot a wounded VC as he crawled away. Now Billy Branson had a score to settle. His brother was killed with the Ninth Marines on the DMZ. He was a great Marine but on the borderline of killing every walking Vietnamese. I usually collared him, but on this tank patrol, he wound up on this VC that crawled in the bush. Ol' Branson came out of the bush wearing a silly grin and nodded. "Job's done, Sarge."

This new lieutenant with the tankers turned to me hollerin, "My God, do something with that Marine."

"Like what?"

"Report it."

These dumb tankers rode around buttoned up so I told 'em they needed to get out in the rest of the world. "I will do no such report. That dead guy was a part of the ambush that was trying to kill you ten seconds ago with you buttoned up in that tank."

With that, the lieutenant reached for Branson. I spat at the lieutenant and warned him, "No, no, Lieutenant, don't touch him."

I spat because Branson would've taken the lieutenant's head off if the opportunity grabbed him.

I told him again, "Leave him alone."

Branson walked over to us, shaking his head, and asked, "What's the problem?"

The lieutenant spoke up. "My God that Viet Cong was wounded."

Branson, staring incredulously, said, "Yes, sir, he was, and I shot him."

"But you killed him."

"Yes, sir, I did just that; I killed him."

Branson got the lieutenant's message so he got six inches to his nose and sure told him. "Lieutenant, he shot at me, not you."

Branson walked away. That was the last we ever heard of it.

Branson was later shot, medevaced home, returned to Vietnam, and was shot up again.

Years later I got a letter from him that read, "I've had it with these civilian pukes."

He committed suicide.

We were supposed to give confiscated Vietnamese money to the ARVN's or the PF's. But when I discovered they were using it as their bank account instead of distributing it to the villagers or buying anything to improve the villages, I said, "Forget that noise, that's the last sack we're turning in." So we stuffed the money inside the hootch of a poor ol' farmer—without his knowledge—that looked like he was a little more down on his luck than the others; or we bought chickens and ducks to give to mammasan.

Yes, I felt that we changed hearts and minds, especially Marine CAP units who were alone in villages with no obvious close support other than a radio. Those brave fellas helped villagers with everyday life. They raised pigs and chickens, built fences and houses, and trained the Vietnamese in infantry and patrol tactics, systems, and weapons. They were also taught how to use a radio to intercept the VC and the NVA. Some suspicious villagers thought the Marines would stay until the NVA or the VC attacked, and then they'd bug out and leave them to be butchered. But they soon discovered when the enemy came, those Marines protected the village. Slowly the villagers said, "Hey, these guys are for real."

One village wore armbands mourning a team of Marines that were killed in their village.

The Marines dropped out of one patrol to walk through a village market and trade C rats for chickens, ducks, and stuff. There was a hoorah behind me as one Marine purchased food from a Vietnamese woman. A Vietnamese gentleman with one leg and crutches pinned this woman by the neck with one hand while holding a grenade with the other—with the pin pulled back—ready to shove into her mouth. I yelled at the Marine ready to shoot the guy, "Cease fire and back off." They did, and we sorted the problem. The Vietnamese lady had cheated the Marine during their exchange. The one legged man—witnessing the exchange—came to the Marine's point of honor. He wasn't going to let the Marine be cheated. This ol' South Vietnamese Army guy had lost his leg fighting the VC. Marines gave him cigarettes or what ever he needed and he gave us information.

Some villagers, genuinely appreciative of American protection and care, quietly gave us information after MedCAP's or clinic calls. They'd signal as we patrolled; like the ol' man sitting on the edge of a well, discreetly showing two or three fingers or nodding left or right. We were ready to turn a VC loose until an elder lady gestured with her hand on her throat. "No, he'll cut your throat." So we latched onto him. But some, despite our help, had fire in their eyes and were ready to slice our throats in a heartbeat.

Thank goodness we didn't have to deal with the ARVNS and PF's often. They just stayed out of our way. And we didn't take them on patrols because they were worthless. Every time—well maybe they had some good ones during the eleven years, but while I was there every time they were assigned as an NVA blocking force, they'd let the NVA escape.

On this occasion, we radioed the PF's that a squad of Marines would be passing through at such-and-such a time as we marched through new country, including an unfamiliar village toward a PF outpost. Well, they disappeared. So those enemy suckers let us get to the end of the village before they opened up and pinned us down in the village crapper. You know, where they went to relieve themselves before scooping it up to put in their gardens. And it stuck to our clothes. Guys puked so bad. We never did get it washed out of our web gear. The aroma was beyond description. We warned the PF's the next time they abandoned us we were going to blow them off their hilltop.

We let one group of NVA walk right through us. They were dressed in the South Vietnamese Army uniforms. We thought they were allies. We gave them cigarettes. We even chided with them. But we all had the same feeling. "Man, we're in the middle of rattle snakes." We knew that hawks circled. The enemy, knowing we sensed them, made their bird down to the bamboo, and we didn't get a one of 'em. They flew out.

One Marine ran into a knee-deep paddy of muck *during* a firefight to carry a little girl trapped in a line of cross fire back to safety. The newspapers never covered those stories. *Marines* did things like that everyday. You just can't beat 'em, I can tell you that.

Lance Corporal Jesse Lyons:

I wish I had the intestinal fortitude to write my own book. Lucia, make sure people understand how fast a Marine makes life and death decisions during combat. All combat situations are orchestrated by the intensity of the firepower unleashed by the enemy. And because things happen so quickly, most engagements follow Murphy's Law; the mission doesn't always go as planned even if you plan beforehand.

Fucking New Guys (FNGs) were treated badly and avoided at all costs. FNGs were stupid. FNGs got you or your buddies killed.

A gook opened fire with an AK47 during my first Antenna Valley patrol as an FNG. I froze. The Marines in front of me were wounded and killed. The FNG that I went to Vietnam with—a big, strapping black Marine—was shot through the head. We could see his pinker than pink brain oozing. I began vomiting.

My Fire Team Leader, Mike Hare, one of the best guys I've ever met in my life, said, "Hey, Lyons, he's lucky."

I was dumbfounded. "Lucky?"

"Yeah," he said. "He's lucky he's dead. He's lucky he doesn't have to suffer. It's better to get killed your first day as an FNG instead of suffering through thirteen months of this shit and never making it home alive."

Mike Hare was killed on patrol with three days left in his Vietnam tour.

Combat is about crawling through mud and blood, sticking your fingers in someone's head or neck to stop the bleeding and watching your best friends get killed.

I spent twelve years getting beat up by the nuns and priests of Catholic school. I'm not sure which was worse, going to Vietnam or enduring the olden days of Catholic school.

I had second thoughts about killing people. I spoke with the VA chaplain who said it was okay to kill for your country. Many years later, a Catholic priest sermoned that killing during an undeclared war meant that you murdered. Vietnam was an undeclared war. I walked out and never returned. I was born again but that only lasted a few years. Today, I visit the VA chaplain and chapel to receive communion.

Lucia, please let the world know about my friend, Mike Hare. He was a true hero. Mike Hare was a Marine's Marine who sacrificed his life for his country. I'm proud to have served by his side.

FMF Corpsman Roger Ware.

Fleet Marine Force Corpsman Roger Ware:

Marines not attached to the battalion as infantry or grunts busting their butts in the boonies were nicknamed outsiders and skaters.

Wounded Marines, although appreciative of their medical care, felt guilty about deserting their platoon and wanted nothing more than to get back to their squads. Vietnam combat Marines were dedicated to *each other.* Dying Marines asked about their buddies. I'd be overwhelmed with an atrocious injury, while they lay oblivious, asking about Joe, Jim, or Doc. It was always about someone else. Marines fought for each other. Marines performed many heroic acts because they didn't want to let their brothers down.

A Field Medical Tag was a blue five-by-seven paper tag wire bound in a book. One copy tore out, leaving a carbon copy in the book. Tags were pinned to a guy's shirt with his name, rank, unit, date, location, type of injury, was it due to enemy action/hostile fire, what you did, priority of evacuation, and your signature. Although required, rain, mud, and dampness made tags impossible to write in the field. The ink was like grease writing on wet paper. And most of the time, I just didn't have time to write.

Here's a typical scenario. A guy gets hit by a mine on patrol. Marines yell, "Corpsman up." A corpsman runs to the scene as the lieutenant calls for a medevac. A corpsman is patching up a guy with fifteen or twenty holes from a booby trap or grenade shrapnel when someone yells, "Doc, helo's inbound." Corpsmen didn't have time to write a medical tag. That helo's not going to wait; particularly if it's under fire. They'll drag the wounded on a poncho, throw him in the helo, and off they go. In the meantime, you're saying, "Wow, I never wrote a medical tag!" It all happened quickly.

Imagine trying to write in the pitch black of night. And you can't make any light as it draws enemy fire. How do you treat a guy you can't see? Although challenging, by feel.

Battalion Surgeon, Floyd Gonder, MD:

Field medicine was frustrating. I didn't have any equipment. I lived and worked with the pack on my back. I'd stop the bleeding, stabilize, and medevac patients for definitive treatment without knowing who lived or died. Injured Marines were always extremely scared. They'd ask, "Oh, Doc, am I going to die?"

And I would always tell them, "No, you're going to make it."

Gunshot wounds destroyed the anterior portion of the abdomen and left intestines exposed to the elements. Kids stared at their own intestines! I relaxed

*Lance Cpl. Wasson and
Lance Cpl. Underwood
—"Underdog"—Hotel
Company, July 4, 1967.
Underwood lighting a cigarette
for tight buddy Wasson being
medevaced for facial and lung
wounds. Photo entitled
"My Brother's Keeper."*

the wounded with morphine. It wasn't easy. We were on a first name basis with these guys.

Immersion foot—trench rot—was devastating. The tissue between the toes cracked down to the bone. Although secondary infections didn't require surgery, patients were horribly debilitated, and healing took weeks.

But heat stroke frightened me more than getting shot. I constantly sucked on salt tablets even though they tasted horrible. During a heat stroke, temperatures could reach a fatal one hundred and six degrees, and patients could suffer irreversible brain damage. Marines complaining of indigestion and abdominal cramps became weak, disoriented, dehydrated, and passed out. We insisted that Marines fill their canteens with stream water and use iodine and Halazone tablets to kill the bacteria. But combat grunts didn't have the time to worry about fluid intake, iodine, Halazone, and salt tablets. They just didn't have that luxury.

One kid from Philadelphia, who flunked out of four colleges, saved my life. He *fearlessly* dragged me from harm's way after a mortar knocked me unconscious as I loaded a medevac. God, I had a concussion headache for days. That happened twice. No Purple Hearts though. Never. Marines were superstitious about Purple Hearts. Small insignificant Purple Hearts led to a major one.

One Marine appeared at the BAS with a migraine headache before any major field duty. He'd be in agony so Dr. Tom and I, shaking our heads, would place him in sick bay. And sure enough after the troops moved out, he'd perk up. Dr. Tom would counsel him but the kid had agony down. And then he did something heroic during one patrol, and what do you know? He never had another migraine headache. We'd see him in An Hoa and boost his confidence. "Hey, Joe, congratulations. You're a real hero." He'd smile and wave. But we never did see him in sick bay again.

In one hostile area, jets dropped camouflage smoke bombs to cover our landing. Well, the wind blew the smoke *into* the chopper, and we were pelted by bullets the instant we hit the ground. I never ran and jumped into a bomb crater so fast in my life. It took the Marines almost fifteen minutes—an absolute eternity—to secure the perimeter.

Another medevac loaded with wounded crashed while trying to get altitude through a hailstorm of bullets. A round landed in the pilot's chin and we spiraled down twenty-five feet. It wasn't a tremendous crash but we were in no man's land with wounded and an injured pilot and gun crew. Two choppers were sent, one to rescue us and one for the downed chopper.

Vietnam harbors no lingering effects on my quality of life. But I only share my Vietnam experience with other veterans. Civilians don't want to hear about ancient history. I read an occasional Vietnam book. No particular movie. Everything's always neat in the movies. Nothing was neat in Vietnam. You have to smell death to feel combat. We'd walk through rice paddies after big operations, counting decomposed and bloated bodies. The sights and smells were horrid.

Napalm smelled horrible. Everything burned and of course the noise, the screaming and hollering wasn't joyous.

Without a doubt, we fulfilled a purpose in Vietnam. I was one hundred percent in favor of our mission because the alternative was devastating. The people, especially the village chiefs, were gung-ho. They didn't want South Vietnam in communist hands. Vietnam gave me an appreciation for life. Working among the Vietnamese was phenomenal. Dr. Tom and I loved caring for the Marines and the Vietnamese, especially the children. I was astounded to hear the anti-Vietnam rhetoric when I returned home. I was devastated to hear America's declaration that we lost the war; such a tremendous waste. In light of my role in the Vietnam War, I would do it all over again. Would I encourage my children? Yes, I spoke to my son about a possible draft. Losing him to war would be devastating, but running off to Canada is not an option. That's how strongly I feel about serving my country. Although Vietnam is never discussed, my children know that my Vietnam experience is held in a positive light. They've never seen my pictures or know I received any medals. Only my wife knows.

Vietnam matured me in ways I never thought possible. I've learned how to truly appreciate the little things. I thank God for all that I have.

Lieutenant James Meyers:
Lucia, again I tell you, I was grateful to America for sending her finest sons and daughters to protect the innocent from the barbarians. America's ideology was undermined by the anti-war protestors and the ill-conceived political strategists usurping America's military by politically fighting a war that should have been fought by the military. America's military did not lose the Vietnam War.

I met Captain James Graham while I was stationed with a security platoon at the base of Nong Son, our mountain outpost. We dug in below the COC with flanks on each side. Captain Graham asked me to show him our defensive positions. As we walked on this little trail, He called me by my name, "Jim?"

Now, it was unusual for him to call me Jim because I didn't know him very well.

"Jim," he said. "What do you intend to do about Jesus?"

I thought, *Jesus, Jesus, what squad is he in? I don't remember a Spanish kid named Jesus. I didn't have the faintest idea of who he was talking about.* I hesitated before apologizing. "I'm sorry, sir. I don't know what squad he's in. What does he look like?"

Captain Graham laughed. "No, I'm talking about Jesus Christ."

"I didn't know I was supposed to do something with Him, sir."

"When you discover that Jesus is the Lamb of God, you'll know what you have to do."

When I understood the answer as Jesus as the Lamb of God, my faith took a pivotal turn. That conversation burned the innermost part of my being to become the cornerstone of my faith.

Lieutenant William Harvey:

Life sucked in Vietnam. We lived like dirty animals. We drank water from rice paddies fertilized with human feces. We wore our utilities until they rotted off. We had a choice of twelve C rations for one year. It was as an about face of life as I could imagine. We couldn't escape it so we just kept going. We were Marines.

I had a twenty-one year love affair with the Marine Corps. I loved every

Lt. Bill Harvey, USMC, RSVN, 1967.

goddamn day. I'd open up my eyes every morning, anxious to get to work. I learned more about people and life in Vietnam, despite the sadness and trauma, than anyone could possibly imagine.

Lance Corporal Jesse Pender:

I joined the Marine Corps determined to be the best that I could be.

During my early An Hoa days, Corporal Barry (not real name) invited me to socialize. "You're new here, Pender, come to my tent for a drink later, and I'll introduce you to some people."

"Cool."

I met everyone until one Marine, unhappy with the *idea* of me said, "I don't drink with niggers."

My better judgment deviated me from grabbing him by the stacking swivel and beating him. Corporal Barry threw him out. But racial tension or segregation didn't happen often. And when it did, it happened in the rear.

One officer threatened to court-martial me when I refused to turn in my M14 for the damn worthless M16. And that didn't bother me none because if court-martialed, I had to return to Okinawa. So it didn't bother me a bit.

There are no atheists in foxholes. And there's a thin line between cowardliness and bravery. Anyone can go either way. You can be a hero or you can be a zero. I wasn't John Wayne. I wasn't looking for a Medal of Honor. As a matter of fact, I wasn't looking for a medal of anything. I was just doing my job.

We found one kid frozen with an un-blown satchel charge lodged between his legs. It messed his head. No one could bring this kid back to the real world. He was medevaced out. Another kid shot a Chinese soldier point blank, and while dying, the Chinese soldier laughed and smiled at the Marine. The young Marine became so screwed up, he walked around babbling like an idiot. Another Marine drowned as we forged a rapid stream. He washed away before we could save him. We found him several days later.

When I returned home after my first tour things weren't cool. Americans protested, called me names, and blamed me for this, that, and the other.

Americans forgot that I performed the job I was asked and ordered to do. Americans didn't blame the right people, the political administration. Bitter, I went back to Nam. At least I knew who I was fighting. While waiting to pick up my military clothes from the cleaners, I went to Woolworth's five-and-dime store to enjoy a cold soda. But the counter waitress told me that she didn't serve niggers. I didn't say anything. I just left thinking, *What the hell was I doing fighting for a country that tells me that I'm a second class citizen because I'm black?*

Lieutenant Martin Dunbar:
The strangest thing happened to a brand new second lieutenant during his first field operation with his infantry company. We fired flares; thirty-pound canister artillery shells that held a parachute that drifted down to provide light. Well, a canister hit him on the head and killed him.

Name Withheld:
One chaplain wandered the halls of the Battalion Aid Station comforting the wounded, dying, and dead. He prayed as the doctors sewed broad stitches that left huge, pink, healing welts. "Alive at least for now."

And he prayed when the doctors failed to grant the young men another earthly breath. He'd ramble on, drunk at the Club. "Bullshit is what I, the chaplain, give them. Bullshit and God."

Fleet Marine Force Corpsman Dennis Noah:
We discovered hootches packed with tons of rice in no man's land. We loaded one hundred pound bags of rice on choppers destined to friendly

Vietnamese villages and CAP units. An entire platoon stuffed bags until sundown without making a dent. B52s blew the cache to hell. The brass feared an ambush if we stayed any longer. But man, we hauled rice and loaded helicopter after helicopter, leaving enough rice to feed an NVA regiment for six months.

After one harrowing escapade we took turns holding a knife to the throat of a VC sniper pulled from a spider hole as a photo op. "The capturing of a ferocious enemy!" We handed him over to Intelligence nervous and unharmed.

Email delivered by Captain John Newton, USMC, following the 9/11 attacks on the World Trade Center:

Although difficult to begin again following the devastation of 9/11, I must, saddened as an apparent, albeit very small, casualty of the attack. I apologize for yet another ramble by a whiney Vietnam vet, but since it's the yard stick used to measure my life events and an apparent curse to talk about this junk over and over again, I'm going to bore you with my reflections concerning the past two weeks anyway. Feel free to hit the delete button at any time.

> 1. I've spent the past two weeks with an overwhelming need, or urge, or both, to do something. At one point, because I disdain the arms length involvement that writing a check allows, I thought about jumping in the car and driving to New York to help. Fortunately, "they" said don't come, so I was spared a probably meaningless gesture. I'll make do with writing a check. If any of you can direct me to where a check will do the most good, please do so.

> 2. One radio talking head announced that there seems to be a reduction in the fill in the blank _____ rages. Suddenly things that seemed very important on September 10th— like getting "that" parking place or getting to the toll booth first—just don't seem to be as important. I was struck by the parallel of the feelings harbored, and I fear, nurtured, since my Vietnam combat thirty-four years ago. Nothing has been worth getting too worked up about since, because on my peculiar yard stick, nothing was as important; nothing until now.

> 3. I would like to welcome everyone to the world of post traumatic stress syndrome. In large measure, the fear that gnaws the back of one's mind when boarding a plane or riding an elevator beyond a thirteenth floor, is what it's all about. Get used to it. It never goes away.

4. Be careful decorating your car with American flags. From what I've seen in the Massachusetts Commonwealth, it's creating a lot of colorful road litter.

5. How much freedom are you willing to exchange for security? Franklin said that if you trade freedom for security you don't get either, and I agree. When I really want to get depressed, I think about legislative bodies at the federal, state, county, and town level passing laws all year long year after year. Laws are not removed, they are simply added. And with every addition another freedom silently passes away. I am, however, willing to take my chances.

6. A very dark and selfish thought that I feel safe sharing with people I trust . . . Where were all the American patriots in 1967 and 1968 and 1969 . . . ?

That's it. Thanks, I needed that. If I've offended anyone, I'm sorry.
Peace and God Bless!
John

{Roger "Doc" Lansbury mailed a Vietnam Care Package which included several notable books, a video segment of a *Good Morning America* Vietnam Reunion and his diary—a gem that he willing gave me permission to share. I've included only the first six months of his tour to incorporate within my Vietnam time-frame. The contents have been edited—with permission, for grammer and punctuation—Lucia}

April 28, 1967

It's nine p.m. I've spent my first day in An Hoa after two days in Da Nang. An Hoa is surrounded by mountains that arise abruptly. The southern mountains are being defoliated, by chemical or fire I know not which, but they are blackened.

I still don't believe that I'm in Vietnam. I only remember that I'm in a war when the artillery fires—especially when it passes overhead. The building shudders under the impact of the shock waves, and I jump. They fired all morning. I watched artillery hit a few miles from here. I found it hard to believe those puffs of smoke were aimed at people. I'm told I will soon believe it. I must remember I am in a war.

I've been told that An Hoa is worse than the DMZ. I suppose everyone says that about where they're stationed. In a few days I'll be heading to the most booby-trapped place around. War. Will I realize it when I am under live fire?

The doctor had me start an IV on a Vietnamese boy today. Though shaking violently, I did well. The twelve-year-old had shrapnel wounds in his arm and side, and a big bullet hole through his foot. He came from a village known to be infested with VC. He was apparently lying to his questioners. The Marines slapped—gently—and threatened him until he was petrified. Even so he didn't flinch. He was medevaced to a hospital.

The VC are daring, probing the camp often. Two were caught inside the lines several nights ago. The few women I have seen are attractive. The children, as all children, are cute. They appear to be quite independent.

I'll be in the field in a few days to experience, to quote another corpsman, hell. We shall see.

April 29, 1967

Last night was quiet and rather cool. Fire has been more active in the last hour than it was all day. Today a Vietnamese came into the BAS with a high fever. Although he was diagnosed and treated for heat stroke, it was later discovered he had malaria. His temperature was over one-hundred-and-five degrees. The second class corpsman didn't seem to care how we treated this man. He was just another gook. Everyone seems to feel the same way. Apparently many of the Vietnamese fake malaria to get medevaced to Da Nang for a vacation.

A little girl with one brown and one blue eye came in for a shot. She was adorable and offered to shake everyone's hand.

It's quiet now. Everyone figures we will get mortared on May 1st because it's a communist holiday.

May 2, 1967

All rumors of a May Day attack were unfounded. We've finished our orientation classes and wait to join our companies for Operation Union.

We defend the only coal mine in South Vietnam. We are also situated by a route of the Ho Chi Minh Trail.

The Marine CAC program is an opportunity to learn the ways of the people that interests me. A corpsman lives with the people of a village and becomes the village doctor. Training includes thirty days of Vietnamese language school.

It's hot, of course, and more windy than usual. The compound seems more quiet than usual because the companies have left for Operation Union. Our medical gear was issued today, and I find it quite inadequate. But everyone around An Hoa is short of supplies.

If only I could be descriptive about this room in An Hoa where I've spent the last week, and I now spend my last night. It has a beauty all its own. The French room reminds me of a room depicted in the old French Foreign Legion movies. The floor is rough cement that's cracked, pitted, and discolored from age, heat, and mud. The plaster walls resemble the floor in texture. There are two large French windows on the opposite wall and on either side of the doorway. Only one has its panes intact. Through patched screens and piled sandbags I can see the smoke rising from the village fires.

The ten-cot room is lit by two, fly-speckled single neon lights secured by masking tape. A fan on the other side of the room runs constantly or as constantly as electricity runs. Ammunition boxes piled atop of one another make excellent storage space for personal items. The walls are adorned with the usual nudes from girlie magazines. Some are attractive; others aren't. The fan and the flies buzz.

Tomorrow I will enter hell.

May 3, 1967

The German Peace Corps nurses brought a twelve-year-old village girl with a fever of unknown origin into the BAS. She also had an infection on the right side of her face. A Vietnamese doctor treated it with human feces. Animal feces are often used by the locals. The girl was medevaced to Da Nang.

May 14, 1967

Mother's Day in the States; malaria pill day here. I've been back in An Hoa for three days. I joined my company in Antenna Valley on May 5th. As the helicopter landed, sniper fire welcomed me to the field. My first night was spent in a self-dug ditch in between the rows of a farmer's tobacco field. We stayed close to the farmer's house. His house consisted of several large bamboo poles that supported a grass thatched A-shaped roof. One usually finds livestock—a pig pen and a chicken coup—in the corner of a Vietnamese house. Those wealthy enough to own a water buffalo keep it in a pen nearby.

Vietnam and its people must be used to war. The majority of homes include a built-in bomb shelter. The shelter is also used for storage.

May 15, 1967

Hill 90 was our objective. The younger people were evacuated from the farmer's house whose land we dug in on. Two old men, a boy, a small pig, and several chickens and ducks remained. Refugee men and women burdened with ten children came from the surrounding farms, carrying their worldly possessions, chickens, ducks, un-husked rice, tobacco, and beetle nut. The women have black teeth from chewing beetle nut. The shriveled up men and women look twice their age. They remind me of old, weathered farmers. These people waited to be escorted to the safety of An Hoa, sitting as is their custom with both feet flat on the ground eight inches apart, resting their buttocks on their heels. The adults talk and smoke cigars. The children are subdued. The children smoke as soon as they're old enough to walk and talk.

As we prepared to leave, one woman bared her filthy breast to nurse her child.

A Vietnamese police chief who was a former VC joined us. He knew the valley and the people well, spotting booby traps and hiding places without difficulty.

He showed us VC huts which were immediately burned. The Marines got a kick from burning hootches although I fear not all of the burned homes were VC.

One village, terrorized by the VC had three young children shot through the head. One girl, still alive, was medevaced to Da Nang.

May 16, 1967

We moved to Ha Quang III today, a small hill five-hundred meters from the China Sea. It's beautiful. One sits, admiring the sights and sounds, and suddenly all is marred by the sound of a 30-caliber machine gun in the distance. The firing stops, and the children can be heard playing their games. What do they play? They play war.

May 21, 1967

Yesterday the company was sent to a nearby village as security for an American ambassador's inspection tour. The village is a completed sample of American aid to the Vietnamese. The Vietnamese village was built under American supervision. The homes are typically Vietnamese. The fields are well-plowed with a good irrigation system in place. The village, the homes, and the people appear much cleaner. Unlike many other villages I only saw one sickly child.

Many of the Vietnamese children have festering sores, scabies, and other vitamin deficiency diseases. I don't know what kind of sanitation devices, if any, are used. Even here an old woman walked out of her door to squat next to her house.

The children in this village are numerous. While waiting for the ambassador, we accepted the hospitality of a father, his pregnant wife, and their ten children. The children filled our canteens from their large stone bowl where they keep the day's water. Unfortunately the water tastes like rice paddy water.

Senator Tate, a Texas Democrat is due any second. The ambassador's visit was cancelled.

May 30, 1967

We sit in our raised, screened, and galvanized tin-roof quarters, writing letters, playing cards, arguing, sleeping, and waiting for war. A nearby company ran into a sizeable number of VC so we wait to be needed. Yesterday we acted as a blocking force for Popular and Regional Forces. The Marines don't trust the PF's, the RF's, or the ARVN soldiers. These Vietnamese forces are better known for running than fighting.

The relationship between us, especially in the field, appears to be close. The negro-white relationship is interesting. The negroes and whites get along better here than I've ever seen anywhere else. There's little prejudice on either side. The Marine word for negro is "Splib," for white is "Chuck." To address or refer to each as such is perfectly acceptable. I've not heard the word nigger.

I think that *Time Magazine* expressed this relationship well in their article entitled, "The Negro in Vietnam." The piece suggests that negro-white relationships between servicemen in Vietnam are years ahead of race relations in the United States.

June 13, 1967

We just got back from three days of R & R on China Beach in Da Nang.

Da Nang is a huge complex of military installments of Marine, Navy, and Air Force Services, each with its own PX and a Club overflowing with liquor and beer.

Da Nang City is located in the center of these complexes surrounded by shanty towns. Prostitution, pornography, and marijuana sales are the main business endeavors. Five dollars can buy the dubious pleasure of a quick roll in the hay or several hundred pre-rolled marijuana cigarettes. Of course, the prostitution houses, also known as skivvies, are off limits to Marines. But truthfully, few Marines ever get caught.

I'm not surprised at the amount of marijuana smoked by some. It's easy to get, relatively cheap, and makes for a pleasant trip after a few days of war.

We have a beer call every day in An Hoa. Thirty cents will buy your two-can-per-man beer ration. Other than this and the occasional bottle in the mail, there's nothing other than marijuana to turn to.

The beer hall opens soon, and we will all politely push and shove in line to get our two cans. I hope it's cold.

FMF Corpsman Roger Lansbury and FMF Corpsman Richard Stanton (KIA during TET '68).

June 20, 1967

Operation Arizona from the point of view of the unknowing, unthinking pawn was an unorganized and unsuccessful mass of confusion. I'm convinced each step of the operation was planned on the spot. Any pre-planning was disregarded. The morale was the lowest I've seen so far. There were many quarrels. Tempers flared with little provocation. This occurred especially after long and fast marches as the troops dragged with fatigue. The mental and physical strain placed on everyone for the five days was exhausting. To make matters worse, there was no enemy contact other than finding three VC in the caves of the ville where we spent the night. Enemy contact brings the troops together as one fighting force. During a fight, each individual is dependent on the other. The whole unit makes a decisive victory. Each individual has his own task and the responsibility of doing this task well. As a corpsman, I would probably do more harm than good if I were to play Marine by using a weapon during a firefight. If I had to use my .45 it would be as the Marines say, "Time to hang it up."

June 24, 1967

We sit on the uppermost level of the mountain of Nong Son on the Thu Bon River. During the day I sit and live, as others do, dug in a deep hole in the bare earth, surrounded by sandbags and covered by a tin roof that is also sheltered by sandbags. I sit fighting a war on a hot hill; living in a hole, eating the same twelve meals out of green cans. At night we trudge over hills through thick brush to ambush an unseen enemy while fighting myriads of blood thirsty mosquitoes. So it will be for several weeks.

Sitting here, I find it hard to believe there's a war going on. And yet, I believed it three weeks ago when mortars exploded and voices called "corpsman" from every direction. I believed it when a fellow corpsman screamed in agony as I watched helplessly. I believed it while he slowly died, pleading, "Please help me, help me."

I believed in the existence of war melting into the ground to avoid mortars. I remember thinking, *Oh my God, it's for real. It's not a game. It isn't fun anymore; they're trying to kill me*. I almost cried. But that was three weeks ago, and now I sit in a hole on a hill overlooking a beautiful view, and I find it hard to believe there is a war going on.

I wonder if I'm the only one who feels this way. Are flying bullets, exploding projectiles, and torn bodies the only way for me to remember I'm involved in a war in a country halfway around the world? Maybe I find it hard to believe because the only enemy I've seen other than a few dead are the VC we captured in a village during Operation Arizona. Funny, they looked like any other villagers.

I watch fires glow on the surrounding hills; fires that explode with artillery. I find them pretty. Jets swoop down dropping napalm which explodes in red and orange flames with billowing black smoke. I forget that napalm kills people, just as the enemy is trying to kill me.

I know there's a war going on. The newspapers say so.

I wonder if American presence is right or wrong, good or bad. I'm not sure I can answer. Villages are built with American aid near An Hoa. The homes are cleaner than most, with better irrigation systems so the crops are rich and plentiful. The people look cleaner. Gone are the scab-infested children with open running sores covered with flies and water buffalo dung.

But I see a Marine shoot a water buffalo securely tied to a fence. He kills and unties the animal to tell everyone that it charged him. I wonder about the Vietnamese farmers who have no way to plow their fields.

But good or bad or right or wrong is of no importance to me right now. That is a matter of reflection over a cup of coffee or a glass of wine after a home-cooked meal. It doesn't matter because good or bad or right or wrong, I'm here. Even though I find it hard to believe, I'm involved.

June 27, 1967

We never reached our intended ambush site last night. As we were leaving the CAC unit we received a radio report to spend the night. Intelligence spotted six companies of NVA nearby. We also learned that two water buffalo were killed yesterday. Apparently the Vietnamese kill water buffaloes as a sacrifice before going into battle. The hill is defended by one company minus one platoon, now on R & R in China Beach. Everyone is expecting to be attacked at any moment.

The men's spirits are high. Maybe they are covering their nervousness. Everyone is friendly, staying in groups and chewing the fat. We sit and wait. There is joking and talk of old times and home. We even joke about being overrun. Some write letters home saying, "Dear Folks, Everything is fine and there is nothing exciting happening. P.S. This may be my last letter home."

Yesterday during an evening ambush a Marine went crazy. He had been acting strangely—very withdrawn—for the last few days. I kept an eye on him because he had been recently released from the hospital with a diagnosis of malaria. He was immediately medevaced to Da Nang.

Mail just came in. We are expecting ice and ice cream shortly. Spirits remain high while we wait.

July 8, 1967

Our fears were justified on July 4th. At approximately 2340 on July 3rd the upper level of Nong Son was attacked. By midnight—July 4th—the top level was overrun. Fox Company, who had recently lost a platoon on Union II, lost a platoon on top of the hill. Fifteen were killed and twenty were wounded. The hill was overrun by a VC sapper suicide squad.

My platoon had been on top of the hill until July 1st. Foxtrot took over our positions. We went into the Antenna Valley. When Foxtrot was hit, we were called to help. We covered the five-mile distance in one hour and ten minutes—excellent time for a company-sized move. We learned that a two-company NVA-sized ambush waited for us. Fortunately we got on the road a thousand meters below the ambush site. Intelligence sources revealed that Chinese advisors helped with the attack on Nong Son which coincided with a mortar attack on An Hoa.

August 22, 1967

July 8th now seems eons in the past. I've been too busy and lazy to keep up-to-date on my writings. We returned to An Hoa from Nong Son on July 8th. The area was buzzing with reports of NVA battalions in the area. An Hoa was in imminent danger of attack. We embarked on a crash program of strengthening line fortifications, putting up barbed wire, building above ground bunkers, trenches, and fighting holes until an intelligence report stated that a nearby CAC village was to be hit by a company of NVA. Our platoon spent five days in the village strengthening the barbed wire perimeter. Neither An Hoa nor the ville have been hit.

September 8, 1967

Our next base of operations was eight miles north of An Hoa on Phu Lac (6) and My Loc (2). Both had been in our TAOR until April. Because our TAOR was exceptionally large for one battalion to control, Phu Lac (6) and My Loc (2) were given to 1/26 and one week later to 1/7 because 1/26 went to the DMZ. The areas are commonly called booby-trap alley. We suffer almost daily booby trap and mine casualties on Liberty Road.

Our first job was to rebuild the fortifications on My Loc (2). Rolls of barbed wire and thousands of sandbags were brought in. We built fifteen perimeter bunkers, a command post, and an ammunition bunker. The perimeter barbed wire remained intact. Our immediate concern was building a shelter on the barren hill. We spent eleven days on My Loc (2). The troops were exhausted. We couldn't work from eleven a.m. to one p.m. because of the heat. After a hard day's work, we still had the usual night activities of manning the lines, listening posts, outposts, ambushes, etc. The strain showed on the short-handed and undersized platoon. Morale was low. Water was scarce; our only source a two-hundred-and-fifty-gallon container called a water buffalo. Showers were simply out of the question. I've had one sponge bath in eleven days.

My Loc (2) was depressing. My morale's low. I'm tired of an apparently senseless and futile war. I'm tired of eating C rations and sleeping in the dirt. We live like animals and smell worse. I'm tired of seeing fear on the faces of the Vietnamese men, women, and children from the surrounding villages. As we enter a village for a routine patrol, children cry, and the men and women visibly shake. The VC have a very effective propaganda system. The people think Americans rape, savage, and destroy. Sometimes a destruction of property and rough handling happens more than is necessary. An unthinking Marine searching a house will throw things and overturn furniture.

The Marines ask the Vietnamese questions to which the standard reply is, "I do not understand." The angered Marine, tired of hearing this, might give the individual a hard shove or slap and leave disgusted.

The civilian casualties who were inadvertently wounded by our fire also depressed me. We received sniper fire for five days which we replied with machine gun, mortar, and artillery fire. After such incidents civilians brought us casualties from our fire.

On August 1st before our bunkers were completely finished, and before we could enjoy the dubious pleasure of living in our own completed works of art, second platoon moved to Phu Lac (6) and first platoon took our place.

The routine at Phu Lac (6) was a strenuous one. We were concerned with the security of a five mile stretch of road from Phu Lac (6) to An Hoa. This road is feared by the daily convoy drivers from Da Nang to An Hoa. 1/7 had been losing men and vehicles to mines planted on the road. Our luck hasn't been much better. Our convoy's lost an average of one vehicle every three days. Phu Lac (6) has five tanks at its disposal. At one point we had no tanks in operating condition. It's amazing there were not more serious casualties.

One day I was riding the lead tank as a convoy security returning from An Hoa. The second tank was the rear of the twenty-vehicle convoy. About four miles from Phu Lac (6) the rear tank hit a small mine. There were no injuries but the tank had to be towed by our tank. About a mile from Phu Lac (6) the tank we were towing hit a second mine. I was momentarily dazed by the concussion but quickly came to my senses and jumped off the tank to check for casualties. One of the three injuries required evacuation. The tank was almost beyond repair.

Our routine at Phu Lac (6) consisted of daily squad-sized mine sweeps, four man day and night road outposts, night ambushes and platoon-sized search and destroy missions.

On the night of August 10th, I was one of the four man outposts. We set up on the side of the road around a small bush fifteen meters from a foot trail running perpendicular to and crossing the road. At 2000 OP1 joined us. We had no cover and little concealment. Two men stayed awake for watch as the rest settled to sleep.

I couldn't sleep. I missed the constant buzz of mosquitoes. As I got up to urinate, one watch Marine quietly woke everyone. In a barely audible whisper he told us not to make a sound or move a muscle. We froze. I was lying on my back in a shallow gully that was deep enough to block my view of the road. I didn't dare look. The Marine on watch saw a man carefully scan the road. It was a dark night with no moon. We were in the open but they did not see us. He disappeared and reappeared with ten men. They casually walked to the center of the road talking in normal but excited voices. They then split up as though they were setting up flank security for a larger force. Our squad leader decided to wait. Again, in a barely audible whisper, he told us not to move or make a sound.

After an hour, a column of well-armed, well-spaced, and well-disciplined uniformed NVA walked quietly across the road, following a foot path to a gully fifteen feet from our position. I couldn't see but I could hear boots on the dirt and pebbles mixed with the occasional ring of metal or clank of a machine gun ammunition belt. The Marines began counting. One stopped at eighty; another at one hundred and fifty; another counted close to two hundred. How none of them saw us I do not know.

The last man on the NVA column passed us and four men stayed to scan the road. The NVA were apparently waiting for another element to start across the road. As a flare from An Hoa illuminated our position, one Marine rustled his poncho. The squad leader saw one of the four NVA crouch and advance to our position. We had been spotted. The squad leader immediately threw two grenades, yelled for everyone to open up, and fired his M16 on full automatic over my head. Everyone was shooting and throwing hand grenades. Two of the four figures still on the road fell immediately. The other two took cover on the far side of the road. We took one hand grenade and three carbine rounds.

The carbine hit no one. The grenade gave three of us minor shrapnel wounds. We caught them completely by surprise. They did not assault us because they didn't realize how small of a group we were. For all they knew we could have been company-sized. To open up on us would give away their positions.

We decided it was time to withdraw. This we did; at a dead run. It took us about a half hour to return to Phu Lac (6). My main concern was running into enemy flank security. I don't know how, unless they withdrew upon hearing the fire, but we missed them.

A check of the area the next day found two blood trails—where the bodies had been dragged—and our gear which we left behind in haste. We were credited with averting a possible attack on Phu Lac (6).

September 22, 1967

The paper, like everything around here, including me, is grubby. I haven't written anything or to anyone in a month due to low morale. I'm afraid that I am fed up with what I feel is useless bloodshed.

We are at Phu Lac (6) to keep Liberty Road—which runs from An Hoa to Da Nang—open. Unfortunately VC activity has markedly stepped up. Every two days a vehicle hits a mine. I was blown off a tank two days ago when the vehicle hit a mine, despite the daily mine sweep and Marines stationed at strategic points on the road. We lost our platoon commander and a corpsman I knew when the mine sweep was ambushed several days ago. They were completely overrun. Fifteen were killed. It won't be in the papers. I'm tired of treating innocent civilians accidentally shot or bombed. I make it sound more horrible than it is so I can't be quoted.

The CAC villes, now CAP as we discovered that CAC pronounced KAK is a dirty word in Vietnamese, are often probed by VC snipers.

Booby traps between An Hoa and Phu Lac (6) are worse. Stepping on a booby trap guarantees the loss of a leg or two.

On one three-day sweep of Phu Nong we lost two men to booby traps. The first Marine on flank stepped on a perimeter booby trap within the first two hours. His right leg was so badly damaged it had to be amputated at the groin. He also lost the four fingers of his right hand. Another Marine stepped across a trench onto a booby trap. His left leg was severed at the shin and his right foot hung by a small bit of flesh and muscle. We cut the remainder of his foot off. He lost a finger and one, maybe both testicles. Both legs were amputated at the knees.

December 12, 1967

I sit in a room of sandbags. It's not a room in the common sense—bearing a distinct personality of people and memories, familiar and secure. This sand-bagged room is an enclosed portion of the outside, meeting and clashing at tarp-covered windows and doors. The earth on the floor is the same as the earth of the walls and the ground outside. A candle flickers and the water drips inside and out.

I sit and write while watching the rats.

Rats scurry amongst sleeping men; not to harass for they as we, desire only to feed an empty stomach. Man is careless, and rats feed from his carelessness. After all, where would man be without his faithful companion, the rat?

Rats have lived with man's wretchedness and suffering, sharing man's burden. Rats have witnessed the rise and fall of the Roman Empire and the birth and death of Christ.

Rats ventured with Columbus.

Do they remember war, famine, and disease? Is Vietnam just another war for them? This war will end, and these rats will endure, living, suffering, and dying.

The rats have seen this all before and will see it again, in another war, another time, another place. They will see more death and suffering. They will scurry among exhausted boys. Boys tired of fighting; tired of living in fear; tired of not knowing why; tired of unaccustomed dirt and hate. They will live their existence in between these sandbags, searching, sniffing, scrounging, and fighting until death robs them of life.

In this room I sit and write, protected by sandbags among the rats.

I'm tired. Tired of expecting the unexpected and wondering what horrors we might have to face tonight. Tired of wondering if we'll see tomorrow's sun or die under illuminations of burning lead and steel with torn and ragged flesh.

I'm so very tired.

Are the rats tired as well?

December 22, 1967

I left the platoon today to start my tour at the BAS. I was scheduled to leave the field after six months but today it's almost eight. I shouldn't have to go into the bush again except on battalion-sized operations. I don't really like the BAS but it's better than being shot at. The BAS chief has all but promised to assign me to the pharmacy. I don't want to work sick call because the Marines from my platoon will be looking for favors of light duty. I hate to refuse them although I must. Fortunately I think they know it. Unfortunately I know our chief well enough to realize I can't depend on his promises.

December 23, 1967

I'm in the BAS, physically and mentally exhausted. I've had my fill of Vietnam. I was scheduled to leave for in country R & R but was not allowed because An Hoa is supposed to be mortared tonight. They promise that I may leave tomorrow.

We've been told of a Christmas truce but everyone knows that to be a farce. The VC use our holidays for strategic strikes. This is a good morale deflator. I fear if the VC come into An Hoa's perimeter, they'll come through the weakest point in the lines—the BAS.

December 24, 1967

They caught a VA sapper inside the lines yesterday afternoon but could not get any information from him. I watched the questioning but was told to keep mum as the procedures used in his questioning are considered unlawful. The suspect's nose and mouth were covered with a cloth which was kept moistened with soapy water.

I'm going to China Beach for five days of an in-country R & R.

The battalion will move to Phu Bai—north of Da Nang and south of the DMZ in early January.

January 1, 1968

I leave for Da Nang again for ten days of on-the-job training at First Medical Battalion. I will be working at A & S—administration and supply—which receives all casualties from the I Corps.

Epilogue
September 25, 1986

The question of how the Vietnam war affected my life is difficult if not impossible to answer. I have no way of knowing how I would differ today had I not experienced it. I have nothing to compare myself against. My Vietnam experiences are and always will be a part of me.

My combat experiences broadened my world view. I've witnessed the best and worst of man. The Vietnam War was a living horror. People I didn't know and really didn't have anything against were trying with all serious intent to kill me, as we were trying to kill them. We were humans—yet strangers—trying to kill and maim each other.

Fear was my constant companion in Vietnam. Fear walked with me, ate with me, and embraced my sleep. Fear affected my every action. Fear forced me to be forever alert and on guard. Fear caused me to sleep with my boots on. Fear forced me to know that every step may trip a wire or mine that could blow my legs off. Fear taught me not to get close to my comrades because the pain of their loss hurts. This fear forced me to withdraw and become hard, cold, callous, unthinking, unseeing, and uncaring.

Vietnam's fear was invasive, sapping my energy into a state of constant fatigue. Yet, this fear helped me to survive.

Vietnam gave me a new appreciation of life. Vietnam provided the knowledge of how fleeting and tenuous our existence can be. Vietnam taught me how quickly our bodies can cease to exist; how one's living, breathing, thinking life form can suddenly become nothing more than mangled meat, guts, bone, and hair.

I existed in Vietnam with the conscious knowledge that this breath, this moment in time might be my very last. The reality of death in Vietnam was no different than at home. However, in Vietnam we were forced to live with the awareness of death on an active, conscious level of understanding. In Vietnam the reality of death was uprooted from the subconscious to become an everyday thought.

I was plucked from watching TV while drinking a cold beer and dropped in the middle of a tropical jungle among people whose language and customs I had no knowledge of. These people shot me as I disembarked the helicopter. I lived in torrential rain and murderous heat with the ground as my bed and the sky as my cover. I saw devastation and horror. I learned the sickly sweet smell of human blood and the stench of burning flesh. I learned to identify weapons by the sounds of bullets cracking by. I became unaware of flies crawling all over me because I became used to them. I went un-bathed for weeks.

After a year of this existence, I was just as suddenly plucked from the jungle and put back in my easy chair with a cold beer while watching my comrades on TV. I was asked to act as if nothing happened to me. No one was interested in hearing about my living nightmare. I wondered, *Did it really happen or was it an imaginary figment of a warped and twisted mind? Was it real or have I gone mad?*

I went to Vietnam alone, and I returned alone to a citizenry whose disillusionment in their government's actions was growing in leaps and bounds. Faith and belief in Uncle Sam was shaken. I was twenty-four years old and I couldn't get served a drink in a bar because my military ID card was not proper identification.

This was America's first TV war. The public was selectively shown Vietnam's horrors. There were no flags raised over captured ground or maps with lines representing troops advancing victoriously. There were no joyous, flag-waving crowds of liberated Vietnamese throwing flowers at the tired marching troops. There were only numbers of dead and wounded.

There was a newsreel of a naked girl-child burned and fleeing from her accidentally napalmed village. Where were the cameras when I was in a remote village, holding a little girl who had been shot through the head by the local Viet Cong? She was alive but three of her baby sisters lay dead beside me. Their crime? We had camped next to her village two nights before.

I believe we can better appreciate joy by knowing sorrow; happiness by knowing sadness; and peace, unfortunately, by knowing war.

Because of my Vietnam experience, I pray that I am a better person. I pray that I am more tolerant, sympathetic, and empathetic. I pray that I may forgive. I pray most of all that I have learned to love, for love is I believe the Lord personified.

Vietnam
My Diary
December 12, 1967

I sit in a room of sandbags.
A candle flickers.
Water drips,
somewhere.
Inside?
Outside?
But this is not really
a room.
A room has personality
of people, of memories
it evokes.
Previous comforts.
Familiar.
Secure.
This sandbagged room,
is not a room
but an enclosure
of the outside.
Inside.
Outside.
Meet; clash
at tarpaulin windows
and doors.
Floors of earth,
Walls of earth,
Outside earth,
the same.
Amongst sleeping boys,
exhausted,
a rat scurries.
Not to harass,
but only to feed,
as we,
an empty stomach.
This rat has lived
man's wretchedness;
his suffering;
has shared the burden.
He has seen
the rise and fall.
He has known
famine.
Disease.
War.

Some die.
Some suffer.
This rat has seen
it all before,
and will again.
Another time.
Another place.
Boys tired;
of fighting.
Tired;
of fear.
Tired;
of unaccustomed dirt,
of unaccustomed hate.
This room that is.
Not a room.
The sandbags
will crumble.
Earth to earth.

I am tired.
Expecting the
unexpected.
Wondering.
"What horrors tonight?
Will I see
the sun again?
Or die under
man made,
sun bright,
illuminations?"
Flesh torn,
ragged.
Blood,
sickly sweet
from jagged steel
and burning lead.
A candle flickers.
Water drips,
somewhere.
People weep.
Does the rat
also tire?

The Wall
By Roger Lansbury

Black granite.
Somber. Smooth.
Mirrored reflections
from etched stone.
People.
Silent.
Slowly passing.
Like time,
an endless flow.
Care worn hands.
Searching.
Touch.
Caress.
A name.
Old uniforms;
now too small.
Medals worn;
ribbons,
faded.

Features, etched;
Frozen, like the names.
A sob. A moan.
A smile,
soft; private.
Remembering.
I walk and gaze;
vision blurred
by deeds undone;
and done.

Young hopes.
Young dreams.
Fifty-eight thousand
in stone.
Harry.
Frenchy.
Tiny.
Doc.
Names.
Living then;
And now,
in memory.

Between the lines,
the heart
of cold black stone;
Nightmares remembered.
Flashes of light.
Bursts of sound.
Smell of blood.
Agony and pain.
War.
Obscene.
My heart cries out,
"Why?"
I look again.
Black granite.
I see reflected;
me.

🌿 *Dear Daddy* 🌿

I've earmarked today, Friday, April 20th, 2007, the 20th anniversary of your passing, to finalize Dr. Tom's War. My stage drips with an ambiance designed to collectively stir my soul's solace—San Diego's off-beat rain day, perfumed candles, soft music, and cuddled cats. Anxious to purge, sentiment runs high. I've been rehearsing this day for as the grand finale from all that has separated me from my world of norm.

Truthfully, however, it's not quite nine a.m., and I've already piggy-backed Chris for a work-truck, fix-brake, drive me home, Good Samaritan exchange. The rain, unfortunately, deterred his intended bike ride home. As prayer enveloped my silent arrival ride, our return trip was a lesson in a ridiculous Radio Show entitled the "Deaf-Frat-Blog" interview. Without question, I expected Chris, Starbucks-jacked and jovial, to recall yesterday's tearful relay of my somber anniversary intentions. Remembering nada and noticing the obvious, I endured a rationale soliloquy of the comedic talent of this incredibly stupid show. My disdain was palpable to everyone but him which sadly left no one but me.

I now face the page, tea in hand, intentions not yet guttered. But our three hundred pound TV blares TiVo's **Saturday Night Live** *while Chris enjoys an early morning snack. I vacillate between disappoint and the projection of my best pissy face.* **Saturday Night Live** *wreaks of Don Imus and Anna Nicole Smith, figuratively and literally dead in the water. Throw in a couple of political jabs and sexist jokes and I'm ruined. I can't block the volume of idiocy ringing in my ears. My seething glares go un-noticed.*

Add Malaki, my eight-week Panther Bengal kitten, center stage, nibbling on my ear as though it was his mother's teats while his mother, butt-high in heat, woos, coos, and wails. I'm drowning in chaotic disharmony.

I exhale; loudly. I repeat the exhale. No one is listening. I lean back and stare at my surroundings. I give; up that is; but not without smiling at this satire of irony. Prepared to wallow in sympathy and sadness from the void of your absence, I stumble into your realm of wisecracks and jokes. Chicken Little's sky never fell in your world. Your homegrown turf was never, ever ordinary, so why would this arena be any different? You win, Pops. You win.

On the Lighter Side

MAY
ALL THE COLORS
OF EARTH
SURROUND + CELEBRATE
YOUR JOURNEY
Mac

"Retreat Hell! We just got here!"

—*Captain Lloyd Williams to the retreating French Army commander who pleaded with the Marines to flee from the attacking German Army in Belleau Wood, France, 2 June 1918.*

"I've got some bad news and some good news. The bad news is that we will be filling sandbags until the next Japanese attack comes. The good news is that we have plenty of sand."

—*Unidentified gunnery sergeant on Wake Island after the initial Japanese attacks, 11 December 1941.*

"Remember, whatever you write, this was no retreat. All that happened was that we found more Chinese behind us than in front of us, so we about faced and attacked."

—*Colonel Lewis B. "Chetsy" Puller to the media after the breakout of the Chosin Reservoir, Korea, December 1950.*

"Being ready is not what matters. What matters is winning when you get there."

—*Lt. General Victor H. "Brute" Krulak, April 1965.*

Gunnery Sergeant Sam Jones:

When I think about Vietnam, I think about the dumb things, the stupid stuff, the feather brains, and the lies we told. I don't relive the blood and guts or rehearse the close calls. I don't remember names. I remember the good and bad people.

I wasn't a pleasant person to work for. I was demanding and hard-nosed. I wanted things done and done right. Mister nice guys can't discipline two-hundred-and-sixty Marines. Those boys never opened their mouths back to me because I was GOD. Gunnery sergeants had different personalities, and it was my personality to be an SOB. You can't be a nice guy one day and a son of a bitch the next, so I was a son of a bitch every day.

But I'd rather work for an SOB than somebody who was wishy-washy; one day this is okay and the next day it ain't. I was the guy that said, "You walk down that line straight. If you get off to the right, I'm gonna' get on you, and if you get off to the left, I'm gonna' get on you."

While getting ready for outpost duty I told the platoon sergeants to leave the good troops behind because they needed a break. I ordered the shit birds out of mess duty where they were always warm, ate good meals, and got eight hours of sleep. I wanted them to be as miserable as we were.

As the ol' grouch, over-thirty gunnery sergeant, I never paid attention to my age because I grew up in the Marine Corps. But in Vietnam, we'd come back from the field exhausted while the baby-faced grunts cleaned up for inspection and played basketball. We, the officers, went to the staff club for a beer. We, meaning the older guys, couldn't do nothin' but rest and drink. William Cody once threatened to shoot every young Marine on the basketball court.

We grew tired of C rations. Ham and lima beans a.k.a. ham and mothers—were downright awful. But the worst thing about C rations is that we ate them cold. We never had time to heat them. So I demanded that my troops eat hot chow in An Hoa because if they didn't, they ended up messin' with their rations. I didn't want them eatin' those 'cause by the time we got to field they'd have nothin' to eat. I told the company commander that everybody goes to chow. If the lieutenant or troops complained I told 'em, "Okay no one has to go to chow. But everyone has to fall under company formations in the mess hall. And no one has to eat but everyone has to go through that line."

Dr. Viti backed me one hundred percent. I did it for their sake. The troops were like raising kids. If they didn't eat hot chow they deprived themselves. It may not have been cooked their mamma's way but hey, sometimes mamma was drunk when she cooked too.

I didn't get along well with most lieutenants. They were inexperienced and most often wanted to be their own boss. They didn't want some gunnery sergeant tellin' 'em what to do. The captain would say, "Gunny, I want this done," and I got it done with no discussion with no *lieutenant*. One day Captain Graham, one of the finest Marines I've ever worked for, held a meeting to lay out—*in order*—the next day's events. And since Captain Graham didn't miss nothin', at the end of the meeting he asked, "Are there any questions?"

And this second lieutenant says, "Yes, sir, I have a question. Do I have to take orders from Gunnery Sergeant Jones?"

I thought, *Oh shit, here it comes; Sam, you and your big mouth.*

Well, Captain Graham turned around, looked the lieutenant square in the eye and said, "Mister, let me tell you."

I couldn't believe what I heard. If a captain, colonel, or major called a lieutenant "Mister" you knew he was mad. Real mad.

"Gunnery Sergeant Jones is the company gunnery sergeant, slash the company executive officer, slash the weapons platoon commander, slash the weapons platoon sergeant. If you want his job, I'll give it to you."

That left that lieutenant speechless, and me happy.

Once we were crossing the river into the Arizona Territory with a green corpsman who huddled in a wet, soppy, muddy patch of water with Sergeant Marengo. The enemy opened fire and assaulted us from every angle. This corpsman started wailing, "Sergeant Marengo, Sergeant Marengo, Sergeant Marengo."

The kid was ballistic.

Sergeant Marengo yelled, "Doc, what the hell do you want?"

"Leeches, Sarge. Leeches. The water's filled with leeches. There are thousands of them."

Bullets buzzed like bees, and this kid worried about leeches.

Lance Corporal Brenton MacKinnon:

Sam Jones' administrative persona, posture, and banter were consistent; he was provocative, insulting, confrontational, foul, and thoroughly knowledgeable and professional. This façade was Sam's way of sorting and caring for his Marines. Gunnery Sergeant Sam Jones was Marine Corps glue. He was the incarnate high school football coach yelling, grumping, swearing, and publicly displaying imperfections to gradually rid his kids of bad habits. Except, Sam's kermudging helped Marines survive. Sparing no one, we knew that on some level, this mockery was an act of love. This daily, minute-by-minute repartee was his way of taking care of us. No one *really* disliked Sam; we all depended on Sam. We would have been lost without him. *Many* officers sought Gunnery Sergeant Sam Jones' advice. Sam's tone of voice—when lampooning—never changed. "Are you a protestor, you liberal bag of puke?"

I call this memory Soul Music.

During one lunchtime observation as I surveyed the tree line across the dry rice paddy, Robby lamented while consuming his ham-and-mothers. "No, Mac, I'm tellin' you. Jackie Wilson sang that song, not Wilson Picket."

Brenton MacKinnon, 2007.

"Do you think because I'm white, I don't have a memory?"

Robby stared at the last lima bean inside the C-rat can as though it was Frank Sinatra's name on a record label and then glared at me through sweat glistening on his black skin. "You still don't get it. You're okay for a California boy and lucky enough to have a soul station in safe, white suburbia, but Motown's a cultural thing, brother. It's something in our blood. And well, your white blood is yours, and our black blood is ours."

We finished eating in silence. We knew the color of blood by then.

"Check it out, Mac, it's time to call in."

The rest of Foxtrot was dug in two hundred meters behind us. I put my mixed fruit down and scanned the tree line with my binoculars. Nothing.

"Foxtrot Four. This is OP One. Over."

"Copy. Go."

"Sitrep. All clear. Over."

"Roger. Out."

"Hey, Mac, give me your mixed fruit, and I'll sing the whole song so that you can see you're blowing smoke about Wilson Pickett."

"I know the lyrics, Robby, and my voice is better."

"Bullshit! I heard you sing."

"Listen."

I stood up, prepared to belly breathe and belt my song to the sight of more than fifty VC guerillas charging us at full speed.

"Holy fuck, Robby! Let's go!"

I slapped the radio on my back, triggered the phone, and ran.

"Foxtrot Four. OP One. Fifty VC, half a click out, we're moving in. Don't shoot us!"

As I lagged behind burdened by the indescribable heat, humidity, and my twenty-five pound radio, Robby turned, sank to one knee, and emptied an M16 clip into the remains of our lunchtime observation post.

Robby didn't let up. "Come on, Mac!"

He jammed in another clip to the sound of chopper blades. A Cobra gun-ship lined up on a strafing run two hundred meters out was flying in fast.

"Fuckin' A, Mac! They're makin' a run on us! They think we're gooks."

I shivered, thinking we all looked the same from the air.

"Foxtrot. Abort chopper. Friendlies. Do you read me. Abort. Abort."

Nothing.

"Foxtrot. Abort chopper. Do you read me? Abort. Abort."

As the ship closed in, Robby wildly unbuckled and chucked his helmet to the ground. Thrusting his dark face and middle finger at the bird, Robby screamed, "I'm black you Mutha-fucker. Look, I'm black. I'm black."

The Cobra swooped down and swiftly redirected to the VC target.

"Let's go, Mac."

We sprinted to the outer ring of Fox's defensive position and dove safely behind a blasted tree stump. Leaning side by side, relieved, exhausted, and exhilarated, we nervously laughed as our company opened fire.

"Fuck, Mac. I've never been so happy to be so black in all of my goddamned life."

"Yeah. Me too. Me too."

He grinned with a toothy-white beauty I'll forever remember as he laughed. "It was Jackie Wilson you know."

After one successful operation Lieutenant Colonel Jackson awarded each platoon, in rotation, three days of R & R at China Beach. Unshaven and unclean, donning flak jackets, helmets, weapons, and ammunition, we flew from the bush to Da Nang. Our world changed simply by crossing the perimeter checkpoint at China Beach. This resort town sported guys in swimsuits playing volleyball, surfing, and barbecuing. We were C-rat guys now in shock. "Hey, I thought there was a war going on. What the hell is this?"

Drinking was our only desire. So we entered the cafeteria-slash-bar for new arrivals with our rifles, M70s, and pistols, and drank beer until the bartender announced, "Last call."

We defiantly stared. "Who is the enemy, and what are we fighting for? Why are being treated like shit? This is a special award in recognition for our achievements."

So Strong (not real name) stood, pointed his M79 at the bartender, and said, "We're keeping this bar open as long as we want. Give me the keys."

The bartender handed Strong the keys and ran.

Strong grinned. "Gentleman the bar's open."

We grabbed six-packs to celebrate. Five minutes later a squad of armed MPs marched in and ordered us to leave. We stood up and faced the MPs. The MPs looked at each other and left. Awarding ourselves a celebration that would have otherwise been denied, we drank every remaining drop of beer.

Staff Sergeant Tony Marengo:

During Operation Tuscaloosa Dennis Smith (not real name) charged in the wrong direction. We still joke about it today. "Everyone thought I was evading or scared when I was only going the wrong way." Fortunately, I pulled him back.

Chief Hospital Corpsman Lou LeGarie and Fleet Marine Force Corpsman Dennis Noah:

The Marines nicknamed one giant, burly, Ohio farm-boy corpsman, Mule. They loved this guy. Mule carried anything and everything for the Marines who fed him as payback. Unfortunately, Mule stuttered. As chief hospital corpsman I hesitated before assigning him to a line company but since we were so short on manpower, I had no choice.

The Arizona Territory was lethal. I joined the company CP during one brutal firefight when we received a frantic medevac call. Since the NVA often attempted to ambush Marines by speaking perfect American English via a stolen net, we needed to validate the call's authenticity. I suggested that Captain Bowers put the stuttering corpsman on the radio. Sure enough we heard, "Caaaapppptaaiiinnn Boooooowers, tttthhhhiiiiiss thiis is thiiiss iiissss doooc, doc, dddoc, cooommm, eoocmmm aaannnd gggeeett, uuusss, come and get us." We saved them.

Mule stuttered like hell but he became a hero.

Fleet Marine Force Corpsman JP Higgens:

One of the Marines most beloved corpsman stuttered. During one lengthy and lethal encounter, a large piece of shrapnel tore through his left thigh. Despite an infection painful enough to cause a limp, this corpsman refused to return to the BAS. "Nnnnooooooo, I'm noooooot leaviiiiing my MMMMMMMMMMarines."

Steel plates and sandbags covered truck floors with good reason. While riding one truck convoy six trucks back, a *boom* shook us to the core. Smoke billowed from the first truck. My gallant leapfrog from my moving truck caused me to somersault through the dirt, which in itself was comical. I hightailed to the explosion as the convoy defensively lined up with Marines to protect the first truck, now a mangled mess. I hopped on the remains of the truck's running board, expecting to see the driver's legs as two bloody stumps. Thank God, they were fine. He sat frozen, holding the steering wheel with both hands. I yelled, "Are you okay?" Shell shocked, he slowly turned his head. His face was completely black. He resembled a character from the minstrel show. The whites of his eyes were the only things visible. I expected him to say, "Mammy."

FMF Corpsman Doc "JP" Higgins.

Shock and dirt were his only injuries.

While patrolling the lethal Arizona Territory, sniper fire bolted us into a trench occupied by a poisonous, green tree-viper snake. Well isn't this just great. Caught between a snake and a sniper, we played a comical game of whack mole, jumping up to avoid the slithering snake and down to dodge sniper fire. We popped between the viper and sniper until one enterprising, courageous Marine sliced the snake with his Ka-Bar. And to our delight the sniper disappeared, no doubt fearful of the crazy Marines.

Every military man had a love-hate relationship with C rats, alternating between "at least we're eating" to "one more can of C-rat anything, and I'm going to puke."

While stationed in a village loaded with chickens during the latter phase, I was bound and determined to eat a chicken dinner. I knew that my .45 would disintegrate the bird so I snuck behind the herd, aware that running after them would be a waste of time. After several feeble attempts of getting within ten feet before one zoomed off, I spotted a harvest scythe mounted on a long pole. Scythe in hand I was steadfast to wound and kill. Of course, the chickens had other ideas. I chased them through hedgerows, houses, and across a large, dry rice paddy, wielding the scythe like it was a medieval weapon. I swung, and chickens scattered. I swung again. More darted and dashed. Who thought chickens could be that smart? The few that peeled away didn't stop me. I continued hunting as the Marines laughed. I didn't care—I was a man on a mission—to get me a chicken. I didn't give the booby traps and mines a second thought. Finally a swing not only made contact—it sliced its head. Now I trailed a bleeding, zigzagging, headless chicken. I finally caught it as it wildly flapped its wings. To the delight of my Marine audience I was splattered in chicken blood. But I had me a chicken.

Marines never patrolled the lethal Arizona Territory without suffering a booby trap, mine, or sniper casualty. My pineapple story proves how cautious we were.

One Marine spotted a pineapple plant, complete with pineapple, lining the side of the old railroad tracks. Now, this was the only pineapple I ever saw in Vietnam, but this was the Arizona Territory. Anything—especially a lonesome pineapple plant—could be trip wired. We couldn't risk a booby trap but we couldn't ignore a fresh pineapple. Thick sharp leaves blocked all side views, so we searched the ground for trip wires. What a dilemma. After wasting yet another hour deciding who had the stones to pick it, a Marine attached a rope to a grappling hook, determined to hoist the pineapple. We took cover on the other side of the railroad bed. Five Marines and an hour later, still no pineapple. We called in false checkpoints to avoid explaining our pineapple battle. Imagine our relief when we finally snagged the fruit without blowing up. But the damn thing was green. With considerable effort, one Marine sliced the pineapple with his K-bar. It was impossible to chew, and really bitter; all of this time and energy on a pineapple not ripe enough to eat. But thanks to that damn pineapple we returned to An Hoa without a single casualty.

Chief Hospital Corpsman Lou LeGarie:

I threatened to slap the shit right out of a corpsman who got smart with Dr. Gonder. I didn't stand for wisecracking bull or disrespect.

Hell, I'd line my boys up and chew their asses out. One guy made the mistake of coming forward so I flattened him in front of everyone.

Private First Class Bill Patton:

Typewriters were lifelines for office pogues. Our An Hoa office was down to one, which of course, wasn't enough. We couldn't get any more through supplies so I devised a plan with permission from the first sergeant. Sort of. "Hey, Sarge, cut me orders to go to Da Nang. I'll get typewriters."

"How are you going to do that? Never mind, I don't want to know. Just don't get caught."

"Don't worry about that, sir."

A fellow Marble Mountain office pogue made daily mail runs to Marine Air Wing Headquarters in Da Nang. We schemed to wait until noon chow when all but one guy remained in the office, a Quonset hut with a front and back door. While I engaged the duty clerk in conversation, my buddy snuck through the back and grabbed some typewriters. Within minutes, we hauled ass back to the jeep. We drove away as the clerk screamed, "Hey stop, thieves, stop. Come back here, damn it, come back. MP's, MP's they stole my typewriters, thieves, stop them."

Although the afternoon sniper at Phu Lac (6) never hit anyone, he bugged us. The constant *kapow, kapow, kapow* was annoying. This character was relentless, despite our best efforts with a 106, recoilless rifle and its 50 caliber spotting scope. Disgusted, we rolled an M48 A1 tank with a 90mm cannon to hose the tree line. That's like using an elephant gun to shoot rabbits. It worked.

Fifty-five-gallon trash-burn barrels lined every hootch in An Hoa. We, the grunts, discovered that peanut butter C-rat cans exploded when heated so we covertly dropped the cans into the barrels. Fifty yards down the road, *boom!* Smoke and ashes. The colonel forbade it after some guy dropped ammunition.

Name Withheld:

I remember sitting on the crapper at Nong Son, completely incensed at being sniped at. I'm in the damn shitter receiving sniper fire. What goes through your mind? Hurry up.

As strange as this may sound, only once did I question my safe return from Vietnam. I was afraid, yes, but even during combat, I never thought, *This is it, I'm dead.*

And then I got diarrhea from dinner. It was terrible. I couldn't believe that after all of this, I was taking a deep six because I ate a rotten chicken.

Lt. General Victor H. "Brute" Krulak

Vietnam had Nuc Mom sauce that was very, very strong. If you tasted even a little, your breath smelt terrible for a week.

Lance Corporal Jesse Lyons:

Mike Hare bugged me to get a watch in light of the daily, without fail, four o'clock sniper at Phu Lac (6). We didn't know who was shooting, we only knew when.

One afternoon without paying attention to the time, I dutifully sat on the second to the left hole in our four-seater, screened-in latrine. Within minutes a bullet zipped over my head followed by another zooming on my right. Pants down, I dove head first through the screen door onto what felt like a gigantic piece of sandpaper. I ran up the hill getting shot at, wearing my pants on my ankles. I dove down the hill's opposite side on wet clay that shred every inch of my arms and legs. I also twisted my ankle. Although I wasn't hit, I was embarrassed. Everyone laughed, including Mike. "Hey, Lyons, how about that watch?"

I bought a watch at the PX the first chance I got.

We frequently patrolled Antenna Valley, an area once used as a French Game Preserve. One particularly hot day a guy in my squad yelled, "Tiger on the trail, tiger on the trail."

"Yeah, yeah, you saw a tiger."

"Hey, I'm not kidding, man. C'mon look for yourself. There's a tiger right down the trail."

All of a sudden this huge pig, I mean this thing looked like it weighed three hundred pounds, ran oinking through the bushes.

"There's your tiger, only it looks exactly like a pig!"

Not two seconds later this *incredible* tiger charged the pig.

Speechless, we hauled ass.

Private First Class Ken Noonan:

Vietnam was filled with snakes, bugs, rats, apes, and the occasional mongoose. One machine gunner, an animal lover that wouldn't kill a fly, caged a mongoose; a vicious, scurvy little bastard with a mouth bigger than a possum and long, long fangs. Guys put flip-flops in its cage, and he'd chuck right through them. This beast scared everyone even though the gunner kept it harnessed. We tolerated its foul and rancid smell, thinking it would keep the snakes at bay. Well, one night this damn thing got loose in a trench line that connected our positions, and needless to say, created complete havoc. Word got out that the mongoose was loose. Fearing the mongoose, nobody wanted to stay in their hole. Everybody panicked. The lieutenant yelled over the net, "What's going on?"

"Sir, the mongoose is loose, the mongoose is loose."

"What?"

"The mongoose is loose. We have to do something with the mongoose."

Not a very good answer.

Lieutenant William Harvey:

I was medevaced comatose from Nong Son for food poisoning. I went down like a ton of bricks and woke up in Da Nang's Charlie Med two days later. Preparations were underway for Operation Essex, and since I spent more time in Antenna Valley than any round eye since the French, I knew that 2/5 couldn't possibly conduct the operation without me. At the time, I didn't know what a catheter was but I wore one. So I tore it out and escaped down the hall with a long line of blood dripping out of my crank. I rummaged through a bin filled with utilities cut from wounded Marines and ran to the airfield, still bleeding, to hitch a ride to An Hoa.

I was on Operation Essex.

Private First Class Bill Gavin:

Generally, the first night in An Hoa after an operation, Marines were free to drink or sleep until the booze ran out or the sun showed up. We didn't have perimeter duty so we owned this one and only night.

Now Marines never took their clothes or boots off in the field. *Never.* We wore our utilities until we returned or they rotted off, whichever came first. So relatively safe in An Hoa, I removed my boots and trousers to sleep. Since we didn't wear underwear because of chaffing, I slept in nothing but a t-shirt.

One first night, around four a.m., I heard a *VROOOOOM* that was different than the familiar 105 Howitzer and 155 H&I fire that often rattled our rack silverware. The next *VROOOOOM* vibrated closer followed by an even tighter *VROOOOOOOOOM.* All of a sudden, *BAM!* Shrapnel hit the tin roof. Only one word was said. "Incoming."

Imagine fifteen Marines charging through one front or back hootch door into slit trenches three feet wide and seven feet long. First through the front door, I slid belly down into a slit trench filled with six inches of muddy water. Another guy flapjacked on top of me, another on top of him and so on until we pancaked six deep. I could barely breathe. I hoisted my body up with both arms on the ground just to stay alive at the bottom of this mound. The fire finally lulled. We piled out and into the hootch, grabbed our rifles and deuce gear, and waited for the impending attack. Luckily the night remained quiet.

The next morning in chow line I heard one guy four guys up say, "Damn last night. I jumped into a slit trench on top of this guy and the son of a bitch was naked. My face landed right in his ass. Another guy jumped on top of me and another on top of him and another on top of him so I couldn't get my head out of this guy's ass. He hadn't taken a shower in months. He smelled so rotten I thought I was going to die from the stench, forget the rocket and mortar attack."

Guess whose ass he had his face stuck in?

Since An Hoa's base perimeter bunkers deteriorated from the rain, Marines forever hunted for reinforcing two-by-four sheet metal and plywood. Well, the Seabees—responsible for all construction projects—had a five-foot stack of half-inch plywood fifty yards behind one of our line positions. One night, on our way to manning this position, we passed the stockpile with a Seabee perched on top holding a rifle. I couldn't hold back. "Hey, man, what the hell are you doing here?"

"I'm guarding this goddamn plywood."

"Who are you guarding it from?"

"From you, asshole."

"From me, why?"

"Because you'll steal it."

"I wouldn't steal it. I wouldn't do anything like that. Look, I don't even have a saw to cut it."

Now this guy may have heard a round *fired* in anger but he never pulled a trigger in anger. He piped up. "Hey, what's it really like in the bush?"

So we tell him some bullshit sea stories, and he's all ears. Now I'm thinking, *We need this plywood to reinforce our perimeter bunkers. How the hell can I get this Seabee away from this pile?*

I politely asked, "Hey, how long are you supposed to sit on this stack?"

"All night."

"All night?"

"Yeah."

As I leaned closer to tell him another story, I pulled out an illumination grenade. Although this clamshell burns a bright light, an illumination grenade doesn't explode or shatter like an M26 frag grenade. But to the un-initiated, it looks just like a frag grenade. I removed the pin.

The guy panicked. "What the hell are you doing with that goddamn grenade?"

Since I threw the grenade in my story I faked throwing the illumination grenade but "accidentally" dropped it at the Seabee's feet.

That son of a bitch jumped off that wood and winged it back to the Seabee compound. Needless to say, the next morning the plywood was not stacked quite as high.

An Hoa had a bin of letters written by girls wishing to correspond with Marines.

I opened one with a Playboy pinup cutout and pasted on cardboard with an Oatmeal commercial tagline that read, "Nothing is better for thee than me" printed underneath. The girl included her name and address. Oh man, did I rip a letter off to Miss Mary Smith (not real name). Two weeks later I got a letter from Mary. We became pen pals for the next three months. Although I repeatedly asked for her picture, she never included one. Finally Mary sent a photo, and by God, I'm sorry to say, this poor girl was butt ugly. This relationship had to end, but how? So I asked Miglio, our resident college English major. "I don't know what to do, how do I get out of this?"

"No problem, we'll write a letter telling her that you were killed in action. That'll end it."

"That's a great idea."

"It'll start, 'Mary, this is going to be a difficult letter to write and undoubtedly a difficult letter to receive. It is with a heavy heart that I tell you of Bill Gavin's death. Your letters meant so much to him. He was planning to see you after his Vietnam tour.'"

"Miglio that's superb."

"We'll save the best part for last. 'Mary, have no fear, Bill's death will be avenged.'"

"That's gorgeous, just gorgeous."

I carried the letter for days, deciding whether or not to mail it. On the verge of leaving for an operation, I said "fuck it," and threw it in the mail bag.

Upon our return, Sergeant Larson appeared in our doorway hootch. "Gavin, Miglio, Lieutenant Colonel Jackson wants to see you in his office right now."

"Jackson? Damn, Miglio, we did really well on this operation, I betcha' we're gonna' get a medal."

So we brushed off our jungle mud, donned our best utilities, squared our cover, and marched into the company office. There we stood straight and tall in front of Lieutenant Colonel Jackson sitting at his desk holding a letter swimming in highlights.

"Gavin, I just got this letter from a Mrs. Smith, the mother of Mary Smith, and it seems that you were killed in action."

Holy cow! I didn't think we were going to get called in for this.

"Sir, I can explain, sir."

"Explain? Explain? No, let me explain. According to Mrs. Smith, Mary has been crying uncontrollably since receiving this letter. So Mrs. Smith checked with the Red Cross, and you're not listed as wounded or killed. She then checked with the Marine Corps who also had no listing of a William Gavin WIA or KIA. As a last resort she addressed this letter to the company commander of Second Battalion, Fifth Marine Regiment."

"Sir."

So Jackson read the letter—out loud—in front of every pogue in the company office. I swear to God when he finished, there wasn't a dry eye in the house. That's how gorgeous this letter was.

"I don't know what the hell I'm going to do with you two. I should court-martial you both but you're pretty good with your rifles."

"Sir, I would like to explain."

"The hell with your explanation. If I ever walked down the street and saw either of you on the same sidewalk, I'd cross over just not to walk on the same side. You have forty-five minutes to leave a retraction on my desk before we go into the field."

"Yes, sir."

Off we went.

"Shit, Miglio, I can't believe we got off without punishment."

"Yeah, let's keep the apology simple and get rid of this thing."

I can't remember the details of our retraction letter because we had to write it so fast, but it bounced around justifying the first letter.

Two weeks later a re-supply chopper landed in the weeds with a mail bag that included a three-page, front-and-back, handwritten letter from Mary's mother, Mrs. Smith. The opening line read, "You dirty, no good, son of a bitch."

That's as far as I got. We were in a bad situation, and I couldn't handle one more thing. Pissed, I stuck Mrs. Smith's address in a tree instead of burning it. Rumor had it, gooks mailed body parts to Americans from addresses they found in the jungle.

I'm not proud of it, but I never thought it would go beyond, *Oh well, he's dead.*

One brutal four-day operation evolved into nine days of hell straight through Christmas Eve. General Nickerson had earlier ordered the Marine Corps helicopter wing to fly us back to An Hoa—no matter what on Christmas Day—from this lethal area later nicknamed Christmas-ville. Early Christmas morning as though God extended his hands to wash away the monsoon rains, the sun rose into a bright, blue-bird, crispy day. And the good general kept his promise.

Well, during this hell, we had marched through rusty barbed wire that ripped our cotton utility trousers to hell. Mine shred until I wore *nothing* but a belt that held four white pockets. And when the chopper landed in An Hoa, there stood General Nickerson shaking hands with every Marine that piled out. Now I'm half-naked, wearing only a t-shirt, flak jacket and helmet—with my pecker hanging out—and here's a *general* who wants to shake my hand. I thought, *Here*

I stand naked before God, General Nickerson, and my fellow Marines. Oh what the hell, I'm shaking his hand.

I extended my hand to the general's kind words. "Well, son, it looks like you lost something."

"I sure did, General. I sure did."

And I walked away bare-assed and proud as a peacock.

That's why Christmas day; the twenty-fifth day of December is my favorite day of the year, and it will always be my favorite day of the year.

Drunkard stories are Marine favorites, and this is one is mine.

We were stationed on Nong Son's crest, once assumed to be South Vietnam's safest outpost since gooks needed to infiltrate two layers of Marines to reach the summit. Meaner-than-hell monkeys swinging from bush to bush along the mountains bluff posed as our biggest threat.

One night as we lay on top—instead of inside our bunkers—to avoid the heat, rats, and centipedes, we guzzled Vietnamese beer and gook whisky and threw hand grenades at the monkeys. Quickly shit-faced, bored, and dumb, we decided to play hot potato with a *live* M26 frag hand grenade. Four guys, lining each side of a slit trench, had five seconds to pass the potato before chucking it off the cliff. The second the spoon flew, the counting began. Lieutenant Harvey, soon disturbed by the explosions, stormed over. "Who's throwing all of these God damn grenades?"

So one Marine on the brink of throwing the potato yelled, "Sir, there are gooks down there."

"Private, do have a grenade in your hand?"

"Yes, sir, the gooks are climbing up the hill, sir."

"Private, those are monkeys not gooks."

"No, sir, they're gooks. I think I hear another one."

BOOM!!!!!!!!

Lucia, do you know how grateful we were when he threw that grenade?

Name Withheld:

It was not unusual to find a chaplain reading *Playboy Magazine.*

Communications Operator Phil Perozzio:

Let's talk about a small world. I met a Marine in Vietnam—for the first time—who lived around the corner from me in Yonkers, New York.

I never resented the officers because if we were bogged down in a rice paddy, so were they. If I walked mile after mile, Major Esau walked right next to me. He wasn't back at camp saying, "Okay, make a right here."

Name Withheld:

One night we almost got creamed by our own guys *twice.*

Patrols and night ambushes leaving An Hoa notified all defensive perimeter bunkers of their departure to avoid death by friendlies. During one squad-size night ambush, word stopped two bunkers down without our knowledge. We marched in front of the perimeter, and all hell broke loose. The intense Marine fire was incredible. We lay as flat as we could as rounds sliced our packs and killed our radio. Since we couldn't call for help, we screamed for our lives. Within minutes we heard, *ERRRRR. Clink, clink, ERRRR, clink, clink.*

The distinctive sound of our tank zeroing his machine gun on us! Trust me you don't want to get shot by a tank. Sergeant Grey (not real name) quickly popped a good-guy green flare. Thank God the shooting stopped. We returned to the base for a new radio and requested permission to stay. Captain Martin (not real name) refused. We collectively agreed, "The hell with this."

So we settled to sleep in brush and high grass outside the wire. Later that evening, An Hoa's artillery flares lit a hootch on fire in the friendly village beyond our perimeter. Suddenly two Marine platoons and an emergency crew headed toward the village straight through us. We knew we'd be mistaken as the enemy.

"Oh shit, they're going to open up on us again."

Thank God, four Marines guarding the emergency crews stepped in front of us before shooting. "What the hell are you guys doing here?"

"We're the night ambush."

"Okay, hang tight, we won't tell."

We went back to sleep. We returned at dawn, popping green flares.

Lieutenant Wade (not real name) ordered me to guard a news reporter during my first operation. Since I was a By God Marine, I couldn't wait to show off. We boarded a chopper and, despite my fear of heights, I sat on the open ledge with one foot on the skid and enjoyed the rush. We landed and safely jumped off. But instead of staying low, I immediately stood, allowing the ascending chopper to blow me right off the paddy dike. Much to my embarrassment the reporter helped me up.

Lieutenant James Meyers:

One work detail required the transport of old, abandoned, brakeless ARVN trucks down from Nong Son's summit. I insisted that the PF's drive them because I wouldn't let my Marines near them. One PF barreled down so fast his rear end never touched the seat. He could only hold and steer. That probably was the most fun he had ever had in his life. They all arrived safely.

A young, beautiful, blond, buxom, curvaceous German Nurse often dined in An Hoa. Chow hall chatter buzz ceased when she opened the screen door. Marines then dueled in a bench-booty-push to make room for her to sit. It was a sight.

Chief Corpsman Lou LeGarie and Lieutenant James Meyers:

Chaplain Grubbs *always* brushed his teeth. He walked around with his toothbrush, a cup, and his mouth covered in toothpaste. We figured the good chaplain brushed his teeth out of nervousness. But he was a pretty brave chap. He learned radio logistics and called in SITREPs every thirty minutes for the CP.

Second Battalion Fifth Marine Regiment, First Marine Division, United States Marine Corps; An Hoa, Republic of South Vietnam; 1967:

The F word in Vietnam became a way of life. I did nothing but apologize my first month home from this hearty adjective that became a normal mode of communication.

Name Withheld :

Pot was readily available but since I never even smoked cigarettes, I drank my pot mixed with strained local tea. I think I got high. The commanding

Chief Hospital
Corpsman
Lou LeGarie, USN.

Chaplain Grubbs,
USN, brushing
his teeth, An Hoa,
RSVN, 1967.

officers knew about the pot but turned their heads since we didn't fool with it in the field. Hard drugs and pills were available but we steered clear. It was too dangerous not to have your wits about you.

So here's the sorry truth, when I moved into the pogue world as an S3 (intelligence), I joined Joe (not real name) as a frequent flier on the court-martial circuit. I was the prosecutor, and he was a citizen for the defense. He did a great job and as a result loved it. I did a pissy job and therefore hated it. Fortunately the perps usually pled to avoid a trial. Sadly, one monkey insisted on a trial for an illegal weapons' possession charge—a Lambreta 9mm. And since the MP's gun was the same gun used by the kid, a paper trail was needed. And with due diligence I accomplished that task. In court, however, Joe was Clarence Darrow, and I was Gomer Pyle. Although the court ruled in my favor, they seized every opportunity to tell me about my crappy performance. I think the verdict was later overturned which pretty much ended my legal career, proving that all good things come to he who screws up.

Private First Class Ron Powers:
Slimy leeches sucked our blood until they burst. Slimy leeches left their heads in our bodies and blood stains on our trousers. Slimy leeches scared us into thinking we had been shot. Most of the time, we didn't know they were on us. Salt, insect repellant, and fire killed the greasy worms.

Fleet Marine Force Corpsman Ron White:
Vietnam's water went through you like Grant through Richmond. It would go, man. It would go.

Private First Class Steve Zeck:
Here's a Navy story. Two Navy landing crafts carried Marine troops and a tank across the river to Phu Lac (6). One boat transported the tank and several Marines while the other shipped the troops. The driver stood in the open turret. The sailors navigated to drop the door on the river bank in two feet of water, allowing the tank to roll up shore as we walked with it. Well, when the door dropped and the tank moved forward, it and we sank. The Navy guys misjudged the water's depth. We edged land but we were in at least ten feet of water, not two. We screamed, cursed, and dog-paddled as best we could. Thankfully we were close enough to the shore where it was only a problem for the tank. Fortunately no enemy was waiting for us or if they were, they just died laughing. We spent two days getting that tank out of the water.

Nobody wants to be your friend when you're the new guy, the FNG—Fucking New Guy. You'll get yourself and anyone within proximity killed doing something stupid, like I almost did on my first night ambush. I couldn't decide whether the safety on my weapon should be on or off. I

PFC Steve Zeck, USMC, and his record player.

PFC Steve Zeck.

ultimately decided off and clicked it. Smashing a life-size Chinese gong during silent prayer couldn't have sounded louder. I burned the shitters the next day in An Hoa. I knew I had to find something to keep me from shit duty, so I jumped at the chance of being a tunnel rat. After several fearless tunnel excursions I didn't get any more lousy jobs.

You know how John Wayne pulled out grenade pins with his teeth? Well truthfully, teeth can't pull pins. Pulling carter pins required muscle. Carter pins had a metal circle to help yank the pins as we held grenade spoons in place with our fingers and heaved. The grenade, now armed, had eight seconds to explode. As an extra precaution against snagging pins on flak jackets and pouches, we wrapped grenades with black electric tape. The tape held the spoon which held the pin. But since our grenades were left over from the Korean War, we had a lot of blanks. And since I released the spoon *as* I tossed the grenade—just in case in took less than eight seconds to explode—if the grenade didn't blow up, I'd wonder if in my haste, I forgot to rip the tape off or was this really a blank. I crawled back—flashlight in hand—too many times to count. A good grenade couldn't be left behind.

Marines were notorious for carrying cameras into the field. Grenade pouches were checked before every patrol to make sure they were lined with grenades, rather than film canisters and instamatics. We'd be in the middle of a firefight, with three Marines shooting while two guys took pictures.

I inherited a battery-operated record player from Steve Bruner, the former radio man. During our seldom downtime, I played the same two 78 records over and over and over again. My Johnny Cash "Dear John" record was so sad, guys threw stuff at my door, hollering, "Take it off. Stop."

My aunt mailed pints of bourbon and scotch in loaves of hollowed bread. I'm sure the military post office knew she wasn't sending bread, but no one ever said anything. My grandmother sent stockings and candy bars like they did in World War II, suggesting that I trade what I couldn't use.

I swear I saw a UFO one summer night in Vietnam. An eerie light just zoomed across the sky. Although faster than a plane, it wasn't a missile or a shell. This unfamiliar, bizarre light even flew a strange flight pattern. My platoon saw it. I think every Marine in Vietnam saw the UFO. I asked Marines stationed in different places who confirmed the sighting. It could have been an experimental plane but we swore it was a UFO.

While shooting the breeze in our hootch one night, a flying object bounced off my neck and knocked me to the ground. Bill Patton picked it up and by God, it was a stray sniper round. We thought someone hurled it in as a joke until we realized we could see a circle of light coming through the roof. It was one of my luckier days.

Doc Christen (not real name) dragged a wounded Marine off to the side, during a particularly brutal firefight. That evening, while cleaning his .45 he noticed a round had sliced a hole in his leather holster and dented his gun's panhandle. He had no idea he'd even been shot.

Chaplain Von Almen surprised me in the field, threatening to make me his assistant if I didn't write home. I quit answering letters because Vietnam became my only world. I was happy to receive letters but I didn't write back. My parents and grandparents wrote the chaplain to make sure I was okay. I quickly wrote home. Being the chaplain's assistant wasn't on my to do list.

At the end of my first An Hoa haircut, the Vietnamese barber grabbed and twisted my neck until it cracked. At first I thought he was trying to kill me. But the twenty-five cent haircut included a chiropractor-like adjustment. It was over quick. He wrapped his arms around my neck and snapped it before I could even say, "Oh my God."

Captain Gene Bowers:

While stationed at Phu Lac (6) this squawking, squeaking, NVA psych ops loudspeaker blared, "We know you. You're the company that wears bushes and leaves. You are all enemies of the Vietnamese people. You rape our women, kill our cows, shoot our water buffaloes, burn our homes, and kill our chickens."

It was quiet for one second before one Marine roared back, "Hey, we don't kill no damn chickens!"

Eating C rations became a creative sport.

Gunnery Sergeant Yancy had arms that looked like they were filled with guts. Whenever I did something dumb, I could feel his enormous presence.

{Captain Gene Bowers often walked point in his command group.}

I'd look up and see him standing there, shot gun in hand. "Skipper, what the fuck are you doing up here?"

Officers could shout and gesticulate as much as they wanted but nothing really happened until the sergeant moved. Sergeants—mine were all wonderful—are the backbone of the Marine Corps.

Lieutenant Gene Minors:

Everyone thought that our platoon commander, John Hackett (not real name), was mean, but he wasn't. He was just butt ugly.

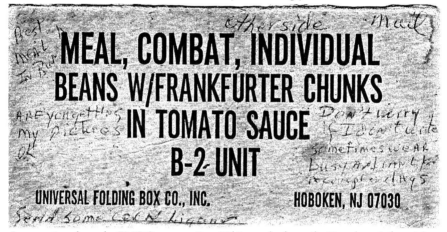

Letter written home by FMF Corpsman Ron White on the front of a C-rat box. Left to right "Best meals in bunch." "Are you getting my pictures ok?" "Don't worry if I don't write, sometimes we are busy cannot write for a couple of days." "Send some liquor."

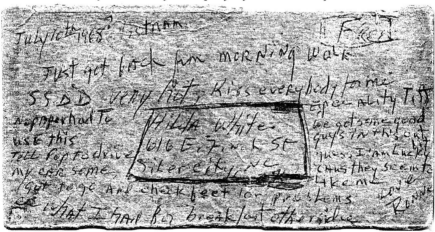

Letter written home by FMF Corpsman Ron White on the back of a C-rat box. "July 10th, 1968 Vietnam. "Just got back from morning walk SSDD very hot, kiss everybody for me, especially Tiff." "I got some good guys in this outfit. I am lucky 'cause they like me." "No paper had to use this." "Tell Pops to drive my car some." "I got to go and check feet for problems." "See what I had for breakfast —other side." "Love Ronnie."

Weapons Platoon Sergeant Harold Wadley:

One of An Hoa's Battalion Sergeant Majors was really stateside. He demanded, in An Hoa, that field jackets, sleeves, and collars be squared away like you were on liberty in San Francisco, for crying out loud. This pain in the rear was a big guy with a voice like a bull moose. He must have been in some rear echelon all of his life. We'd march into An Hoa stripped to the waist with trousers torn off, soles coming off our boots, no socks and our flak jackets slung over our shoulders—remember, it was really hot—and he'd come out blowing a fit. "You're at battalion now, straighten up," and on and on and on. He'd stop guys dragging their flak jackets by the collar—yeah, so they hit the ground. "You guys don't respect Marine Corps property!" God we hated him. I often thought, *Man what a dipstick you are.*

Really. You see, once we crossed the perimeter wire we were supposed to clear our weapons. But gee whiz, we could get shot clear down to the airstrip, and we needed to return fire accordingly. We weren't going to clear our weapons, that dipstick.

He left after Operation Arizona, and we didn't have any more rifle checks straight from patrol. Can you imagine that requirement coming out of the muck and crude of the jungle and paddies? We thought he was Donald Duck and wondered how he managed to get himself *into* the Marine Corps. My guys were tough. Marines are a special breed. Men die for each other without ever a thought.

I never figured who instigated this story, although I have my suspicions.

The Air Force went along with this sergeant major's orders to be in clean clothes with jackets buttoned and cuffs squared away with no weapons at their slop shoot, our beer garden. The Air Force ran these slop shoots, the Marine entertainment spots, in a big twenty-four-by-thirty tent. One time we came in after losing several Marines. Nothing had gone right, and everyone was ticked off, so some guys went straight to the slop shoot.

I said, "Fine go ahead. I'll see you later." I reported to the CP.

Now this Air Force tent was a plush set up complete with a refrigerator—good grief. Our jarheads shouldered their weapons, but the Air Force guys were going to court-martial this one and that one for not being squared away. "You violated this one," and man, these guys didn't understand. Just clearin' our weapons in case the sergeant major called for rifle inspection angered us. Gosh, it just angered us. Soon I heard this hoorah in the slop shoot and thought, *Dang gosh, that sounds serious.*

One mouthy Air Force airman ordered my guys outside until they squared away their gear, so one Marine yanked him over the bar and threw him into some boxes. Pissed, my boys exited. I heard them cussin' from across the airstrip.

I yelled, "What in the thunder happened?"

They told me. They were darn angry.

I told them, "Okay, leave it alone. You didn't need any hot beer anyway."

But the more they thought about it, the more it bothered them. So, in the middle of the night they burned the slop shoot. The Air Force guys barely got out of their hootch. The next day, the Marines that took care of that slop shoot were all smiles. And nobody knew a thing.

The sergeant major and the Air Force airmen asked, "Who did this to the slop shoot? Who ordered that fire?" Hotel stood smiling. That was the enjoyment of it. No one got in trouble. Everyone knew because they heard the ruckus. We didn't frequent that spot of recreation again.

Lieutenant John Newton:
Lessons that second lieutenant Sam learned in Vietnam:
1. There really is a difference between the quick and the dead.
2. There's really nothing you can say to someone who's just been shot in the nuts.
3. Your ears never really stop ringing.
4. It really sucks being wet.

Battalion Surgeon Floyd Gonder, MD:
The CO ordered me to find Jane Mansfield—the only brave soul who ventured into An Hoa to entertain the troops—and her LA-lawyer boyfriend whiskey as per their request. Jane drank whiskey while singing with her band in onc-hundred-and-ten-degree heat. She was well-received. God, we so seldom saw women.

I really admired Major Esau. About four a.m. during one Bald Eagle mission, shrapnel sliced his cheek. Based on the size of the hole, I dreaded looking into his mouth. I thought, *God, it must be in his brain.* Funny enough, there was another hole in the roof of his mouth, but he was okay. An x-ray showed shrapnel embedded in his hard pallet. I covered his cheek with a band-aid. He didn't miss a single day of work.

The contrast from horrible field conditions to downtime in An Hoa complete with a warm meal and a bed were unimaginable. *Everything* was relative in Nam. During those rare moments of drinking with the guys, I was on cloud nine. We'd also play poker with the artillery officers to break the monotony of evening inactivity. We were terrible but we had fun.

Sometimes, we were simply bored until incoming casualties arrived or mortars struck, then it was complete chaos. Vietnam vacillated between hours of boredom and moments of stark raving terror; nothing in between.

My dad sent care packages with Bourbon, Wild Turkey, and Southern Comfort in baby bottles packaged so the liquid wouldn't gurgle when the Post Office shook the boxes, checking for booze. We'd remove the nipples and pass the bottles.

We'd barter booze for equipment with Charlie Med in Da Nang. One guy showed up in An Hoa with an injectable antibiotic that Dr. Tom and I wanted and since going through the system took forever, we personally bartered a case of liquor.

Centipedes were virtually harmless other than bites causing acute pain. Centipedes loved to snuggle in combat boots so we always shook our boots. My kids think I'm nuts. I belong to a hunting club, and to this day, I shake my boots, embarrassed to tell anyone why.

Rats were big, bad, and difficult to control in the presence of food. They'd run across bunkers at night and, if pushed, they'd bite. Rats were potentially rabid so we administered painful rabies shots. Rabies can be fatal if not properly treated. And Marines panicked over vipers. They were small, fatal, and we didn't have counteracting venom. We'd see the occasional three-foot cobra slither by, stop, sit up, look at you, and return to slithering. They were neat to watch.

George was An Hoa's Vietnamese house mouse who worked as our Vietnamese interpreter and BAS helper. For some reason, the village chief from the ville outside of An Hoa's wire imprisoned him in a cage. I don't know what he did, but he sure pissed somebody off. He was in a cage for weeks until I asked the village chief to release him. The chief did the next day.

Lieutenant James Meyers:

I medevaced one Marine suffering from an allergic reaction from a biting centipede—they were hairy little unpleasant mothers—lost in his shirt. His lip curled, his eyes swelled shut, and he had trouble breathing. This kid sat whacking himself until this hairy centipede the size of a hotdog crawled out. I have work shoes in the garage that to this day, never go on without a tap search.

Motor Transport "cumshaw-ed" everything in Da Nang. The colonel wanted An Hoa to look "Christmas-y" so he sent me to Da Nang, promising to disavow his order if I got caught. My team returned with green and red paint and a wreath wearing a label for the commander of the 15th Arial support. The good colonel hung the wreath on his door.

One Marine was almost carried away by a tiger in Antenna Valley—a one-time game preserve. While asleep, his hole-mate, supposedly on guard duty, did the same. The tiger grabbed and dragged the kid away by the shoulder. His buddy woke up and shot but his rifle jammed. So he sunk his bayonet into the animal. The monstrosity measured some un-godly length. It didn't take long for a division chopper to snag the tiger. I'm sure he's still hanging on some general's wall.

Private First Class Roger McDowell:

James Meyers was not only the best officer I served under, he was the most unique. Lieutenant Meyers spent as as much time in the field as a grunt officer as he did running the motor transport pool. I volunteered for everything and anything that involved working with him.

A sniper at My Loc (2) took a potshot at Lt. Meyers in the CP bunker so we kidded him about his big, tall body making a good target. But we secretly worried that he would get his balls shot off; he so loved the boondocks.

James Meyers was all about the safety of his men; of his Marines.

Lance Corporal Jesse Pender:

We were ordered not to *return* sniper fire from one "friendly" village because they were "friendly." So my radio quit working.

One time my punishment—a month's worth of shitter duty—didn't last long because one shitter *accidentally* caught on fire and blew up.

In the middle of one three-hundred-and-sixty-degree perimeter sat the captain, the first sergeant, and the platoon commander. And when we received incoming, those three big guys had to get into one tiny little hole. And I laughed my ass off.

If we ever got discouraged, we'd say, "Ain't nothin' but a thing."

I made only one deal with God. "Let me go home in one piece, and I'll be a good boy." And I was for a while.

We passed one hootch where an old man, a woman, and some kids sat crying. As we turned the corner I grabbed my sergeant. "Sarge, shits gonna' hit the fan in a few."

He shook his head. "Ah, you're just nervous."

"No, it's going to happen in a few."

Within seconds, all hell broke loose. We jumped into a ditch. Man, they had us dead as rice. And the company gunny ordered the first platoon into the nearest tree line.

I couldn't believe it. I told him, "Are you out of your damn mind?"

We could see the rounds flying by with tracers so we knew there were at least five bullets in between those tracers that we *couldn't* see.

The guy yells back, "Pender, I'll have you court-martialed!"

"Well, you've got two choices. You can court-martial me or you can take the tree line. But we ain't moving."

About that time ol' big Jim White lifted up to command his rocket unit when a bullet ripped *through* his lips. Now White was tall, dark, and already had big lips.

And those puppies swelled up like soup coolers, my God. Lord have mercy, he looked like a Ubangi. That was one of the funniest things I had ever seen. And I never did get court-martialed.

This was the first thing out of Lieutenant Mauro's (not real name) dumb mouth. "I'm in charge, and there are three things that you don't do while I'm in charge. Number one, never arm wrestle superman. Number two, never wee-wee in the wind. And number three, never mess with the kid."

I had to ask, "So, who is the kid?"

Mauro stood real tall. "I'm the kid. And what's your name?"

"Lance Corporal Solo."

Solo—short for soul man—was my nickname.

"Well, Lance Corporal Solo, blah, blah, blah."

And he went on and on and on.

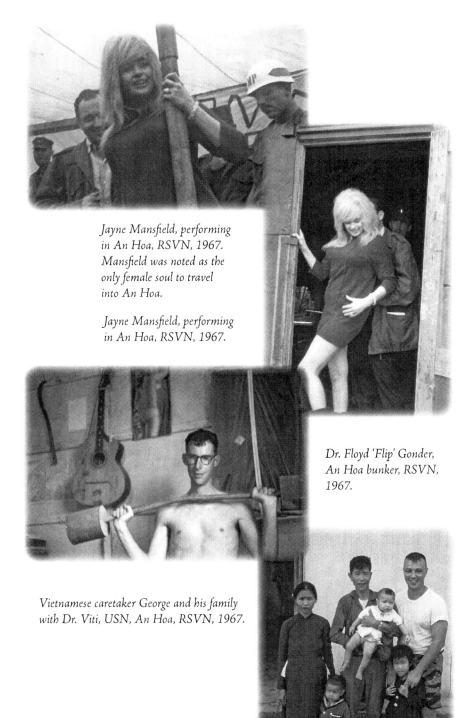

Jayne Mansfield, performing in An Hoa, RSVN, 1967. Mansfield was noted as the only female soul to travel into An Hoa.

Jayne Mansfield, performing in An Hoa, RSVN, 1967.

Dr. Floyd 'Flip' Gonder, An Hoa bunker, RSVN, 1967.

Vietnamese caretaker George and his family with Dr. Viti, USN, An Hoa, RSVN, 1967.

Vietnamese Family that handled laundry for the BAS, Motor Transport and Supply, An Hoa, RSVN, 1967.

Montegnarde Children on Nong Son.

"Hey, you souvenir me two cigarettes."

Lt. Commander Dr. Floyd "Flip" Gonder, USN, 1968.

Days later, we received sniper fire during a cakewalk around the perimeter. Everyone, including me, hit the deck. And this kid lieutenant buried his face in a pile of buffalo dung. Lieutenant Mauro howled for my radio to call artillery on this sniper, but I refused. I wasn't letting him near my radio. He continued hollering and spitting dung like he had nasty sesame seeds caught in his mouth. I called the sergeant. "Hey, man, show Lieutenant Mauro what to do. I ain't gonna die because he's an idiot. And keep his face away from my radio."

I'll do anything for my country but die, just like General Patton says, "The idea of war is not to die for your country. It is to get the other guy to die for *his* country."

Name Withheld:

Trouble usually started with alcohol. One night, after running dry in An Hoa, we headed to a local store outside of the wire. We bullshitted the guards about being on a mission for the skipper. When the store owner wanted to charge us too much for the booze—even at three a.m. if you could believe it— we twirled our Ka-Bars and took what we wanted. We didn't steal it, stealing is when people ain't looking. We took it right in front of him, drank what we could, and buried the rest. Now mind you, we were drunk. The unhappy store owner came to the battalion the next morning for restitution or maybe just our heads. The lieutenant colonel wanted names of the guilty party but a veil of silence fell over the company. Our escapade was known at the company level so the captain fined and chewed us out. "You guys have to snap out of your shit." And that was the end of it. Maybe the transaction would have gone smoother had we twirled our rifles.

Lieutenant Martin Dunbar:

One day a Vietnamese elder rode his bicycle past the artillery battery, set a box in the middle of the road, and peddled off. As the ranking officer, I was called to check the likelihood of this explosive booby trap. I timidly walked up to the box, observed, and listened. The box ticked. So I threw it six feet in the air and scrambled away—fast. Silence. After a twenty-minute decision discussion, we flipped the box top open with a long pole. And still nothing happened. After a closer examination, the box was filled with some Army guy's alarm clock, clothes, and personal items. The Vietnamese was returning it.

But that ticking sound scared the crap out of us.

Name Withheld:

An Hoa had a joke on that grunts got penicillin for clap and officers got it for sore throats.

Lt. James Meyer, An Hoa, NEW washrack for troops 1967.

An anonymous email—Second Battalion, Fifth Marine Regiment, First Marine Division, United States Marine Corps; An Hoa, Republic of South Vietnam; 1967:

An old southern preacher from Georgia had a teenage son old enough to be thinking about choosing a profession. But like many young men, the boy didn't yet know. And he really didn't appear to be concerned about it.

One day during school the preacher placed four objects on the boy's study table—a Bible, a silver dollar, a bottle of whisky, and a *Playboy* magazine.

I'll just hide behind the door, the old preacher thought, *and when he comes home from school this afternoon, I'll see which object he picks up. If it's the Bible, he'll be a preacher, like me. What a blessing that would be. If it's the dollar, he's going to be a businessman, and that would be okay; but if picks up the bottle, he's going to be a no-good drunkard. Lord, what a shame that would be. And worst of all, if he picks up that magazine he's gonna be a skirt-chasin' bum.*

The old man waited anxiously. Soon, he heard his son whistling as he entered the house and headed for his room. The boy quickly spotted the objects on the table and inspected them but for a moment. He placed the Bible under his arm, dropped the silver dollar into his pocket, and took a long drink while he admired the *Playboy* centerfold.

"Lord have mercy," the old preacher whispered, "He's gonna be a Marine!"

❧ Dear Daddy ❧

Dr. Tom's War introduced me to Vietnam's Marine Corps private first class 03—grunts. Serving as the very backbone of the Corps, grunts sacrificed their lives in Vietnam—as did their forefathers during World War II and Korea—because it was the right thing to do. Often erroneously portrayed under the guise of the wayward kid by the media and Hollywood, these men remain bonded by a culture of legendary valor where failure is not an option.

Dr. Tom's War also introduced me to Bill Gavin—a Vietnam Marine Corps grunt. Courageous, resourceful, disciplined, and spirited, Bill Gavin belongs to a corps of men that survived Vietnam's complexities while defending America and South Vietnam from communism. Although issues concerning the righteousness of their cause were never discussed in the combat zone, Bill Gavin and his grunt brothers understood that survival of American democracy was dependent upon the success of Marines in battle.

Bill Gavin spoke candidly about Vietnam. Anywhere and everywhere was a front line of harsh terrain and inhospitable living conditions. These boys battled in every conceivable way—ambushes, sniper fire, bombings, company-sized and multi-battalion conflicts and small and large patrols. But within Vietnam's daily trials and tribulations, Bill shared an unconditional loyalty which prevailed as a benchmark to who these men would become.

During Vietnam's terrorizing, brutal, and inhumane moments, Bill Gavin and his Marine brothers shared a devoted, unyielding camaraderie that rose above the severe ravages of Vietnam. Bill told tales of constant teasing through a veil of unspoken understanding that grunts fought to save each other from death. Theirs was a war fought not only to protect America, but to "save the guy on my left and the guy on my right." Never ending days evolved into weeks without Sundays, all of which were dutifully checked off on a calendar. For these boys not old enough to shave, Vietnam existed as a fundamental lesson of mortality. And sadly, as thousands lay dead, undistinguished by the courageous manner in which they died, Americans protested and labeled them "baby killers." Once home, America shamelessly spat, accused, and abandoned those following in the footsteps of the "Greatest Generation."

But despite Vietnam's carnage and America's betrayal, Bill Gavin is among the many grunts sustained by his Marine Corps pride. Bill Gavin spoke with an air of confidence and honor about his rite of passage in becoming a Marine.

Bill Gavin knows how to survive combat. And he offered to share his perspective with the world.

GRUNTS

Cpl. William F. Gavin, USMC, An Hoa, RSVN, 1967.

Dear Lucia,

It was so nice talking to you yesterday. You are part of a USMC family that you never realized until you began this journey into your father's past. Marines ALWAYS take care of their own. Try this, wear a USMC cap, and every former Marine will salute you with a "Semper Fi" or a "hoorah!"

The only ex-Marines are dead Marines. Know that all Marines hold their heads in high respect and reverence. I still get goose bumps at the sound of the Marine Corps Hymn, even on TV!

All Marines have sea stories. My grandfather, John Francis Gavin, was a World War I Marine in France in 1918. He spoke of Marines pushing the Boshe back across the Marne River where the Germans were on one side and the French on the other, since 1915. Huge bunkers were dug on both sides, some with grand pianos and crystal chandeliers. On Mondays, the Germans would walk down to the river and wash their clothes. The French wouldn't shoot. On Tuesdays, the French would do the same and the Germans wouldn't shoot. Well, Grampa said when the Marines got to the river, nobody washed their clothes, and the fight was on!

Forty-eight years later I fought in Vietnam with same regiment as Grampa, the Second Battalion Fifth Marine Regiment. The Fifth Marine Regiment is the most famous or the most infamous regiment in the Marine Corps. Please feel free to use my essay, "A Discussion of the Realities of Life in Combat."

Good luck and stay happy. Semper Fi!

William F. Gavin CPL USMC (Retired)

A DISCUSSION ON THE REALITIES OF COMBAT

I've lived in Alaska as a professional hunting and fishing guide for the past forty years. I've experienced more adventure than most, guiding clients in pursuit of Alaskan King Salmon, Caribou, Dall Sheep, Moose, and Alaskan Brown Bear, the largest land carnivore on earth.

The foundation of my life in Alaska began over forty years ago in Vietnam as PFC 0311, assigned to Golf 2/5, Third Platoon, Third Squad. I'm proud to have served as a 03 island warrior grunt in the toughest combat outfit in the world. Marines are masters of combat and grunts *are* the foundation of the Marine Corps. Technology may change the weapons of war but the Marine infantry companies will always take and hold ground.

I think of Vietnam, my toughest life experience, every day. Sights and sounds trigger memories of nasty fire fights, company-sized battles, fire maneuvers, night ambushes, and sniper rounds shot by men that were true marksmen and those that were not. And my stomach still balls into knots.

I'm not an expert on combat, I'm a survivor. And after a firefight, the dead and the survivors are all that's left. So I pass on the following lessons, mental attitudes, disciplines and crafts I learned in combat so that others can become a functional part of a Marine rifle squad.

William Gavin hunting bear in Alaska, 1985.

William Gavin and long-time friend, Richard 'Doc' Blanchard, USN, enjoying Alaska, 1995.

MENTAL ATTITUDES IN COMBAT

Corporal William O'Brien a.k.a. OB, my squad leader and mentor, taught me well. Corporal O'Brien died in Vietnam, gut shot at close range. I'll never forget OB or any other brave Marine that I served with.

OB taught me that blind shithouse luck, although out of my control, played a role in surviving. But add to that what one can control, attitude, discipline, training, and leadership, and one has the ability to spot booby traps, mines, and ambushes plus the competency to win firefights. OB said, "Learn quickly, stay alert, and remember when shot at:

    1. Find close cover.

    2. Determine where the fire is coming from.

    3. Return fire.

    4. Stay in contact with the man ahead of you in the column. When he moves, you move."

DEALING WITH COMBAT FEAR

All front line 03 Marines face fear in combat.

I thought I was brave but during my second patrol I found myself frozen to the ground, eyes closed, head buried deep in the dirt, waiting for the bullets to rip my flesh. I was quickly kicked and cursed as the FNG for not staying with the Marine ahead of me. I was ashamed. I had failed. Marines could be killed because of my actions. I vowed to never, ever allow fear to control me again.

That evening OB assured me that fear was a good thing. "Fear alerts one to danger, so use it to your advantage."

By daylight OB and I were convinced of my new found courage. As we left the bunker he slapped me on the back. "Welcome to Vietnam, Gavin, you're in a world of shit now."

By learning how to control my fear, I learned how to survive.

I didn't over think. Everything became black and white; life and death; kill or be killed. There was no gray in the bush. I controlled my fear in three ways: through a fear of failing my fellow Marines, as a payback for the loss of my brothers-in-arms, or I simply considered myself dead.

THE FEAR OF FAILURE

Vietnam was a personal war like WWI and WWII because of the long months exposed to combat. Keeping communism out of South Vietnam was bullshit. We killed gooks to keep each other alive. I fought for the survival of my fire team and platoon. They were my world, and nothing else mattered.

PAYBACK

Revenge overpowered fear and drove me to kill. Every VC I killed meant that one more Marine would live. The VC weren't human. They were gooks, zipper-heads, and gooners. My heart was consumed with hatred. They killed my brothers.

DEATH

I considered myself dead already. I had nothing to lose.

PROVING ME TO ME

FNG's had a "point" monopoly, thus learning how to be aware of one's surroundings spotting ambushes, booby traps, mines, and anything out of the ordinary. If an FNG screwed up on point he killed himself and his fellow Marines.

Initially I was awful walking point. I was too loud and cautious for my platoon commander trying to get from point A to point B before dark. OB walked right behind me to ensure that I didn't kill the whole platoon. Luckily our patrols didn't make contact for the first two weeks. Not even sniper dings. The short timers enjoyed the quiet after life at the DMZ. We knew it wouldn't last. My adrenaline kept me guarded as I learned to expect what I knew lay ahead. We patrolled every day, never using the same trails twice.

I deer hunted on point, quietly moving, senses alert to sights and sounds like I did in Missouri.

One morning I walked under a trip wire. A piece of mono fishing line was tied to a Chicom grenade and lashed to a tree. Morning dew caused the line to glisten in the sun. The gooks had an exaggerated idea of the height of American Marines because the line was seven feet high.

We continued. To my left lay a trail. Six gooks squatted thirty yards away around a small cooking fire. I knelt down, stopping the column. Instinct took over. I brought up my M14, put the front sight on their feet and triggered a 3-5 round short burst. All hell broke loose. Gooks recoiled. I sighted low on one VC aiming his rifle at me. He fired and missed. I didn't. Another fired and missed. My burst blew him backwards. It was over in seconds. Gooks ran through the jungle as Marines down behind me hollered, "What are you shooting at?"

Only I could see up this trail. I kept firing. I wanted the gooks running away to think that the entire First Marine Division was on their ass. I eased up the trail, still firing and reloading, yelling to those behind to back me up. It was over.

I shook as we collected weapons and equipment from the dead. My CO made his way up, patted me on the back, and rewarded me with two Camel cigarettes. Smokes were in short supply in a grunt squad.

With luck and straight shooting I survived my first combat. I didn't know what lay ahead, but I proved myself to myself. I could control my fear and reactions under fire. To be considered a good Marine by my peers was all of the confidence that I would ever need.

DAILY STRESS OF COMBAT LIFE AND DEATH

Facing potential combat day after day, week after week for thirteen months was an emotional nightmare. I built defensive walls to maintain my sanity and keep my emotions at bay. When I killed, I killed scum. I didn't dwell on the loss or wounds of my fellow Marines. Feelings drove me nuts so I walked away.

I became tight with my squad as we lived, fought, and bled together in blood and mud. We caused and cheated death. We were young Eagle Scouts with guns and a license to kill.

COMBAT LIFE AS A 03 GRUNT IN VIETNAM

Marines humped in one-hundred-plus degrees through mountainous jungles and waist-deep rice paddies fertilized with human shit. We burned villes we took fire from and shot their buffalos, pigs, and chickens. We swept through countless bunker tunnels for VC, weapons, and rice caches. At night, we went on ambushes and LP's and formed defensive perimeters in two-man holes, standing fifty-percent watch.

People tried to kill us where ever we went. We were thirsty, dirty, and bone tired. We dreaded the next patrol out of Phu Lac (6) or Nong Son. But like the Marines before and after us, we did it. We never lost a fire fight.

Vietnam had no front lines. The VC surrounded us. We didn't take and hold ground as we did in other wars. We only controlled the ground we stood on. Battle success was measured in body counts. We won if we killed more.

There were no safe areas. A trail used yesterday could be mined today. The ARVNS mined areas but didn't map them. It was extremely dangerous wherever we went. Rockets, RPG's, mortars, snipers, booby traps, mines, and ambushes could be anywhere. Mines and booby trap were the worst, especially on point. One second of inattention caused mangling and death.

The Vietnamese we were sent to protect hated us. These rice farmers by day were VC men and women who fought us at night. Vietnamese kids sold Coke filled with ground glass and offered us bananas stuck with needles.

The water, infested with parasitic worms, caused diarrhea, a.k.a. the screaming GI. Men with severe screaming GI used Ka-Bars to split the crotch of their trousers to be able to squat anywhere. We never wore underwear because it chaffed. It was insane.

We eagerly ate C rats and shared pogey boxes from home. Marines learned how to create culinary masterpieces with hot sauce and accessory packets. Base camp chow was awful, but hot.

The ARVN's and the PF's (Popular Forces—Civilian Militia) a.k.a. Rough Puffs were supplied with American arms and equipment. Many were VC passing information and weapons. The ARVN's were gutless troops. Whenever possible, we put them in front of our lines.

Marines were filthy, invisible, and silent in the bush. Bleached, ragged, and torn, we blended with the jungle floor. Our utilities rotted off. The supply sergeant in An Hoa never had enough utilities to go around so we cannibalized sea bags of the dead for clothes and equipment. Flak jackets, deuce gear, and ponchos were stained with blood. Many Marines wore utility shirts with names of the dead. It was demoralizing, but we learned not to notice. Survival was the priority.

My protective walls could only be breached by the few remaining Marines that I began my tour with. The sight of a dead Marine angered me. I needed to kill as payback. Although strangely enough, I could also look at a dead Marine and think, *better you than me*. I wanted to survive.

ADRENALINE, PHYSICAL EXHAUSTION, AND THE MENTAL STRESS OF VIETNAM

Measured in dog years, every day alive was a good day.

Call it an adrenaline rush or the desire for payback but I liked being on point.

However, I will say that blind shithouse luck kept me alive on point. One afternoon, I stepped on an M8 Bouncing Betty land mine that smoked without exploding. The Marine behind me thought I dropped a lit cigarette butt until he saw three prongs sticking up through the grass. Another time, I unknowingly pissed in a booby-trapped 105 artillery round.

Two weeks prior to Christmas of '66, we set up a defensive perimeter around a downed chopper. Torrential monsoon rains hampered the chopper rescue and re-supply. Surrounded by VC and NVA, we took constant sniper fire. On Christmas Eve as the enemy disregarded the Christmas truce, I was a part of a four-man fire team sent to kill the gook snipers. I killed two gooks carrying U.S. rifles, which really pissed me off. My fire team and I then shared a blood-soaked rice ball found in a gook pack. It was good. It was insane.

I recall running the five-mile length of Antenna Valley under a barrage of fire. We collapsed halfway behind a dike, physically depleted and unconcerned with the rounds popping round us. We rested until we found the energy to continue.

One Marine committed suicide after receiving a "Dear John" letter.

One FNG couldn't hack his first patrol and broke down crying. We treated him like he had a communicable disease that infected our walls of discipline. A Marine who couldn't hack it endangered everyone around him.

Grunts dealt with the stress by mercilessly badgering each other with racial, family, and ethnic slurs. Nothing and no one was sacred. What we were before Vietnam didn't matter. Now we were Marine brothers, living in shit hour-to-hour, day-by-day. Psychologists explain the bonding of combat men as the strongest bond one could ever experience.

FNG'S AND MENTORS

I have a recurrent and chilling dream that PFC Zilch, fresh from boot camp, is right behind me on his first patrol, scared, pointing his rifle at my back, safety off, with his finger on the trigger.

Or better yet, this tragedy among one too many:

Two FNGs were placed together during one night ambush. Scared and nervous, they decided to stay awake. They spoke in whispers. Several hours later, one had to shit so he left his position to go a few yards away. Minutes passed. He didn't return. It was pitch dark. The Marine left behind became even more frightened. He panicked at the sound of a gook walking through the brush. The Marine fired. The gook fell on top of him. But it wasn't a gook. It was the other FNG. Dead. The surviving Marine went crazy with grief. They had to gag him to quiet him. He wanted to commit suicide.

Mentors are essential to FNG's. We were all FNG's and will continue to be whenever we need to learn something new.

DAYDREAMING DEADLY MEMORIES OF HOME

Letters and pogey boxes from home were morale boosters. I knew almost everything about the personal lives of the men in my squad. We kept our sea bags filled with extra clothes, personal items, photo albums, writing material, etc. in An Hoa. Free time was spent reading and writing letters and talking about everything we would do once back in the world. Guys collected magazine photo ads of the latest Mustang or Corvette they planned to buy complete with extra options. An Hoa was a time of high spirits until the working parties began. NCO's and officers bombarded grunts to burn crappers, fill sandbags, dump trash, and build bunkers. Add to that perimeter watch and night ambushes. Apart from the occasional mortar round or rocket, An Hoa was fairly safe. We could walk around without worrying about snipers. The stress of bush life was eased temporarily.

When I first arrived in Vietnam OB told me to leave my memories in my An Hoa sea bag. This was the roughest discipline next to fear. During long hot days of humping without contact it was almost impossible not to wonder about life at home. Standing perimeter watch was easier if I could occupy my mind with memories of people and things I loved back in St. Louis. But I learned that if I didn't keep my mind on business people could die.

VIETNAM AMBUSHES

Night ambushes were dangerous. Even today, those memories give me cold shivers. Everything had to work together perfectly, or we'd kill each other. The teamwork, preparation, practice, and discipline necessary to make it work took time and trust. Sadly, in Vietnam, we didn't have the time to train properly. Ambushes were hastily put together after a day of humping in unfamiliar terrain and locations often found at night by map. Thank God, we seldom made contact. On the two that we did, we lost several Marines. I hope that the lessons paid for in blood were truly learned.

DEADLY ATTITUDES

Marines with a death wish were aggressive and took stupid chances. Some short timers were too cautious as others developed a cocky, false sense of security. Over confidence caused deadly mistakes that affected everyone. That was the reality of screwing up. People died. I made more than my share of mistakes, and some could have killed people. But I learned from all of our mistakes and tried awfully hard not to make the same one twice. Although shithouse luck gave me another chance, luck couldn't replace staying focused, alert, and aware.

MY PERSONAL CODE OF ETHICS

Don't think that all American Marines were above acts of cruelty. Some collected gold teeth and ears from dead gooks. Others did worse. I didn't participate but I didn't try to stop them either. Every man had to know how far he would go before he could no longer live with himself. "Payback" tempted me many times, but I resisted. I had no qualms finishing off a mortally wounded gook, but I couldn't torture or kill unarmed VC prisoners. I was ordered to do so once but I refused. I told my platoon sergeant that if he wanted them dead he would have to shoot them himself. I guess he had a code of ethics too, because he didn't shoot them either.

FRIENDLY FIRE

Marines mistakenly killed Marines, thinking that they were VC or NVA.

Remembering death by friendly fire breaks my heart. No part of combat was more horrible than one Marine accidentally killing another. Friendly fire caused deaths that weighed heavily on the heart of another for life. Misjudgments, stupid mistakes, confusion during a fire fight, safety is off, fear, panic, and a quarter-inch pull on the trigger is all it takes.

During a firefight, anything can happen. Confusion reigns for the first few minutes. Men scream orders as others scream in pain. No one knows what's happening. Adrenaline's pumping, rounds pop, visibility is poor, and it's hard to see where the fire's coming from. It was insane and only worse at night.

Marines were wounded by artillery and mortar fire beyond our control. Fire missions called in from An Hoa had to be exact. I remember lying on my back, watching 105mm rounds roar overhead to enemy targets. Several exploded in short round bursts directly over me. It was just shithouse luck that no one got hit. At times I was more afraid of getting killed by Marines than by VC.

COMBAT

Think Like A Marine.
1. Practice pre-arranged hand signals with the squad.
2. Prepare, arrange, and silence your deuce gear and equipment.
3. Where ever you are, look for the best and nearest cover.
4. Look for possible ambush sites when ever you're in the field.
5. Estimate ranges to various objects.

PREPARING FOR COMBAT

Remember your training at the onset of fire. Expect confusion and noise.
1. Take cover and turn outboard toward the fire.
2. Determine the point of fire.
3. Return fire and mark targets with tracers.
4. Keep contact with the men ahead of you in the column. When they move, you move.

DON'T MAKE YOURSELF A MOVING TARGET

New and clean utilities, helmet covers, backpacks, deuce gear make you obvious. Stay dirty in the bush. In Vietnam grunts were silent and dirty.

Remember, snipers target Radio Operators so watch your antennae. Other targets:

> A. Squad leaders, NCO's—men shouting orders.
> B. Officers—directing troops.
> C. CP groups—clean uniforms, men talking together, antennas.
> D. Special weapons, machine guns, anti-tanks etc.
> E. On patrol, whenever the column stops, get down on one knee and face outboard. Keep your distance so one round doesn't get all of you—fifteen- to twenty-feet apart.

CHECKS

Marines shot seriously wounded VC in the head. Always check the dead by touching the eye with a rifle muzzle, just like a grizzly bear. If it blinks shoot. The dead usually have their eyes open so beware of closed eyes.

All Marines should know how to work radios, read maps, and compasses, and operate all weapons. I've seen PFC's take over squads, and lance corporals take over platoons. Rank and responsibility can change quickly in combat.

Expert marksmanship is combat salvation. Practice until you're an expert with your service rifle. In combat, if you don't hit what you aim at, you're useless. It's just a fact, man. Shoot with both eyes open to consistently hit moving targets. Gunner shots—don't close one eye. It's easy to retrain. Keep both eyes on the target, bring the rifle up to your master eye—aim and shoot.

All M16s look alike. Mark yours with tape so you don't grab PFC Zilches. Periodically sight your rifle in combat. Don't assume it hits the mark. During a lull in the fire fight, if a target presents itself—a gravestone or a rock—that would register a hit, take a pop at it. It's reassuring.

TIPS AND EQUIPMENT

Once in the Vietnam shit, we could tell if a Marine knew what he was doing by how he wore his deuce gear. I arranged my deuce gear for easy access. During a firefight, I pulled the most accessible mags *last*. I taped mags to my butt stock or helmet to prevent jams. I reloaded during a lull in the firefight (that's when a drop bag became handy). I pinned charger clips, important for reloading the magazine quickly, all over my deuce gear to avoid loss. Every Marine kept one mag of tracers—used for spotting snipers or direct rifle fire—on his web belt.

I'm right-handed so I didn't tape anything that could block raising my rifle to my right shoulder strap. Jungle clips didn't work for us. I taped two mags together upside down and put one in the mud if we were prone during a firefight. I carried one quick mag in the left pocket of my flack vest.

Neck towels, used to wipe sweat and protect one's head and neck from bugs, became indispensable. Most were dyed green and brown and sent from home.

Guys carried knives taped upside down on the shoulder strap of their weak side. This was too bulky for me so I carried a smaller knife, upside down, tied around my neck by a para cord. I liked it so much I still carry one today.

The U.S. didn't provide all that we needed. If you're preparing for deployment, take what you need with you. Mail what you can't carry. Ask family and friends to send pogey boxes filled with your favorite food on a regular basis. Waiting pogey boxes raised our spirits in Vietnam, especially after long operations.

Remember, it's a long way to the nearest K-Mart so even the smallest creature comforts will make living out of your helmet somewhere out there more tolerable.

NIGHT RULES TO AVOID FRIENDLY FIRE

Night Rule #1

Never, ever walk to another platoon, company, or Marine position without first letting them know that friendly forces are approaching. Radio, shout, and holler to make sure that everyone gets the word. Remember Marines can shoot and shoot well.

Night Rule #2

Never, ever, ever leave your position or foxhole unless it's a life threatening emergency. If you need to shit or piss, crap or pee in the bottom of your hole and cover it with dirt. If you must leave, let everyone know that you're coming.

Night Rule #3

When setting in night perimeter positions don't accidentally wander out of the perimeter. Know *exactly* where you are.

Night Rule #4

Use grenades or claymores first. Don't fire unless you have a valid target, then use semi-auto only. Use full-auto unless you're getting over run, fast, furiously, and at close range. At night, reload your rifle, using hand finds hand.

SHIT BIRDS IN COMBAT

Like drunk drivers, Shit Birds cause death but aren't injured themselves. They are the ten percent that assume ninety percent of your time.

What is a Shit Bird?
1. Shit Birds cause Marines death and destruction.
2. Shit Birds cower in a fire fight.
3. Shit Birds are untrustworthy.
4. Shit Birds cannot be found for working parties.
5. Shit Birds complain and whine.

6. Shit Birds try to get out of the field.

7. Shit Birds don't maintain their rifles, deuce gear, or equipment.

8. Shit Birds are poor shots.

9. Shit Birds refuse to take responsibility for their actions.

10. Shit Birds almost never climb the ranks.

Most Shit Birds can be turned around. They must be confronted and dealt with ASAP as their actions affect Marine combat readiness, effectiveness, and safety.

SHIT BIRD SQUAD AND SHIT BIRD FIRE TEAM LEADERS IN COMBAT

What is a Shit Bird Squad or Shit Bird Fire Team Leader?

1. Shit Bird Squad and Shit Bird Fire Team Leaders don't assign their buddies dangerous jobs.

2. Shit Bird Squad and Shit Bird Fire Team Leaders *always* associate with their buddies in another squad when given a chance; *your* squad is your family, you spend time with them.

3. Shit Bird Squad and Shit Bird Fire Team Leaders take the best chow.

4. Shit Bird Squad and Shit Bird Fire Team Leaders don't check for required gear and equipment.

5. Shit Bird Squad and Shit Bird Fire Team Leaders care about themselves and their comfort.

6. Shit Bird Squad and Shit Bird Fire Team Leaders don't care about the safety and welfare of their men.

7. Shit Bird Squad and Shit Bird Fire Team Leaders don't stand night watch.

8. Shit Bird Squad and Shit Bird Fire Team Leaders only talk to their men when giving orders.

9. Shit Bird Squad and Shit Bird Fire Team Leaders don't control their fear.

10. Shit Bird Squad and Shit Bird Fire Team Leaders degrade their men in front of others.

Shit Bird Squad and Shit Bird Fire Team Leaders should not be tolerated. Use the chain of command to remove those who hold the rank but lack the ability to lead.

In the final analysis, leadership is the ultimate result on any field battle. It is one thing to command, quite another to lead. Without question, long overlooked, seldom praised, few times decorated, and quickly forgotten, the United States Marine squad leader carries the spirit of freedom on the sword of his country.

A BACKWARD GLANCE

William F. Gavin

Their eyes glance back at me, piercing the years,
confirming our bond.
As a photograph frozen in time,
yet flowing in memory's stream,
I see each face,
as arms reach out pulling me up to solid ground.

Vietnam forged our youth and took their lives,
as we shared the best and worst of the inferno.
A stronger bond is known only but to God.

Now hesitating as I stumble over life's setbacks,
I welcome their backward glance from under steel helmets,
For I will always return it with one of courage.
A promise to press on, for they would expect
no less.

❧ Dear Daddy ❧

I've chosen to highlight An Hoa's June and July, 1967 for two reasons—your friend Captain James Graham, recipient of the Medal of Honor—and you. I asked my now "Uncle Mac" (Captain Graham's radioman and constant companion) to describe Captain Graham—a hero so revered tears shamelessly fell from those willing to share. Those who couldn't speak of Captain Graham simply walked away, leaving me silent and embarrassed to have scratched and bled the still raw nerve.

As far as you're concerned, suffice to say for the twenty-six years that you were mine, nothing could make me more proud of the man I had the privilege of calling Daddy.

JUNE

Captain James A. Graham, USMC, Official
Marine Corps Photo, Camp Lejeune, NC, 1966.

Lance Corporal Brenton MacKinnon:

I joined Foxtrot 2/5 in January 1967; assigned as a rifleman to the first platoon. In March, I was transferred to the Command Post as Captain Graham's radioman and translator. I was ordered by the gunny to trade my life for Captain Graham's. I was replaceable, Graham was not. Captain Graham's serious demeanor and compassionate humor was respected and popular among his fellow officers and NCO staff.

Until his death on June 2, 1967, I was Captain Graham's constant companion, shadow, and relay voice to Foxtrot Marines.

Looking older than twenty-seven, Graham reminded me of a hawk, a predator caged in a body—intense and hungry—released into his own personal hunting ground, Vietnam. I believe that he deemed himself anointed to embrace a special destiny. It wasn't ambition per se; the promotion ladder was not his personal mission. Jim Graham was driven by a powerful inner force.

Skillfully dancing with the ever-present shadow of death using electric senses and soaring spirits, this aggressive and tactical leader led Foxtrot Company to many victories in the midst of chaos and attrition. Captain Graham's ambition for combat was almost childlike. He continuously studied sitreps and maps, remaining cognizant, at all times, of the flowing stream of intelligence. Captain James Graham was, as the saying goes, "Born ready."

Jim Graham carried a Bible and toiletries into the field when no one else did. He'd wash, shave, brush his teeth, and change into clean, pressed fatigues in the middle of nowhere to be at his best. This archetype projected a missionary vision—donning his robes, making his absolutions, and saying his prayers. He was ready to die at all times. I respected his professional and private disciplines and obsessions. His confidence made us better warriors.

On June 2nd, the rice paddy of death lay before us. A ripple of apprehension traveled through the entire company. For the first time, I witnessed Captain Graham hesitate and question his direct orders to advance. Evidence suggested that formidable enemy forces were waiting in the trees lines across the open rice paddy. And indeed, they were.

Captain Jim Graham was courageous when the opportunity presented itself, not with guns blazing to assault and destroy, but in a doomed effort to save Foxtrot's second platoon, ambushed in a dry rice paddy. He is an authentic hero who sacrificed his life doing the impossible.

The last time I saw Jim Graham he was dead on a poncho. He had given his all in the face of certain death. For me, our family died that day. Our Captain Graham was gone, taking with him the heart and soul of Foxtrot.

Operation Union II aimed to uproot the NVA from the southern rim of the South Vietnam's Que Son Valley. Serving as a response mechanism to Operation Union I, this multi-battalion operation continued a bitter crusade to terminate enemy existence in the fertile and densely populated region. Although Operation Union I loosened the foothold of the NVA, communist forces maintained a political and physical stronghold on the people and their rice-rich harvest.

Foxtrot 2/5, commanded by Captain James A. Graham, was under the operational control of Lt. Colonel Peter L. Hilgartner's 1/5 for the eleven-day undertaking that began on May 26th. The Sixth ARVN Regiment, the First ARVN Ranger Group, and Lt. Colonel Dean E. Esslinger's 3/5, Companies I, L, and M were also included in the coordinating efforts.

Intense enemy fire did little to thwart Marine victory during the operation's initial days. June 2nd, however, transformed lives through acts of obedience, regret, heroism, victory, and grief for An Hoa's Second Battalion, Fifth Marines.

Prior to noon, Companies D and F advanced northwest of the basin with the objective of landing Fox Company in the Vinh Huy Village. With Company D on the right and F on the left, the companies traversed a mile-wide exposed horseshoe-shaped

clearing to reach a bordering hedgerow. Captain Graham led Fox
Headquarters Group (HQ) fifty yards behind two platoons. An
additional platoon served as the company's rear security.

*Fox Company Lance Corporal Brenton MacKinnon, Captain Graham's radioman
and constant companion:*

With monsoon season over, the rice paddy was a sheet of rock-hard dirt that
bore no vegetation. Forward scouts, led by Staff Sergeant Tony Marengo, crossed
this massive field and killed several NVA enemy observation posts. Staff Sergeant
Marengo unearthed a crank phone and wire running across the paddy into the
tree line. As Staff Sergeant Marengo lifted the wire to show Captain Graham, a
single sniper shot and horrific screaming bellowed through the ears and fears of
all. Our OP scout had been hit in the groin. The sophisticated sniper and com
line were markers of a regular NVA unit who didn't care about being discovered.
Captain Graham notified Lt. Colonel Hilgartner of the sniper and wire.

Fox Company Staff Sergeant Tony Marengo:

Initially Captain Graham requested air and artillery strikes on the tree
line furthest from the horseshoe opening to prep the area for protection. Lt.
Colonel Hilgartner denied the request. Captain Graham then requested an
artillery strike as predetermined coordinate to rouse and weaken enemy concentration. Indignant, Lt. Colonel Hilgartner once again denied Captain Graham.
Lt. Colonel Hilgartner was satisfied with his on call 81mms. Captain Graham
disagreed; the 81mms were insufficient. Lt. Colonel Hilgartner's scenario would
trap, without cover or concealment, Fox 2/5. Lt. Colonel Hilgartner ordered
Captain Graham to advance; Delta 1/5 was engaging the enemy. A heated
disagreement ensued.

Lt. Colonel Hilgartner remained unconvinced. "I'm giving you a direct
order, move your troops."

End of discussion. Collectively we felt as though we were walking into a
firing squad.

Fox Company Lance Corporal Brenton MacKinnon:

When Lt. Colonel Hilgartner gave his direct order to "deploy and engage,"
Captain Graham stared doubtfully at Gunnery Sergeant Green. For the first
time in six months as Captain Graham's radioman, I witnessed his bravado
evaporate into hesitation. Fox entered that paddy with a collective gut feeling
that the order and decision to proceed was very, very wrong.

Fox Company Staff Sergeant Tony Marengo:

We continued forward, killing several NVA soldiers stationed at a machine
gun outpost. Their clean uniforms and high-cropped haircuts indicated that
we were dealing with fresh NVA soldiers, not local VC. As we pressed on, our

Kit Carson scout shot miscellaneous humps of straw, unveiling NVA soldiers buried in spider holes.

Midway, NVA troops hidden by rice thatches in the hedgerows to our front and back, opened with heavy, heavy fire. With nothing to stunt or smoke screen the enemy, we marched into a meat grinder of pelting fire. People fell, including me. The low paddy dikes were useless for cover. If I could've removed my belly button to hover closer to the ground, I would have. I knew we needed the immediate concealment of higher ground.

Enemy bullets blitzed the front and left flank, entangling the platoons in a cross fire. Heavy automatic weapons fire stunted further efforts of the Marine reserve platoons.

Fox Company Lance Corporal Brenton MacKinnon:
We were ambushed within minutes by the Third Regiment of the North Vietnamese Army. It was sheer chaos and mass mutilation. The second platoon was decimated and the 3rd platoon now pinned, suffered major casualties. In frustration, Captain Graham ordered his ten HQ men with rifles to follow him to aid the second platoon.

Because radiomen carried only pistols and radios, Captain Graham ordered me, artillery spotter Ron Devore and First Sergeant Cleo Lee to remain and coordinate communications. We had two radios and three pistols.

Fox Company Anti Tank Assaultman Patrick Haley:
Every Marine hit the deck hard, straining, clawing, and scratching for depth. Staff Sergeant Marengo, wounded but functioning, shouted commands, scattered and flattened as we were, to re-group so the platoon could bear all of its weapons on the NVA. As we crawled under mortar shell and flat trajectory fire, Captain Graham dove into our midst with his runner.

Fox Company Staff Sergeant Tony Marengo:
I ordered Corporal Melvin Long and the remainder of his squad—four of his seven men were seriously wounded; three wounded but functioning—around and up the reserve slope to surprise and destroy the NVA firing into the First and Second Platoon. The Third Platoon hunkered in the rice paddy to support Corporal Long. Captain Graham approved. We simply had no other choice.

Fox Company Anti Tank Assaultman Patrick Haley:
Instead of retreating to either of two comparatively safe hills to direct the battle, Captain Graham returned to the First and Second Platoons where his chance of survival was slim. Shouting orders, he charged and eliminated an NVA machine gun nest positioned to prevent moving First and Second Platoon's wounded Marines. Surviving members of the Foxtrot HQ unit joined in this courageous effort, most of who were wounded or killed in that assault.

With enemy pressure now slightly diminished, the men transported the wounded to a secure area as the NVA pummeled the out-gunned and out-numbered Marines. Captain Graham's attempts to silence the second automatic weapon were stalled by his wounds and lack of ammunition. He ordered his men to E and E—evade and escape, to friendly positions while he shielded Thomas Donovan, a seriously wounded corpsman.

Fox Company Staff Sergeant Tony Marengo:
Captain Graham called me on the radio. "Grey fox, they look good; they're firing and maneuvering."
I asked if I could help, but once he heard what I had going on, he told me to stay put.

Captain Graham's final radio transmission stated that twenty-five enemy soldiers were overrunning his position.
Captain Graham received the Medal of Honor posthumously for his heroism.
Lieutenant Colonel Hilgartner's CP suffered heavy mortar, recoilless rifle, and RPG fire. The communists were too large and well-situated for the battalion to dislodge.

Fox Company Anti Tank Assaultman Patrick Haley:
Hours passed before we saw Corporal Long standing on the hilltop's outcropping rock and firing an automatic weapon into one of the two machine gun emplacements. Corporal Long made an incredible silhouette, inserting magazines into his weapon like a wind-whipped flame, saving the lives of his fellow Marines. He was wounded but unquenchable.

The battle continued although diminished in ferocity once Corporal Long spearheaded the third platoon to secure the hill by flanking the enemy.
Fox Company Corporal Long received the Navy Cross for his actions.

Fox Company Staff Sergeant Tony Marengo:
Although I pressed at every level, I lost most of my elements that day. Adding to the day's chaos, the 1/5 Battalion commander had ordered us to remove our flak jackets in an effort to move faster. Yes, flak jackets were cumbersome but without it, we felt naked. It was the one piece of equipment that I bitched about having the most.

I organized a nucleus of wounded and dead to be carried back to the lines. I had to reassure the living that we were going to be okay all night. The night was endless.

Fox Company Lance Corporal Brenton MacKinnon:

The day was endless; the battle continued for over sixteen hours. Late air strikes offered little relief from close NVA heavy-weapons fire. All attached units were on the defensive including the 1/5 engaged across the ridgeline. Friendly fire killed several Marines from the second platoon. Radioman Diesel died as we spoke on the radio. Devore, Lee, and I buried ourselves using our radios as shields from incoming machine gun fire, impotent to the pleas of the wounded and dying two hundred feet ahead. I connected with a radio operator who lay gut-shot and crying for someone to kill him before the enemy captured him.

Devore and I decided to rescue our brothers while Sergeant Lee monitored the radios. Within one hundred and fifty feet, enemy tracers pinned us prisoner. I relaxed, convinced that death was imminent. A tracer ripped through Devore's foot and flipped him midair as he dashed back to the protection of the tree line. He lay motionless. Dead, I thought, but to my surprise, he dragged himself into the bushes under enemy fire.

The intense barrage ceased as the sun set, allowing me to crawl through this graveyard in search of the living. I tied a tourniquet around a Marine wounded in the leg. We limped forward and found a guy shot in the head, conscious but blind. The bullet had cracked his skull. I positioned a gut-shot Marine on the blind guy's shoulder. I shouldered a Marine shot through both legs and found another kid peppered with arm and head wounds, shocked and disoriented, but ambulatory. Like a band of exhausted old men, we inched forward and collapsed into a pile, resting before our next effort, terrified of being caught weaponless by NVA death squads. The NVA squalled threats while executing our wounded lying on the perimeter. I found a serviceable radio and contacted Chuck Connolly now huddled on a small hill with survivors. "Connolly, where are you? I've got seven wounded."

"We're on the hill on other side of the creek. Do you remember the creek?"

"Yes."

"Well, for God's sake, when you're within hearing distance of the creek, call me. I'll come and guide you across."

Although paranoid that the gooks were on our net, Connelly and I shared a visible landmark that would enable us to stagger across a stream into the protection of an emergency LZ. We, the survivors, now approaching an unknown count of NVA in the thick of the night, heard guys crying for help.

I yelled, "What unit are you in?"

Every Vietnamese accented response kept me moving. But I'm forever tortured by what may or may not have been a real Marine. Once at the creek, I called Connolly who met me in the middle, sidled by another Marine. Connolly was also blind. A bamboo grenade had concussed his eyeballs.

He laid his hands out. "I can't see but I'm the only guy who knows you. So they sent me down."

We made our way back to the perimeter. I could smell the fear inside the small hillside perimeter, but hell, these guys were healthy and armed. Listening to the sorrow of the wounded lying tortured and executed on the battlefield, I insisted on returning to our dead and wounded. No one listened to me. I was the only one from Fox's CP group not shot. My aura was fifty feet in every direction. I was an animal with acute senses.

Lt. Colonel Hilgartner questioned me. "Who were you with?"

"Captain Graham, now dead."

"You're safe now, son."

"No one's safe."

"Son, we don't know where we are."

"Fuck you! We don't leave anybody, goddamn it!"

I bore witness to a terrified, fucking lieutenant colonel in combat trying to save his own shit. I lost control. Me—the calm, cool, collected control freak who held his shit together during crises, lost control. Screaming wildly to retrieve the wounded, I was physically subdued until I promised to be quiet. I thought then as I do now, they were cowards.

The regimental commander colonel, Kenneth J. Houghton requested help from An Hoa's division reserve under the command of Lt. Colonel Jackson. Supporting elements included Echo Company 2/5, Delta Company1/7, and Echo Company 2/7.

Lt. Colonel Jackson and Major Esau expeditiously organized a bobtailed helicopter placement of two companies plus the command group as Colonel Houghton prepped the LZ with ninety minutes of air and artillery strikes. Landing unopposed, the units waited for the third company. By evening, the additional leg had not yet arrived. Lt. Colonel Jackson then requested and received permission to initiate the assault minus the company. Leaving a security platoon in the landing zone, Lt. Colonel Jackson and Major Esau maneuvered their forces south against the enemy.

Major Richard H. Esau Jr.:

Lieutenant Colonel Jackson assembled the remainder of the battalion to proceed in column, covering our flanks with continuing artillery fire controlled by the regimental operation's officer (S3) instead of using our own flank security. Although unusual, this was a cognizant, tactical decision made to get to Jim Graham, Fox, and Hilgartner as quickly as possible. A helicopter entering our airspace requested a smoke to pinpoint our exact position. The multiple-smoke response indicated that the NVA were on our frequencies, thus adding to the danger of moving through the regiment's protective fire without flank security. Dick Alger, the regimental S3 tracking our progress on radio, and I creatively labeled our journey to Hiep Duc, our final destination. Hiep Duc became New York's Battery Park, located on Manhattan's southern tip. Alger, a fellow New Yorker, understood my directives for moving south on the Henry Hudson Parkway to Columbus Circle down to Times Square, across to the Flat Iron Building and ultimately east down the FDR Drive into the tip of Battery Park. Not only did Alger provide flank cover fire, he assured that none of the regiment's protective fires threatened our men. I also spoke to Gunnery Sergeant Green who advised us of the gravity of their situation and the death of Captain Graham. I assured him in no uncertain terms to "hold on, we're on our way. We are on our way."

We arrived outboard of the enemy's ambush site and splintered the NVA command post. We surprised an enemy shocked at the onset of a Marine unit's commitment and swift arrival. Our forces engaged the enemy who attempted a rear guard action, careful not to strike with weaponry that would hit our troops on the other side of the NVA.

Marine presence in the northern flank of the NVA CP caused the communists to disengage and flee from the protection of their fighting holes through an open battlefield. Now caught in a Marine cross fire, the NVA were easy prey for devastating Marine artillery and air fire.

Major Richard H. Esau Jr.:

We radioed for a CH-34 medevac-bird in the middle of this madness. Inadvertently a CH-53, loaded with reinforcements, picked up our guiding strobe light instead of its intended destination two-thousand meters east. Although the NVA ripped more than fifty-eight holes into this big bird, the pilot persevered, and like manna from heaven, dropped off its platoon and transported our wounded to Marble Mountain. The pilot received the Distinguished Flying Cross for flying through the hail of bullets.

The 2/5's Command Chronologies note two F-4 aircrafts that operated in tandem. The first aircraft approached its target slowly, donning landing and running lights in order to draw 50 caliber enemy machine gun fire. The second F-4 followed in trace, without lights, targeting and eliminating the enemy weapons crew with a napalm strike. The pilots exchanged several such runs, ultimately destroying two of the enemy 81-82mm mortars that caused the majority of the 2/5 casualties.

Echo Company Ammo Humper Denny Curtain:

Serving as Sparrow Hawk, we, Echo Company, grabbed our haversacks and rifles and bolted to An Hoa's airstrip. As we boarded the choppers the mess hall fed us fried chicken, oranges, and milk, like death row inmates eating their last meal.

Midair, I could see squads of NVA running wildly, undaunted by our choppers. We landed and waited in a B-52 bomb crater depression—without being fired on—watching Phantoms dropped bombs, artillery-fire and napalm.

Echo Company Fleet Marine Force Corpsman Roger Lansbury:

Echo Company headed out after receiving word that Foxtrot 2/5 and Delta Company 1/5 had been ambushed and were now engaged in a full-scale battle. After refueling at Tam Ky, a failed engine forced my bird into an emergency landing. Five Hueys passed before we rejoined the remainder of the company at 1600. Our position was reinforced by Delta 1/7; eight UH-2 helicopters, equipped with two M60 machine guns and two 20mm cannons; and four Phantom jets that carried rockets, bombs, and napalm.

At dusk, Echo 2/5 and Delta 1/7 marched in column to flank Foxtrot, now rumored to have been annihilated. The enemy continued their automatic weapons fire despite the tracer rounds that gave away their positions. But enemy ground-to-air fire ceased with Puff the Magic Dragon's six-barrel gun firing six thousand rounds a minute.

That's one hundred rounds per second with every fifth round serving as a tracer, allowing one visible, impressive solid red line.

Echo Company Ammo Humper Denny Curtain:

When ordered to move out, we walked a tree-lined dirt road and made a sharp left onto the paddy dike. Another tree line lay ahead with banana trees and jungle foliage encompassing our sides. Exploding grenades and rifle fire from the tree line forced us behind the paddy dike. An NVA machine gun strafed the dike, shooting one A-gunner three times. Hell and chaos followed as a second machine gun strafed our line.

As the muzzle flash swung from left to right, I knew I had only one chance. I aimed above the muzzle flash and shot. The enemy machine gun ceased. My M16 jammed after that shot, and I didn't have my cleaning rod, so I locked my bayonet. Our front guys returned, dragging our wounded gunner.

John Payne, a close friend and fellow ammo humper and I continued right on the dike running parallel to the tree line ahead. The night was so dark and thick, our platoon somehow separated, leaving us with a mortar team and two squads ahead. As we stretched along that rice paddy, we were hammered with mortars. We entered the backside of Fox's earlier ambush and into the rear of the NVA ambush. We surprised the NVA as much as they surprised us. It was pure chaos and confusion in a concentrated time frame. JP and I watched an NVA forward observer fire direct mortar from behind a rock. Stranded and isolated, we were afraid. We took more casualties. One corpsman was killed; five of the eight mortar men were wounded, three seriously. A medevac came to retrieve the wounded. I could see Echo's Gunnery Sergeant Arthur Fitzgerald, a World War II and Korea veteran, behind us, directing the medevac bird in. He was struck by a mortar round—bad—but survived.

E cho Company's Gunnery Sergeant Arthur Fitzgerald was awarded a Silver Star for his actions.

Echo Company Fleet Marine Force Corpsman Roger Lansbury:
Additional enemy sniper fire continued to wound. Delta 1/7, moving into our right flank, fell under a mortar barrage that followed the departing medevac. Agonizing screams and cries of "corpsman up" followed the explosions. A mortar attack is horrible. No one knows where the rounds are coming from so everyone panics and scrambles for non-existent shelter. One hugs the ground to become a part of it. Fortunately, most of us were dug in. I stayed busy with casualties. Two men died as I tried to save them. I felt so utterly helpless. Echo Company: twenty wounded and one dead. Eight were medevaced immediately while the others waited until morning. Delta Company 1/7: eighteen wounded and three dead.
At three a.m. I fell into an exhausted sleep.

Echo Company Ammo Humper Denny Curtain:
The NVA pummeled Delta 1/7 as they tried to relieve us. The fighting endured for hours. Phantoms finally dropped heavy bombs—snake eyes—and napalm on the tree line. The napalm—dropped seventy-five yards from our position—singed off my eyebrows. The NVA pulled out by three a.m., so we held our position. One rifleman crawled to gather grenades from the remaining Marines and then slinked in front of our listening post and stayed until daylight.

Fox Company Anti Tank Assaultman Patrick Haley:
By dawn, the surviving NVA had departed the rice paddy which now lay in a deathly, ominous, unforgiving silence. We struggled to lug the wounded from the rice paddy to the helicopter loading area. Remarkably, the NVA had already buried their dead in tunnels, trenches, and shell holes.
What a gut-wrenching and unforgettable experience. Regardless of our exhaustion and reluctance to face and identify our dead, we, the surviving Foxtrot Marines, tearfully did what needed to be done.

Echo Company Ammo Humper Denny Curtain:

As we searched for bodies at daylight we found an NVA soldier chained to his Chicom machine gun, a heavy enemy arms cache in the tree line, and a large bag of opium in one of the hootches. Where Fox lay ambushed, we found opened M16s with bolts strewn in the field. Marines, aware of their impending death, stripped their useless rifles rather than leave them for the NVA.

The sight from the crest of the hilltop was unbelievable. Marine bodies were piled like core wood, seven feet high.

The Marines and the NVA gathered bodies during an unconditional cease fire. Both sides, realizing the severity of the consequences from such a bloody battle, simply backed off.

Fox Company Lance Corporal Brenton MacKinnon:

We retrieved our dead and laid them in rows. The toll: fifty-four from F Company swollen, yellow, and purple with grotesque faces on the verge of exploding. Among the dead lay Diesel, Sugar Bear, Red, Driscoll, and Captain James Graham.

Seventy-three lay wounded and fucked up.

Back at An Hoa, I walked silently into my hootch and stared at a shaving mirror into the face and eyes of a stranger.

I asked, "Who the fuck are you?"

I no longer recognized the sole Marine returning to the enlisted HQ hootch from Operation Union II. Sometimes when I permit my memory to crawl through that slaughterhouse, I hear gooks taunting, "Marine you die."

Fox Company Lance Corporal Brenton MacKinnon received a Bronze Star with a combat "V" for his heroism.

Echo Company Ammo Humper Denny Curtain:

Not a day goes by that I don't think about June 2, 1967. I can see, hear, and smell that day in perfect detail. June 2, 1967 is my benchmark. I'm a man driven, with extremely high standards. You do something right or you don't do it at all. If you don't, you will get you and the guy next to you killed.

Unions I and II were noted as the bloodiest battles fought to that point during the Vietnam War. The Fifth Marine Regiment was awarded a Presidential Unit Citation for their heroism on Operations Union I and II.

*Graham family Portrait John Graham, Mrs. Janice Graham, Jennifer
Graham, and Captain James A. Graham, August 1966.*

*Official Photo for
Major MAF
Operations.*

*Cpl. Patrick "Waterbu" Haley,
Fox Company, anti-tank assault-man,
An Hoa, RSVN, 1967.*

Operation Union II Defense Department photo "Marines on Operation Union II advance along the dikes between flooded rice paddies," June 1, 1967.

Operation Union II Defense Department photo "The 5th Marines on Operation Union II" proceed across rice paddies in search of enemy snipers," June 2, 1967.

MY ORIGINAL— WHAT IT DOESN'T SAY
CITATION   IS THAT THE "ACHIEVEMENT"
             INVOLVED 16 HOURS OF A
             DAY & NIGHT

UNITED STATES MARINE CORPS
HEADQUARTERS, FLEET MARINE FORCE, PACIFIC
FPO, SAN FRANCISCO 96610

In the name of the Secretary of the Navy, the Commanding General, Fleet Marine Force, Pacific takes pleasure in presenting the NAVY COMMENDATION MEDAL to

PRIVATE FIRST CLASS BRENTON EDWARD MACKINNON

UNITED STATES MARINE CORPS

for service as set forth in the following

CITATION:

"For heroic achievement while serving as a Radio Operator with Company F, Second Battalion, Fifth Marines, First Marine Division in connection with operations against insurgent communist (Viet Cong) forces in the Republic of Vietnam. On 2 June 1967, during Operation Union II, Company F came under intense enemy small arms, automatic weapons and mortar fire and sustained numerous casualties while conducting a search and destroy mission in Quang Tin Province. Disregarding his own safety, Private First Class MACKINNON repeatedly exposed himself to the heavy volume of fire to assist in the evacuation of the wounded. On one occasion, he was temporarily pinned down by enemy fire as he attempted to move to the side of an injured Marine who was lying in an unprotected position within fifty meters of an enemy fortification. With resolute determination, he continued to maneuver across the fire-swept terrain until he reached his wounded comrade and moved him to a place of relative safety. His heroic and timely actions in the face of extreme personal danger were an inspiration to all who observed him and saved the lives of nine Marines. By his courage, bold initiative and selfless devotion to duty, Private First Class MACKINNON upheld the finest traditions of the Marine Corps and of the United States Naval Service."

Private First Class MACKINNON is authorized to wear the Combat "V".

FOR THE SECRETARY OF THE NAVY,

V. H. KRULAK
LIEUTENANT GENERAL, U. S. MARINE CORPS
COMMANDING

TEMPORARY CITATION

LUCIA ASK ME WHAT
HAPPENED AFTER I
RETURNED WITH THESE
WOUNDED...

Original Bronze star with a Combat "V" citation awarded to Cpl Brenton MacKinnon with notes written to Lucia Viti.

PHOTO TIMELINE BY DENNY CURTIN

USMC, Echo Company 2/5; June 2, 1967. An Hoa LZ waiting for transport into the Que Son Valley to assist Fox Company 2/5.

USMC, Echo Company 2/5; 60mm mortar teams with rifleman Tom Walden 3rd and Denny Curtin waiting for transport into the Que Son Valley to assist Fox Company 2/5.

USMC, Echo Company 2/5; 60mm mortar teams boarding choppers in An Hoa.

Denny Curtin, USMC, Echo Company 2/5; E 2/5 leaving An Hoa.

USMC, Echo Company 2/5; E 2/5 entering the Que Son Valley.

USMC, Echo Company 2/5; June 3, 1967 60mm mortar team left to right Michael Obregon, Denny Curtin, John Payne, "Sitting at NVA spider hole after a long night of battle at sight of Fox 2/5 ambush."

USMC, Echo Company 2/5; November 9, 1987 Washington, DC. E 2/5 Union II Marines, left to right: Leonard Ramirez, John Willis, Denny Curtin, Harry Boyce and Patrick Blessing. Kneeling left to right: Dan Rotar, Bob Worra and John Payne.

June 13, 1967

Dear Doctor Viti,

Your kind letter about our Tommy was most welcome to me and his family. It is good to know that others shared with us a feeling of respect for him as a man.

We knew he loved his work and desired to return to school to further his education in the field of medicine when he left the service.

While his loss is heartbreaking it is lessened by your statement that he died keeping his buddies.

We certainly want you to visit us when your tour of duty ends.

Respectfully yours,

Joseph J. Donovan

Letter written from the Donovan Family to Dr. Viti. Dr Viti wrote to the Donovan family in light of the death of their son, FMF Corpsman Tom Donovan. Captain James A. Graham died while protecting Corpsman Donovan on Operation Union II, June 2, 1967.

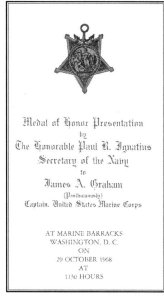

Medal of Honor Ceremony in
honor of Captain James A.
Graham, Washington, DC,
October 29, 1968.

Daily News *Photo,*
Wednesday,
October 30, 1968.

The man stepped forward and showed the medal, inside a blue case, to the little boy. The boy looked at it somberly. "This is for your daddy," said the man. And so Marine Captain James A. Graham of Forestville, Md., was honored in death by Navy Secretary Paul Ignatius at the Marine Barracks in Washington. The nation had given its highest award, the Medal of Honor, to a man who'd given his life for a wounded comrade in Vietnam, June 2, 1967. Graham's wife, Janice, holding back tears, accepted the award for the family.

Capt. James A. Graham—a hero is honored.

Associated Press Wirephoto

Mrs. Graham shows medal to daughter Jenifer, 4, and son John, 5, as Secretary Ignatius looks on.

'This Is for Your Daddy...

The man stepped forward and showed the medal, inside a blue case, to the little boy. The boy looked at it somberly. "This is for your daddy," said the man. And so Marine Capt. James A. Graham (◄—) of Forestville, Md., was honored in death yesterday by Navy Secretary Paul Ignatius at the Marine Barracks in Washington. The nation had given its highest award, the Medal of Honor, to a man who'd given his life for a wounded comrade in Vietnam, June 2, 1967. Graham's wife, Janice, holding back tears, accepted the award for the family.

"Marine Gets Honor Posthumously"

The President of the United States in the name of The Congress takes pride in presenting the MEDAL OF HONOR posthumously to
Captain James A. Graham
United States Marine Corps
for service as set forth in the following
Citation:

For conspicuous gallantry and intrepidity at the risk of his life above and beyond the call of duty as Commanding Officer, Company F, Second Battalion, Fifth Marines, First Marine Division, in the Republic of Vietnam on 2 June 1967. During Operation UNION II, the First Battalion, Fifth Marines, consisting of Companies A and D, with Captain Graham's company attached, launched an attack against an enemy occupied position, with two companies assaulting and one in reserve. Company F, a leading company was proceeding across a clear paddy area, one thousand meters wide, attacking toward the assigned objective, when it came under heavy fire from mortars and small arms which immediately inflicted a large number of casualties. Hardest hit by the enemy fire was the second platoon of Company F, which was pinned down in the open area by intense fire from two concealed machine guns. Forming an assault unit from members of his small company headquarters, Captain Graham boldly led a fierce assault through the second platoon's position, forcing the enemy to abandon the first machine-gun position, thereby relieving some of the pressure on his second platoon and enabling evacuation of the wounded to a more secure area. Resolute to silence the second machine-gun, which continued its devastating fire, Captain Graham's small force stood steadfast in its hard won enclave. Subsequently, during the afternoon's fierce fighting, he suffered two minor wounds while personally accounting for an estimated fifteen enemy killed. With the enemy position remaining invincible upon each attempt to silence it and with their supply of ammunition exhausted Captain Graham ordered those remaining in the small force to withdraw to friendly lines, and although knowing that he had no chance of survival, he chose to remain with one man who could not be moved due to the seriousness of his wounds. The last radio transmission from Captain Graham reported that he was being assaulted by a force of twenty-five enemy; he died while protecting himself and the wounded man he chose not to abandon. Captain Graham's actions throughout the day were a series of heroic achievements. His outstanding courage, superb leadership and indomitable fighting spirit undoubtedly saved the second platoon from annihilation and reflected great credit upon himself, the Marine Corps, and the United States Naval Service. He gallantly gave his life for his country.

News Release United States Marine Corps
Release No. CS-243-68

Washington, DC, October 29 (USMC)—A Marine Captain who was killed in Vietnam when he refused to leave one of his men during a fierce enemy attack has been awarded the Medal of Honor.

Captain James A. Graham today became the 17th Marine to receive the Nation's highest decoration for gallantry in Vietnam.

His widow, Mrs. Janice Graham of Forestville, Maryland, received the award from Secretary of the Navy Paul R. Ignatius in ceremonies at the Capital's Marine Barracks.

Captain Graham died June 2, 1967, while serving as Commanding Officer of Company F, 2d Battalion, Fifth Marine Regiment, First Marine Division, during Operation Union II in the vicinity of Quang Tin, Republic of Vietnam.

His unit was leading a battalion assault across a clear paddy area when it came under heavy machine gun, mortar, and small arms fire, which immediately inflicted a large number of casualties. Company F's second platoon was hardest hit by the enemy fire, and was pinned down in the open fire from two machine guns.

Captain Graham formed an assault unit from his small company head-quarters and according to the citation, "boldly led a fierce assault through the second platoon's position, thereby relieving some of the pressure on his second platoon, and enabling evacuation of the wounded to a more secure area."

Although the second machine gun continued its devastating fire, the small group held is position throughout a long afternoon of fierce fighting. Capt. Graham suffered two minor wounds while personally accounting for 15 enemy killed.

The citation continues, "with the enemy positions remaining invincible upon each attempt to silence it, and with their supply of ammunition exhausted, Captain Graham ordered those remaining in the small force to withdraw to friendly lines, and although knowing that he had no chance of survival, he chose to remain with the one man who could not be moved due to the seriousness of his wounds."

The last radio transmission received by Capt. Graham reported that he was being assaulted by a force of about 25 enemy.

"Captain Graham's actions throughout the day," the citation concludes, "were a series of heroic achievements. His outstanding courage, superb leadership and indomitable fighting spirit undoubtedly saved the second platoon from annihilation and reflected great credit upon himself, the Marine Corps and the United States Naval Service. He gallantly gave his life for his country."

James A. Graham was born in August 25, 1940 in Wilkinsburg, PA., and graduated from Gwynn Park High School, Brandywine, MD., in June 1959. He earned a B.S. Degree at State Teachers College, Frostburg, MD., in June 1963.

He joined the Marine Corps Reserve in July 1961, following two year's service in the United States Army and subsequent service with the District of Columbia National Guard and U. S. Army Reserve.

He was commissioned as a Second Lieutenant on November 1, 1963 and, following assignments at Camp Lejeune, North Carolina, was transferred to the Republic of Vietnam in December 1966.

Captain Graham is survived by his wife, Janice, a son, John, and a daughter, Jennifer, all of 7031 Beech St., Forestville, MD. His parents are deceased.

Green, John S.
Gunnery Sergeant, U.S. Marine Corps
Co. F, 2nd Bn., 5th Marines, 1st Marine Division
Date of Action: June 2, 1967
Citation:

The Navy Cross is awarded to Gunnery Sergeant John S. Green, United States Marine Corps, for extraordinary heroism in action against enemy forces while serving as Company Gunnery Sergeant, Company F, Second Battalion, Fifth Marines, First Marine Division (Reinforced) in the Republic of Vietnam on June 2, 1967. During Operation Union II, Company F came under intense enemy small arms, automatic weapons and mortar fire from a well entrenched enemy force and was temporarily halted. Gunnery Sergeant Green, with complete disregard for his own safety, led a frontal assault against the enemy positions. Leading his men across 800 meters of open, fire-swept rice paddy, he quickly overran the Viet Cong machine gun position and personally accounted for ten enemy killed. After seizing the objective, he immediately established a hasty defense and began redistributing ammunition to his men. He fearlessly braved the intense enemy fire by exposing himself in carrying wounded to positions of relative safety. By his daring initiative, valiant fighting spirit and selfless devotion to duty in the face of insurmountable odds, Gunnery Sergeant Green was responsible in great measure for saving many of his comrades and thereby upholding the highest traditions of the Marine Corps and the United States Naval Service.

Remarks by the Honorable Paul B. Ignatius
Secretary of the Navy
At Posthumously Medal of Honor Presentation
To Captain James A. Graham, USMC
Marine Barracks, Washington, DC
Tuesday, 20 October 1968.

On behalf of the President and in the name of Congress, it is with pride that I present the Medal of Honor to Captain James A. Graham, United States Marine Corps.

Although Captain Graham gave his life in battle, he shall continue to live in the minds and memories of his comrades as an inspirational example of courage, duty and sacrifice. For all who knew and loved him, the memory of James Graham will remain a source of pride and strength.

James Albert Graham was born in Wilkinsburg, Pennsylvania. Following his graduation from High School in Brandywine, Maryland he attended Teacher's College, Frostburg, Maryland. He was graduated in June of 1963 with a degree of Bachelor of Science in Mathematics. He attended the Officers of Candidate Class, Marine Corps Schools, Quantico, Virginia, and was commissioned a Second Lieutenant on November 1, 1963.

While serving with the 3rd Battalion, 6th Marines, 2nd Marine Division; Fleet Marine Force at Camp Lejeune, North Carolina, Lieutenant Graham participated in the Dominican Republic Expedition during the Spring of 1965.

Promoted on September 1, 1966, Captain Graham reported to Camp Pendleton, California to await transfer. In December of 1966 he joined the 2nd Battalion, 5th Marines 1st Marine Division in combat in the Republic of Vietnam.

On June 2 of last year, while in command of Company F during Operation Union II at Quang Tin, Captain Graham chose to remain with one of his men who was too seriously wounded to be moved. He was mortally wounded when this position was overrun. His indomitable courage and supreme sacrifice enabled the company under his command to save its beleaguered platoon and to safely evacuate its wounded in the face of devastating enemy fire. He died to protect the men under his command.

The memory of his gallant sacrifice is an inspiration to his family, to the United States Marine Corps, and to all Americans. He will live forever as a part of this Nation's History of the valiant and brave.

The Medal of Honor earned by Captain James Graham will now be presented to his widow, Mrs. Janice I. Graham.

General Chapman, the Commandant of the Marine Corps, will read that citation.

Houghton, Kenneth J.
Colonel, U.S. Marine Corps
5th Marines, 1st Marine Division
Date of action: May 26-June 5, 1967
Citation:

   The Navy Cross is awarded to Colonel Kenneth J. Houghton, United States Marine Corps, for extraordinary heroism as Commanding Officer, Fifth Marines, First Marine Division (Reinforced) in the Republic of Vietnam from 26 May to 5 June 1967. The Fifth Marine Regiment was launched on Operation Union II to track down the remnants of the 21st North Vietnamese Regiment, which had been thoroughly decimated by them nine days previous. Responding to the intelligence reports that the enemy was attempting to withdraw to the western mountains, Colonel Houghton committed two battalions in pursuit. The First Battalion swept overland while the Third Battalion was enveloped by helicopter near Cam La. The Third Battalion met with heavy resistance, but completely overran the enemy positions, causing many casualties. He was constantly in the operational area, bravely exposing himself to all the hazards of the battlefield. Colonel Houghton revised his tactics when intelligence reports indicated a much larger enemy force in the area, which was identified as the 3d North Vietnamese Regiment and pointed to a buildup along the Suio Cau Doi River, in the vicinity of Vinh Huy (2). Instantly reacting, he launched his attack from the east, with the First and Third Battalions abreast and the Second in reserve. On 2 June, the First Battalion came under intense enemy mortar, recoilless rifle and automatic weapons fire, indicating contact with the main force of the 3d North Vietnamese Army Force. While the First and Third Battalions maintained heavy pressure on the enemy, he committed the Second Battalion to assault the enemy's flank. Although wounded at this time, he continued to aggressively advance on the enemy with renewed determination. Colonel Houghton launched a bold night attack which smashed through the enemy defenses, and annihilated the large enemy force. By his outstanding leadership, gallant fighting spirit and bold initiative, he contributed materially to the success of the First Marine Division, thereby upholding the highest traditions of the Marine Corps and the United States Naval Service.

Long, Melvin M.
Sergeant, U.S. Marine Corps
Co. F, 2nd Bn., 5th Marines, 1st Marine Division
Date of Action: June 2, 1967
Citation:

The Navy Cross is awarded to Sergeant Melvin M. Long, United States
Marine Corps, for extraordinary heroism while serving as Second Squad Leader,
Third Platoon, Company F, Second Battalion, Fifth Marines, First Marine
Division (Reinforced) Quang Tin Province, Republic of Vietnam, during
Operation Union II, on 2 June 1967. While advancing toward a designated
objective, Company F came under an intense volume of enemy mortar, recoilless
rifle, automatic weapons and small arms fire. Due to its exposed position, the
Third Platoon was temporarily pinned down. Sergeant (then Corporal) Long
was ordered to seize a critical piece of high ground in the tree line on the left
flank. He moved his squad under intense enemy fire across 200 meters of open,
fire swept terrain into the tree line. With complete disregard for his own safety,
he maneuvered his squad in an enveloping movement and assaulted the well-
entrenched enemy position from the rear resulting in six enemy killed. Though
painfully wounded, he led his men in overrunning the position and organized
a hasty defense. From his newly won position, he observed another enemy
machine gun position which was delivering accurate fire on the platoon. With
complete disregard for his wounds and the intense enemy fire, he led another
assault which resulted in two more enemy killed. He then organized a defensive
position and defended their key terrain feature for three hours until the enemy
finally withdrew.

Upon learning of the enemy's withdrawal, Sergeant Long led his men into a
landing zone some 600 meters to the rear and supervised the evacuation of his
wounded. By his outstanding courage, exceptional fortitude and valiant fighting
spirit, Sergeant Long served to inspire all who observed him and upheld the
highest traditions of the Marine Corps and the United States Naval Service.

Private First Class Brenton Edward Mackinnon
Navy Commendation Medal
Citation:

For heroic achievement while serving as a Radio Operator with Company F, Second Battalion Fifth Marines, First Marine Division in connection with operations against insurgent communist (Viet Cong) forces in the Republic of Vietnam on June 2, 1967, during Operation Union II, Company F came under intense enemy small arms, automatic weapons, and mortar fire and sustained numerous casualties while conducting a search and destroy mission in Quang Tin Province. Disregarding his own safety, Private First Class Mackinnon repeatedly exposed himself to the heavy volume of fire to assist in the evacuation of the wounded. On one occasion he was temporarily pinned down by enemy fire as he attempted to move to the side of an injured Marine who was lying in an unprotected position within fifty meters of an enemy fortification. With resolute determination he continued to maneuver across the fire-swept terrain until he reached his wounded comrade and moved him to a place of relative safety. His heroic and timely actions in the face of extreme personal danger were an inspiration to all who observed him and saved the lives of nine Marines. By his courage, bold initiative and selfless devotion to duty, Private First Class Mackinnon upheld the finest traditions of the Marine Corps and of the United States Naval Service.

Private First Class Mackinnon is authorized to wear the Combat V.

JULY

JULY 4TH 1967

Nong Son's Apex transcended the Tinh Yen River and bordered Tu Xuan and Ninh Hoa, villages known to sport an atmosphere as agreeable as their freshly-baked French bread. The six-story high lofty peak towered as South Vietnam's sole coal mine. Harvesting the rich black-diamond resource intended to employ one thousand Vietnamese workers, support six thousand Vietnamese families per year, and supply electricity to An Hoa's Industrial Complex. The An Hoa complex would in turn manufacture fertilizer as a by-product; a key ingredient for the agricultural economy. In 1967, however, the anthracite lay untapped due to communist activity interrupting transportation and delivery.

The 2/5 rotated line companies on the three-tier defensive position. Infantry platoons safeguarded the lower ridge and middle plateau complete with bunkers, heliport, and a command post rimmed with concertina wire. A 106mm recoilless rifle and a 4.2 mortar platoon shared the summit with an Army Search Light Team responsible for aerial spotlighting through pea-soup fog. Nong Son's right-angle cliff afforded the Marines spectacular views and the illusion of tranquility. Thick jungle canopy and rock-throwing monkeys known to steal food, saturated the sheer descent as its only threat.

Daylight NVA movement was stunted for miles between Nong Son's outpost and the First Marine Division Recon unit stationed on a neighboring, even higher mountain. Nong Son also towered within An Hoa's protective artillery range. Generals and dignitaries staked their reputations on Nong Son as South Vietnam's crown jewel.

Until July 4, 1967.

According to 2/5s After Action Report, Lieutenant James Scuras, Foxtrot's company commander reported that terrified Vietnamese were evacuating Nong Son's bordering villages in the wee early morning hours of July 3rd. Villagers rumored of an impending attack. Lieutenant Scuras requested and received artillery fire and fixed wing support on an NVA regiment spotted approaching the area. The rest of the day remained ominously quiet. Around midnight, the uppermost listening post reported, "I have movement to my right." Silence. "They're all around me." Chaos. "We're being overrun."

A VC suicide unit had scaled Nong Son's vertical cliff, exploding satchel charges, AK-47s, and Chicom grenades onto the mountain's crest. Within minutes the guerilla sappers had decimated the mortar ammo dump, the army post, and Foxtrot's First Platoon. Private First Class Melvin E. Newlin, F Company's machine gunner now wounded, lay among the dying and dead. Newlin's subsequent actions altered Nong Son's history, earned him a Medal of Honor, and cost him his life.

The injured Marine propped himself on his machine gun and riddled a deadly stream of fire into the charging VC sappers. Despite the continued onslaught of enemy small arms fire, PFC Newlin twice repelled the VC from overrunning his position. Losing momentum, the VC sappers chucked a Chicom grenade which rendered Newlin unconscious. Assuming him dead, the guerillas bypassed the young Marine and resumed their deadly assault. PFC Newlin regained consciousness, crawled back to his machine gun, and fired. The VC sappers continued their offensive in an effort to utilize the 106mm recoilless rifle on the remaining defensive positions. PFC Newlin then alternated fire between the guerillas attempting to engage the captured weapon and the VC force assaulting the bunkers. PFC Newlin persisted until killed. The young Leatherneck had single-handedly disengaged the enemy long enough for his comrades to organize their defensive positions and repel a second attack.

Without a doubt, Newlin's heroic actions stalled the enemy from pulverizing Nong Son. But he wasn't the only Marine answering the call to duty. Lieutenant Scuras immediately radioed An Hoa for Bald Eagle support. Lieutenant Colonel Jackson ordered Echo Company—operating in the western end of Antenna Valley—to Nong Son as Major Esau directed An Hoa artillery to the mountain's apex and suspected escape routes. A Spooky aircraft was added to the mix as Lieutenant Scuras commandeered squads from the middle defensive positions to the mountain's crest.

Foxtrot Company Lance Corporal Brenton MacKinnon:
I heard the radioman broadcasting screams for help as dynamite exploded in his bunker. We bolted up the back side footpath to witness the execution of Marines. The ensuing battle became a nightmare of hand-to-hand carnage. We killed every breathing VC guerilla. Our brothers were slaughtered. This was our revenge. I tackled one unarmed sapper running from the bunker doorway and battered his head with my empty pistol until someone screamed, "He's dead, Mac." Morning light revealed my victim to be a kid no older than thirteen.

Foxtrot Company Lieutenant James Scuras established advantageous gun positions and rolled the enemy down the slope by dawn's first light.

Foxtrot Company Lance Corporal Brenton Mackinnon:
The next morning, I hauled and tossed what had once been intact human beings onto a pile. I kept an official score of the dead VC. On top of the hill my dead comrades were laid in a tidy row. I said good-bye to each companion. An eighteen-year-old survivor from First Platoon lay in a fetal position mumbling gibberish while sucking his thumb. The loss of each Marine, living and dead, severed my soul.

Confiscated items included enemy weapons, ammunition, miscellaneous documents, and vials of drugs. The guerilla sappers had performed their suicide mission doped.

Lieutenant Colonel Jackson and Major Esau later arrived from An Hoa. Major Esau's recollection sustained a heavy heart.

Major Richard H. Esau Jr.:
Nong Son was a beautiful mountain outpost that provided security for the Marines and the civilian populace. Foxtrot Company was assigned to Nong Son in an effort to recoup from the devastation of Operation Union II which included the heart-wrenching loss of their company commander, Captain Jim Graham. Although surveying the massacre was gut-wrenching, I witnessed friendship, love, and bravery in the purest sense at the sight of Salt and Pepper.

Two of Foxtrot's Marines were the best of friends. One was very black, the other very white. They grew up in Army camps, the sons of career Army men. Together at age eighteen, they joined the Marine Corps to avoid a military life in their fathers' shadows. Nicknamed Salt and Pepper, the friends served as one of 2/5's finest machine gun teams.

The ill-suited comments spawned at their friendship rolled off their backs like water off a duck. During Operation Union II, the brothers-in-arms acquitted themselves admirably, saving the lives of many of their fellow Marines.

But fate was not theirs, on July 4th. Salt and Pepper occupied one of the first bunkers assaulted. The force of the satchel-charge explosion in their bonsai-shared space magnified the number and severity of their wounds. By the time we reached them, both were bloodless. Their lifeless bodies bore an identical almost-colorless blue-gray resemblance. Although difficult to differentiate between black and white, it was obvious that the boys tried to protect each other at the slaughter's onset. I remember thinking, Dear Lord, if only we could all live and love the way these two young men did. If we could only see ourselves in life as one as these two appear in death, what a wonderful world it would be.

General Donn Robertson flew in with a visiting division bird colonel to assess the unthinkable.

Major Richard H. Esau, Jr. locked jaws with the colonel in a tension convention of words:
This visiting colonel found it necessary to shit-chip in front of my Marines. Not only was he out of line and unprofessional, this insidious talk was bad for morale. I quietly suggested that his comments were inappropriate. These boys had already suffered one too many combat casualties in less than two months. The colonel responded with a who's who in rank. In his face, I assured him in no uncertain terms, "If you don't shut your fuckin' mouth I will throw you off the top of this mountain, do you understand that, Colonel?"

Lieutenant James Meyers and his men sided Major Richard H. Esau Jr.:
The visiting colonel's wise-ass speculations were ill-suited in the face of these heroic, surviving Marines. Major Esau squared this bird directly in the eye. I watched the Major's quarter-inch neck veins burst to at least half-an-inch of anger that extended to his ears. My men and I were only too eager to help Major Esau chuck the colonel off that cliff.

Nong Son sustained a hotbed of enemy probing for days.

Nong Son
Marine outpost,
RSVN, 1967.

Marine Outpost
of Recon Hill
viewed from Nong
Son Outpost,
RSVN, 1967.

Nong Son coal mine
west of An Hoa over
the Song Thu Bon,
RSVN, 1967.

AN HOA

In an effort to distract and thwart additional artillery support to the mountain under siege, the enemy simultaneously mortared An Hoa's combat base. Counter mortars fired from An Hoa and several Marine support systems halted the diversionary tactic, but not before creating havoc.

Lieutenant John Newton:

Oddly enough I woke up before anything happened. Within seconds I heard, *vhit, vhit, vhit, vhit, vhit, vhit, vhit.* Twenty mortars were air born before the first one even landed. I bolted to the COC. Because of the simultaneous attack on Nong Son, the COC was a hotbed of efficiency. Major Esau commandeered, and counter mortar attacks ran smoothly.

In the meantime Dr. Viti could be seen policing casualties under mortar fire. The good doctor ran into the COC—a twelve-foot deep, twenty-foot long pit with a twisting, rising stairway entrance—as a mortar round exploded. The concussion somersaulted him head first down the stairwell. We could hear his inevitable "those sons of bitches" as he landed on his back with his feet at the foot of the stairs.

Lieutenant Colonel Jackson, already wired and pacing from the night's events, rushed from the COC and knelt down by Dr. Viti with a warning. "Doc, you've got to be careful. That's incoming." I could see Dr. Viti's priceless, no-shit Sherlock expression as he hurried the colonel into the COC. Tom spoke briefly to Major Esau before dashing back into this war zone, no doubt to aid those wounded.

Major Richard H. Esau Jr.:

Needless to say, my hands were full when I received word that my OPS chief and master sergeant lay wounded. Before I could react, Dr. Viti was on my tail with his, "What's up?"

I couldn't believe it. "What the hell are you doing here? For Christ's sake, you're not supposed to leave the safety of the BAS in the middle of a god damn mortar attack."

"Anybody hurt?"

"Yeah, my OPS chief and master sergeant. I'm on my way."

"Hell, no, you stay here. I'm the doctor."

"This is not the night for you to be running around . . ."

Before I could argue, Tom was out of the damn bunker. Although I cringed at the thought of my battalion surgeon running through intense mortar fire— and this was intense—Dr. Viti allowed me to focus on counter battery across the river while supporting Nong Son now pressured from the West.

Major Richard H. Esau Jr. documented the evening's events for a Bronze Star with a Combat "V" award citation:

On the night of 3 July 1967, Lieutenant Viti was attending wounded Marines in the Battalion Aid Station at the An Hoa Combat Base when it suddenly came under a vicious enemy mortar attack which inflicted numerous casualties. With complete disregard for his own safety, he immediately moved from the aid station to an area adjacent to the Combat Operations Center bunker, a distance of approximately seven hundred meters all the while exposed to the intense enemy mortar fire. Steadfastly refusing cover for himself, he quickly moved from one casualty to another expertly rendering first aid to the wounded Marines and supervising their evacuation to the aid station. After determining that all of the casualties had been safely moved from the area, he returned to the aid station and assisted in the treatment of thirty-five Marines until they were medically evacuated. By his prompt and heroic action, numerous wounded Marines received immediate medical attention, undoubtedly limiting the effects and seriousness of their wounds.

Major Richard H. Esau Jr.:
"And of course, Tom's corpsmen as always rallied around him."

Fleet Marine Force Corpsman Richard Roger "Country" Ware:
Dr. Viti and I hustled our gear and a driver to the area being mortared. Dr. Viti was hyper. We brainstormed with no information other than the obvious: An Hoa was under an intense mortar attack. We split up and ran through open spaces under the illumination of candle flares that filtered down like floating angels. It was sheer bedlam. I administered to the walking wounded and dragged those unable to walk back to the jeep and drove to the BAS. Medevac choppers arrived with even more wounded. Chief LeGarie had the BAS staged and ready.

Chief Hospital Corpsman Lou LeGarie:
The airstrip became a hot fire zone with the arrival and departure of medevac choppers. Dr. Viti, the BAS corpsmen including Roger Ware, Lieutenant Meyers, and his Motor Transport Team and I hustled the wounded into the BAS. Through this chaos, Dr. Viti and I watched corpsman Ware shield a wounded Marine with his body and carry him to safety.

"Country" Fleet Marine Force Corpsman Roger Ware then volunteered to board a chopper to Nong Son. The bird was pummeled by small arms fire and the impact of an RPG upon landing.

Fleet Marine Force Corpsman Roger Ware:

The impact of the RPG blew me thirty feet back like a rag doll. I lay unconscious until machine gun fire woke me up shell-shocked, dizzy, and light-headed. My ears rang. I didn't know what just happened. It was pitch black, I didn't know what level of Nong Son the bird landed on, and to my surprise it was still in one piece. I staggered back, worried that mortar fire would hurt those already injured. We stabilized the wounded, loaded the chopper, and returned to An Hoa. I was bruised and disoriented for several days until I asked Dr. Viti to examine me.

Dr. Viti laughed. "Country, you've got yourself a concussion."

Chief LeGarie kept me on light duty at the BAS, teasing that I wouldn't be able to move my head fast enough to dodge a sniper's bullet.

Fleet Marine Force Corpsman Roger Ware was awarded a Bronze Star for his heroic actions.

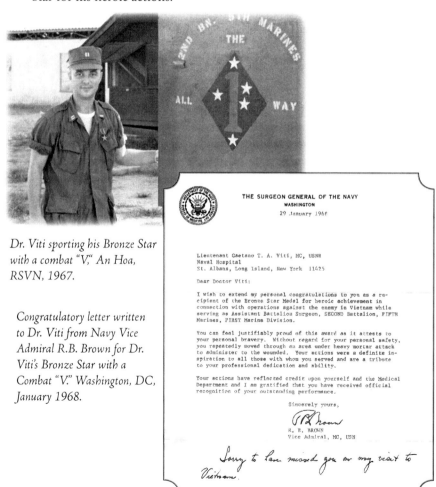

Dr. Viti sporting his Bronze Star with a combat "V," An Hoa, RSVN, 1967.

Congratulatory letter written to Dr. Viti from Navy Vice Admiral R.B. Brown for Dr. Viti's Bronze Star with a Combat "V." Washington, DC, January 1968.

THE SURGEON GENERAL OF THE NAVY
WASHINGTON
29 January 1968

Lieutenant Gaetano T. A. Viti, MC, USNR
Naval Hospital
St. Albans, Long Island, New York 11425

Dear Doctor Viti:

I wish to extend my personal congratulations to you as a recipient of the Bronze Star Medal for heroic achievement in connection with operations against the enemy in Vietnam while serving as Assistant Battalion Surgeon, SECOND Battalion, FIFTH Marines, FIRST Marine Division.

You can feel justifiably proud of this award as it attests to your personal bravery. Without regard for your personal safety, you repeatedly moved through an area under heavy mortar attack to administer to the wounded. Your actions were a definite inspiration to all those with whom you served and are a tribute to your professional dedication and ability.

Your actions have reflected credit upon yourself and the Medical Department and I am gratified that you have received official recognition of your outstanding performance.

Sincerely yours,

R. B. BROWN
Vice Admiral, MC, USN

Sorry to have missed you on my visit to Vietnam.

DAILY NEWS, WEDNESDAY

The late Marine Pfc. Melvin E. Newlin

Daily News *photo; Medal of Honor ceremony PFC Melvin E. Newlin.*

"July—A Nation Remembers—And So Does She"

Mrs. Joseph Newlin of Wellsville, Ohio battled tears in the White House yesterday as she heard her son, Melvin, praised. He was killed at his machine gun in Vietnam on July 4, 1967, as he fought off waves of Viet Cong. When President Nixon presented Medal of Honor, Mrs. Newlin gave way to tears.

A Nation Remembers —And So Does She

Mrs. Joseph Newlin, of Wellsville, Ohio, battled tears in the White House yesterday as she heard her son, Melvin, praised. He was killed at his machine gun in Vietnam on July 4, 1967, as he fought off waves of Viet Cong. When President Nixon presented Medal of Honor, Mrs. Newlin gave way to tears.

Newlin's wife collapses in tears as her husband shows her the nation's highest medal. The President tries to comfort her.

Memorial Service, An Hoa, RSVN, 1967. Helmets of those deceased line the stage.

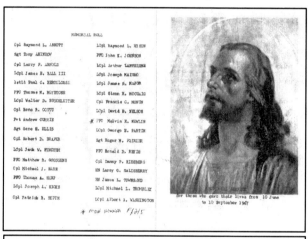

Memorial Service pamphlet remembering those who died
from June 10 to September 10, 1967, An Hoa, RSVN, 1967.

In the name of the President of the United States, the Commanding General, Fleet Marine Force, Pacific takes pleasure in presenting the Bronze Star Medal to

Lieutenant Gaetano Thomas Anthony Viti
Medical Corps, United States Naval Reserve
For service as set forth in the following
Citation:

For heroic achievement in connection with operations against the enemy in the Republic of Vietnam while serving as Assistant Battalion Surgeon with the Second Battalion Fifth Marines, First Marine Division. On the night of 3 July 1967, Lieutenant VITI was attending wounded Marines in the Battalion Aid Station at the An Hoa Combat Base when it suddenly came under a vicious enemy mortar attack which inflicted numerous casualties. With complete disregard for his own safety, he immediately moved from the aid station to an area adjacent to the Combat Operations Center bunker, a distance of approximately 700 meters all the while exposed to the intense enemy mortar fire. Steadfastly refusing cover for himself, he quickly moved from one casualty to another expertly rendering first aid to the wounded Marines and supervising their evacuation to the aid station. After determining that all of the casualties had been safely moved from the area, he returned to the aid station and assisted in the treatment of thirty-five Marines until they were medically evacuated. By his prompt and heroic action, numerous wounded Marines received immediate medical attention, undoubtedly limiting the effects and seriousness of their wounds. Lieutenant VITI's selfless concern for the welfare of others, courage and unwavering devotion to duty at great personal risk were an inspiration to all who observed him and were in keeping with the highest traditions of the Marine Corps and of the United States Naval Service."

Lieutenant Viti is authorized to wear the Combat "V."
For the President
V. H. Krulak
Lieutenant General, U. S. Marine Corps
Commanding

Melvin Earl Newlin
Rank and Organization: Private First Class, U.S. Marine Corps, 2nd Battalion
Fifth Marines, First Marine Division.
Quang Nam Province, Republic of Vietnam, July 4, 1967
Citation:

For conspicuous gallantry and intrepidity at the risk of his life above and beyond the call of duty while serving as a machine gunner attached to the 1st Platoon, Company F, 2nd Battalion on 3 and 4 July 1967. Pfc Newlin, with 4 other Marines was manning a key position on the perimeter of the Nong Son outpost when the enemy launched a savage and well coordinated mortar and infantry assault, seriously wounding him and killing his 4 comrades. Propping himself against his machine gun, he poured a deadly accurate stream of fire into the charging ranks of the Viet Cong. Though repeatedly hit by small-arms fire, he twice repelled enemy attempts to overrun his position. During the third attempt a grenade explosion wounded him again and knocked him to the ground unconscious. The Viet Cong guerillas, believing him dead, bypassed him and continued their assault on the main force. Meanwhile, Pfc Newlin regained consciousness, crawled back to his weapon, and brought it to bear on the rear of the enemy causing havoc and confusion among them. Spotting the enemy attempting to bring a captured 106 recoilless weapon to bear on other Marine positions, he shifted his fire, inflicting heavy casualties on the enemy and preventing them from firing the captured weapon. He then shifted his fire back to the primary enemy force, causing the enemy to stop their assault on the Marine bunkers and to once again attack his machine gun position. Valiantly fighting off 2 more enemy assaults, he firmly held his ground until mortally wounded. Pfc Newlin had single-handedly broken up and disorganized the entire enemy assault force, causing them to lose momentum and delaying them long enough for his fellow Marines to organize a defense and beat off their secondary attack. His indomitable courage, fortitude, and unwavering devotion to duty in the face of almost certain death reflect great credit upon himself and the Marine Corps and upheld the highest traditions of the U. S. Naval Service.

{Fleet Marine Force Corpsman Richard Roger Ware was awarded The Bronze Medal in 2010—Lucia}

The President of the United States takes pleasure in presenting the Bronze Star Medal to
Hospital Corpsman Third Class Richard R. Ware
United States Navy
for service as set forth in the following
Citation:

For heroic achievement in connection with combat operations against insurgent Communist forces in the Republic of Vietnam while serving as a Corpsman with Battalion Aid Station, 2d Battalion, 5th Marines, 1st Marine Division, on 4 July 1967. When the An Hoa Combat Base came under intense mortar attack and probes by enemy ground units, Petty Officer Ware left the relative safety of the Battalion Aid Station and began treating wounded Marines at the airstrip as medevac helicopters dropped them off. As enemy fire intensified and additional personnel were wounded, Petty Officer Ware ran to the most seriously wounded Marines under heavy enemy mortar fire. Initially shielding one of the wounded Marines with his body, he carried the Marine to the safety of a bunker and immediately returned to the other wounded Marine lying in the open and while still under heavy fire, he carried the second wounded Marine to safety. He continued to stay near the landing zone and assisted in the evacuation of wounded personnel and administered aid, thereby saving several lives. After returning to the Battalion Aid Station, a Marine casualty arrived by medevac and Petty Officer Ware started open heart massage to save the Marine's life. When the Battalion Aid Station received word that there were numerous serious casualties at the Nong Son Outpost that was under heavy attack by an enemy unit, Petty Officer Ware volunteered to go to the outpost on a medevac helicopter. On arrival at Nong Son, the helicopter was hit multiple times and he was rendered unconscious for several minutes from the close impact of a rocket propelled grenade. After regaining consciousness and ignoring his own wounds, he provided medical care to several wounded Marines, ultimately saving several more lives. He remained at the outpost until all casualties were evacuated and only then returned to the base at An Hoa. Petty Officer Ware's outstanding professional skill, fortitude in the face of enemy fire and total dedication to duty reflected great credit upon him and were in keeping with the highest traditions of the United States Naval Service. The Combat Distinguishing Device is authorized.

❧ Dear Daddy ❧

Harold Wadley is as they say, "history in the making." After serving in the Korean War—a Silver Star ranks among several medals—this American Cherokee Indian descendent received his Forestry Degree and became a U.S. Forestry Agent in Idaho. While watching TV during the Vietnam War, he decided that "the Marines needed me." So he wrote a letter to the Marine Corps Commandant requesting approval to be assigned as a combat machine gunner. Wadley was ordered to hone his skills in Camp Pendleton before being allocated to Hotel 2/5 as a weapons platoon commander.

I asked Harold Wadley to describe Operation Swift, one of 2/5's deadliest details of 1967. I said nothing for the next forty-five minutes as Harold narrated a tale of unwavering tenacity, bravery, and sheer lunacy.

At this point in my journey, I understood all but one thing. How the heck is this man still alive today?

SEPTEMBER

OPERATION SWIFT

Harold Wadley

During Operation Swift, an NVA Regiment passed through a South Vietnamese Army who couldn't or wouldn't stop them. We—Hotel Third Platoon—were called to reinforce Hotel's First Platoon. Lieutenant Herman was in charge. I was the weapon's platoon commander. Carrying six machine guns and 60mm mortars, we were geared for bear. Lance Corporal Leo Auckland, my mortar kid from South Dakota, was on the barrel. His team fanned out. John "Juice" Jessmore, our machine gunner, stayed up ahead.

Generally one Marine led point, but due to the gravity of the situation, we beefed up point to a three-man, V-point wedge that included Sergeant Stutes, Lance Corporal Braswell, and Corporal Wolf. I tried to get Stutes, my buddy and platoon sergeant off point, 'cause Stutes, quiet and prone to be violent, had been having funny premonitions. His behavior was obvious and it worried everyone enough to ask me, "Do something with Stutes."

So I did.

"Stutes, platoon sergeants shouldn't be on point. Get one of the other guys and stay here where you're needed."

He ignored me so I pulled Lieutenant Herman over and told him to get Stutes off point. "Stutes needs to be with his platoon." But Stutes even challenged Lieutenant Herman. I should've told Captain Bowers to tie Stutes down, handcuff him, do something, just keep him out of this until we can get him out of here.

But of course, should haves are always great.

We forged an area filled with freshly dug gun bunkers and tunnels, knowing the enemy was close. The towels they used to wipe the sweat off their brows hung on tree limbs. But we couldn't find them, because they were dug *in* those tunnels. Dear Lord, we did soon enough. One NVA, figuring he was exposed, got edgy and jumped from his tree-line position. Juice opened up his M-60 and flipped the guy in the air. And then the whole world nearly came to an end.

This was a reinforced company of NVA. Jiminy whiz, they had more weapons than Santa Clause could have ever brought them. Our world unraveled. Lead shredded everything, everywhere. Trees and foliage disappeared. Stutes, Braswell, and Wolf were immediately torn up. Wolf was killed instantly, and Braswell was shot through the neck. I grabbed Doc Noah and said, "Keep your skinny ass right behind me, Doc." I thought I could shoot my way out and give Doc Noah a chance to work on the wounded. But we were gravely outnumbered. This was an entire regiment of heavily armed NVA. I bet eighty NVA were dug in across trenches and bunkers; we had barely thirty-six guys with jammed M16s and machine guns.

I spotted an empty hole four feet to my right and reached for Braswell thinking, *Great, I'll throw Braswell in there for Doc Noah.* But as I grabbed him, a gook shot his face and splattered my eyes with his bones and brains. Now I couldn't see. I thought, *Oh no, I lost my eyes!* The thought of losing my eyesight terrified me. I raked this stuff off and when I could see, I thought, *Good.* But of course, I lost Braswell.

Within seconds, a gook machine gun twenty yards ahead fired, knocked my helmet off and just about broke my neck. Another burst hit my left leg and tore the rubber lining from the gas mask that was strapped to it. But here's the thing—that mask and leg pouch once held four grenades!

Earlier Lieutenant Herman had emptied me out. "Wadley, let me have your grenades."

"I'll loan them to you, but don't bring them back used."

"Don't worry, I'll take good care of them."

One burst from that gook's 50-caliber machine gun smoked the rubberized lining. Can you imagine what that machine gun would've done to those four grenades? Well, I wouldn't be sitting here right now, that's what. Lieutenant Herman saved my life. Man, that was a great, great lick.

Another fifty hammered to our left. I heard the clink of a gun jamming, so I opened up big. That was the last we heard of them.

Steve Rader, my rocket man started hammering his LAW, but I tell you, those LAW's were worthless compared to the old 3.5's for dependability; just worthless. But that didn't stop Rader. Surrounded by quads of dirt, as trees, leaves, and real estate big enough to put a for sale sign on rained down, Rader knelt, assembled, and aimed his LAW into the enemy gun bunker. And it didn't fire. So he yanked the trigger on that sucker and just as calm as a Sunday school teacher, wet his fingers in his mouth. He reached back to hold the magazine needle switch that connected the wires and powered the trigger. And the trigger generated a spark. Good thing.

So as I tried again to get Braswell, an NVA crawled up the hole, fired, and blew right through me. I was hit. I wasn't dead, but that gook sure smoked me up. Again, bits and pieces of bone and blood were in my eyes. "Dawg gone it." I raked the mess to find the world tinged red. With the sun shining and blood in my eyes, everything had a rosy, sun-glass look. When I could see enough, I recognized this big, white bone as a shoulder blade. I've skinned enough wild game and cattle to know what a shoulder blade looks like. But it took me a few seconds to realize that it was mine.

My left arm hung by shreds of ligaments and bones dangled beneath my chin. Afraid that that my left hand would fall off, I held it with my right and ran my left arm underneath my cartridge belt. I reloaded my rifle, but it was pretty hard to do with one hand. Oh well. But here's the good thing, Doc Noah and I were still *alive*.

It was okay because the good Lord takes care of things in strange ways, even in dire circumstances. You see, earlier the officers had ordered us to dump our flak jackets on the LZ to alleviate weight so that we could move faster. If I'd been wearing a flak jacket, I'm convinced I'd be dead. The angle of those AK rounds would've bounced off my jacket at the shoulder and taken my head off.

I looked back to see Auckland with his 60mm mortar thirty yards from the enemy position. That young Marine sat there with the world falling down around him hollering, "I'm going to cover for you, Sarge." With that, gee whiz, I looked up to see one of our mortars landing on earth, fins first, so slow, it was like he tossed it up in the air. I thought, *Oh man, this is going to drop on top of us.*

But the last ten feet from the deck, that mortar round slowly but barely turned—it must turn to detonate—and hit the deck on the gook holes within ten yards of Doc Noah and me. And I tell you, Auckland dropped five more tubes—barehanded with no base plate or bipod into the barrel. You can't duplicate that kind of courage or skill.

You see, the tube is hot when the round discharges, so it's hard to hold; mortar crews use mittens to grab the barrel. And it usually sits on a base plate on a bipod. But Auckland sat with his leg wrapped around the tube with no base plate, held that barrel bare-handed and pumped out five rounds before they killed him. If you could believe it.

Doc Noah, bless his boney ass, now crawled up beside me. This was a bad day. My rifle dangled from my right hand. I was worthless on my left. Intense battle fire destroyed every tree and piece of bamboo, leaving nothing more than a shredded desert. Doc Noah stuffed battle dressings into my shoulder cavern as hot smoke poured out from the round hitting so close and so hard. I later learned that the round had pierced the lining of my heart sack and stopped an eighth-of-an-inch from my spine. I should've been dead but the good Lord had other plans.

Every time Doc Noah raised his arm to unwrap a battle dressing, the enemy cut loose.

Lance Corporal Benny Byrnes shot his way through two feet from us and said, "Sarge, I'm going to get you help."

Byrnes—bless him. He was a character and a crazy Marine all right—pumped lead into enemy positions. But the gooks shot a vein in Byrne's left arm as it lay on the forearm of his rifle. Blood flew every where.

Byrnes yelled, "Gosh I'm hit, Sergeant Wadley, I'm hit."

"All right," I said. "Put your arm down. See if you can clamp your left arm with your right to shut off the blood."

And he hollered, wearing a big ol' grin, "By gosh it worked."

But then he ran out of firepower, so he jumped up in a hail of disaster runnin' and yellin', "I'm going back for ammo, Sarge."

Sergeant Roy Gibson then shot his way to my left. It suddenly got quiet. They shot Gibson. I figured he was dead but he stirred. "Gosh, Sarge, they got me in the back."

I rolled him over—as best I could with one arm—using my right hand to check his back. "Gosh, Gibson," I said. "I can't find anything." The lead kept flying.

Gibson was in pain. "They hit me in the head." I rolled him back and saw the bullet trail from the helmet liner above his left ear to the exit wound *beneath* his scalp. His face instantly swelled up like a big, black balloon. Even his eyes swelled shut. But Gibson wouldn't give up.

"I can still see, I'm headed back."

"Go for it."

He jumped up, in the middle of a gook position, without getting hit—if you can imagine that—and made his way back to the Marines a few yards behind him. Meanwhile Stephen—another great Marine on his way to help—died before he got halfway out.

I yelled at Lieutenant Herman to get a left flank assault coming. "Don't come the way we did."

Lieutenant Herman, a strong weight-lifter guy, shot his way out and scooped me up.

I right on told him, "Lieutenant, I'll shoot you myself if you pick me up. Don't do it. You leave me laying right here. Get those troops around on the left flank. I'll hold right where I'm at."

Lieutenant Herman wouldn't listen, and of course it was a death sentence. Charlie wasn't but fifteen feet away. Herman, now shot in the head, landed on my back and pinned me down in the dirt. I could hardly turn over. Doc Noah got around Lieutenant Herman—who was still under fire—and fixed Herman's body so that it shielded me from incoming. I was amazed that Doc Noah was still alive. By this point, his back was a map of blasted shrapnel.

I heard Corporal Carr cussing and knew he'd been hit. His arm was nearly shot off when he raised it with a cleaning rod to knock the jam out of his worthless M16.

I yelled to Juice, "Try to get that gun to my left."

But Juice's machine gun had quit him. Juice and Corporal Johnson, the machine gun section leader, exchanged grenade fire with the enemy. Corporal Johnson was hit in the shoulder. Grenade shrapnel sliced-up Juice's neck. *Daag damn*, I thought, *We lost Johnny*. But Johnny soon yelled for ammo. He fired on as many gooks as he could with one hand. Johnny had the dag-gone gun working, but here's the sad part.

The malfunctioning M16s were a worthless, dag-gone deal. I wrote a letter to the Marine Corps Gazette after reading an article about malfunctioning weapons that described our battle. Man, they were talking about my dead Marines. And not only the M16s, but the bolt plug pins in the M60s crystallized. So here's what I did. Before Operation Swift, I asked the Seabees to cut twenty penny nails five-eigths of an inch; the same diameter of the bolt plug pin that held the machine gun bolt. Of course we test fired the penny nails that replaced the bolt plug pin. The penny-nails lasted two hundred rounds before we had to change them. So that's what we used. Now if that isn't a heck of a way for Marines to fight a war, I don't know what is. My machine gunners carried cut nails to replace when necessary. That's what Juice was doing when they shot him.

But Juice was still alive and managed to grab the radio. By this time my radioman had been shot through both lungs and was, of course, in no shape for talking.

And here's another good deal. Earlier, Lieutenant Herman and I looked over the map and since I've always been good at remembering numbers, well it was thanks to the Lord that I remembered, I could give Johnny airstrike coordinates to give to Captain Bowers. But every time I yelled, the NVA chopped up on Doc Noah and me. So I crawled under the dead bodies of Braswell and Herman, I knew they wouldn't mind if I took cover under them, while Doc Noah stayed on my right.

Here's the funny part. Juice gave coordinates without coding the messages. And believe it or not, An Hoa scolded this young Marine for not shackling his message under enemy gunfire.

Juice yelled, "Do you think these expletives, expletives, English, expletives or not?" An Hoa got our gist.

In fact, a pilot radioed in. "Sarge, where do you want this napalm?"

"Dump it on us."

"But you have alligators all around you."

"So what."

"Okay."

Doc Noah and I watched the silver eggs fly down. Dag-gone that heat just sucked our breath away.

Doc Noah shook his head. "We're going to burn alive."

"Scrape a hole and get your nose into fresh earth. Don't raise your head or breathe that super heated air."

We survived the napalm strike but artillery rounds, landing hardly ten feet away, nearly buried us. But at that stage you aren't worried about such a thing. Pretty soon we heard enemy movement on our right front.

Doc yelled, "Sarge, there's a gook in the hole."

"Dag-gone it, shoot him."

The gook crawling into the protection of a crater was ready to finish Doc and me. But Doc hesitated.

Earlier, Stutes scolded Doc Noah about his dirty .45. "If you don't clean that pistol, I'm going to break it over your head."

"This thing is nothing more than a bag of rocks that gets in the way of my medical supplies," Doc says.

Stutes wasn't gonna let up. "That has nothing to do with it. Corpsman, you get that .45 clean enough for inspection."

Doc Noah knew Stutes was serious and mumbled about "cleaning that blankety-blank .45 that he couldn't hit a house with so he'll just throw it at somebody because he couldn't shoot with it."

"Shoot him, Doc."

Doc froze.

"Doc, shoot him! You got your .45, shoot him."

It got really quiet. I could hear this NVA breathing, coming up from the side. And then I heard the roar of a .45. Doc Noah had to force the action back into his rusty .45 before he emptied it out. He nearly deafened me. He then threw his gun at the next crawling gook. That ended their attempts on killing us. Ol' Doc Noah hung in there. We were pinned for hours. A band of wounded men.

At sundown I heard Rader.

"Sarge?"

"Yeah, Rader, keep your head down and stay behind Lieutenant Herman's body."

He crawled over. "I'm going to get you out of here."

"Yeah, well, don't raise your head. There's one machine gun left, and I know he's just waiting. Stay right where you're at."

"Sarge, we can crawl out, can you move?"

"Lieutenant Herman's on my bad arm. I can't feel it. I'm afraid he's going to pull it off if I try to pull it out from under him."

I didn't know how much of my arm was left. But dag-gone, Rader yanked Lieutenant Herman off me.

"By gosh, Rader, I think I've got enough strength to crawl if you crawl in front of me. Keep where I can touch your heel with my right hand."

"Doc, crawl on the other side, so we can all go at the same time. We'll move an inch at a time."

We did, and of course they shot at us.

But here's the interesting part of that story. Before Rader arrived, the skies rained buckets of the coldest water ever to fall on the face of the earth without being sleet. I thought I'd freeze to death. Our hole filled with water so frigid, we couldn't keep our faces down. So when we crawled out, the mud was hell. But I knew what the good Lord was doing after all. You see, I would've had a hard time pulling myself on hard ground with my swollen right hand. But since we were dragging like alligators through the rain and mud, I made it. God, it was so very cold.

Artillery flares popped all around us. Rader—wearing glasses—looked up. Oh no.

"Rader, don't look up. Your glasses will reflect the light, and they'll open up on us." Boy, did he ever get his head down in the mud real quick.

Doc Noah crawled between me and the enemy until we reached Captain Bowers and Mike Company. Doc Noah moved the wounded to relative safety—while under direct enemy and mortar fire—to organize the LZ and prioritize evacuations. The hot LZ could only fit one bird. Doc Noah was the salt of the earth, I tell you. I'm surprised with how courageous he was that he made it home alive. The guy was wounded, you know.

While being loaded on the helicopter, Doc Noah told the door gunner not to take off the way we were headed—over enemy positions. Well, dag-gone, the pilot didn't listen. And if you could believe, an NVA machine gunner shot the bottom of the chopper and tore off my boot and sole down to the last three inches. "Dag-gone it!" I didn't feel it, but I knew my foot was ripped up. Guys threw flak jackets on the wounded. I yelled for Johnny.

Johnny yelled back, "Sarge, I'm still with you. This is one heck of a ride out."

We made it to Da Nang.

Our company's casualty rate for Operation Swift was pretty high. Sergeant Gibson got hit on the side of the head. They sewed his face. Juice was hit in the back of the head so his face was swollen too. They led each other, two blind, shot-up Marines to visit me in the intensive care unit. I was the only one in that short meeting that was able to see. Juice made it home but Sergeant Gibson was KIA the following month.

The doctors couldn't operate in Da Nang because my fever spiked to one hundred and four. I was diagnosed with three kinds of malaria. I had been suffering some bad headaches. I had been asking Doc Noah for aspirin, and it had gotten so bad, I dug holes inside my foxhole to place my forehead against the wet, cool earth to ease the pain. I didn't realize I had malaria.

I was in triage for awhile. Finally a Navy surgeon—a bird—came by and asked me if you could believe it, "Sergeant Wadley, are you still with us?"

I could barely talk but I motioned for him to pull his ear down. "Colonel, I've done my job now it's about time that you did yours!"

Now, Navy birds don't like Marines calling them colonel. I made his day. I was placed in a rubber body bag filled with ice and alcohol with a spigot that could be opened and drained when my body heat melted it. It was torture, but it reduced my fever. I hate the sound of ice and alcohol to this day.

The concussion of those rounds blew my shoulder blades to pieces. I had a big patch of nothing but bone fragments holding what was left of my upper chest. The doctors braided the torn ligaments and muscles rather than removing them from the shoulder. Although the doctors did a wonderful job, my arm has never been the same. But at least I have an arm. Loose bone and metal fragments float through my chest and shoulder. I feel the nerve ends growing and twisting with no connections. Do you know what TV snow looks like? That's what my chest x-ray looks like. I lost ninety percent of the shoulder bone and half of the collar bone. Two pieces of my collarbone calcified and periodically break, depending on what I do. It hurts constantly.

The top half of the left arm, the ball and socket, is still lying in that rice paddy. My wife made me a heavy-duty sling so I can saw and chop wood. I made a forked stick to lay my hunting rifle on, so I'm good to go.

Fleet Marine Force Corpsman Dennis Noah was awarded a Silver Star for his heroic actions.

{Lt. Colonel Gene Bowers USMC Retired, who served as Hotel Company's Captain during Operation Swift, provided the following post fact account from the COC—Lucia}

OPERATION SWIFT
Captain Gene Bowers
Hotel Company (2/5)

Company H 2/5, under command of Captain Gene W. Bowers, was assigned OPCON to M Company 3/5, commanded by Lieutenant Colonel W. K. Rockey, on 8 September, 1967 for Operation Swift. On the afternoon of 10 September, Company H swept through a small village northeast of Hill 43. The village was empty with the exception of several women and children and heavily fortified with interlocking trenches and bunkers covered by barbed wire. Company H swept 1500 meters beyond the village before pausing in a defensive perimeter on a small hill to receive helicopter-borne re-supplies.

Captain Bowers dispatched Lieutenant Alan Herman's Third Platoon to conduct a circular, one-mile security patrol around the company position. As the 3rd platoon entered the village, the lead squad was pummeled by concentrated surprise fire from a reinforced NVA company, now occupying the village's reinforced fortifications. The remainder of the platoon was pinned down by heavy automatic weapons, including 50 caliber and 60mm mortar fire. Captain Bowers left a small contingent on the hill to guard the supplies and moved his company to relieve the Third Platoon. En-route, Captain Bowers established radio contact with a wounded, Third Platoon corporal and was advised that Lieutenant Herman had been killed trying to rescue wounded Marines from the rice paddy in front of the fortified village. The Second Platoon had maneuvered left of the village to prevent enemy escape. Company HQ, with the remaining 1st platoon advanced and made contact to achieve fire superiority. Military mortar and artillery fire bore down on the enemy and landing within fifty meters of friendly positions. Helicopter gun ships rocketed and strafed the NVA while artillery sealed the rear of the village. Company M 3/5 approached from the rear for a combined assault on the village. After several air strikes with two-hundred-and-fifty-pound bombs, napalm and tear gas, Captain Bowers led a coordinated assault into the village. Forty enemy bodies were identified above ground. No search was conducted for buried bodies as the trenches and bunkers were collapsed by artillery and air strikes; nine friendly KIA's. Six dead Marines were found with their M16 rifles broken apart in an attempt to remove ruptured cartridges jammed in the chamber. The Marines had powder-burned bullet holes in their heads.

Captain Gene W. Bowers, USMC, RSVN, 1967.

Sgt. Harold E. Wadley, USMC, Retired, 1951 - 1954, 1967 - 1972; and FMF Corpsman Dennis Noah, April 2007.

Dennis "Doc" Noah was awarded the Silver Star for his heroism during Operation Swift on April 7, 2010. As a result of *Dr. Tom's War*, Gene Bowers reconnected with Harold Wadley and Dennis Noah and submitted "Doc" Noah's required paperwork. As though guided by divine intervention, witness letters, military forms, and redo's culminated in this long overdue recognition. General James T. Conway, United States Marine Corps Commandant presided over a glorious award ceremony and reception celebrated at the National Museum of the Marine Corps located in Quantico, VA. Dennis Noah accepted his award surrounded by his wife, Susan, his son, Bill, family members, and friends, including me. Doc Noah remained unwavered in his humility of the Marines and corpsmen that he served for and with.

I was overwhelmed with emotion as Dennis accepted his accoladaes with a dignity befitting a king.

And as I sensed Dr. Tom's presence standing in the lobby of this magnificent museum, I silently thanked him for giving me the fortitude and courage to answer my call of duty in writing *Dr. Tom's War*. I marveled at how Dr. Tom continues to serve as a conduit of acknlowedgement, healing, and hope for those who surrounded him in Vietnam decades ago. The following article was one of many printed in honor of "Doc" Noah.

The Quantico Sentry
The Marine Corps News
"Former corpsman honored for heroism"
4/9/2010 By Lance Cpl. Lucas G. Lowe, Marine Corps Base Quantico

TRIANGLE, Va.—In September 1967, the 1st Marine Division headed Operation Swift, a search-and-destroy operation the division undertook in Vietnam's Que Son Valley.

The valley, a narrow strip of arable rice land bordering the South China Sea, became a battleground where the 5th Marines and at least two regiments of ferocious, well-disciplined North Vietnamese Army regulars converged, resulting in 114 American deaths and approximately 380 North Vietnamese.

Former Navy Hospital Man 2nd Class Dennis "Doc" Noah, a 20-year-old corpsman with Company H, 2nd Battalion, 5th Marine Regiment, 1st MarDiv, found himself at the heart of the fighting the night of Sept. 10, only six days into the operation.

Noah began treating wounded Marines while his platoon was within 10 meters of the enemy position. Badly wounded himself, he crawled from man to man, and used his own body for cover while he administered treatment. He quickly depleted most of his medical supplies and had to improvise tourniquets with the cloth from Marines' uniforms. When an NVA regular tried to infiltrate the platoon's perimeter, Noah shot him in the face at point-blank range with his sidearm, a .45-caliber pistol. Then he moved all the wounded away into relative safety before they were evacuated.

That was 42 years ago. Today Noah is as far removed from the physical stress and horror of combat as the average commercial banker, which is what he was for 39 years after his discharge from the Navy. He now lives comfortably as a professor of international business at Towson University in Maryland.

Even with his considerable combat credentials, Noah was nervous when he arrived at Quantico a day before he received the Silver Star for his actions during an April 7 ceremony at the National Museum of the Marine Corps.

"I'm humbled by the fact that a four-star general is going to pin a medal on me," he said as he stood in the lobby of his hotel.

As far as Noah is concerned, what he did all those years ago was nothing extraordinary.

"I didn't expect to get an award," he said. "The Marines I was with were doing their jobs, and I was doing mine to keep them alive."

That wasn't exactly retired Lt. Col. Gene Bowers' point of view. Bowers was Noah's company commander in Vietnam, and saw what he did to save the lives of his men. Two years ago, he nominated Noah for the Silver Star.

"He [Noah] was 20 years old, trained in triage and highly skilled," recalled Bowers.

Bowers' memory of the day Noah helped save his company remains vivid.

"When he finished treating the men, he was covered in blood—not his," said Bower. "The whole time he never realized he was wounded. He was the only guy who was moving around the whole time."

For Noah, the choice to join the military amid the chaos of Vietnam came naturally. His family immigrated to the American colonies in the 17th century, and has fought in most major conflicts throughout the country's timeline.

Noah's ancestors fought in the Revolutionary War, and his father, a World War II veteran, always flew an American flag at their home during Noah's childhood in St. Louis.

"Going to war is kind of a family tradition," said Noah.

Noah wanted to study medicine, but was admittedly too immature for college. Instead he joined the Navy. At the time, he was worried his chances of going to combat were too low. In a later talk, a recruiter assured him that Vietnam was full of corpsmen, and he was hooked.

He attended training at Naval Training Center Great Lakes, Ill., and was assigned to the Fleet Marine Force at Camp Pendleton, Calif.

When he got orders to Vietnam with the rest of the division, he knew he was where he needed to be. However, as the daily grind in Vietnam wore on and the casualties piled up, Noah began to feel disillusioned.

"Vietnam kind of took the motivation out of me," he said. "It was a funny war. It's not the Marine Corps' fault that that particular war was fought the way it was, so I don't blame the organization."

As a young corpsman, Noah was unprepared for the psychological impact of seeing so many Marines die in front of him.

"I got to know these guys," he said. "A corpsman is more than just a field doctor. We did preventive medicine and kept the Marines well. But when, for example, a guy got a dear john letter from home, he would talk to his corpsman. Or they'd have fears about the fighting and come talk to you."

In this way, Noah became more than just the caretaker of the Marines' physical well-being. He was an anchor of emotional stability for the men under his care.

"When you lost these guys, it just tore you apart," he said. "A part of you died, too."

Noah said he remembers looking down at his hands after he had lost a Marine and asking himself why he couldn't have done more.

"I reached a point where I didn't even want to know their names anymore, especially when a new guy came along," said Noah. "Because first you learn their names, then the names of their girlfriends or wives back home, and then they're like family. I needed to distance myself emotionally to be able to do my job."

As for the day that would bring Noah to Quantico four decades later, he still remembers every move the platoon made on its patrol through the small valley in southern Vietnam.

"We ran into several machine gun positions," he remembered. "These guys were well-disciplined NVA troops—not guerrilla fighters."

The ceremony on April 7 was a quiet, low-key affair. There was no color guard or band on call. And only about 40 seats had been reserved for Noah's family, friends and colleagues.

Having his award ceremony at Leatherneck Gallery in the museum was Noah's choice. He had traveled there before on the occasion of its opening.

"To me, the history that's in those halls—the information, the memorabilia that's there—it's just double the honor to be in such a tremendous place and in the presence of the commandant," Noah said. "It's almost hallowed ground to me."

SILVER STAR CEREMONY—APRIL 7. 2010

Gene Bowers, Lucia Viti, Dennis Noah, General James Conway, USMC Commandant.

Bill Noah, Dennis Noah, Sue Noah.

Sgt. Major Carlton Kent, USMC, Dennis Noah, USN, Retired, and General James Conway, USMC Commandant.

Dennis Noah, U.S. Navy Corpsmen and women.

The President of the United States takes pleasure in presenting
the Silver Star Medal to
Hospital Corpsman Second Class
Dennis L. Noah
United States Navy
for service as set forth in the following
Citation:

For conspicuous gallantry and intrepidity while serving as the Senior Corpsman of Company H, 2d Battalion, 5th Marines, 1st Marine Division engaged in operations against the enemy in the Republic of Vietnam, on 10 September 1967. During Operation SWIFT, the 1st Platoon of Company H, with Petty Officer Noah attached, conducted a security patrol separated from the company by 1000 meters. The platoon came under heavy close range small arms, machine gun, and mortar fire from a numerically superior enemy and was temporarily pinned down. Without hesitation, Petty Officer Noah, with total disregard for his life, crawled among the dead and wounded Marines on the field of fire to render aid to many severely wounded Marines within 10 meters of the entrenched enemy. Although he was painfully wounded, he repeatedly crawled from one wounded Marine to another and administered medical aid while shielding each Marine from enemy fire with his own body. Petty Officer Noah remained in an exposed position for more than four hours, dragging bodies of dead Marines in front of the wounded to give them cover. After his medical supplies were depleted, he packed open wounds and fashioned tourniquets with pieces of utility uniforms. When one enemy soldier crawled forward and attempted to capture a wounded Marine, Petty Officer Noah shot him in the face at close range. Upon the arrival and attack by the remainder of Company H, while still under direct enemy fire and within 40 meters of impacting friendly fire, he and others evacuated all wounded Marines to relative safety. He then immediately organized a casualty collection point, prioritized the wounded, and arranged for emergency helicopter evacuation of the casualties. By his bold initiative, undaunted courage, and unwavering dedication to duty, Petty Officer Noah reflected great credit upon himself and upheld the highest traditions of the United States Naval Service.

Sgt. Major Carlton Kent, USMC, Bill Noah, Dennis Noah, Sue Noah, and General James Conway, USMC Commandant.

🌺 *Dear Daddy* 🌺

I must find closure from Vietnam's theater of war. Five years ago, I didn't know how to begin **Dr. Tom's War.** *Now, I don't know how to stop. You didn't. You continued your Vietnam humanitarian efforts years after returning to the Bronx as noted by newspaper clippings found in your box.*

I understand why Vietnam never ended for you, your officer colleagues, and Marine sons. For I, as they, have allowed Vietnam to penetrate every waking moment. Life, even for me, has become nothing more than a series of events, and Vietnam its point of reference. Visiting the good, the bad, and the ugly served as a constant reminder to not sweat the small stuff. I am a woman forever changed by your Vietnam.

And despite the what-in-God's-name-am-I-doing-here days, enjoying She-Crab Soup with the Esaus, Frozen Yogurt with the Newtons, Bloody Marys on Doc Noah's boat, a Gator Game with the Meyers, or dinner with the "Chief" at the Marengos'—was pretty terrific. Throw in Lake Tahoe with Uncle Mac and a serendipitous tea with the **New York Times** *reporter Bernie Weinraub more than forty years post your interview with him. Kind strangers, like Bernie, willing to share Vietnam's good stories; the good that came from 2/5's benevolent compassion amid the chaos of America's controversial war.*

But the ease didn't offset the sorrow or horror of war. It simply added a complacent line for me to continue. And the end is just my illusion, for it's my heart that needs to stop. Every Vietnam day remains a powerful reminder of your absence; a piercing symphony of frustration and tears. And since this isn't Iowa or heaven, there are no sappy endings of you and me chatting on 2/5's 1967 Vietnam baseball diamond against the backdrop of a glowing sunset. That's okay. We'll save that for heaven.

Daddy, **Dr. Tom's War** *is a testament of my love to you. These pages, fueled by determination, endurance, and resolve, capture the courage, fortitude, and bravery of you and yours in this place called Vietnam. I'm so very proud of 2/5's Dr. Tom and immensely grateful that the stars aligned with the heavens to afford me the privilege of calling you Pops.*

And although it is without regret that I embraced this journey, I must confess, unabashedly, I welcome its closing.

I love you. More than you'll ever know.
Love,
Lucia a.k.a. your jellybean.

Epilogue

• "In December of 1967, Dr. Tom was assigned to St. Alban's Naval Hospital in New York. He did not, however, forget Vietnam. As would be expected, the amputees at St. Albans were Dr. Tom's first concern. To overcome the psychological shock of missing limbs, he arranged parties for all amputees—some of who were operated on only days before. Jimmy Devine and Marty Gilligan, boyhood companions and restaurant owners, joined forces to welcome the wounded. Dr. Tom also continued his campaign to raise funds for his An Hoa area clinics. In November of 1968, Dr. Viti left the Navy, returned to New Rochelle Hospital in Westchester County and subsequently completed his residency requirements at New York's Bellevue Medical Center. In addition to his constant requests for clothing and medical supplies, he personally supported five Vietnamese orphans and their Vietnamese nurse who served as their caretaker."

• Richard Esau's Letters written to Colonel Ridderhoff; September 1970

• Letter written on October 23, 1970, from Dr. Nguyen Xuan Trinh, Official Commissioner of the Ministry of Health of the Republic of South Vietnam thanking Dr. Viti for the medical supplies donated to the orphanage at Duc Duc District Headquarters.

• Letter from Congressman Mario Biaggi written in 1982 regarding the New York State Militia Association's annual banquet for presentation and recognition of Dr. Viti's Congressional Record and New York Conspicuous Service Award.

Lt. Commander Gaetano T. A. Viti,
MC, USN, Burper Orders, 1968.

*Official orders for Dr. Viti's promotion
to Lt. Commander, USN, 1968.*

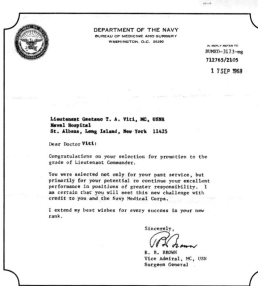

*Vice Admiral Brown's Letter
of Commendation for promotion
to Lt. Commander for
Dr. Viti, 1968.*

DEPARTMENT OF THE NAVY
BUREAU OF MEDICINE AND SURGERY
WASHINGTON, D.C. 20390

BUMED-3175-fc
712765/2105

2 6 JUL 1968

Lieutenant Gaetano T. A. Viti, MC, USNR
Naval Hospital
St. Albans
Long Island, New York 11425

Dear Doctor Viti:

I have been informed that you are due for release from active duty in a
few months, and I wish to convey to you my appreciation for the service
you have rendered. I sincerely hope that your tour of active duty has
been rewarding, both professionally and otherwise.

As you return to civilian life, I wish to extend to you my best wishes
for a happy and prosperous career; and I hope that you will maintain an
active interest in the Navy Medical Department in which you served.

With kindest regards,

Sincerely yours,

R. B. BROWN
Vice Admiral, MC, USN
Surgeon General

Congratulatory letter from Vice Admiral Brown regarding Lt. Commander Viti release from active duty, July 1968.

Letter of recognition for Lt. Viti, written by Major Richard E. Esau to Lt. Col. David Ridderhoff, September 8, 1970.

REK:rg
8 Sept 1970

LtCol David M. RIDDERHOF, USMC
Counterinsurgency Branch
Headquarters Marine Corps (Code 4035)
Washington, D. C. 20380

Dear Col. Ridderhof:

In response to your request, I have composed a scenario of Dr. Viti's
activities on behalf of the Vietnamese people both during and following
his deployment as BnSurgeon for 2/5. The great majority of the information contained in the scenario is personally known to me. A few
anecdotes were supplied by other Marines and Corpsmen who served with him.

The picture, slides and newspaper article enclosed would be next to impossible to replace. It is, therefore, respectfully requested that you
maintain a chain of custody so that I may insure their safe return.

Col. Mallett C. JACKSON Jr., USMC, presently assigned to HQMC (Code
DFA), was Battalion Commander of 2/5 at the time of Dr. Viti's tenure
as Bn Surgeon. I'm sure he will be able to answer any additional
questions you might have concerning Dr. Viti's activities.

It is my sincere wish that Dr. Viti, our "Tom Dooley of An Hoa", receive the accolades due him. I hope my scenario helps.

Sincerely,

R. E. ESAU JR.
Major   USMC

OFFICE OF THE PERMANENT OBSERVER
OF THE REPUBLIC OF VIET-NAM
TO THE UNITED NATIONS
866 UNITED NATIONS PLAZA
SUITE 942-B
NEW YORK, N.Y. 10017

November 10, 1970

Dr. Gaetano Viti
3064 Otis Avenue
Bronx, N.Y. 10465

Dear Sir:

I have the honour to send you the
attached letter from Dr. Nguyen Xuan Trinh,
Official Commissioner of the Ministry of Health
of the Republic of Vietnam, thanking you for
the medical supplies donated to the children
of An Hoa Orphanage.

We all feel grateful to you, Dr. Viti
and Mr. Ward for making the donation possible.

With kind regards,

Sincerely,

PHAM HUY BACH
First Secretary

PHB:al
Encl/1

"Thank you" letter written by Dr. Nguyen-Xuan-Trinh, Official Commissioner, Minister of Health, Republic of Viet Nam to Dr. Viti, thanking him for his continued donation of medical supplies and support for the children of Duc Duc District Headquarters, RSVN, 1970.

VIỆT-NAM CỘNG-HÒA
BỘ Y-TẾ

Saigon, ngày 23 tháng 10 năm 1970

Số 454 BYT/ KHNV(NV)

Dear Doctor :

We have the honor of informing you that we have received the medical supplies which you graciously donated to the Vietnamese chiłrens in Duc-Duc.

We hereby express to you our thanks for this humanitarian gesture, which has greatly promoted the Vietnamese and American friendship.

Sincerely yours,

VIỆT-NAM CỘNG-HÒA BỘ Y-TẾ

Dr. NGUYEN-XUAN-TRINH
Official Commissioner
Ministry of Health
Republic of Viet-Nam

- DR. GAETANO VITI .

Thank You Letter from the United Nation's First Secretary Pham Huy Bach, 1970.

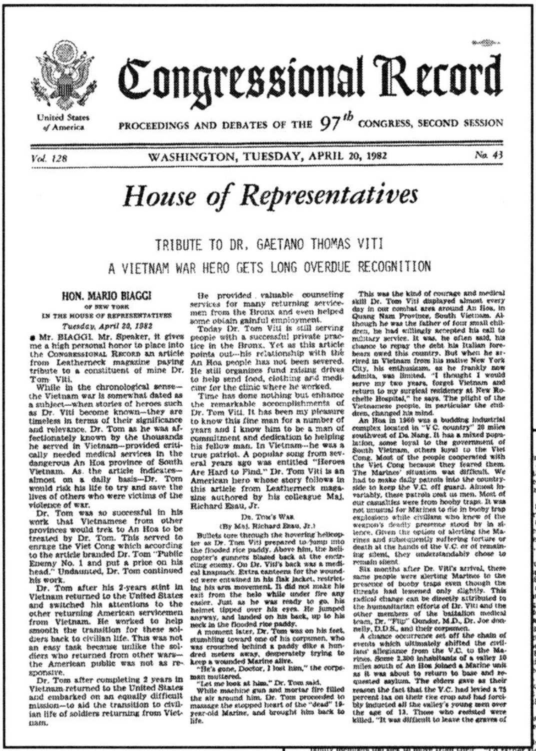

Congressional Record

United States of America

PROCEEDINGS AND DEBATES OF THE 97th CONGRESS, SECOND SESSION

Vol. 128 — WASHINGTON, TUESDAY, APRIL 20, 1982 — No. 43

House of Representatives

TRIBUTE TO DR. GAETANO THOMAS VITI

A VIETNAM WAR HERO GETS LONG OVERDUE RECOGNITION

HON. MARIO BIAGGI
OF NEW YORK
IN THE HOUSE OF REPRESENTATIVES
Tuesday, April 20, 1982

● Mr. BIAGGI. Mr. Speaker, it gives me a high personal honor to place into the CONGRESSIONAL RECORD an article from Leatherneck magazine paying tribute to a constituent of mine Dr. Tom Viti.

While in the chronological sense—the Vietnam war is somewhat dated as a subject—when stories of heroes such as Dr. Viti become known—they are timeless in terms of their significance and relevance. Dr. Tom as he was affectionately known by the thousands he served in Vietnam—provided critically needed medical services in the dangerous An Hoa province of South Vietnam. As the article indicates—almost on a daily basis—Dr. Tom would risk his life to try and save the lives of others who were victims of the violence of war.

Dr. Tom was so successful in his work that Vietnamese from other provinces would trek to An Hoa to be treated by Dr. Tom. This served to enrage the Viet Cong which according to the article branded Dr. Tom "Public Enemy No. 1 and put a price on his head." Undaunted, Dr. Tom continued his work.

Dr. Tom after his 2-years stint in Vietnam returned to the United States and switched his attentions to the other returning American servicemen from Vietnam. He worked to help smooth the transition for these soldiers back to civilian life. This was not an easy task because unlike the soldiers who returned from other wars—the American public was not as responsive.

Dr. Tom after completing 2 years in Vietnam returned to the United States and embarked on an equally difficult mission—to aid the transition to civilian life of soldiers returning from Vietnam.

He provided valuable counseling services for many returning servicemen from the Bronx and even helped some obtain gainful employment.

Today Dr. Tom Viti is still serving people with a successful private practice in the Bronx. Yet as this article points out—his relationship with the An Hoa people has not been severed. He still organizes fund raising drives to help send food, clothing and medicine for the clinic where he worked.

Time has done nothing but enhance the remarkable accomplishments of Dr. Tom Viti. It has been my pleasure to know this fine man for a number of years and I know him to be a man of commitment and dedication to helping his fellow man. In Vietnam—he was a true patriot. A popular song from several years ago was entitled "Heroes Are Hard to Find." Dr. Tom Viti is an American hero whose story follows in this article from Leatherneck magazine authored by his colleague Maj. Richard Esau, Jr.

DR. TOM'S WAR
(By Maj. Richard Esau, Jr.)

Bullets tore through the hovering helicopter as Dr. Tom Viti prepared to jump into the flooded rice paddy. Above him, the helicopter's gunners blasted back at the encircling enemy. On Dr. Viti's back was a medical knapsack. Extra canteens for the wounded were entwined in his flak jacket, restricting his arm movement. It did not make his exit from the helo while under fire any easier. Just as he was ready to go, his helmet tipped over his eyes. He jumped anyway, and landed on his back, up to his neck in the flooded rice paddy.

A moment later, Dr. Tom was on his feet, stumbling toward one of his corpsmen, who was crouched behind a paddy dike a hundred meters away, desperately trying to keep a wounded Marine alive.

"He's gone, Doctor, I lost him," the corpsman muttered.

"Let me look at him," Dr. Tom said.

While machine gun and mortar fire filled the air around him, Dr. Tom proceeded to massage the stopped heart of the "dead" 19-year-old Marine, and brought him back to life.

This was the kind of courage and medical skill Dr. Tom Viti displayed almost every day in our combat area around An Hoa, in Quang Nam Province, South Vietnam. Although he was the father of four small children, he had willingly accepted his call to military service. It was, he often said, his chance to repay the debt his Italian forebears owed this country. But when he arrived in Vietnam from his native New York City, his enthusiasm, as he frankly now admits, was limited. "I thought I would serve my two years, forget Vietnam and return to my surgical residency at New Rochelle Hospital," he says. The plight of the Vietnamese people, in particular the children, changed his mind.

An Hoa in 1966 was a budding industrial complex located in "V.C. country" 28 miles southwest of Da Nang. It has a mixed population, some loyal to the government of South Vietnam, others loyal to the Viet Cong. Most of the people cooperated with the Viet Cong because they feared them. The Marines' situation was difficult. We had to make daily patrols into the countryside to keep the V.C. off guard. Almost invariably, these patrols cost us men. Most of our casualties were from booby traps. It was not unusual for Marines to die in booby trap explosions while civilians who knew of the weapon's deadly presence stood by in silence. Given the option of alerting the Marines and subsequently suffering torture or death at the hands of the V.C. or of remaining silent, they understandably chose to remain silent.

Six months after Dr. Viti's arrival, these same people were alerting Marines to the presence of booby traps even though the threats had lessened only slightly. This radical change can be directly attributed to the humanitarian efforts of Dr. Viti and the other members of the battalion medical team, Dr. "Flip" Gunder, M.D., Dr. Joe donnelly, D.D.S., and their corpsmen.

A chance occurrence set off the chain of events which ultimately shifted the civilians' allegiance from the V.C. to the Marines. Some 2,300 inhabitants of a valley 10 miles south of An Hoa joined a Marine unit as it was about to return to base and requested asylum. The elders gave as their reason the fact that the V.C. had levied a 75 percent tax on their rice crop and had forcibly inducted all the valley's young men over the age of 13. Those who resisted were killed. "It was difficult to leave the graves of

hamlets doubled monthly. A lesser man would have turned from these problems. Dr. Viti just solved them all.

Price on his head or not, Dr. Tom traveled daily into the surrounding villages. While accompanying the battalion on patrols deep into enemy territory he would aid women and children we all knew might be the family of a V.C. Once he found a young girl suffering from spinal meningitis. He brought her back to An Hoa, cured her and returned her home. Immediately the price was taken off his head. She was the daughter of the V.C. District Chief. The V.C. threats of violence soon lost their desired effect when it became obvious that the civilians, without the V.C. could not hope to survive, would rather face death than have one of their children die of a disease which the Bacsi could cure.

Dr. Tom wrote to the staff at St. Albans Hospital in Yonkers, New York and to numerous drug firms. He soon received medical supplies worth thousands of dollars, par-

...munizations for the children. ...of numbers he solved by open... ...hat included a operating the... ...d from a partially destroyed ...ractor.

...when the V.C. shelled the ...he gathered his young patients ...r where the Vietnamese nurses ...told them stories. Then he ...clinics far from the combat ...d by Marine Combat Action ..., a Marine squad plus a corps... ...three squads of Popular Force ...ovide hamlet security. By using ...g clinics as bases of operations, ...ister to those too sick to travel. ...of Dr. Tom's humanitarian ex... ...ued to spread, casual things ...ppen. The incidence of booby ...ies began to drop. V.C. and ...amese Army movements were ...ight by people he had aided. ...nificantly, the rural populace ...derstand that the Americans ...help and not to colonize them. ...ing this medical revolution, Dr. ...d to fight a very nasty war. ...hundred Marines were killed ...oa during this period. He saved ...many by constantly putting ...he wounded ahead of his own

...st 8 months in the field, Dr. ...en an opportunity to leave An ...relative safety of the First ...on Headquarters. He declined. "I'd rather ride a helicopter into a hot zone than fly a rear area desk any time," he said. A few days later, he "borrowed" General Foster C. LaHue's helicopter and flew into one of the heaviest actions of the year.

Finally, in December 1967, Dr. Tom's two years' service was almost over and he was reassigned to St. Albans Naval Hospital in New York. He did not, however, forget Vietnam. No sooner had he arrived home than he began a continuing campaign to raise funds for his clinic.

Dismayed by the average American's distorted view of he Vietnamese war, he attempted unsuccessfully to give an opposing view. He soon found out that a doctor who believed in what he had done in Vietnam was just not news. He also found out that his views on service to one's country were not shared by all of his fellow doctors. One, an orthopedic surgeon, who had just prepared the stump of a Marine's leg for an artificial limb, complained to Dr. Viti that he would have earned $2,000 for that operation if he hadn't been drafted. Dr. Tom suggested a first-hand visit to Vietnam before making any more such rash statements.

As would be expected, the amputees at St. Albans were Dr. Tom's first concern. To overcome the psychological shock of a missing limb, he arranged parties for amputees who had only been operated on days before. Boyhood friends who owned restaurants in the Bronx, Jimmy Devine and Marty Gilligan, joined forces with their neighbors to welcome the wounded home.

In November 1968, Dr. Viti left the Navy, returned to New Rochelle Hospital and subsequently completed his residency requirements at Bellevue Medical Center. Today, Dr. Tom is busily engaged in building the private practice he recently opened in the Bronx. But Vietnam is not forgotten. In addition to his continuing drive for funds, clothing and medicines for the An Hoa clinic, he supports five Vietnamese orphans and a Vietnamese nurse who cares for them.

The eternal optimist, he feels that incidents like the September 1970 North Vietnamese raid against his clinic which killed eight of "his" children and wounded 30 others will not be repeated now that a cease fire is in effect.

It was this same type of optimism which carried him safely through our own mine field the night we returned from an operation and he found one of his patients missing. She had been in a sedative-induced deep sleep when we left the combat base and needed only rest to help her recover from an advanced case of dysentery. Her parents waited 24 hours and when she did not awaken assumed she was dead and buried her. Not 35 minutes later Dr. Tom knowingly took the most direct route to her hamlet, which happened to be through the mine field surrounding our combat base, uncovered her grave with his bare hands and attempted unsuccessfully to breathe life back into her. When later asked about the mine field, Dr. Viti said the issue was never in doubt. He knew he'd get through safely.

Regardless of the final outcome of the Vietnam War, some 50,000 Vietnamese treated by Dr. Tom and the battalion medical team will remember the Bacsi who was willing to risk his life to care for the sick whether the color of their skin be red, yellow, black or white. No matter how Vietnam is recorded in the history books, one thing will remain clear: Dr. Tom Viti won his war for the hearts and minds of the people of An Hoa.●

Congressional Record, *Tuesday, April 20, 1982, pages 1-2.*

"Tribute to Dr. Gaetano Thomas Viti. A Viet Nam War Hero Gets Long Overdue Recognition"

Tom Viti
with his mother
Helen Colucci-Viti,
Brooklyn, NY,
May 4, 1974.

Daddy, Lucia and Mom Viti
celebrating Lucia's Sacred Heart
Grammar School Graduation Day,
June 1974.

Cardinal Spellman High School Father
and Daughter Dinner Dance, Bronx, NY,
April 1976.

Text from Esau's letter written to Lt. Col David M. Ridderhof, USMC, Counterinsurgency Branch, Headquarters Marine Corps, Washington, DC, September 8, 1970.

Dr. Gaetano Thomas Viti M.D.
His Continuing Service to Mankind

Dr. Viti was drafted into the U.S. Navy in November, 1966. He was pursuing a surgical residency at the time, but willingly interrupted his medical education when called to serve. Following Field Medical School, he was assigned to West PAC Ground Forces and subsequently to 2/5 as Bn Surgeon. He arrived at the An Hoa Combat Base in December 1966 and remained there until he rotated in December 1967 although offered an assignment in the Da Nang area on numerous occasions.

To understand the extent of Dr. Viti's obligations on arrival at An Hoa, one must be familiar with the tactical situation at that time. Two/five OPCON to the First Marine Division was responsible for a 144-square mile TAOR or roughly the same area now controlled by the Fifth Marine Regiment. Included in this area was the coal mine at Nong Son, Antenna Valley, An Hoa, Duc Duc District Headquarters, the Arizona Territory north to the Son Vu Gie, the Song Thu Bon, Liberty Road and Go Noi Island. In December, 1966, most everything in the area was controlled by the Viet Cong, and the BN (Rein) had to operate constantly to keep the Viet Cong and the NVA off-guard. Movement as might be expected was restricted and the danger of ambush and booby traps always high. Into this unreal situation, Dr. Viti, along with Dr. Gonder and their corpsmen, brought the marvel of true Christian charity.

It was about Christmas time 1966 that Drs. Viti and Gonder realized that the German Red Cross working in the vicinity of the An Hoa Industrial Complex was not equipped to handle the multitude of refugees in the area. Refugees who had voluntarily left their homes in Viet Cong controlled areas to escape communism. Operation Mississippi in November 1966, for instance, had resulted in the exodus of approximately 2300 people from the Antenna Valley. Invariably, these refugees settled near the Duc Duc District Headquarters, swelling the population in that area to about 15,000 people. USAID, 2/5 and the Seabees provided needed assistance to get them settled, but medical services were at a premium. The need was alleviated when Dr. Viti constructed his first clinic and began ministering to the needs of the civilian populace. One year and 50,000 patients later, Dr. Viti and his men had built additional clinics at Nong Son, at Ninh Bin (3) and Mau Chanh (5) CAP locations, and at Phu Lac (6) near Liberty Bridge. He had also modernized his An Hoa clinic.

Throughout his tenure as Bn Surgeon, Dr. Viti consistently moved into the field during BN (-) (Rein) Operations. On one occasion he ministered to a

Vietnamese "civilian" who later attempted to kill him. His composure under fire was proven time and time again. On more than one occasion while under fire, he performed a medical miracle saving the life of a young Marine who would not have survived the trip to the BAS. As always, his concern during operations centered around his Marines and his VN children, orphaned by the conflict. He still supports five of these children who were found in the TAOR and nursed back to health at his An Hoa clinic.

No request for medical help was too small, whether that request came during an afternoon MedCAP or late at night. Dr. Viti frequently ventured into the surrounding villages at night to deliver babies and treat those too sick to travel to his clinic. On one occasion, he departed the An Hoa combat base to treat the sick children of a man who was later identified as a Viet Cong leader. From that time on, his travels into the country side were rarely impeded. The local Vietnamese came to love the "Bacsi" and his name was known throughout Duc Duc District. Dr. Viti had proven that dedication of a medical doctor to the cause of mankind transcends all political boundaries.

Since leaving Vietnam, Dr. Viti has not forgotten the clinic he began. Along with the support of his five special children, he presently provides assistance to 25 others. While working at St. Alban's Naval Hospital, he coordinated programs to send money, food, medical supplies, and clothes to An Hoa. He also initiated a program to bring servicemen amputees to parties in his old neighborhood so that they could see first-hand how much their sacrifice is appreciated by the average American. There is no doubt that the reception of these young men did much to aid their ultimate recovery.

On 12 November, 1968, Dr. Viti left the Navy and returned to his surgical residency at New Rochelle (New York) Hospital. Active in community affairs, he continues to give many speeches to local groups re-assuring them as to the necessity of the American presence in Vietnam. On a phrase, this young doctor is the anti-thesis of the "darlings" of the news media (i.e.) Dr. Levy et, al. Dr. Viti takes his Hippocratic Oath seriously and is a credit to the American way of life.

Text from the *Congressional Record*
Proceedings and Debates of the 97th Congress, Second Session
Washington, Tuesday, April 20, 1982
House of Representatives

Tribute to Dr. Gaetano Thomas Viti—
A Vietnam War Hero Gets Long Overdue Recognition

HON. Mario Biaggi of New York In The House of Representatives, Tuesday, April, 20, 1982

Mr. Biaggi, Mr. Speaker, it gives me a high personal honor to place into the Congressional Record an article from *Leatherneck Magazine* paying tribute to a constituent of mine, Dr. Tom Viti.

While in the chronological sense—the Vietnam War is somewhat dated as a subject—when stories of heroes such as Dr. Viti become known—they are timeless in terms of their significance and relevance. Dr. Tom as he was affectionately known by the thousands he served in Vietnam provided critically needed medical services in the dangerous An Hoa province of South Vietnam. As the article indicates almost on a daily basis Dr. Tom would risk his life to try and save the lives of others who were victims of the violence of war.

Dr. Tom was so successful in his work that Vietnamese from other provinces would trek to An Hoa to be treated by Dr. Tom. This served to enrage the Viet Cong which according to the article branded Dr. Tom "Public Enemy No. 1" and put a price on his head. Undaunted, Dr. Tom continued his work.

Dr. Tom after his two-year stint in Vietnam returned to the United States and switched his attentions to the other returning American Servicemen from Vietnam. He worked to help smooth the transition for these soldiers back to civilian life. This was not an easy task for unlike the soldiers returned from other wars—the American public was not as responsive.

Dr. Tom after completing 2 years in Vietnam returned to the United States and embarked on an equally difficult mission—to aid the transition to civilian life of soldiers returning from Vietnam.

He provided valuable counseling services for many returning servicemen from the Bronx and even helped some obtain gainful employment.

Today Dr. Tom Viti is still serving people with a successful private practice in the Bronx. Yet, as this article points out, his relationship with the people of An Hoa has not been severed. He still organizes fund-raising drives to help send food, clothing and medicine for the clinic where he worked.

Time has done nothing but enhance the remarkable accomplishments of Dr. Tom Viti. It has been my pleasure to know this fine man for a number of years and I know him to be a man of commitment and dedication to helping his fellow man. In Vietnam he was a true patriot. A popular song from several years ago was entitled, "Heroes Are Hard To Find." Dr. Tom is an American hero whose story follows this article from *Leatherneck Magazine* authored by his colleague, Maj. Richard Esau, Jr."

"Dr. Tom's War"
By Maj. Richard Esau Jr.

Bullets tore through the hovering helicopter as Dr. Tom Viti prepared to jump into the flooded rice paddy. Above him, the helicopter's gunners blazed back at the encircling enemy. On Dr. Viti's back was a medical knapsack. Extra canteens for the wounded were entwined in his flak jacket, restricting his arm movement. It did not make his exit from the helo any easier. Just as he was ready to go, his helmet tipped over his eyes. He jumped anyway, and landed on his back, up to his neck in the flooded rice paddy.

A moment later, Dr. Tom was on his feet, stumbling toward one of his corpsmen, who was crouched behind a paddy dike a hundred meters away, desperately trying to keep a wounded marine alive.

"He's gone, Doctor, I lost him," the corpsman muttered.

"Let me look at him," Dr. Tom said.

While machine gun and mortar fire filled the air around him, Dr. Tom proceeded to massage the stopped heart of the "dead" nineteen-year-old Marine, and brought him back to life.

This was the kind of courage and medical skill Dr. Tom Viti displayed almost everyday in our combat area around An Hoa, in Quang Nam Province, South Vietnam. Although he was the father of four small children, he had willingly accepted his call to military service. It was, he often said, his chance to repay the debt his Italian forebears owed this country. But when he arrived in Vietnam from his native New York City, his enthusiasm, as he frankly now admits, was limited. "I thought I would serve my two years, forget Vietnam and return to my surgical residency in New Rochelle Hospital," he says. The plight of the Vietnamese people, in particular the children, changed his mind.

An Hoa in 1966 was a building complex locating in "VC country" twenty miles southwest of Da Nang. It had a mixed population, some loyal to the government of South Vietnam, others loyal to the Viet Cong. Most of the people cooperated with the Viet Cong because they feared them. The Marine's situation was difficult. We had to make daily patrols into the countryside to keep the VC off guard. Almost invariably, these patrols cost us men. Most of our casualties were from booby traps. It was not unusual for Marines to die in booby-trap explosions while civilians who knew of the weapon's deadly presence stood by in silence. Given the option of alerting the Marines and subsequently suffering torture or death at the hands of the VC or of remaining silent, they understandably chose to remain silent.

Six months after Dr. Viti's arrival these same people were alerting Marines to the presence of booby traps even though the threats had lessened only slightly.

This radical change can be directly attributed to the humanitarian efforts of Dr. Viti and the other members of the battalion medical team, "Flip" Gonder, MD, Joe Donnelly, DDS, and their corpsmen.

A chance occurrence set off the chain of events which ultimately shifted the civilians' allegiance from the VC to the Marines. Some 2,300 inhabitants of a valley ten miles south of An Hoa joined a Marine unit as it was about to return to base and requested asylum. The elders gave as their reason as the fact that the VC levied a seventy-five percent tax on their rice crop and had forcible inducted all the valley's young men over the age of thirteen. Those who resisted were killed. "It was difficult to leave the graves of one's ancestors unattended," they said, "but one can no longer bear the yoke of communist rule."

Taken to District Headquarters next to the Marines combat base, they were graciously received by the District Chief, Major Ham. The resultant housing shortage was quickly alleviated by the Marine and Seabees, while food was supplied by USAID.

Medical help, however, was another story. The Vietnamese had no doctors and only one nurse. The German Red Cross had a clinic in the area but their doctor, a gracious lady and authentic baroness, could not handle the multitudes flocking to her clinic each day. Dr. Viti and the battalion medical team immediately came to her aid. The three MD's would often treat 500 persons a day while Dr. Donnelly pulled 250 rotting teeth. Their efforts quickly produced more patients as Vietnamese came from miles around to be treated by the American "Bac-si" (Vietnamese for doctor).

Then came the inevitable Viet Cong reaction. Seeing their hold on the civilian populace begin to slip, the VC made Dr. Viti "public enemy number one" and put a price on his head. They threatened reprisals and posted circulars in every hamlet. One mother who chose to ignore the threat and seek aid for her dying baby was killed with her husband and four other children on the night she returned home.

Medical supplies ran short. Additional requests for asylum raised the population to over 20,000. Refugee requests for aid for family members to sick to move their hamlets doubled monthly. A lesser man would have turned from these problems. Dr. Viti just solved them all.

Price on his head or not, Dr. Tom traveled daily into the surrounding villages. While accompanying the battalion on patrols deep into enemy territory he would aid women and children we all knew might be the family of a VC. Once he found a young girl suffering from spinal meningitis. He brought her back to An Hoa, cured her and returned her home. Immediately the price was taken off his head. She was the daughter of the VC District Chief.

Some 50,000 Vietnamese treated by Dr. Tom Viti and the 2/5 medical team will remember the "Bac-si" who was willing to risk his life to take care of the sick and wounded.

VC threats of violence soon lost their desired effect when it became obvious that the civilians; without whom the VC could not hope to survive, would rather face death than let one of their children die of a disease which the "Bac-si" could cure.

Dr. Tom wrote the staff at St. John's Hospital in New York and to numerous drug firms. He soon received medical supplies worth thousands of dollars, particularly immunizations for the children. The problem of numbers he solved by opening a clinic that included a protected operating theater fashioned from a partially destroyed amphibious tractor.

Nights when the VC shelled the combat base, he gathered his young patients in the tractor where the Vietnamese nurses in training told them stories. Then he opened three clinics far from the combat base in villages protected by Marine Combined Action Platoons, i.e., a Marine Rifle squad plus a corpsman who joined three squads of Popular Forces soldiers to provide hamlet security. By using these outlying clinics as bases of operations, he could minister to those too sick to travel.

As word of Dr. Tom's humanitarian exploits continued to spread, unusual things began to happen. The incidence of booby trap casualties began to drop, VC and North Vietnamese Army movements were brought to light by people he had treated and most significantly, the local populace began to understand that the Americans had come to help and not to colonize them.

While running this medical revolution, Dr. Viti continued to fight a very nasty war. More than a hundred Marines were killed around An Hoa during this period. He saved at least that many by constantly putting the lives of the wounded ahead of his own safety.

After months in the field, Dr. Tom was given an opportunity to leave An Hoa for the relative safety of the First Marine Division Headquarters. He declined. "I'd rather ride a helicopter into a hot zone than fly a rear area desk any time," he said. A few days later he borrowed General Foster C. La Hue's helicopter and flew into one of the heaviest actions of the year.

Finally in December 1967, Dr. Tom was reassigned to St. Alban's Naval Hospital in New York. He did not, however, forget Vietnam. No sooner had he arrived home than he began a continuing campaign to raise funds for his clinic.

Dismayed by the average American's distorted view of the Vietnamese war, he attempted unsuccessfully to give an opposing view. He soon found out that a doctor who believed in what he had done in Vietnam was just no news. He also found out that his views on service to one's country were not shared by all of his fellow doctors. One, an orthopedic surgeon who had just prepared the stump of a Marine's leg for an artificial limb, complained to Dr. Viti that he would have earned $2000 for that operation if he hadn't been drafted. Dr. Tom suggested a first-hand visit to Vietnam before making any more such rash statements.

As would be expected, the amputees at St. Albans were Dr. Tom's first concern. To overcome the psychological shock of a missing limb, he arranged parties for amputees who had only been operated on days before. Boyhood friends who owned restaurants in the Bronx, Jimmy Devine and Marty Gilligan, joined forces with their neighbors to welcome the wounded home.

In November 1968, Dr. Viti left the Navy, returned to New Rochelle Hospital and subsequently completed his residency requirements at Bellevue Medical Center. Today, Dr. Tom is busily engaged in building the private practice he recently opened in the Bronx. But Vietnam is not forgotten. In addition to his continuing drive for funds, clothing and medicines for the An Hoa clinic, he supports five Vietnamese orphans and a Vietnamese nurse who cares for them.

The eternal optimist, he feels that incidents like the September 1970 North Vietnamese raid against his clinic which killed eight of "his" children and wounded thirty others will not be repeated now that a cease fire is in effect.

It was the same type of optimism which carried him safely through our own mine field the night we returned from an operation and he found one of his patients missing. She had been in a sedative-induced deep sleep when we left the combat base and needed only rest to help her recover from an advanced case of dysentery. Her parents waited 24 hours and when she did not awaken, assumed she was dead and buried her. Not thirty-five minutes later, Dr. Tom knowingly took the most direct route to her hamlet, which happened to be through the mine field surrounding the combat base, uncovered her grave with his bare hands and attempted to unsuccessfully to breathe life back into her. When later asked about the mine field, Dr. Viti said the issue was never in doubt. He knew he would get through safely.

Regardless of the final outcome of the Vietnam War, some 50,000 Vietnamese treated by Dr. Tom and the battalion medical team will remember the "Bac-si" who was willing to risk his life to care for the sick whether the color of their skin be red, yellow, black or white. No matter how Vietnam is recorded in history books, one thing will remain clear: Dr. Tom Viti won his war for the hearts and minds of the people of An Hoa!

Bronx, New York
October 1982
"War Hero Wins Award 15 Years After Service"
By Michael Haber
Associate Editor

Gaetano Thomas Viti remembers an era and a place in which all different types of people were united for a common cause. And although the characterization may not be the most popular one of an historical episode that has come to be known simply as "Vietnam," Viti's job was unusual.

Alongside the destruction that claimed the lives of 56,000 Americans and left more than a quarter-million wounded, Viti's goals was to save lives.

Dr. Viti, a Bronx-native physician, will be honored this week with the New York State Conspicuous Service Cross in recognition of his service in Vietnam, which earned him the Bronze Star Medal with a Combat "V."

Viti was so fiercely determined and so successful in his fight to save lives that the Viet Cong labeled him as "Public Enemy Number 1" and swore that he would die. The crusade to kill Viti was called off only after he saved the daughter of a high-ranking Viet Cong official.

Today, Viti is recognized as a war hero by the U.S. Marine Corps, and as a "true patriot," by Rep. Mario Biaggi, who paid tribute to the Bronx doctor in the pages of the Congressional Record.

Known to the civilians of the An Hoa Province of South Vietnam as "Dr. Tom," he routinely risked his life to serve others, and, on one occasion, dug up a grave with his bare hands in hope of discovering that a victim of a disease might have been mistakenly thought to be dead.

Dr. Tom, however, is as modest today as he was brave and determined in the jungles of South Vietnam 15 years ago. "I'm accepting the award that I am getting not just for myself and my family, but for everyone who fought," he told the News. "They're really the forgotten veterans. We came back and people said, 'You fought in that unnecessary war.'

"You had all of the Jane Fonda's who went over to Hanoi and said how bad we (members of the military) were and yet a lot of people (more recently) died in the boats coming over here. So we must have been fighting suppression."

There were a number of occasions when Viti was convinced that he would never live to see the wife and four children he left behind half-a-world away on Otis Ave in the Bronx. But he casts off any commendation for his bravery and risking his life countless times. "You had to, everybody did. It was a daily occurrence as far as I'm concerned.

"You didn't think about it at that time, but you sort of realized it afterwards," said the 44-year-old Bronx doctor who now has a private practice at 3147 Bruckner Boulevard. "It's very strange how you become accustomed to things.

"Vietnam was unique," he recalled in a News interview. "There weren't any front lines. Where ever you were—were the front lines," he said.

For all the destruction that Viti saw in Vietnam he clung to hope throughout his 14-month stint in that country, doing everything in his power to help the people of that land, even helping the enemy. "I'm a doctor," he said. "You treated your own first, but everybody's a person."

Never during all his time in Vietnam did Viti become hardened to the needs of others or to the death and pain that surrounded him continually. "You never get hardened to it," he said. "Nobody ever does. I don't believe there was a man who served over there who got hardened to the death around him. You don't get hardened to children being hurt, young Marines and servicemen being hurt."

"But, returning home," Viti said, "meant fighting a whole new war all over again." He said that he was not ashamed of the war "because deep down inside you felt what you were doing was right." But, others, he conceded, tried to make him and other returning veterans ashamed after coming back home.

"That's where the war really was," he said of the home-front. "Those (families of servicemen) are the people who really suffered."

An article in *Leatherneck Magazine* written by Viti's war buddy Col. Richard Esau, Jr., recounts Viti's experiences and dedication. Entitled, "Dr. Tom's War," the article tells how Viti established a clinic and orphanage to care for civilians who were victims of the war.

Viti described his friend Esau as "my big German leprechaun, standing up and carrying wounded to the chopper while getting shot at."

"Tribute to a War Hero"
By Angela Canaday
Home Reporter and Sunset News
Long Island, New York, May 28, 1982

Memorial Day is a soulfully patriotic day that is dedicated to the untold number of servicemen who died for their country, VFW and American Legion ceremonies and honors to the Unknown Soldier. It seems timely, therefore, to speak of a war hero, one who was fortunate to survive the Vietnam ordeal and be honored by the 97th Congress of the United States on April 20, 1982. He is Gaetano Thomas Viti, M.D., a former Brooklyn-ite who continues to have many friends in the area.

Sponsored by Congressman Mario Biaggi, the act as recorded in the Congressional Record is titled, "The House of Representatives: Tribute to Dr. Gaetano Thomas Viti. A Vietnam War Hero Gets Long Overdue Recognition."

Biaggi stated that "while in the chronological sense, the Vietnam War is a somewhat dated subject, when stories such as Dr. Viti become known, they are timeless in terms of their significance and relevance.

"Dr. Tom, as he was affectionately known by the thousands he served in Vietnam, provided critically needed medical services in the dangerous An Hoa province of South Vietnam. On a daily basis, he risked his life to save the lives of others who were victims of the violence of war."

Part of the citation honoring the Naval Officer who was attached to the Marine Corps included an article from *Leatherneck Magazine* authored by his colleague Maj. Richard Esau, Jr. The eyewitness recounted the surgeon's many heroic deeds during the death and disease days of 1966. Under the most adverse conditions, Dr. Tom established clinics, ran through explosive mine fields to visit villages and battle zones, refused to accept a safe desk job behind the front lines, massaged the stopped heart of a "dead" 19-year-old Marine, bringing him back to life, and much, much more.

Having left his wife and four children to answer his country's call to duty, he returned safely to them, after a two-year stint in Vietnam. But, not one to forget, he immediately began to work with American servicemen returning from Vietnam, amputees at St. Alban's Naval Hospital and organized fundraising drives to provide clothing and medicines for the people of An Hoa.

Presently in private practice in the Bronx and associated with Westchester Square Hospital, he is the son of the late Dr. and Mrs. Felice Viti, his father having been a respected physician at Madison Square Garden and the ILA Medical Center where his proud sister, Agnes Viti Ogonosky of Fort Hamilton Parkway, is chief of the X-ray Department.

Congressmen Biaggi summed up the essence of the man when he described Dr. Tom as "a man of commitment and dedication to helping his fellow man." In Vietnam, Biaggi said, "he was a true patriot."

Bronx Times Reporter
May 28, 1987

Gaetano T. A. Viti, M.D., a well-known and respected Throggs Neck-Pelham Bay Physician/Surgeon passed away on April 20th at the age of 51. Born in Brooklyn and a resident of Pelham since 1974, Dr. Viti's practice was at 3147 Bruckner Boulevard.

Dr. Viti was best known for his expertise in vascular and abdominal surgery and was affiliated with Pelham Bay General Hospital, St. Barnabas and Westchester Square Hospital. He studied in Italy at the University of Padova and spent 1966 to 1967 as battalion surgeon in South Vietnam attached to the 2nd Battalion 5th Marines, 1st Marine Division.

During his tour of duty, Dr. Viti received the Vietnamese Medal of Honor, the Vietnamese Cross of Gallantry, the Bronze Star with a Combat "V," two Presidential Citations, a Vietnamese Service Medal, and the National Defense Medal. In 1984, Dr. Viti was appointed Medical Director of Madison Square Garden's Medical Department and Physician for the New York Rangers.

Dr. Viti was waked at Giordano's Funeral Parlor, where hundreds of people including District Attorney Mario Merola were in attendance to pay their last respects to this extraordinary man. His long-time friend and combat buddy Major Richard Esau Jr., gave the eulogy to the family and friends on Saturday, April 25th. Dr. Viti was buried at Rose Hill Cemetery in Putnam County with full military honors. As the funeral procession moved up the Bronx River Parkway, to the Bronx/Yonkers border, a police honor guard marked the way and saluted this distinguished gentleman.

Dr. Viti is survived by his wife of 30 years Louise and their four children Felice-John, age 29, an Assistant District Attorney; Anthony, age 27, a physician and graduate of West Virginia University; Lucia, age 26, a journalist; and John, age 25, an attorney.

The Throggs Neck Ambulance Corp will be dedicating their June Journal to the memory of Dr. Viti. He was the first surgeon to support this worthwhile, non-profit community organization.

As a respected and valued member of the community, Louise Viti expressed her husband's feelings for the area when she said, "He practiced here because he fell in love with this part of the Bronx." And surely, this part of the Bronx fell in love with Dr. Viti.

Bibliography

Canaday, Angela. "Tribute to a War Hero." *Home Reporter and Sunset News*, Long Island, New York, May 28, 1982.

Daily News Photo. "A Nation Remembers—And So Does She." *Daily News*, March 19, 1969.

Daily News Photo. "This is for Your Daddy . . ." *Daily News*, October 30, 1968.

Dzubak, Susan L. "Operating Room Nurses Share With Readers Inspiring Reports From Vietnam," *The Herald Statesman,* 1967.

"Fifth Regiment Aid Station Aiding Marines and Villagers : Da Nong." *The Sea Tiger,* November 17, 1967, vol. III, no. 46.

Haber, Michael. "War Hero Wins Award 15 Years After Service." *Parkchester News*, October 1982.

Krulak, Victor H. *First to Fight: An Inside View of the U.S. Marine Corps.* Annapolis, MD: U.S. Naval Institute Press, 1999.

Lowe, Lance Cpl. Lucas G. "Former Corpsman honored for Heroism." *The Quantico Sentry*, April 4, 2010.

Noah, Dennis L. "A Grunt Corpsman's Prayer." *Reflections on the Vietnam War: Experience of a Marine Corpsman.* unpublished manuscript, c2005.

Noah, Dennis L. "An Old Corpsman's Dream." *Reflections on the Vietnam War: Experience of a Marine Corpsman.* unpublished manuscript, c2005.

"Thumbing a Boat Ride." *The Sea Tiger*, February 8, 1967, vol. III, no. 6.

United States Marine Corp. "Release No. CS-243-68." October 29, 1968.

U.S. Congress. "Tribute to Dr. Gaetano Thomas Viti: A Viet Nam War Hero Gets Long Overdue Recognition." *Congressional Record.* 97th Cong., 2d sess., 1982, Vol. 128, pt. 43.

Viti, Tom. "Nurses at St. John's Hospital Send Ex-Interne Supplies Needed in Vietnam." Letter by Dr. Tom Viti. *The Herald Statesman*, September 1967.

Weinraub, Bernard. "Navy Doctor from the Bronx is 'No. 1' to South Vietnamese Village Children; An Incident Last March." *New York Times*, November 24, 1967, sec 11/24/67, page 4.

Illustration/Photo Credits

All photos and illustrations are courtesy of Lucia Viti, except for the following list.

page:
9—courtesy of Gary Lee Webb
13—courtesy of Richard H. Esau, Jr.
41—photo 2, courtesy of Dennis Noah
42—courtesy of Dennis Noah
45—photos 1 & 2, courtesy of Dennis Noah
46—photos 1 & 2, courtesy of Dennis Noah; photo 3, courtesy of Anthony Marengo
47—courtesy of Harold Wadley
48, 50, 60—courtesy of Dennis Noah
67—courtesy of James Meyers
74—photo 3, courtesy of Operation Care
75—photo 1, courtesy of James Meyers
89—courtesy of Martin Dunbar
94—courtesy of Daniel Meyers
95—Superman, reproduced with permission from iStockphoto
97—photo 1, courtesy of Janet Newton, photo 2; courtesy of John Newton
98—courtesy of John Newton
99—photo 1, courtesy of John Newton
108—courtesy of Dennis Noah
111—photo 1, courtesy of John Newton, photo 3; courtesy of Richard H. Esau, Jr.
125—photo 3, courtesy of Richard H. Esau, Jr.
126—photo 1, courtesy of Gene Bowers, photo 2; courtesy of John Newton
132—photo 1, courtesy of Janet Newton
158—courtesy of Phil Perozzio
167—New York Times article, reprinted with permission
185—courtesy of Tony Marengo
187—courtesy of John Petersen
205—courtesy of Gene Bowers
211—courtesy of Roger Ware
212—courtesy of Harold Wadley
235—card, courtesy of Brenton MacKinnon
252—courtesy of Steve Zeck
260—photos 2 & 3, courtesy of Gene Bowers
262—courtesy of James Meyers
265, 266—courtesy of Bill Gavin
267—courtesy of Doc Blanchard
281—courtesy of the United States Marine Corps
292—photo 3, courtesy of Richard H. Esau, Jr.; photo 4, courtesy of Patrick Haley
293—photos 1 & 2, courtesy of the Department of Defense
294—Denny Curtin
295—photo 1, Denny Curtin
297—Daily News Photos, reprinted with permission
313—Daily News Photo, reprinted with permission
334, 336—courtesy of Dennis Noah
357—Lisette Omoss, photographer

Photo by Lisette Omoss

About the Author

Lucia Viti was born in Brooklyn and bred in the Bronx, NY and has a B.S. in Journalism from the University of West Virginia. She spent over twenty years in New York as both a copywriter and program director in marketing, advertising, and public relations in the health and wellness profession. In 1999, she moved to San Diego to pursue a career in publishing. Ms. Viti has worked as a certified fitness professional in group exercise and personal training for thirty years and continues to write for health and wellness trade journals and publications. Her Sweet Kitties calendars demonstrate her passion for photography and cats.

When not writing, taking pictures, teaching, and running along the majestic Pacific near her home in Carlsbad, California, Ms. Viti shares a happy home with her significant other and their brood of Bengals.

The Boot Campaign is a grass roots initiative that provides an easy and tangible way for all Americans to show support for the United States Military. Proceeds from all boot sales fund partner charities which assist returning war Veterans suffering with physical and emotional disabilities. So get your boots on!

"When they come back, we give back."

CPSIA information can be obtained at www.ICGtesting.com
Printed in the USA
LVOW091503150212

268849LV00004B/31/P

9 781934 452516